AF483606

THE GIRL AND

Apple Martinis

THE GIRL AND

Apple Martinis

JEREMY TAYLOR

Andean Publishing
New York City

Andean Publishing
1420 York Avenue
New York, NY 10021

Published by Andean Publishing

Publisher's Note: This is a work of fiction. Names, characters, places, and incidents are a product of the author's imagination. Locales and public names are sometimes used for atmospheric purposes. Any resemblance to actual people, living or dead, or to businesses, companies, events, institutions, or locales is completely coincidental.

Book design © 2024 Andean Publishing
www.andeanpublishing.com
The Girl and Apple Martinis / Jeremy Taylor
1 2 3 4 5 6 7 8 9 10

Identifiers:
Library of Congress Control Number: 2024908952
ISBN: 979-8-9905189-9-5 (hardcover)
ISBN: 979-8-9905189-5-7(e-book)
Printed in the United States of America

To Murat

THE GIRL AND

Apple Martinis

CHAPTER ONE

Where Are Them Fries?

THERE'S NOTHING LIKE A STRONG DRINK AFTER A DAY OF HARD work—a statement—hardly evaluated by the Surgeon General, but heartily evaluated by me, Surgeon Particular. I rarely discriminate my alcohol, but today I decide to stick to generation-proved staples of comfort and problem solving: vodka and whiskey. Starting in reverse alphabetical order, I take a shot of cinnamon whiskey, which sails down smoother than the *Titanic*, leaving traces of familiar warmth in my stomach for a minute straight, tongue pleasantly on fire.

Next comes a complimentary and mandatory apple martini (Friday night's special for the ladies), provided a particular lady orders ten dollars' worth of food. With a liver that has seen better days, I'm not sure if I could qualify to be called a lady at this point, but bartender Mario doesn't seem to mind. I order a dinner-size portion of fried chicken with fries on the side. After the shenanigans at work, today for sure is the day when I need my fries (my comfort food) the most. I feel extra hungry too, courtesy of a skipped lunch to save up calories for drinking.

While waiting for food, I sit at my table and munch on dried Turkish apricots, a favorite snack that I bring with me in a sandwich bag from home. I must be dumb for ordering such a massive amount of food while eating another pouch of the apricots because I'm already so constipated there's traffic in my ass all the way to Chicago. If it's anybody's business, it's been three days and counting. But comfort food will make me forget what happened at work.

Spider webs with fake spiders, glowing pumpkins, skeletons, and other Halloween junk is thrown around the perimeter, disguised as decorations. These are the same decorations Mario used last year, laid out in a similar, disorganized manner. New York City gets crazy when it comes to Halloween, each store gets decorated, pumpkin spice lattes are sold by the cauldron-full, and people in zombie costumes roam the streets without notice. Being a secretary taught me two skills: how to be somewhat organized and how to dress slutty, the latter skill will come in handy for Halloween, but today I'm wearing slacks.

Cheerful smells of food waft toward me from the kitchen, the sizzling of the fryer can be heard all the way out here. Pedro Grande (Mario's barback/cook/waiter) comes in from the kitchen from time to time and the two of them mutter in Spanish, occasionally looking in my direction, watching carefully as the apple martini slowly being consumed will soon turn this beauty into a beast.

Bored, I pull out my phone to check the call log and text messages, both empty. Then I log in online to my dating website. My friend Chloe created a profile for me on some dating website for young single Jewish women. As opposed to what? A dating website for old married Jewish women as though somehow they haven't suffered enough? Chloe promised me it didn't matter I wasn't Jewish or that I was no longer "young." Chloe claimed she'd been talking to one handsome gentleman, so it must be legit. In theory. Two weeks have gone by and I've talked to one and a half men on that lousy website. Even though the date with the half man went quite well and even though I felt emotionally connected to him, I was still skeptical of his alarming set of unruly red hair and couldn't fathom seeing him naked mostly because he ended up being nine years my junior and was into older women. I'm thirty. Who's an older woman? He also somehow must have managed to realize I wasn't Jewish because he went to use a water closet without ever coming back. Yes, I was stuck paying for his food. It wasn't expensive since we ate at a diner near his NYU campus. Since then I distrust men who use words "water" and "closet" in the same sentence. Moshe apologized later by a text message, claiming the food made him sick. To apologize for calling me an older woman and for leaving me alone, he sent me a bouquet of flowers as a peace offering, not realizing a bottle of vodka would suffice. Somehow, in between his online payment for the flowers and the delivery man knocking on my door, I was informed his debit card was declined due to insufficient funds. Yes, I paid for the flowers and the tip. Carnations will never again smell the same.

My slightly older, therefore wiser, Russian friend Natalia said I should have seen it coming: Men who hide behind their keyboards and who can't start a conversation with real women are liars, child molesters, and have penises curved to the right. Natalia has a strict belief in finding real men in casinos, claiming men in casinos have money, and I can't argue with her on that. Men with money, she claims, have power to have their red hair cut, perhaps bleached, and they, therefore, are confident. Most of those men offer to pay for dinner and drinks because they like to seduce their women. Confidence is attractive, Natalia claims, and again, I can't argue with her on that. It comes down to a simple test: Has she met any men at casinos? The answer is yes if you count being devoid of sobriety while with such men. The only real men I personally had met at casinos, however, could be divided into two categories: Category one includes men I wasn't attracted to because they smoked, nursed their liver implants from all the drinking, or simply because they could be my grandfathers; category two were men I was attracted to, but even though according to Natalia their penises didn't curve to the right, the men were either already married to eighteen-year-old bombshells or were halfway into category one.

For me, I keep coming back to this bar. Since I have not enjoyed my online experience and have not won a jackpot, it seems meeting people at bars is the most traditional way. The more I wonder why I don't choose a better, different bar instead of this hole in the wall, the more I'm assured it must be the ugly baby phenomenon. Ugly babies all come out bald, needy, resembling a hairless rat—some even look like their neighbor, Mister Wang—yet, regardless, parents adore those ugly babies (all babies in general, that is). Our neighbor, Mister Wang, was a strange specimen of a man, and who Aunt Sarah kept telling me was my father and that one day he'd kidnap me. First of all, I was scared because Mister Wang was—shockingly—Asian and I wasn't Asian. The joke worked because Aunt Sarah's daughter (my cousin Christina) was assembled with the help of an Asian man or two, and, therefore, Christina was not dissimilar to a little Mulan. I never could understand why she disliked Jackie Chan's movies so much. As a child, however, I was terrified I'd turn Asian by the age of thirty, and I would look in the mirror from time to time, wondering why I was so good with chopsticks. Truth be told, I never met my father, but I do know he's of Middle Eastern descent, a fact that explains why

Chloe calls me Princess Jasmine, saying I'm her twin. With whatever is happening to my stomach's nonexistent abs buried under a thick layer of fat, Natalia claims I look more like Jasmine's father.

So as any parent would adore their ugly child, I also adore my Upper East Side bar for its cute men, cheap drinks, and music. By Upper East Side, I mean, of course, Spanish Harlem; by men, I mean, of course, the baseball players on the sports channel across the bar; and by music, I mean, of course, hearing Pedro Grande say, "Here's your fried chicken, ma'am," which is music to my ears.

Pedro Grande fails to notice the rage I'm in, how hunger turns me into a cranky bitch while he, whistling a tune, casually stops by the table as though strolling around Central Park with a baby carriage, an indication of his laziness and lack of customer service skills. When Pedro Grande dumps fried Foghorn Leghorn on the table, I scan the plate, searching for the taters.

"Where are them fries?" I ask Pedro Grande, offended.

"The potato man no come yet," he announces in his broken English. I was looking forward to getting the fries all day.

"Are you serious?" He nods somewhat honestly. "Let me know as soon as the potato man comes."

"Maybe an hour."

Pedro Grande dismisses himself back to the kitchen. Completely devastated, I try to come up with a way to get my hands on a basket of fries. Since my mind works better on a full stomach (and during sleep), I jump on my food with a passion more appropriate for a first-time kiss by two teenagers.

When the poultry is eaten and the plate is licked clean, up pops an email in the middle of my phone's screen. A web of tiny lines created by a crack in the screen cover the body of the email, but I can see it came from a retail store, subject line advertising an upcoming sale. The crack makes me wince each time I pick up the phone in my hands.

This is my very first adult smartphone, an upgrade from a brick phone, which as a real philanthropist I donated to my cousin Christina, who is unemployed and could never afford one of her own. How I managed to smash the new one already beats me. Glass screens are more vulnerable than I thought. The salesman had that superior smile when I declined insurance and a protective cover. He told me horror stories of how often screens get broken, but at the time, I thought he was trying to upsell. Now it haunts me that I was such a dupe. The battery level is only 90 percent full, meaning a tenth of the charge has evaporated since I charged it this morning. It was hardly used today at all. This lithium battery business is absolutely ridiculous, just a ploy to drive customers into purchasing portable battery cases. Why they call them smartphones is a serious question. With the phone in my hands, I check the text message log, but it appears empty, as neither Chloe nor Natalia have left me any messages. Next, I open the Internet browser. The flight status, according to the website, is on time, departing at 9:00 P.M. sharp. The temperature is fifty-five degrees, unusually cold for October, and in a few hours, the temperature will drop to fifty. No new messages from any Jewish men. I sit back and think of French fries, how a carbo-load would help me forget about work.

Still hungry and anxious after finishing the food, let alone sober, I flag down Mario with the hope he's got my fries. He gives me one of those death stares to let me know he ain't got any. After finishing my only entertainment —food—I get bored. Chloe and Natalia won't get here until later. I must be stupid for leaving work early today. I could have been productive or could have worked on more of my Photoshop experiments. It was not because of laziness that work was the last thing on my mind, but because I'm a secretary (which is a defense on its own), and since Adam who I "secresit" is on vacation, I had a legitimate reason to slack off and leave early.

Besides, I needed a break after a certain fiasco. Adam's been gone for five days, a long enough stretch in time for problems to begin to accumulate. For months, I've been having issues with this rat, Babette, who secresits the company's president, Chuck Petticoat. Today she and I had a big fight. Two hours later, Mr. Petticoat sent me an email that he wants to see me first thing Monday morning. I quickly forwarded the email to Adam but he failed to respond, neither did he return any of my calls. I constantly check the poor smacked screen, paranoid Adam would call and I'd be stupid enough to miss him. I need to bring him up to speed and make sure he hears my side of the story first. He's the only person who can stand up for me if things go to hell and judging from Mr. Petticoat's email they will.

With the phone in front of me in case Adam calls and no fries, I watch the door, wishing at least once a man would get here before the evening crowd to chat with me, among other things I can think of he could do to me. Maybe because men who respect themselves prefer real bars, but I've noticed how on rare occasion some rare Caucasian would surprise me by being all dolled up and ready to tango. As misfortune would have it, he'd turn out to be married or, more realistically, I'd be too drunk to remember. Since I'm in an early position before anyone else shows up, and since even Mario hid somewhere in the supply closet due to no patronage, tonight promises to be boring. I'm longing for a quick catnap from all the food that came inside of my body and a legitimate fear that none of it will ever come out. My left elbow is on the table, palm holding my left cheek, a pose boring people came up with to look bored. To entertain myself, I strum my lips with an index finger.

I need to get them fries one way or another, a task for which I open the Internet browser on my phone. The entrance door swings open, hinges crying loudly like an old, drunk lady who smoked for forty years, moaning to be oiled and to get laid. The light from the outside brightens up the interior of the bar. In walks Chloe, with a tote bag in hands, scanning the prairie of the bar as though an eagle searching for dinner. Her eyes lock on me, the chipmunk. She reaches the table in three jumps, breathing heavily. Her tote is stuffed to its full capacity, amounted to approximately two weeks' worth of clothes. In her white wife-beater underneath a blue denim jacket, she looks like Jean-Claude Van Dyke.

"Moving to Vegas?" I say, squinting for an unidentified reason. We are going away for a weekend, not a month, is what I really want to tell her. Into my gooseberry-colored Michael Kors leather tote, which I simply nicknamed "the Gooseberry," went the essentials: makeup, two pairs of panties, a tee shirt, and one dress. Chloe went one step further, apparently. She sits down across from me, occasionally looking back at the door in a sketchy manner, placing the lumpy tote on the table near my drink, almost spilling it on my work slacks. Thankfully, they are black anyway.

"This will blow . . . your . . . mind," she says, stopping for three seconds after each word. "I need a splash first."

With two fingers in her mouth, she whistles toward the bar where Mario waves back, indicating he's got it. As frequent Friday night guests at this dirty saloon, we're sort of privileged and Mario acknowledges it by remembering each patron's poison, same as remembering someone's name, which means I'm out. Mario knows Chloe's getting a beer, one of those, consistency of maple syrup, darker than her fake tan, and smellier than engine oil. Beer lacks class if you want to know the truth. When the beer arrives in a footed pilsner glass together with a pitcher for refills, Chloe gulps half the glass as though to oil her own engines, to rehydrate. Foam from the beer paints her upper lip white, as though a mustache, and she licks it off with her tongue.

"Dig this. Pocket got arrested today, see? I saw the whole thing through the pee-hole: He was handcuffed and all. The cop was so hot I almost peed *my* pants." She highlights word "my," as though by mistake she could have peed someone else's pants. She finishes the beer, loudly placing the glass down on the table.

"And then," she adds, "guess what happened?"

"I had such a terrible day. Let's play the guessing game some other time." I sigh to emphasize. To emphasize even further, I lift up my drink and take a long sip.

She keeps cruising the entrance door and turns back around. "I just woke, see?" she whispers as though it became illegal. "Pocket brought my weed and left. Two minutes later, after I ate a brownie, I heard this hubbub happening in the hallway. I saw zero through the pee-hole, so I lay on the floor and peeked under the door. Pocket must have told the fuzz about me, see, because two minutes later—boom—the doorbell goes and I see boots an inch away from my nose. I stood up carefully, see, looked through the pee-hole, and guess who I saw?" she finishes with her eyes wide open, blinking rapidly. Goodness, what big eyes you have, Grandma. I think of all that "see, see" she's giving me. If I learned nothing else from knowing her since May is the fact that "see, see" means she's lying, but I decide to play along.

I have a sip of my drink first, again just for the emphasis and say, "Just tell me." If she asks me to guess one more time, I'm going to flip my cork.

"Who else? It was the cop who rang the bell. The funny part is we both know him. Garry Straddle. Remember how we met him in Times Square after we ate sushi?"

I nod, but I don't remember. She keeps pimping out the idea I eat sushi when inebriated, and I keep telling her I've never had sushi before in my life.

"And?"

"I saw him and said to myself: holy ship. In his uniform, he looked unyielding. And who knew he was a cop, right? I knew he was going to arrest me, see, so I ran to the bedroom, packed the tote, grabbed the fish, then Matilda and I fled using the fire escape."

"What fish?"

"Matilda is catching up, by the way. Last I saw of her, she was on the 72nd Street. Another cop was following me, so I had to trick him, see? I went to McDonald's, ordered some chicken nuggets and taters, locked in the bathroom, and waited for about an hour. When I exited, he was gone."

"Wait a minute, what fish were you talking about?"

"Here."

She lifts up the tote, making a grunt only bodybuilders managed to learn and puts the bag on the floor next to her. After throwing three books from the top of the bag onto the floor, after Wonder Woman panties fly on top of the books, she digs deeper into the tote and produces a condom filled with water before my eyes. With my right hand holding the drink I freeze while

Chloe takes my left hand, straightens it out, and places the condom on it. The condom, from the way it holds itself together, must be tied at the top and weighs about three pounds. Putting my drink down, I hastily grab the top of the condom with my right hand to prevent it from rolling out, noticing a fish the size of a shark inside. When the fish sees me, she swims closer to me and becomes teeny, courtesy of water or condoms and their ability to multiply everything. On closer inspection, my fingers on the other side of the condom appear massive and there—crook's worst enemy—my friction ridge can be seen, triple in size.

"I broke the fish bowl while packing," Chloe says, "but I found the condom in haste."

I stare at the fish and at Chloe, wondering whether I'm being *Punk'd*. I'd rather do an appearance on *Jersey Shore,* though. I circumvolve my head around in hopes to find a hidden camera stashed behind the curtains someplace. In reality, I hope to find Ashton Kutcher stashed behind the curtains. Better if naked. Or Mike the Situation. Whoever comes first; I'm not picky.

"Matilda was electrified when we stole it," Chloe adds. "She saw the fish and pointed her finger, saying how much you'd love it. We got it for you yesterday. Tell me how much you love it."

"I love it a lot," I say carefully, wondering if I can be put in jail for accepting a stolen fish. What the heck am I supposed to do with this thing? The smell of latex hangs strongly in the air, my hands oily with lubricant. I peek at the condom closer, moving it around, playing with the light. The fish, perhaps scared to death, swims as far away from my eye as possible, then returns. If she appears giant and fancy to my eye, imagine how giant and fancy my eye must be to her?

"You get to name the fish?" Chloe states, asking. Besides "see, see," what I've also noticed since the time we met (in May) is her sentences: even the firm statements end with imaginary question marks, as though she's unsure whether she wants to ask a question or to answer it. This is the second time Chloe has supplied a present, and from the past experience, I gauge she'll request a return on her investment. The fish is her idea of bribery.

After balancing the fish on my palm for thirty seconds, I realize the condom sits perfectly fine without the need to hold it from the top with my other hand, so I release the top, picking up my apple martini.

"Well, tell me her name," she says excitedly.

With the condom on my left, drink in my right, I say, "Can we do the name thing later?"

"Fine. I need to go potty. I had way too much coffee at McDonald's. By the time I'm back you better come up with a name for the fish, Calyssa."

With the mess still on the floor, she picks up one of the books and stands up, leaving toward the bathroom with the book in hand. I simultaneously place both the condom and the drink on the table, slowly, to avoid breakage. I hate when people take books to bathrooms, as though to do what with them? Read? The only reason I take books to bathrooms is when I run out of toilet paper.

On the table, the condom gets squishy. Lack of elbowroom for the fish is eminent. She needs a fish bowl or an aquarium. What if I ask Mario for an empty bottle, stick the fish in the bottle, order another apple martini, and deal with questions as they come up, including what to name the fish and how to transport her to Vegas, to name a few?

Sounds legit.

Unwillingly, I plant myself in the upright position, bones cracking like a bag of chips. By the bar, I notice how Mario has already started making me a drink, juggling bottles twenty feet in the air to impress me. Please, I think. I always want him to drop a bottle so I can laugh at him, and long ago I would have said something like "Hurry up" or "Who taught you how to bartend, Sarah Palin?" Which could also be a great name for a TV show. Mario, however, gives me free drinks here and there, so I tape my blabbermouth shut. Sometimes, when I'm totally crapulous, Blabber—my mouth—won't listen to me and acts of its own accord.

Mario rarely speaks. He nods or puts on a smile by stretching his lips without showing teeth, his flabby cheeks usually as red as the sclera of his oculus. That makes me wonder if he has the teeth to show in the first place or if he has a black hole in his mouth. It's also possible he has bad breath and wants to hide it. Last, his English is worse than my Spanish. When the cocktail materializes before me, I try it right away. The drink is so strong that I only taste vodka in it, exactly what I asked for without asking. Mario probably gathered from the look in my eyes that I no longer wish to be sober.

"Could you give me an empty liquor bottle?" I politely inquire. "Preferably from some expensive liquor." Might as well do it right. "And more importantly, did you receive the fries?"

Shaking his head, Mario gives me such a stare I assume that's a no for the fries. Without saying a word, somewhere from under the bar, Mario fishes out a big bottle of Patrón. He removes its easy-to-recognize mushroom cork pronto, which leaves a hollow echo in its wake. He rinses the bottle for me using a bottlebrush I never knew he had, at the end replacing the wooden cork back on. Good customer service, all I'm saying. Mario then hands me a funnel. It smells of tequila and lime juice.

"What's the funnel for?" I say. "And, are you sure you don't have any fries? I'll even eat them cold; I don't care. I'm super depressed."

Mime he is, Mario puts the funnel on top of the Patrón bottle after removing the cork, and I understand in a New York minute the funnel will help with filling in water.

"No . . . Fries . . ." he says. I understand he's serious because when people stop for three seconds after each word, they either think you're stupid or because they want to get their point across.

At the table, after removing the wooden cork, I put the funnel into the Patrón bottle and pointlessly try to untie the top of the condom. If you're trying to do the same right now—and of course who wouldn't do it on a regular basis?—I can tell you to quit trying now, because it's impossible.

I return to the bar with a new plan. "Do you have a pair of scissors?" Mario looks at me askance as though I have a cucumber up my nose.

"I need to cut the condom somehow," I clarify. On top of that clarification, I even create a pair of scissors with my index and middle fingers and pretend to be cutting air by bringing the two fingers together a couple of times. Mario fishes out a pair of manicuring scissors from under the bar and passes them to me. Weird, but they should work regardless, I think, taking the weapon.

Back in surgery, I cut a little opening at the top of the condom and, as though pumped, the water instantly starts pouring out on the table like a volcano. I clip the opening with my fingers as fast as I can, which prevents "the wound" from leaking. With my left hand, I remove the funnel away from the bottle while trying to come up with a plan how to put the shark inside (the bottom part of the funnel is too small for her to fit into). I bet she's dialing her emergency number, asking a shrink to help deal with strange anxiety she's been having lately. Anxieties like a broken fish bowl, being tucked next to Wonder Woman panties, a condom that served as a carrying case, and a liquor bottle into which this crazy lady is trying to place her. Can this day get any worse or what?

To my surprise, the fish accelerates from one side of the condom to the other, unwilling to give up without a fight, a little trooper she is. Her fins raise, her gills tremble, her aggressiveness imminent. I'm 98 percent sure she comes from Jersey Shore: She looks fearless and ready for a fight. If I were fish and next to her, right about now she'd be gladly smashing my face, pulling out my hair, and ripping off my clothes. I think of a name Snooki, which is very Jersey Shoresey, but for some reason, it doesn't quite fit. If I pour the fish directly into the bottle, she may miss the rim, fall on the table, and break her bones (should she have any). I need to come up with a safer plan. Pleading with my eyes, I lure in Mario to help me with the fish. I hand him the condom, saying, "Watch out for the cut over here."

He takes the condom in his hands while I create my own funnel with a thicker bottom part: I grab the rim of the bottle with my left hand and stack my right hand on top it.

"Now, slowly let her in," I say.

Mario leans the condom into my hand funnel, and slowly the fish water starts seeping through the cut into the bottle. The fish fights till the very end, backing out farther and farther, vigorously swinging her fins in what could only be a ballet performance, the Fish Lake. Finally, she gets plunged inside. Several drops of water full of fish pee fly back in my face. The fish swims happily, however, not at all hurt, or hurt but impossible to tell without an X-ray. Her bottle is almost full to its capacity with more than enough elbow room for her fishiness, and man does she use the bottle accordingly, swimming at an accelerated rate back and forth, up and down, crisscrossing the bottle, zigzagging the bottle. Mario wipes the table with paper towels. I reward myself with a sip of apple martini and look at him with my "where-are-my-fries" look (my normal look), but he pretends to ignore me.

I make my way to the restroom to wash the fish water off my hands. Even after rinsing, I realize the latex smell seems to have clung to my skin. Not to embarrass myself later to be called "a condom lady" by all the boys, I rub my hands harder, pointlessly soaping and rinsing several times only to discover that latex is now a part of my natural scent. The liquid soap also does little to help, being it smells like a cute mango, proved by a sticker on the dispenser that says: Cute Mango. I guess ugly mangoes, just like everything ugly, will stay untouched at Walmart.

Suspicious of the complete quietness in the bathroom, I bend over to find Chloe's legs in one of the two stalls, her panties down to her ankles together with jeans, meeting a pair of blue Crocs at the bottom, book on the floor. I knock on the door of her stall. "Is everything okay?" After a failed response, presuming the worst, I pull the door to open, but it won't budge. Quickly I detour to the other stall. Holding my breath and praying to Jesus, I lie down on the dirty floor, disgusted by myself, afraid this will end up on TV while I will not end up in bed with Ashton Kutcher.

I crawl under the wide opening between the two stalls toward Chloe, cussing silently and thanking Mario for keeping the bathroom spotlessly clean.

With one of her fake lashes peeling off, Chloe fell asleep with her hands crossed in front of her chest. *Latent Tramplet*, I read the name of the book as I pick it up off the floor. Chloe's high school reunion invitation, which is scheduled for next Tuesday, four days from now, works part-time as a bookmark. I always attended my high school reunions, just to laugh at all the losers who have no jobs or steady incomes. My eyes find the following sentence in the book: "Her beautiful locks were as wavy as the Pacific Ocean. Not yet a star but a starlet, not yet a tramp but a tramplet, Ouchita looked across the ocean, asking the king of the waters to make her the next Dixie Evans. Ouch, you have a long way to go."

Putting the book under my arm, I slightly slap Chloe's cheek, which wakes her up. I'm sure she mistakes me for Matilda based on the confusion on her face.

"Are you okay?" I ask her.

"Sorry. I ate too many brownies."

I unlatch the door and wait outside. Chloe splashes her face to wake up. What a pain it is always to be the responsible adult between the three of us. Last month when we were in Atlantic City with Chloe and Natalia, I had to drag them both to our room, a workout I wasn't prepared for when tipsy myself. Natalia is lightweight, but Chloe is somewhat on the heavy side, so you can imagine the struggle.

When we return to our table, I eye the fish, admiring the work Mario and I put in. The fish swims around, perhaps cleaning her new house. She must be happy we didn't sell her to the Japanese for sushi or pissed off we weren't careful enough. I sit down with a sigh of relief like I never worked harder in my life. That is a true statement.

Chloe, now fully awake, refills her beer and starts working on the unshelled peanuts she stole from the nearby table. She presses on the shell, retrieving two peanuts simultaneously, throwing the shells on the floor. At the end of the night, the floor is one giant peanut carpet that squeaks under your feet with a crunchy finish. Just like Mario, she entertains me by throwing the peanuts in the air one at a time and they both land in her mouth, same as would metal chess pieces fall onto a magnetized chessboard. I roll my eyes. How is it fair to people like me who are allergic to nuts? I deliberately put the bowl away from our table when I first got here so I wouldn't have to be reminded of the injustice. Plus, the peanuts are free and I'm furious Mario put no free fried chicken in my bowl. I imagine myself juggling that chicken like Chloe though. I'd be black and blue all over by now. One last time I bug Mario with my fries-eyes, but he averts his gaze, pretending not to know me.

"How's work?" Chloe asks me. "You've been there awhile now, haven't you?"

"Yes, almost five months, but work's been miserable. Babette is spreading rumors I sleep with Adam and other married guys at the office."

"Babette? What an ugly name. Who's she?"

"She's Mr. Grunt's secretary, so she thinks she's the boss. Jessica said she'd overheard Babette discussing me during lunch where Babette said I had crabs, which was the reason behind why Adam left for vacation to get treated before his wife found out. She's also saying I got knocked up from sleeping with him."

"Who's saying, his wife, Babette, or Jessica?"

"Babette. Can you believe it?"

"Yeah, I can." She giggles for thirty seconds. "What's her problem?"

Where do I even start? "Well," I say, "her breath is horrifying, for starters. She needs to learn how to brush her teeth, or better—how to floss. I bet she's got crumbs of some burger patty still sitting between her teeth from a July 4th barbecue. Anyway, this past Tuesday, some chick from work told Babette I was discussing her breath with Jessica, so she grabbed me by my hair in the bathroom, which made me fall."

"Who grabbed you, some chick, Babette, or Jessica?"

"Babette. It was so gross."

"What was gross?"

"The bathroom floor. We had a little fight until the girls stopped us. Today, Mr. Grunt sends me an email that his majesty wishes to see me on Monday morning. I'm sure Babette has set it up. Mr. Grunt was vague in the email, but I can tell it didn't look like he wanted to discuss my raise. Mr. Grunt will probably want to fire me."

"What kind of a name is Grunt, anyway?"

"Well, his name is Chuck Petticoat, but everyone calls him Mr. Grunt, behind his back, that is."

"That's a name of a sex offender right there. Who is he?"

"He's the president of our company—a CEO, founder, blah blah blah— an older man, perhaps sixty-one, married but flirts with the younger girls, maybe even rents hookers with his money. He's obviously a creep. Rumor has it he just bought a duplex penthouse for his wife and kids, but keeps his old place for hookups."

"Why haven't you mentioned him?"

"I never had to deal with him until now. Babette will make sure to tell him what I did and I'm out the door next week. However, only Jessica saw us fighting, so it's my word against hers."

"Against Jessica?"

"Against Babette. Are you paying any attention to me?"

"Yes, sorry." Chloe snorts, sitting up straight. "I couldn't sleep last night, see? I knew something bad was going to happen to Pocket."

See, see. I might as well tell the story to a wall. Did I become this boring to her? I sigh. "Babette can't prove anything, but Mr. Grunt, of course, will be on her side, since she's his secrehooker. I'm planning to fight with her till the very end though."

"Caly, explain to me something. Why is it every time you talk about your work you always happen to have a fight with somebody or you suck up to some manager by buying him lunch or fighting with some stale-breath gals?"

"Because that's what we do in the working world. It's called a career ladder," I say, mad at her for not understanding how I feel. "I'm afraid that my name will be a synonym for failure again."

"How do you mean?"

Images of that day come back in a quick, unpleasant flash. "When I worked as a babysitter in Orlando, Bella, one of the older kids, finished high school. She refused to go to college. She wanted to be an actress and live in New York. Her mother had told Bella that she'd be waiting tables in New York rather than auditioning for movies. She didn't believe in Bella's talent. Her mother insisted she go to college instead. In one of those heated arguments between the two, her mother yelled at her and said: 'Is your goal to become Calyssa? Do you want to babysit kids your entire life? Do you plan to live without having any savings, without having your own home, without having any respect for yourself? Do you want to be a failure?'"

"What happened then?"

"Bella went to college."

"Oops."

"I quit and moved in with Christina and Aunt Sarah. When I found the position at Shred Unread through my friend Jessica, I finally realized my life's back on track. I'll do whatever it takes to keep my chair, even if it means dueling Babette. Even if I loathe this job, it doesn't matter: I refuse to associate with failure. I want to live alone. That would make Mom proud."

Chloe purses her lips, contemplating a response while I quickly refresh my breath with the apple martini. "So basically you want to be Mr. Grunt," Chloe says after thirty seconds of silence. "Make all that dough, live in a duplex penthouse, have a husband and kids, and be this creepy when you turn sixty-one."

"You totally missed my point."

"Or maybe you missed your own point, Pettycash. You'll be like this fish," she points at the Patrón bottle, "sitting at a bar like this, in this bottle, trapped at a job you hate, lonely but married, rich but miserable. Ever since you found this job, you're not yourself. You're like this crazy, job-obsessed Calyssa."

"We can't have it all."

"Pointless swimming with no goal, Toozyboom. Do the math," she says with a whisper before pausing to check her watch, scanning the door right after.

Looking at the *Latent Tramplet* book, exhausted, I decide to switch the theme of our conversation. "Are you going to your high school reunion?"

"I probably must get out of town for a while, stay low," Chloe responds with eyes attached to the door, voice humming quietly as though we might be bugged.

"You completely ignored my question."

"If that cop catches me, I'm history. They're probably searching through my stuff as we speak, digging for evidence." She turns her face around. "May I stay with you?"

"I live in this city. I thought you said you should get out of town." What I meant to say was: I just got that apartment all to myself and I want to keep it that way.

"You live in Queens and Queens is a different borough, you know. All I need is a place to stay away from my crib."

"You're being silly. Why would Pocket tell on you? The cop probably wanted to talk to neighbors, that's all."

"Right. That's why he was following me through the concrete jungle like a monkey just to chat about the weather."

"I mean, talk to neighbors about Pocket. You're just jumping to conclusions. What's your plan after we're back from Vegas?"

"Why is there always got to be a plan? The plan?" She throws her hands up in the air, eyes attached to the ceiling. "God, why didn't you create me like everybody else, with a plan?"

"Stop being melodramatic. What's your problem?"

She studies my face. If she were able to cry, I swear she would because her eyes swell up. "Because I do wish to attend the stupid high school reunion. But I'm not going."

"Why?"

"I was chatting with this guy online. He didn't have his picture and neither did I, but we talked anyway. It was so easy with him, you know? We had a great conversation about cats—he loves cats—and he's thirty too, a bit taller, according to his profile. We talked about our perfect date and he mentioned the planetarium. I love planetariums. I told him the zoo. He loves the zoo, especially tigers, elephants, and all the good stuff. We'd set up our date at the Bronx Zoo, but after I sent him my picture he stopped responding. I'm unattractive, I'm not in shape, and nobody will remember me at the high school reunion. That's why I'm not going."

I swallow. "You're not unattractive just because the guy never responded back." Sometimes I want to take her by her shoulders and give her such a violent shake and say: Wake up from your imaginary world and face reality. "You should go to your high school reunion."

"I will not."

"You're good enough, but you're acting like a child, Chloe."

"Oh, really, Pussyfish. If you're so confident in yourself, if you're good enough, then why should you worry about Mr. Grunt firing you?"

Just as melodramatically, I sigh at my new nickname, trying to come up with a sophisticated explanation. "Because I have a lease and bills to pay."

"Pussyfish, why does it always come down to money with you these days?"

"Stop!" I say, suddenly tired and irritated. "Stop calling me Pussyfish. You can stay with me for a couple of days. Deal?"

"Deal. Now I can relax a bit." She sits back and finishes her glass of beer in one take. "Thanks for letting me stay?" she says, as though asking again, the way a child would: cute, unsure of herself, impossible to resist. Just want to take a belt and smack her ass.

First time Chloe stayed over, helping me get home after I'd consumed an exuberance of cocktails, she wouldn't leave for two days, pretending we were sisters. It reminded me of the second grade all over again while in reality we're both thirty. It's unbelievable she tricked me into letting her stay using such a sneaky way as—what?—mind control?

"Something must have happened to Matilda because she was supposed to be here like twenty minutes ago. I'll go check on her. If they caught her, go to Vegas without me. And, oh, pay for the beer," she says fast before she throws her belongings off the floor into the tote. Just as fast she sashays toward the door, unable to see other tables as though they became invisible, bumping into at least three before she exits. I wonder how many brownies she'd eaten that she managed to lose her imaginary friend Matilda. Her reality is my nightmare.

One table falls down with a whooping sound. Peanuts, salt shaker, and an empty glass Mario failed to put away smash all over the floor in a merry chorus, rhythmic as the strum of an electric chainsaw guitar. The glass magically survives, but the metal bowl that was holding the peanuts rolls on its side toward the bar, as far away from people as possible, back to his papa and mama, Mario and Pedro Grande, respectively. What a mess this dame can make, I think while looking at the floor. In the past, the floor could have been cedar or maybe even birch (the lighter kind), but now, after living in this neighborhood for this long, or after being treated carelessly, or after the many drink spills, the floor is no longer Caucasian. With all the peanut shells scattered around the dark floor—sprinkles on a cone of chocolate ice cream—it really is a disgusting spectacle. Due to his heritage, Mario washes the floors every day, out of habit more than anything, but the wood is stained for good.

The door slowly closes behind Chloe, hinges squeaking from the boredom of their job while a draft of cold fall air finally reaches me about thirty seconds later, a whiff of freshness people manage to bottle into this ridiculous "Irish Spring" scent. I always admire inventors and how they manage to prepackage the scent of spring into a bottle. Come to think of it, what does the air of Ireland smell like after we stole most of it? Beer? Cute Mango? For the sixth of October, however, I'm very disappointed with the weather, how this cold and gloomy New York prepares itself for winter without giving us a chance to enjoy summer just a little longer.

To be polite, I stand up to fix the table Chloe flipped, but Mario waves me away like he's got it, like he's the man, like it's his job, not mine. Good customer service is what I call it. I have to smile in return to sort of thank him for being patient with us. He smiles back, showing me his teeth, also barely Caucasian. I close my eyes, take a deep breath, and sit down, thinking of what to do with the fish. Instantly, for whatever reason, the name Guadalupe comes to mind, not too inappropriate, mind you, being we're in Spanish Harlem. Guadalupe or Lupita is also a name of Natalia's housekeeper.

Bored, I examine the fish, thinking Guadalupe sounds okay, but way too long, the reason why, maybe, pet owners pick up sharp names for their pooches like Scud, Toto, or Pluto (which also happens to be an amazing name for a nonexistent planet). What about the name Elizabeth? Elizabeth sounds, however, like a name you must earn by pedigree and money, by being a prostitute to the Kennedys or by living in a thirty-million-dollar house. Just compare famous people: Queen Elizabeth I and II, Elizabeth Taylor, Bess (Elizabeth) Truman, Liz (my hairdresser). Come to think of it, Elizabeth is my favorite name after all. Since the fish is kind of a green color, like money, maybe a royal name will be suitable after all. "Are there any other names besides Elizabeth?" I ask my brain, but receive a hollow, empty response, an echo that goes cuckoo, cuckoo, lalaley. I'm really either a person who lacks class or imagination, maybe both, or maybe the switch that turns my brain on is now completely shut down like I forgot to pay my thinking bill (among the others). Will my liver start charging me fees for putting it through so many cheap apple martinis?

How did Mom pick the name Calyssa? I wonder. Did she sit at a bar, pregnant with me, thinking of all the syllables and endless combinations and meanings? Or was it fast, like the knock on Chloe's door—boom—and she named me Calyssa?

Fine, Elizabeth it is.

With two fingers, I quickly tap on the glass to get her attention. "You like your new name, Elizabeth? Are you proud of me?"

Swimming toward me, aggressively, I swear she nods. She's a live one, that fish, from the look of things. To cheer with Elizabeth I raise my drink, touching my martini glass slightly with the bottle until I hear a ding. She probably thinks what a dummy I am for doing so, or maybe she likes it if she indeed drinks like a fish. Elizabeth is the color of an olive, extra virgin olive, of course. Tastes better. Her fins are spread out, Mohawk making her look angry like she's ready to slap me.

The first (and last) living creature I've ever had was a cactus in a tiny planter, which had a magnet on its back. My cactus lived a long, happy life.

Or at least that was true until I bought it.

That happened drunkenly, without further attached thought while the cactus got attached to my fridge. Somehow, a week later, it fell off the fridge. Marble floor destructed the small and fragile terracotta pot and the cactus died. The worst thing of all? It happened while I was taking spinach out of the fridge to make a salad, something I never do since it's so healthy. And this happens. Lesson learned: I didn't need any spinach in my fridge and I didn't need a cactus to tell me that.

"Elizabeth," I tell her, "brace yourself, girl. I hope you do much better than the cactus."

After another unconcerned look from Mario in terms of having my fries, I get agitated enough and leave for the bodega across the street. I buy a five-pound mesh bag full of red potatoes and throw the whole thing on the bar to get my point across. Now Mario can't make any more excuses. At the same time, our potato guy comes in with a satchel full of potatoes. With a smile on his face, Mario exits the supply closet, carrying potatoes in a large bowl. It means they've had potatoes all along, but Mario missed them somehow. Good timing, I want to yell out but decide to hold my horses. No need to get irritated now.

Regardless, I'm getting my fries one way or another.

Pedro Grande shows up, wearing an apron. "Freidora rompió," he tells Mario. Even though I don't understand what he says, I swear I hear him being dubbed: "The fryer broke."

CHAPTER TWO

Present

THE POTATO GUY LEAVES MAD, TAKING MY FIVE-POUND BAG OF potatoes as a down payment because Mario refused to pay him. I have nothing to eat but my dried Turkish apricots. Mario promptly calls his chicken guy and cancels the order of fresh pollo, which he has no use for. Tonight they'll focus on sandwiches and guacamole. Pedro Grande brings me the first batch of guac together with corn chips, as a substitute for the fries I never had.

I receive a picture message from my cousin Christina in the middle of checking out a crooked guy who seems to be passed out at the bar. He must be one of the earlier patrons who came in already drunk while I was busy naming my fish. I pick up my phone in my hands. Christina wants to know which color outfit she wears best, the peach or the maroon. I remind myself to buy a present for her belated birthday, thinking she looks good in neither. I type, "Maroon," because Christina hates when I ignore her messages. She types back, "Thanks, but I think the peach is better."

Then why ask me? Christina claims I'm unoriginal when it comes to picking up presents. One lesson she learned the hard way: insulting me won't net her anything at all.

First, to stretch my legs, and more importantly to take a closer look at the guy, I get up, casually strolling in the direction of the bar and ease myself into a stool, two seats away from him. The guy is suspiciously too quiet, face dipped neatly into a peanut bowl. The scattered peanuts have created a halo around his head to inform us he may be dead. Drool is evenly distributed around his mouth. I can't help but wonder what made him want to drink so much. Was it a breakup, a family loss, or is he just an alcoholic who likes sleeping in peanuts? Drool aside, the man appears cute, and by cute I'm being generously nice. His face is rugged, and he's around my age, thirty. If he were awake, I'd totally flirt with him out of courtesy if nothing else. What I mean by courtesy is, if there are only two people at a bar, and one of them happens to be a man, and one happens to be a woman, you talk, regardless of whether you're attracted to each other or not. Too bad all decent men are in jail, married, cheaters, alcoholics, or unemployed. Out of boredom more than anything, I'm half-tempted to sneak into his pants to find his driver's license just to learn his name. Ever since I discovered the magic of walking and cussing, I remember craving to be in the loop of everything, a snoopy little child with a nose that could smell secrets from a mile away. If something were being kept away from me, I would turn ecstatic, electrified, cry until I received what I wanted. And his wallet is just two feet away from me, bulging in the side of his jeans.

As much as alcohol tempts me to do silly things, for the moment I decide better of it. There's still a chance he'd wake in the middle of me rummaging through his pants and then what? I could laugh and explain to him that since childhood I snooped but would he really fall for that? I must be puppy-cute not to deserve a punch after that, and God's the witness puppy cute I ain't. Besides, what if he becomes a regular patron? What if he keeps coming back here every Friday when I'm here? Soon I'll be famous as Miss Sticky Fingers. Instead, I switch my gaze from the guy toward the bar, thinking I could entertain myself by having another apple martini. My search, however, shows that Mario and Pedro Grande hid themselves someplace discreet, where the clientele isn't allowed. I'd bet thirty cents they're in the bathroom making love. They also switched my baseball men to a cooking show, and I can't take this on a thirsty stomach. I need to figure out what original present can be bought for a thirty-something-year-old woman who lies about her age. I open my phone browser and type in "Cute Mango."

The entrance door opens. I know this because the hinges announce each patron with their loud signature shriek. A girl in sunglasses walks in. She surveys the perimeter, letting her eyes adjust to the darkness. Behind her, like a good dog, sits a skinny pink suitcase on wheels. A suitcase of such a small size could probably fit one of Chloe's books, a pouch of dried Turkish apricots, and possibly my fish if I downgrade her back to a condom. Why did she decide to get a rolling suitcase instead of carrying a handbag like mine? She seems quite disoriented at first, but a bar is a bar: you must be an idiot not to know what to do here. The absence of the bartender or a waiter must have startled her. Without any more doubt, I just presume she's stupid, and why she's here is nobody's business.

She parks her skinny pink suitcase near the bar and positions herself on an empty stool. Her wavy blonde bob goes well with the glitter-sparkling pink bandeau, denim booty shorts, and black high heel stilettos, an outfit perfect for girls who need to turn tricks. Her ass does a little peekaboo, shamelessly smiling at me from underneath the shorts. She resembles a hooklet who just jumped out of a gentlemen's magazine, and I bet thirty pesos she's not even twenty-one yet.

"Hello?" she says toward the empty bar.

No response comes, so the girl lifts her head up toward the screen, watching a fat bearded guy putting marinara sauce on spaghetti, followed by meatballs that look too good to be true. Mario emerges from the bathroom right as he flushes the toilet, failing to wash his hands.

"Make me a margarita," she tells him in a voice more appropriate for a three-year-old girl. Mario shrugs as though he has no idea what she's talking about, but he keeps staring at her. Little does she know that his English is a train wreck, so I must intervene.

"She wants a margarita," I tell Mario in Spanish, "and I'm ready for a refill."

"Skinny, if possible, no salt," she amends the order.

Mario retrieves a margarita glass from under the bar and starts throwing bottles in the air. He mixes tequila with a liquid from their special "house mix," which the Department of Sanitation would frown upon. He then violently jolts the shaker in a rhythmic rhumba. He checks out the young girl —whom he doesn't even understand—his eyes sparkling. One way to interpret the sparkle is that Mario's somehow amazed hookers know their way to Spanish Harlem. "Maybe she'll have sex with me," Mario must be thinking, "if I pay her more attention."

If you pay her period, moron.

Mario puts the margarita in front of her, with salt unlike she asked, and decorates the rim with a wedge of lime that was previously squeezed into the guacamole by Pedro Grande. Don't forget, Mario never washed his hands after the bathroom. I'm sure, though, this girl is used to dirty men touching her. Fortunately, my drink comes without any decorations. Mario makes me an apple martini and disappears into the supply closet possibly to refill his amphiprotic house mix.

The girl pulls out cash from inside of her bra. She carelessly throws several crumpled one-dollar bills next to her drink, overpaying and overtipping by a good five bucks. She picks up her margarita, annoyed look on her face. She either hates salt or is simply stupid. Why in the world would Mario have a skinny margarita? She stands up, picks up her skinny pink suitcase, and sits in one of the two booths.

I return to my table with the martini in hand. Elizabeth greets me by swimming two rounds in the Patrón bottle while I wonder whether she's just hungry. I decide the best way to kill time is to play the dollar lottery I impulsively purchased with the five-pound bag of potatoes. With seven games of different kinds, I get into position and start with the first game, a pink one. Here, I have to scratch question marks one by one with a penny to reveal three identical numbers to win. No match. I go for the second game, a green one, this time scratching off little sacks with dollar signs. Nothing. The third game, ditto. The lottery is a preview of how much I'll lose this weekend in Vegas. Even though my budget is only a hundred bucks, in the past I won with much less.

Instead of scratching the last four games, I decide to spend some money and order a present for Christina. I open the Internet browser on my phone. An ad pops up, advertising a cleaning service called "HAPPY ENDING," which offers a twenty-minute massage as a bonus. On later inspection, I realize this is a bargain, having looked up competitors, none of who offer free massages. Mei Fun, my masseuse at the "4 U MASSAGE" on Canal and Elizabeth, charges sixty bucks an hour, and that's without any cleaning.

In the middle of me ordering my first twenty-minute massage/cleaning service with Happy Ending, I start wondering who gives the massage, the cleaning lady or an extra person she brings along with her. I put in my address and credit card information, typing "don't bring massage oil, I have my own," in the special notes box. A shadow covers my table, smell of margarita impossible to miss.

The girl, sunglasses on top of her head, stands in front of me. Her blonde hair has been changed to brown, signifying a change of a wig. She appears tall or so because I'm sitting. She's skinny with raccoon eyes, skin sparkling with glitter. Raccoon eyes are evidence of prolonged sunbathing with sunglasses on. Her stomach possesses a pierced belly button with a legit-looking diamond.

"Sister, do you know how to get to LaGuardia Airport from here?" she asks in the same voice I'd expect a child using on a doggy. I put in effort to hear her. She must be stupid. Her skinny pink suitcase next to her proves she's indeed stupid. I hate when people turn relatives on you. I'm not your sister is what I want to shout.

"Just take a cab."

"Cabbies overcharge. If I took one, it would be exorbitant in my situation. Someone told me there was a bus from here, M60, but I have no sense of direction. I walked forever, hoping to get a sense of my life and I got lost. It feels as though I sprinted for twenty-five miles without stopping. This city is exhausting."

Land the plane already is what precisely I wish to say.

"When I saw you with this fancy schmancy phone," she continues, "I thought you could help me find directions on the Internet." She takes a sip of her margarita, disgust, like peanut butter on bread, spread on her face. "I asked for no salt. What is wrong with people these days? Nobody is listening to me. Nobody is paying attention. I'm Lindsay, by the way."

"So you know, it's the bottom-shelf tequila they use here. You'll need a whole bottle of Advil in the morning. Stick to a vodka drink. Apple martini is way classier."

Without asking for permission, she sits down across from me. She places her legs on top of each other, a pose, hookers came up with to look more sophisticated. "You're right. I can't drink this crap shrap. When he's back, I'll order something else. What drink would you recommend?"

"Okay," I say, picking up my phone. "You said your name was Chastity?"

"No, it's Lindsay."

In the first place, I should've listened. In the second place, she should speak up because it's hard to hear her. In the third, I thought she'd have a hooker name anyway, like at least Chastity.

"Okay, Chastity, I'm Calyssa, but call me Caly."

"It's Lindsay," she says, "but call me Lindsay."

"Okay, you said you were going to the Newark International Airport?" I open the web browser on my phone as she interrupts me.

"No, LaGuardia. I'm leaving for Omaha today."

"Oh, sorry." In the Internet browser, I type: "hooker names."

"Thanks for helping me out," she says. "I have a crappy phone I inherited from some homeless person for twenty-five bucks. I wish I had yours." You and 99 percent of the population.

The first result that pops up in the Internet browser is Aunt Jizzy. Then a list of names goes on: Squeeky McBoink, Dee Lite, and my personal favorite, Bunnie Pye Thang.

I notice Chastity's long pink-painted nails, crafted with embroidery on edges. She's changed her wig again while I was looking up hooker names. Her hair now looks too hot to touch, a rich bouquet of all shades of red, which makes me want to fire-extinguish her. She's also sprinkled some perfume all over herself, one of those perfumes designed by a singer like Britney Spears whose career needed a new direction, and it wasn't perfume, from the smell of it. I'm also being nice calling her a singer.

"You sell wigs?" I ask.

"Oh, that," she laughs without producing any noise. "I hated the brown wig on me. But no, I'd never sell wigs. I worked at a strip club here."

Her last sentence catches my attention. Is it not cool to sell wigs or what? "Continue."

"Do you like this red wig better? I'm not crazy about it, but everybody keeps saying it looks awesome."

"No, continue about a strip club. I'm intrigued." I've never met anybody working as a stripper.

"I quit because I'm leaving for Omaha so I'm technically not doing anything at the moment. What's this?" She points at the fish, laughing. She then taps the bottle.

Her face is full of confusion: eyes narrowed, brows squished. She must be one of those people who sees a banana and laughs about its sexual reference to a penis.

"A fish," I say.

"Oh, how funny," she laughs and taps on the glass once again. "Does she have a name?"

"Chastity, I've never been to a strip club before. What do you do there besides the lap dances? Do you have to sleep with clients? This is my first hooker experience and I need to see the whole picture."

She seems insulted by my question. "It's Lindsay, not Chastity. I don't mind giving lap dances, but I'd never sleep for money." She says it as convincingly as a hooker saying: "I don't mind sleeping for money, but I'd never take the bus."

"And you said you're moving to Idaho, right?" I say, burying my eyes in my phone.

"Omaha," she says or doesn't say. I'm confused because somehow my brain only registers her voice in waves. "I'm over New York, girl. And it was such an easy decision because my friend Candy said I could stay with her for free in Omaha. On top of that, I broke up with this guy Ian."

I realize I like how she uses the phrase "on top of that." She must be a pro at that pose.

"Why did you break up with Luke?" I say and almost add, Bunnie Pye Thang.

"It's Ian, not Luke. He was like dead fish in the sea." She pauses to give Elizabeth a stare. "Ian was not the perfect guy for me, but who is? He appeared out of nowhere when it was convenient. I needed comfort; he needed a girlfriend. I needed a place to stay; he needed to play. He came without instructions in his package on how to break up with him or how to use him properly."

She pauses, waiting for a response. Instead, I have a sip of my drink, yawning without even covering my mouth, like a real lady. She moves her hands behind her head and starts playing with the curly red mop as she tilts her head back, so casually, so flirtatiously.

"The thing is," she says, "at twenty-five, I imagined I'd have a place of my own. You know what I mean? I wanted to have a steady job and a nice place to live. Reality is not quite like it. I stay on people's couches; sometimes flirt with a guy so that he will take me home. I've worked in a stupid club shmub as a dancer, but there was no raise, no movement up."

I always presumed strip clubs involved a lot of movement. I was wrong.

"To what end?" she continues. "My friend introduced me to this strip club where we make enough money a night to make a salad out of it, but I have no idea how to toss it. It's ridiculous. But it's not like I'm a hooker, you know," she says as though reading my thoughts while I casually keep looking at the web browser on my phone for more names, some of which include Ebony Blowregard, Shafty Crispington, and my new personal favorite, Boobsy Tamarack.

"I'm sure I'll find some other job in Omaha. I'm smart. I know I sound stupid for running, but I'm done with New York. I'll start from scratch. I'll write my blog or do something respectable. You know what I mean? I have nowhere to go, so I might as well go to Omaha. I don't even have a plane ticket yet because Candy was supposed to order it. I tried calling her but the sister doesn't pick up. Stupid?"

She mentioned being smart once and being stupid twice. You do the math.

"Very impulsive," I say.

She looks down, as though embarrassed, which gives me a feeling something is scratching her, hopefully not an STD. She tastes her margarita with a slight slurping sound. Chastity turns away toward the TV while I take advantage of the situation and search for more hooker names. My eyes play tennis between Chastity and the screen of my phone.

"I just want a place to call home. You know what I mean? I never wanted to be a stupid dancer."

She has to be careful using word "dancer," because a dancer she ain't. I think about what she said and simultaneously look at my fish, wondering if I could ever train Elizabeth to make me drinks one day. Elizabeth has sunk to the bottom of the bottle, head turned toward the TV set, watching her relative, salmon, being poached.

"I'm over stripping. I'll go to Omaha and see if it fits. Maybe I can go back to school or study cooking. I always wanted to do that. Maybe I could learn to be a writer. Maybe do both. Why not? There's plenty of time to decide."

"I skipped college altogether and started working at nineteen. The idea of college never fascinated me."

"Oh, how funny."

Chastity positions her skinny hands behind the flaming red wig and begins to play with her hair while I wonder what was so funny. She shapes her hand like a comb and uses it to brush her wig. It beats me how I hadn't noticed, but her lipstick is a color I never knew existed. I want to say blue, but then why would anyone wear a blue lipstick? Her skin is bronze and perfect, not a zit in sight.

She eyes the ceiling. "Are you there, God? It's me, Lindsay. Please have Omaha work out for me. Their zoo, they say, is fabulous. I've never even seen a monkey."

"Is that where you're from, Ohio?" I ask her, wondering why Chastity can't just leave already so I can go back to figuring out an original, perfect present for Christina.

"Not Ohio, Omaha. But no, I was born in Florida."

"Is your family still there?"

"I don't have a family. My mom left me in the delivery room." And she, of course, drank a lot during her pregnancy, I just fancy her adding silently. "She was an orphan herself and she didn't need another burden, or so I imagine the reason why she left me. Growing up, like a ball I was passed from one foster family to another, hardly a quality life as a tumbleweed. You get respect nowhere. When people learn I was adopted, they assume I'm mean and uneducated. Nobody wants to remember my name."

"Then don't tell people you were adopted."

"That would be lying."

"Exactly!"

She groans, but keeps playing with her red locks.

"Lying is wrong, Caly. Lying is the beginning of denial. Soon after, you find yourself thinking this is what life was meant to be, denying the truth. I know I have no home, but I don't lie to myself. See, I never learned how to save because I make easy cash. Easy come, easy go. But still, after everything I've been through, I've managed to stay true to myself and I accept life as it should be: To be respected you must work and be honest. People hate liars."

"You can't make people like you by simply being honest. In fact, if you don't keep your mouth shut, you could make some people very angry. Without lying you can't be good at," I say, giving it a thought, "anything. From astronomers to weather forecasters, everyone lies. If Adam hadn't lied to Eve about being a perfect gentleman, she wouldn't have been penetrated is all I'm saying. I'm talking about my boss here just so that we're clear."

I wonder what's worse though, Chloe with her compulsive, pathological lying, or Chastity with her denial of lying. For me it has always been the middle ground: You lie here and there, and then you tell the truth here and there, which is what I call a perfect world balance. Regardless of their point of view, both Chloe and Lindsay seem to have a lot of baggage, whether literally or figuratively. So lie or tell the truth, emotional baggage follows. I motion for Mario to make two apple martinis, one for me and one for her.

"Chastity, do you ever wonder about your mom at all? Maybe she's still in Georgia."

"No, girl, I don't wonder about my mom at all. It was in Florida, not Georgia. My name is Lindsay, not Chastity. And what's more, why would I wonder about her? She left me, so she was a bitch. Obviously."

Her cheeks turn red as it took her strength to raise her voice so much. I look at Elizabeth, wondering why that alone makes a person a bitch. Unless she was a dog? But I don't remember talking about a dog. I ponder upon why she howled the last sentence like a prairie dog out in the wild. I just asked her a question to be polite, not to get yelled at.

"I always wondered what Mom would think of me if she were alive," I say. "Regardless of what I do, I wonder if she'd approve. Sometimes, I imagine her peeking at me from above until she gasps with disbelief, ashamed. I want to prove her I've become an adult, and I even bought a couch this week to prove it. Though now my bank account is a big blind and I don't want to know what's left there."

"How a couch makes you an adult?"

"Couch is what we put into our first adult apartment, right after our bed. Next come the dishes and the rest, but Aunt Sarah purchased those for me as my housewarming present."

"Girl, you've been properly brainwashed by the TV. It's easy to be confused by the media telling us what makes one an adult. You're wrong. You just live with the fear of rejection, trying to be what society tells you to be. My friend Delight, for example. She has her own apartment in the Village. She's an adult, but she's also such a crybaby. She's just like you when it comes to being insecure."

It almost offends me being compared to somebody named Delight, but I try hard not to let it bother me. "Well, does Delight have a good job? Let me make it easier: does she have a job?"

"She's one of the bigwigs at Morgan Stanley, making $250,000 per year. We've known each other since high school. Delight is book smart, but I'm telling you, she's so dumb when it comes to dealing with men."

"Well, duh, with a name like Delight."

"I said it was Delilah, not Delight. Are you listening to me?"

Chastity is getting on my nerves. Mario brings our drinks, almost stumbling as he failed to watch his feet the way his mama taught him. But he eyes Chastity with the same enthusiasm I save for Oprah marathons.

I take a sip of my freshly made drink. "What I meant to say was: I'm trying to make a life on my own after living with Aunt Sarah and Christina. I'm afraid to lose my job, because if I do what would Mom say?"

"You need to be proud of yourself, girl. Act as if. Act confident." She scratches her head with such vigor that I suspect the worst. Maybe it's not an STD but lice she's trying to scratch off. But I like how she preaches me about confidence. "I work to exist, not to be existed. A gaggle of materialistic things made no one an adult. I have none, and I consider myself grown-up."

Yes, I can see where she's going with this. I have none, and that's why I have no place to live.

"'This is a material world,'" I say, "'and I am a material girl.' You've never listened to Madonna or what? I started working at nineteen because I wanted things to call my own. Yes, I never attended college, why I worked in many places, as a waitress, as a babysitter, and even as a janitor. I earned money, but I was too young and knew nothing about saving. So I returned home, defeated. In the meantime, all of my girlfriends started getting married and started making babies, and a lot of them started full-time jobs as housewives. I want none of that. My mom was a hardworking woman and if she taught me nothing else, she taught me that to truly own something you want to call yours is to work for it."

"I hate those women who exchange their lives for children."

"My cousin Christina will be one of them. She's pregnant. She'll be a single mom."

"That's tough."

"She lives with Aunt Sarah. She doesn't want to grow up. She works as a waitress and never saved no money. I gave her my cell phone when it was time to retire that brick. Who doesn't have a cell phone?"

"You want to prove to your cousin you're better?"

"It's not a competition."

"Sounds like it is. It all comes from fear of rejection. You want to be what your mom told you or what your schoolteacher told you. You want to be a good girl, so not to be rejected by society. What do you do now, by the way?"

"Well, almost five months ago, I found this well-paying secretarial job. A friend of mine works for HR so I'm sure she pulled some strings. I signed a one-year lease in a one-bedroom in Astoria, Queens just in July, foolishly thinking I could afford it. Today I question whether I made a mistake." I close my eyes for a second and breathe in deeply. "If not for Babette."

"Babette?" she interrupts. "Who's that?"

"She wants me fired. She's another secretary, but she works for the owner and CEO of our company, Mr. Grunt. She thinks she's better than me. I photoshopped her face to a chimpanzee this morning to get even with her. She didn't say anything to me, but the steam out of her nose was a pretty good indication she was furious."

"What an ugly name, Babette."

"Exactly. Babette is one of those people who don't use vulgar language. I mean, seriously, grow up. I know every line of her face and what it stands for. For instance, her lips pursed means 'screw you.' Eyes squinted, mouth as a capital O: 'what the hell?' The last one she used on me this afternoon. Eyes big open and nostrils wide apart means she pooped her pants."

Chastity starts suffocating from laughter, and I know she's laughing because she makes a face as though she's laughing, even if no sound escapes her mouth.

"Minds yet I can't quite tell but body language shows it well. Face is all you need if you want to see the person from the inside. Of course, scalpel would do just fine. That sounds like a lot of fun, actually, because if given a chance I'd prop that bitch open like a can of tuna in nothing flat."

"You sure like talking about her. Gossip is toxic."

I roll my eyes and sigh. Out of my bag, I take a picture of photoshopped Babette, which I printed out earlier at work. The picture looks just like I described it: a cute gorilla and an acute profile with a thick mustache above her lips. Babette's face is attached to a black and hairy monkey's body. You can see the reproductive organ too, which I did not remove in Photoshop. This picture was supposed to be a mood elevator, to be seen by the help only, including mailman Bob.

My crafty photoshopping makes Chastity continue her signature laugh, which involves an open mouth, closed eyes, and body shaking. She takes the picture in her hands as soon as her hysteria attack is over and examines it closer.

"Chastity, you said you've never seen a monkey. Now you have."

"You made this? It looks amazeballs, but it's so childish."

I get offended, but not enough to kick her in the knee. "What do you mean, childish? I spent three hours on this piece of art," I say, at the same time questioning why this picture was never hung at the Met next to Monet.

Chastity finally starts on her drink and gulps half of it, spilling a few drops here and there. She makes a face as though she just ate horseshit wrapped in gross kale leaves.

"Excuse me," she says, standing up.

Chastity unzips her skinny pink suitcase, where she finds a comb and a toothbrush. She zips the suitcase right back, locking it with a tiny padlock. She heads for the ladies' room and stumbles once. She took the drink with her, and for whatever reason also took the skinny pink suitcase. I decide to first-name her Ruby for her red hair representing the ruby red slippers, and last-name her Sprinkles due to the amount of glitter sprinkled on her pink bandeau and now all over the table.

Meanwhile, I examine the details of the chimpanzee picture. What an ugly face, I think, and automatically shake my head in disbelief. Babette's hair was for sure cut under a bowl of ramen noodles. Her bangs are two inches from the top, something I saw poor kids wear in third world countries, their naked bellies protruding from dehydration, according to *The Secretary Times*. Babette's got only one eyebrow, spread above her eyes, which resembles a centipede sitting on her forehead. If I were her, I would want to punch myself in the face every time I saw myself in the mirror.

"Mirror, mirror, on the wall," Babette says in her bathroom upon awakening.

The mirror interrupts her, "You, scary bitch, turn away."

"But it didn't rhyme!"

"I'm a mirror, not a poet."

Her parents left her in a basket in the jungles where Babette grew up with wolves, munchkins, or snakes, possibly with all three species at the same time. One way to rule out the problem at work is to tell Mr. Grunt it simply wasn't me who photoshopped this monkey. This will excuse me from an explanation. I mean, how could Babette prove I did it? No fingerprints found, no crime committed. What, she never watched *How to Get Away with Murder*?

Hiding Babette's picture as deep in the Gooseberry as possible, I reflect upon what Ruby Sprinkles told me. Her immaturity, her impulsiveness, her inability to act like an adult is who I can never become. At nineteen, it was expected. At twenty-five, it was decent. At thirty, it's unacceptable. I must fight for my job and prove Mr. Grunt how irreplaceable I can be. In two months, in December, we're getting our annual evaluations for proposed promotions. I can just imagine how much money I'll be making, enough for buying top-shelf alcohol from then on out. If I win this war against Babette.

This will be the time when Mom is finally happy for me, because after all the years of failing and living with Christina and Aunt Sarah, I have a place to call home. When I lived with them on Staten Island, how could I bring anyone home when I had a pregnant woman sleeping next door to me? I would not be making love, I would be making quiet. Christina can also be so annoying sometimes, nagging me with her questions about men I'm seeing and preaching at me about too much drinking, about not having any savings, and about not being original.

While alone, I take advantage of the situation and open my phone browser, thinking a book would be an appropriate present for Christina. I personally don't read anything but subway ads and magazines, so picking a book is like having a side of fries in front of me without eating them. Completely inappropriate. In my defense, I offered to take her out for a drink as a present but she keeps using the same stupid excuse about being pregnant.

Ruby Sprinkles returns from the bathroom in five minutes, again distracting me from picking a present. What's her real name? Was it Chastity? She assembles herself on a chair, hooker pose on, blue lipstick she had on earlier substituted with bright gold. Clumsily she places her empty martini glass on the table. Her motions became inept, as though she's consumed several martinis in the bathroom, which can't be true since she only had one. In her vindication, she's skinny and lightweight and obviously gets drunk quicker. Involuntarily, I check my watch and then notice that Ruby's got a pink sweater atop her pink tee. Her booty shorts have been changed to a skirt.

"You keep looking at your watch," she says. Her voice, just like her attitude became different, on a softer side, almost impossible to hear.

"I'm going to Vegas for the weekend with some girlfriends. I don't want to miss the flight."

"Anyone getting married?"

"No. My friend Natalia is a professional gambler. She hates traveling alone. And she doesn't have any other girlfriends, as far as I know. Whenever I fly with her, she buys my ticket. You'd be surprised how inexpensive they are. But also, she's rich."

With three hours before the flight, we still have plenty of time. After a lack of response from Ruby, I check my phone, noticing how my charge has gone down to 80 percent. That's 10 percent worth of looking up hooker names and presents for Christina.

Ruby clears her throat loudly to get my attention. "I know it's out of blue. I've been watching your face all evening long and let me tell you this: the eyeshade you're wearing is too pale, girl. Same goes for that makeup you've got on. It makes your face uberwhite like you're some clown. You need a darker shade."

She reaches into her suitcase and pulls out a flip phone. It's ringing. I didn't know anyone used those ancient phones anymore, besides my cousin Christina. But she's a lost cause anyway. While mouthing something indecipherable, Ruby flip-opens her phone, pushes a button, and stands up, walking toward the exit door. She leaves her skinny pink suitcase by the table as a reminder she'll be back. Her heels click against the wood floor, a cause for a few guys sitting at the bar glance in her direction. I silently thank Ruby for the clown comment, instantly getting a compact to find myself looking exactly the way I normally do.

Now that Ruby's gone, I take advantage of the situation and give Chloe a call. She doesn't pick up. I make another call, but it goes straight to voicemail. I send her a text message. Patiently, I wait for a reply back, though receive none. I give up. If Chloe and Matilda are late, I'm leaving for Vegas without them. Out of anger, I may even leave Elizabeth here, under the parental guidance of Mario and Pedro Grande. Having thought that, I take the fish in my hands and realize how easily I'm able to get attached to such an innocent, small living organism. No, I'll regret if I leave her here, the poor green thing. I wonder if she understands what she's got herself into as my pet. Four score and seven years ago, Chloe and Matilda tried to pimp me a cat. That beast I gave right back, despite the fact it was kind of cute, kind of black, and kind of furry. By my best calculation, Chloe's still got the cat around her apartment someplace. Hopefully, not as a rug.

Once again, I decide to admire the photoshopped picture. Alcohol is such a great invention; my senses are now heightened, I automatically have more trust in myself, and I trust that everything will work out. All I need is to have trust in Adam that his influence in the company is enough to save his favorite secresitter. Men have this special way of communicating with each other, which we women will never understand: They shake hands, have a Scotch, and the deal is sealed. We women don't have a special ceremony like that. We just smile, wag our lashes, and make eye contact, praying our booty looks good in those jeans.

With Babette's chimpanzee picture on the table, I think of how to present myself to Mr. Grunt on Monday. Babette's sly attitude somehow appeals to the executives. She's always right because she knows how to kiss the right ass. What if Babette can prove how terrible I am at work? (Which is not entirely true.) Or how late I am all the time? (Mostly true.) Or how many free donuts I can shove in myself during breakfast? (True.)

Right away I call Adam, my heart racing from fear of being fired. I don't even know the time difference between New York and Hawaii and I don't care. While his phone's ringing, I think of what Ruby told me, about me having a fear of rejection and how my insecurities come from such fear. However, how many people can say they are certain, confident, and courageous? After seven rings, voicemail kicks in. I try his number again with no luck. Have people stopped answering their phones or what?

I could potentially stop by his place on Sunday evening and have a chat with him and his wife. Adam and Eve (how pathetic?) have both swallowed the apple (the pay-cut) and moved out of Eden (Manhattan). Now they live in Bayside, Queens. Plus, I will send Adam an email tomorrow to warn him about the shenanigans that happened at work, so he's in the loop.

For some reason I feel ashamed about what I did and if I knew how to blush, it'd be the time I would. I blame Mom because she loved pranks, a quality I inherited from her. Sometimes impulsiveness attracts irrationality, as in photoshopping people's faces on monkeys. My second favorite is to send an email to the girls in the office with a subject similar to: "Tori's eyeliner is leaking," while I carbon-copy Tori. Right away, I'll send an email to Tori, saying, "Sorry, I meant Vicky," and watch her look in the mirror all day, paranoid. Last, I can never get enough of making fun of the lobby guy who works as a receptionist. He's got this perfect geek face for whoopee cushions. He also blushes every time he sees me, avoiding eye contact at this point. How can you miss an opportunity to have a good time, especially when such an opportunity jumps at you first?

Given the chance, I decide to mock the chimpanzee picture once more. I take it in my hands, admiring my Photoshop skills, something I've picked up on my own without any guidance. If I were a taxidermist, I'd skin her alive. Drunkenly, out of anger, I go to the ladies' room and act like a real lady when I drop the photo into the toilet and pee on her. I have another copy at work, one I wish to frame and hang in the bathroom incognito so everybody can make fun of her.

The origami-like ruffles of my work blouse somehow got unwrinkled while my face is a stark resemblance to a clown, exactly what Ruby said. The green in my cheeks goes well with the green on the blouse, and I decide to blame it on my lack of imagination for failing to buy Christina's present. I wash my hands with Cute Mango soap, wondering if it's okay to smell so exotic in a dirty bar. Doing some fifth-grade math, I decide the couch I bought wiped me of my financial assets needed for Christina's present, which is why I take the whole Cute Mango dispenser and place it under my blouse. Now she'll have to admit I'm original after all.

CHAPTER THREE

Escaping the Jungle

I RETURN TO MY TABLE. THERE'S NATALIA SITTING IN AN UPRIGHT position in the chair next to mine, eyes shut closed. Ruby's skinny pink suitcase got knocked off, its edges ripped from wear and tear of endless traveling between the strip club and wherever she gets to spend the night.

Natalia seems to be sound asleep, proved by deep and loud snoring. With her elbow on the table for support, she holds an empty glass in her hand. During the thirty segundos I spent in the bathroom, she managed to order herself a drink and finish it up. I call her name and shake her shoulder. Natalia opens her eyes, the two red communist flags heavy with sorrow. She sits up straighter and drops the glass on the floor by accident. Without breaking, cushioned by wood, the glass rolls on its side toward the bar, running away for dear life. I remove Elizabeth from the table and put her in my bag together with the soap dispenser I quickly recover from underneath my clothes, careful watching for Mario and Pedro Grande. I give Natalia a look indicating how annoyed I am at her. She's an hour late, and she assumes she's privileged to be late. Rich and Russian people are arrogant like that. And she's both.

"I'm late," she says like I don't know. "I had to attend a stupid bris."

"As opposed to what, a smart bris?"

"I don't understand what you mean."

Annoyed, I drop my ass on the chair. Natalia's wearing a black tunic under a fuzzy gray sleeveless jacket that looks more like a sheepskin rug. Her lips are generously stained with red lipstick, smudged just a tiny bit at the right corner. What's unfair is how her brown hair falls flawlessly on her shoulders, unharmed by New York humidity. A double silver chain hangs in her inviting, recently purchased cleavage. She told me she'd been transitioning from a man to a woman, working on one part of her body at a time. I knew she looked somewhat weird when I first met her, mostly because she's loud and her accent is strong, but if I met her on the street I'd never suspect she had a penis. She's done plastic surgery on her cheeks, injected her lips with silicone, and bought the biggest pair of titties last year in Brazil. She's naturally beautiful, with an hourglass figure, but she's clueless how to dress or accessorize. Several silver bracelets that don't match are hanging on her arm.

Eyes opening and closing in a tick-tock manner, Natalia's fuming the air with her alcohol breath, trick-or-treating as a bottle of moonshine. She's Donnie Drunko, but I know for sure she can still outdrink everybody within a fifteen-mile radius. She stares at my drink and humiliates it with a look of disgust. She hates apple martinis.

"You're such a sissel," she says. "When will you drink the good stuff?"

"When the apple martini is blue."

"I don't understand you. Speak English."

She whistles toward the bar. Mario acknowledges with a nod and starts fixing her a Manhattan, hopefully in a plastic cup before she manages to break something else. Her eyelids slide halfway down her eyes, due to (but not limited to) the heavy weight of gin, rum, maybe vodka, all mixed together of course, yet a hero she is, she's trying to look at me with her eyes half shut. Mario promptly delivers the drinks and escapes. He's scared of her, for sure. But who isn't?

"Here," she says, handing me the drink.

"No, thank you. I have my own."

"Don't chicken, Calyssa. Chickens don't get laid, chicks do."

Laughing, she snorts up a neigh while I roll my eyes. Even looking at her drink makes me want to puke. Manhattan is primarily Canadian whiskey, sweet vermouth, and Angostura bitters, a kind of drink that could potentially explode in flames should there be a source of fire.

"No, thanks," I repeat, raising one eyebrow. "Even my boss wouldn't dare drinking something this manly."

"You're such a pussel."

She swallows the Manhattan in three gulps and slams the glass down on the table with a juicy smack. Next I hear a certain suspicious sound you're afraid to hear when the USPS delivers dishes you ordered from the Internet.

Natalia fishes out a lighter from her red Burberry clutch and pointlessly tries to make it work. Even though the gold lighter sparks, it fails to produce flame. When a steady flame finally comes, she realizes there's no cigarette in her mouth, why she fishes one out of her bra. She carries a small clutch but no bag, so there's no room but in the titties for whatever else she wishes to carry with her. She finally lights up the cigarette despite the "NO FUMAR, PER FAVOR" sign neatly placed on our table, complete with a picture of a lit cigarette in a red circle with an X mark over it. The sign, common sense, and the fact it's illegal to smoke in public places never seem to bother her.

The smoke from the cigarette manages to find its way to my lungs, making me cough from the unexpected bitterness. I melodramatically fan the area near my face, which does nothing in terms of reducing the milky cloud in front of me.

"Natalia," I say, blowing the smoke away from my face, "can you put it down?"

"He doesn't mind," she says, pointing at the general direction of the bar where Mario pretends not to notice us.

"He minds but he's scared of you. That's why he put the sign on each table. You see the sign?"

"I don't freaking speak Spanish," she says, picking up the sign in her hands and fanning her face. She then drops it on the floor. Her speech is becoming more slurred with each drag of cigarette.

"Are you okay? Why are you drunk? We're supposed to go to Vegas tonight. We have tickets."

"Don't talk to me like I'm eleven. I know we have tickets."

"Then what's the matter with you?"

"I'm upset. Lupita is such a pussel. I hate those Mexicans."

I look around, wondering if Mario heard us. Natalia is not a racist, but she has no filter. Lupita is her housekeeper she hired a few weeks ago.

"Hey, cut that out," I whisper. "What did Lupita do?"

"The bitch eloped."

"Natalia, she was not your slave. She's allowed to quit. And word 'elope' means escaping for a wedding. Just say she left, not eloped."

"Why not just tell me?" She collects her hands into fists, and gives the table a blow. "If she wanted to quit I'd let her."

"You tend to intimidate people without realizing it."

"I didn't do anything to her. I'm sure she just pretended to be Mexican so

I would feel sorry for her and her ten kids. If I find that Mexican rat, I'll shave her pussel and drown her in the Hudson."

I can hardly wait to read the headlines in *The New York Times*: "Pussel-shaved Mexican rat drown in the Hudson."

That will most definitely stop illegal immigrants from sneaking through the border and jumping through the fence. I look at Mario, knowing realistically that without hard-working people like him, clean floors and cheap margaritas would come at a stiff price.

"Who in this country would pretend to be Mexican? Lupita must have had her reasons."

"What reasons? She had no rights and no reasons. She's Mexican: She can't afford to have reasons. She's a rotten sissel is who she is. And I was so nice to her, you know. I bought her a laptop, for Russian's Christ sake. I'm such a nice woman."

I nod. "You're a nice woman. Just cut down on the Mexican talk. Natalia, listen to me. We can find you another housekeeper, but you can't buy loyalty with a laptop. You can't just buy people things and expect them to like you."

"But I miss her empanadas," she says loudly, making Mario duck his head in fear. "What am I going to do without help?"

Shut up, I mouth, afraid to say it out loud. "You will survive."

I like how rich people react to problems that don't exist in the middle class. Correction: problems that don't exist in any class. Natalia rarely explains anything, giving abrupt instructions. She expects people to read her mind. No wonder Lupita "eloped," perhaps scared for her safety.

With a gesture of my hand I order two more drinks from Mario, one for me, one for Natalia. Mario delivers them in less than a minute. The bar is somewhat empty so service is fast. Natalia gulps hers as a shot and places the cigarette butt inside the glass. She lights up another cigarette while I exaggeratedly blow the smoke back in her face. Whenever she's angry or nervous she chain-smokes, which is what she seems to be doing now. I wish I could comfort her, but maybe once we're in Vegas we'll see a magic show. She loves those.

Having smoked half a cigarette, Natalia's eyelids make a complete shutdown and she gradually falls asleep, just like Aurora after she pricked her finger on the spindle of a spinning wheel. I relieve the cigarette carefully from her fingers, trying not to get the fishy chemicals all over me, after which I stab it out on the floor with Natalia's black suede Prada pumps. Nothing in the world, besides money and dried Turkish apricots, would make me stab out a cigarette with my own shoes.

Her classic jeans are rolled up to her ankles, and I notice a few bristles of hair sticking out because Natalia neglected to shave. Maybe Lupita is scared of unshaved legs. I shake Natalia's shoulder several times, but get nothing except for Russian mumbles. She'll fall in and out of sleep periodically, say something in Russian, laugh, snore, and once in an upright position, she walks while talking nonsense.

What am I going to do with you, Natalia?

Ruby Sprinkles gets back. She's crying quietly, not a tear in sight.

"What's wrong?" I say, annoyed.

She falls down on a free chair and shakes her head while staring at the floor.

"I'm such a fool shmool, Caly. I'm not going to Omaha. I called Candy, my friend who I planned to stay with, but she said her landlord just kicked her out of her apartment for not paying rent. I knew she was a flake. This proves it."

I can't exactly tell you how I know whether she's crying or not, because truth be told she could be laughing, potentially. Reading between the obvious lines of her sentences I must presume she's crying, all I'm saying.

"So now I'm homeless again."

I don't know why I feel sorry for her, something about that high-pitched voice of a three-year-old.

"I can buy you a drink?" I say, unsure what else people say in such situations.

"Candy was going to pay for my ticket because I told her I was broke. I was actually thinking, Caly, since your friend paid for your ticket, will she be able to pay for mine?"

My eyes pop open in surprise. "What do you mean?"

"You know, like, I could go with you to Vegas and try it there. I've never been. And I'll make some money at a strip club there and pay you back."

"I'm sorry . . ." I say, realizing I forgot her name.

"Lindsay," she says as though she understands the reason for my pause. I thought it was Chastity.

"I'm sorry, Ruby, but I doubt so. Natalia is drunk but she'll suspect something fishy is going on."

"Is that her?" She points with her pinky at Natalia. "The tunic doesn't fit her at all."

"Yes."

"Is she okay?"

"Yes."

"Did somebody just smoke here?"

"Yes."

"Can I come with you?"

"No."

Lindsay slowly breathes in, wiping off invisible tears.

"I'm sorry, Caly. I'm an idiot to even ask for a favor of such magnitude. I forgot all sense of human decency. I hate Candy."

"Maybe you should switch to chocolate?"

"I knew it: the only way to get anything in this world is by hard work. You can only rely on yourself. Good things don't come on a free plate. I'll go order another drink."

She slowly gets up, making her way toward the bar. She positions her skinny tush on a stool and starts watching a local news channel, occasionally flipping her hair.

Meanwhile I look at Natalia, wondering how I'm going to deliver her to the airport by myself without Chloe's help. I also need to pay for her drinks with her money because I can't afford to pay for two Manhattans out of my own pocket. Natalia always picks up the tab and last time it was no exception. Several times she mentioned she loves buying people stuff because, I believe, she thinks friendship and loyalty can be bought. She's trying to fit in as a female, always talking about doing something "girly." When we hang out it's doing something "girly," so she pays for us. Also, somehow, she's entrusted me to be in charge of her when she gets drunk, just like now.

I like Natalia's company because she's interesting, not because she's paying for everything. She's had such a rough life. She emigrated from Russia in her twenties and started gambling for a living. She drinks a lot. Now she's transitioning to a woman and started electrolysis, a painful procedure wherein each hair follicle on her face gets burned out. I'd never have enough guts to go through that. Even though I've known her for about two months, it seems I've known her for years. Somehow, when you get drunk together, you instantly become best friends or even family. It depends, of course, on which drinks you order and the amount.

Chastity is trying to get Mario's attention, but for him she's invisible. Like she mentioned, people don't notice her.

Maybe the little skinny hooklet was right and maybe she could help me after all. She can help me carry Natalia to the airport and through security. Of course, Natalia would have to buy her a ticket, which I can purchase on her behalf using her credit card. If we don't go now, we're staying in the concrete jungles of Manhattan, and that will not make Natalia or me any happier.

Traveling to another setting helps people forget about their current problems, which is why it is important we leave town tonight.

I open up Natalia's clutch and search for some cash. The color of the clutch is called military red, whatever defines that. It looks the same as period red, fire truck red, or simply red red. Inside, there's a Prada wallet, also red, tucked next to a cell phone. Like in every rich Russian woman's wallet, there are three bundles of one hundred dollar bills, stacked in nice, thick, juicy rolls and held by rubber bands. To keep the clutch safe, I place it in my bag next to the fish. With a Benjamin in my hand, I approach the bar and pay our tab, tipping Mario a much-deserved 30 percent.

"Listen," I tell Ruby, whispering for some reason. "My friend Chloe bailed on the trip, so you can take her ticket if you wish."

"Don't joke with me," she says excitedly.

"But you'll have to work for it." I swear she starts to undress but I stop her. "Help me get Natalia through the airport security and whenever needed. Get ready to lie a lot, starting with: if anyone asks, you're my older cousin Christina from Staten Island. Roger that?"

"Calyssa, I can't tell a decent lie. I never lie."

"Then you better start today. Or better yet, sometimes the best way to lie is to keep your mouth shut. Just follow my lead."

"Wait, why am I the older cousin? I'm only twenty-five and you're at least thirty."

I raise one eyebrow, annoyed. "Because Christina is three years older than me. And I'm not thirty. It's none of your business how old I am."

"Okay, I'm the older cousin," she amends.

"Good. Now, give me your driver's license."

"Why?"

"So when I call to get your ticket, I spell your name correctly, Dumb Dumb. We need to hurry because the flight's at nine."

I'll call to cancel Chloe's ticket and get Ruby's while we're in the cab.

"Ruby, grab my bag off the chair and go hail a cab. I'll be right out with Natalia."

"I'm Lindsay."

She hands me her driver's license and I pocket it promptly. We exchange phone numbers, which is always a good idea when you hire help. Ruby is now my employee and if I need something I'll call her.

At the table, leaning down, I clutch Natalia's waist and on the count of three I pick her up. In the upright position, which is rare for her, Natalia is like a sequoia, tall and ancient. I barely reach her shoulder. Natalia holds on to me like a baby koala bear to her mama. She talks about Lupita but her words are gibberish. Before Ruby leaves the bar with my bag, I catch her halfway out the door and pull out Elizabeth. I don't trust her life to no one. Fish in left, Natalia in right, I stumble out of the bar, somehow manage to open the door with my hip, and hold it open with my foot. Then I deposit a singing Natalia outside.

THE TEMPERATURE HAS DROPPED SIGNIFICANTLY SINCE THE TIME I left work, now running somewhere in the high fifties. Not my favorite temperature range. Besides us three, the street is packed with the Friday night crowd, people who are as drunk and obnoxious as we must be. Due to the approaching Halloween in three weeks, people who dress in all sorts of abnormalities become the new norm, and I spot Batman and Robin leashed by Catwoman who looks as good in her tight leather suit as President Bush trying to look smart on stage.

As though completely ordinary, the Queen of Clubs walks by, or someone who attempted to look like the Queen of Clubs. The three black cloverleaves are pointed out in three directions, her black crown slightly askew, and the most disturbing thing of all is the mirrored version of her that's dangling upside down. The costume is fitted into a white rectangle for the purpose of looking like a card.

I know at least one Queen who ain't fitting in no cab tonight.

Ruby is unsuccessfully trying to hail a cab with her hand at a wrong ninety-degree angle. Everybody knows your hand must be solid sixty-five degrees, a perfect angle seen easily by cab drivers. Even though Third Avenue is packed with cabs, most are unavailable with their roof lights off. Ruby's failing the only job I've assigned to her, and as one cab after another zooms by without noticing her, Ruby throws her hands up in the air, maddened. Natalia keeps singing a Russian tune while I keep her upright.

"Hot goddammit," Ruby screams. "Why none of them stop?"

I raise my left hand, one with the fish, trick-or-treating as the Statue of Liberty. One of the cabs stops nearby in about three seconds.

"Finally, I got us one," Ruby says, taking all the credit for herself.

"Where are you going?" Muhammad asks her, talking through an opening in his spotless window. Instead of answering, I order Ruby to open the sliding door. If Muhammad knows we're going to a borough, he'll never take us. By law, the cab drivers are required to take you anywhere you wish but only *after* you're in the cab.

"JFK," Ruby declares proudly.

My jaw drops. She leans in to slide the door to open but Mohammed, not surprisingly, drives away, going through the red light in the process.

"Ruby, what is wrong with you?" I almost yell. "You don't tell them anything until you get inside. Nobody wants to drive to a borough."

"I'm sorry. I didn't know."

"Now shut up and get another one."

I suddenly feel embarrassed for yelling at her, though I decide not to indicate that. Another cab stops by in a minute, an SUV van.

"Where are you going?" the second Muhammad asks us.

Ruby silently opens the sliding door and takes a seat near the front, holding her skinny pink suitcase in her hands together with my bag. I step in and neatly place Natalia in the rear, taking a seat next to hers, fish in hand.

"JFK," I say. "Please."

Muhammad gives me a look I catch reflected in the mirror—his eyes narrowed, lips pursed, nose steaming—as a simple reminder that cab drivers never betake themselves to a borough. He makes his knuckle crack by pushing his fingers outwards the palm. My throat gets automatically dry. With a hump, droopy mouth, big brown eyes the size of my fists, and an orange complexion, Muhammad resembles a camel. I cover my face in case he decides to spit at me.

But if Manhattan is a jungle, then this is the beginning of our Safari.

Ruby slides the door to close.

"Rev 'er up," I yell from the back seat.

I need to order Ruby's ticket, for which I get my bag from Ruby's hands and find Natalia's red clutch. Slowly we start moving. I hear a loud, violent bang on the back of our window, which scares me to death. In this neighborhood creepy things happen and not only do you have to lock up, zip up, and never drop the Cute Mango soap, but owning a black belt in karate would also be a good idea. With Elizabeth between my legs, I look back behind my shoulder without being able to tell what's going on due to a dirty window Muhammad failed to wash.

We stop and whoever was behind the cab smashes into the back window. The sliding door opens and in steps Chloe, along with her tote bag, her cat Anubis in a carrying case, and an oversized pumpkin.

"Go, go," she loudly says. "The faster, the better."

Muhammad shakes his head while I indicate she's with us. Chloe squats and moves forward in such a position.

"Are you okay?" Chloe says to the invisible Matilda. "Good, keep your head down."

She reaches the back seat and plants herself next to Natalia. We're so cramped I can hardly breathe. When Chloe is talking to Matilda it usually means she's stoned, and she looks it too. Something squishes into the back window, something resembling a tomato. Someone's attacking us. Muhammad revs up the engine and switches two lanes, carefully avoiding other cabs. All of a sudden it feels like we've relocated to an action movie set.

"What's going on?" Ruby asks.

Chloe makes a surprised face. "It's you."

"I don't think so," Ruby says. "Do I know you?"

"Hell yeah, you know me. You're the one who abused the animals. You're the animal abuser."

"What are you gabbing about? I've never had any animals."

"I'll never forget your skinny face. Caly, what is she doing here?"

I clear my throat. "Chloe, actually, you don't know her. She's my cousin, Christina."

"I thought Christina was Asian," Chloe says.

"She's done plastic surgery. What's with the pumpkin?" I say, trying to avert the focus from Ruby. Now that Chloe is stoned she's probably hallucinating.

"That dude over there and I got into a fight. I was picking watermelons and I pressed one harder than needed and it cracked, see? It splattered all over my face, so I told him I deserved something for free, but he just laughed in my face. So I stole a pumpkin as a payment."

That's her way of bringing attention to herself.

"Why did you pick the biggest pumpkin?" I say. "We're going to Vegas, if you're unaware. You can't bring that thing with you."

"Sure I can and I will." Chloe breathes deeply and yawns deeper, causing a chain event for all of us.

"I'm starved. Brownies, Caly?" She fumbles in her tote, fishing out a Ziploc bag. After she takes one brownie, one still remains inside. Ruby's watching while Chloe puts half a brownie in her mouth, and while I take the other one from the bag. Her brownies serve the same purpose as fries, but they work faster.

"These are with weed," I tell Ruby. "I'm not sharing, sorry."

"What are you doing?" Ruby whispers. "Do you want to get arrested?"

Chloe gives her a stare, her mouth opening and closing like Elizabeth's, tasting whether or not it's dry, something I noticed potheads do a lot. "Calyssa, you told me Christina loves brownies. Who is this clown?"

"All right, she's not Christina. She's a friend of mine. And she's not the animal abuser you were talking about."

"Oh," Chloe says. "I know where I know her from. She must be the fugitive from the FBI's Top Ten Most Wanted. I'm telling you. I know her from somewhere."

"No, you don't," Ruby says. "I'm wanted, but not by the FBI; by men. Calyssa, put the brownie back before we get arrested. It's illegal."

"You know what's also illegal?" Chloe whispers. "Your face. Ever thought of auditioning for *Scary Movie*?"

"Huh? Your story makes no sense. Watermelons are not in season."

"You know what's also not in season? Sunken-chested girls like you."

"With your fake F-cups, everybody you come in contract with is sunken-chested."

"I know where I saw you last. You let me borrow your hair to wash floors in the public bathroom."

"Why don't you spray more fake tan? Maybe you'll reach the color of your cat."

"Dry up you two," I say, annoyed. "What's the matter with you? You never met each other, so shut up before I kick you both in the balls."

How crazy are they? They don't even know each other. Sure, they're both drunk and/or high but it's not an excuse for anger tantrums. Ruby turns around while Muhammad accelerates the engine once again. I read somewhere in a magazine we like or dislike somebody within the first five to ten seconds, our decision based fully or partially on our judgment and previous human interactions. If someone resembles somebody you hate, on a subconscious level you'll hate that person too. Chloe is perhaps jealous of Ruby's skinny body and soft side while Ruby must be jealous of Chloe's strong exterior and self-respect. While in reality they both feel inferior and absolutely lack confidence in themselves.

Chewing on the brownie, I look at Chloe, whose eyes are now closed. "Why did you bring Anubis with you?"

"I can't leave him alone. He's a cat, not a plant." When she speaks, her mouth smells like Quarter Pounder with cheese, my favorite meal at 2:00 A.M. on a Friday night.

"Why do you always have to bring attention to yourself?"

She sticks out her tongue at me and turns away. Anubis has creepy green eyes and kinky-looking white fur around his neck for a scarf; otherwise, he's so black you won't notice him in a dark room. His eyes are aimed at Elizabeth in a way that suggests he hasn't been fed in weeks.

The brownie puts my thoughts together and I suddenly realize I need to book a hotel for the weekend (plus I need to buy Ruby's plane ticket). True, it would be easier to kick her out of the cab—now that Chloe's back—but it would be mean. Besides, a ticket to Vegas only costs $150. You can't even hire a good masseuse for that much, let alone a whole live striplet. She'll help me with Natalia so long as I help her.

I get Natalia's phone and dial the number located on the back of her credit card, putting the phone between my left ear and my shoulder. I get on hold. My own phone starts ringing in the depths of my jacket, and hanging up Natalia's phone, I pick up mine.

"Caly, it's Adam."

Adam who? I think for about thirty seconds, opening and closing my mouth to check whether it's dry, until I realize I'm talking to my boss, Adam Klutz.

"Is everything okay?" he says. "I saw you called me and I just listened to a voicemail from Mr. Grunt. He told me he wanted to discuss your employment."

"He wants to discuss my employment? That's it. He wants to fire me. You must be there on Monday or alone I won't be able to rule it out."

"Tell me what happened."

"I photoshopped Babette's face on a monkey. She annoyed me, and you know how she can get on people's nerves. I wanted to print out only a few copies for me and Jessica, but my computer froze and it printed out hundreds of copies until the printer was out of paper."

"So what?"

"So everyone saw that picture. Babette got insulted and she swore I did it. She said I violated the harassment code."

"What harassment code?"

"Title VII, the one that states that it is illegal to harass an employee because of sex, race, face, color, religion, or bad breath. She can't prove anything. But before she finds a way to tear me apart, I want you to put a word on my behalf to Mr. Grunt and tell him how good of a secretary I am."

Adam clears his throat. "Forget about it. Everything will be okay. He can't fire you for such a trivial thing."

"Trivial? They just fired that girl Kathleen for taking print cartridges."

"Those were expensive. Don't forget it's called stealing. What does Mr. Grunt say about stealing?"

"Stealing is unappealing."

"Right. What you did was a mistake. What does Mr. Grunt say about a mistake?"

"Mistake is a delicious cake. After burning you get to learning." Adam once told me Mr. Grunt had been a poet but gave it up to build Shred Unread, the company we're working for.

"Exactly. Forget about Mr. Grunt. I'm your boss and I'm the only person who can get you fired." He clears his throat again even louder.

"He owns the company. He can fire anyone he wants."

"Calyssa, you're asking for a huge favor. I was going to call out on Monday."

"Right after a vacation? People will point fingers at you. Can you please show up for just the meeting and leave right after?"

"Um, hungover? That's what you're asking?"

"Or drunk. Whatever. I will need your help. He'll eat me alive."

"You'll be fine. Listen, I have to go now. I'll see you on Tuesday."

Adam hangs up. I keep the phone in my ear without letting go, hoping he'd call back. Unfortunately, he doesn't.

I sober up in a second.

If Adam is ditching me on Monday, I won't have a job on Tuesday. One thing clicks with me: not because he wants to call out on Monday but because he's afraid of Mr. Grunt. Unless I come up with some sort of plan, Adam will not put in a word for me, not even a letter, to preserve himself in the company. What I did was wrong and being wrong by defending me sounds unappealing to him. I want to cry. Mistake is not a cake. Mistake is a big and ugly snake. Once you have so much class, then it snaps you in the ass.

Instantly, something clicks in my brain: I need to gain some advantage. Leverage is all I need. Leverage on Adam. But how? He's in Honolulu until Sunday night, however. I ordered his tickets, even though it wasn't a corporate trip. The nonstop flight takes eleven hours, or up to twenty if with a layover. I found him the best available rate, a nonstop, round-trip flight to Honolulu. I do all these personal tasks for Adam, but a moment ago he talked to me as though I was no more than just a replaceable, not-worth-fighting-for secrehooklet.

So Honolulu?

The leverage plan unfolds in my mind. Adam is fond of alcohol—so fond of alcohol you'd think he invented it. I'll get him drunk and take pictures of him naked to use as blackmail to make sure he's on my side in this war against Babette.

This suddenly sounds like the best idea I've ever had.

I'll cancel our tickets to Vegas and we'll go to Honolulu. Natalia will be happier on the beach than in dry Nevada weather. None of us has ever been there either. I pick up Natalia's phone and dial the number on the back of her credit card. She uses the free personal concierge service to make travel reservations, and calling from her phone means less of a hassle because I don't have to go through the verification process. The several times we've been to Vegas, the concierge put Chloe and me on file, so Natalia doesn't have to remember our personal information.

"Hello, Miss Romanova. Thank you for calling personal concierge this evening. I apologize for the wait. My name is Ted. How may I assist you this evening?"

He even thanks me for calling. Good customer service is what I call that. Little Teddy sounds like he's around thirty, has freckles, and smells like Cute Mango. This is my only chance to make sure we Peter Pan all the way to Hawaii, instead of Vegas.

"Teddy, could you get me four tickets to Honolulu? The first available flight." I disguise my voice to sound Russian, and I believe I'm pretty good at this because I sound sexy, harsh, and arrogant.

"You're flying from New York, ma'am?"

"Of course." I pretend I'm the Queen of Russia circa 1850: elegant, powerful, filthy rich.

Little Teddy taps on his keyboard, which sounds quite distant as though he's out in Oregon or somewhere far away.

"There's a flight with available seats leaving in an hour and a half. Do you have time to make it?"

I look at my watch. "Of course." Needless to say, Natalia would say "of course," if she were to speak. She believes people should know answers to their own questions.

"Perfect. Per your preference, I notice you choose first-class seats, but, unfortunately, there are only two first-class tickets untaken. Plus, they're next to each other. There are several empty seats in economy, but none of them are together. I apologize for that. What do you wish me to do?"

"How about two first-class tickets and two economy?"

"Just say a word and I'll do it."

I think for no longer than a second. "Word."

Teddy cancels the trip to Vegas. After he gets two tickets for me and "Calyssa," he gets one for Chloe. I add Ruby to the list, telling him not to save her information. I read Ruby's information off her Florida driver's license and learn her real name is Lindsay Goldplenty. Bitch lied about her name, calling herself Ruby! On the mugshot her hair color is pink and purple; I wonder what hair color brings her best tips at work.

"We'll also need a hotel," I tell Teddy when the tickets are booked.

"For how many nights?"

"Saturday. One."

"Per my liberty, I suggest a hotel on the shore called Waikiki Beach Palace. My wife loved it."

Of course he's married. Ugh. What else is new? "Get it," I say arrogantly, suddenly imagining Little Teddy to be seventy, scrawny, and without any freckles. Freckles are my favorite, so suck it, Teddy.

"Great. The ocean view room—with two double beds, private lanai, and all modern amenities—is $495 per night. You'll arrive at seven in the morning and check-in is at three, so I will book it for tonight as well as for Saturday night. This way, when you arrive, you don't have to wait for eight hours before your check-in and your room will be ready. I'll arrange transportation for you from the airport. They have shuttle busses. I'll call the hotel to explain the situation."

What a smart man is all I'm saying. If I arranged the trip myself, under the influence of those apple martinis and the brownie, the four of us would probably end up in four different cities without a reserved room. Three of us would most likely be pregnant while Natalia, without recollection of why or how, would end up at a casino.

"All done," Little Teddy says, breaking my wild fantasies. "To remind you, Miss Romanova: the flight departs in an hour and a half. Have a great night."

I hang up the phone, thinking I'll talk to Adam face to face. He'll be surprised when he sees me in Honolulu, sure, but I doubt he's smart enough to suspect anything. Tomorrow I'll call him, apologize for freaking out, and nonchalantly ask where he plans to spend the evening. And I'll make sure I'm there too.

Previously, during company parties, Adam and I drank together. He can probably outdrink Natalia, but his memory is of a chicken. When he's passed out from alcohol, I'll undress him and take pictures on my phone. Maybe I'll hire Ruby to strip naked, in which way he becomes a cheater. Even more fun! Of course, I can't drink with him as much—which will be a challenge—but I'll hold my horses.

.   .   .

I look at my watch. We need to make this flight but we're running out of time. Grand Central Expressway, however, is free of traffic. We're pushing a steady fifty miles per hour, and Muhammad for no reasons switches lanes, driving around imaginary cars in what appears to be an imaginary car chase. I wonder if people get so bored in their lives that they must imagine things to spice it up. Muhammad, perhaps, has an imaginary harem; he drives a Maserati (or whatever the coolest car is these days); his net nears one billion dollars (mostly stashed away into bonds and investments) and he won a Nobel Prize for inventing yellow cab. In reality, he's just an angry camel.

Manhattan appears with its skyscrapers to my right. The night has consumed the city, the lights came on. Manhattan skylight is perhaps the most beautiful sight to see, especially from Brooklyn where we're at now.

Muhammad, even though he looks like a terrorist, speeds up even faster as though he knows what he's doing. I start to like him. He'll earn an extra tip so he can buy himself a new turban, because the one he's wearing looks almost as solid as a seashell.

Traffic suddenly gets heavy by Flushing Meadows Lake and my heart sinks. Unable to see what's happening, I imagine some stupid driver running into another stupid driver, which turned into a fender bender, and police is holding up all the other stupid drivers in between.

To my right, as our speed descends, we stop next to a black sedan. The driver is missing behind a cloud of smoke while his music makes the sedan jump. When guys need this much attention, according to Natalia, it means they have small penises. She knows all about penises: who has the curved one, who has the big one, or who's just a big pussel. Fortunately for me, my lane moves faster than his and soon enough the guy's place is taken by a Mazda filled with the cast from the Modern Family: two dads and an adopted Asian girl.

In about five minutes, we merge to J Robinson Parkway where traffic flow is better but we drive not as fast as I wish we could. We speed up a few minutes later as we pass through Jamaica, Queens. Natalia and Chloe are both snoring away, and how they do not wake each other up I will never know. Natalia won't notice we're going to Honolulu because when drunk her attention span is of a three-year-old. Chloe won't mind since she just wants to be "out of town." But I'm worried about Lindsay (or Ruby or Chastity; by now I'm completely lost). She either accepts the ticket as her birthday present for the next thirty years or she can kiss my ass and take the train back to

Manhattan. But since I hired her to be on my side I decide to fill her in, why I sit in the chair next to her.

She gives me such a stare, which works as a reminder that I resemble a clown. I try not to look at her directly before she insults me more. Out of her kinky-looking leather bag she fishes out a cranberry juice bottle filled with red liquid.

"Want some?" she asks me.

"Cranberry juice? You must be out of your mind. Empty calories without a buzz. What's the point?"

"It's red wine, disguised as cranberry juice so nobody can tell I'm drinking. I always take a roadie with me. Wanna have some?"

Red wine tastes disgusting and it stains your teeth. She unscrews the top and drinks some, releasing a satisfying sound at the end.

"I never used to drink," she says, "until I moved to New York. Here with the stress of the job and having to move from couch to couch there's no better way to drown your sorrow. What's up?"

When she hands me the bottle I take it promptly, because nobody cares about stained teeth when the booze is free.

"Ruby," I say, wondering if that's her real name. "Is it Ruby or Chastity?"

"Call me Ruby, I don't care anymore."

"Change of plans, Ruby," I say, almost gagging after a sip of the wine, which is dry and so acidic it might as well be balsamic vinegar. "We're going to Hawaii." From the disgusting wine aftertaste my body profoundly shakes, and I imagine I must look like a wet Anubis trying to dry himself up after a bath. I quickly hand her back the wine, making a mental sticky note not to drink it again.

"Why Hawaii?"

Why is the question I wasn't prepared to answer, unless I tell her the whole truth. Since I pay her, I expect no judgment. Maybe Natalia was right and it's possible to buy loyalty with money.

"Remember I told you about Babette?" I say. Ruby nods. "I just got off the phone with Adam and he doesn't want to help me fight her on Monday. He wants me to go to the meeting with Mr. Grunt by myself. So I switched tickets and now we're going to Honolulu where he's on vacation. I'll get leverage on him there."

"How?"

"I'll find him, make him drunk, and take pictures of him dancing with some naked girl. Possibly you. This will be my leverage on him. I want to make sure he defends me in front of Mr. Grunt on Monday. Good, huh?"

"It's fine with me and I can help, but it sounds like you're betting on the river."

"It's my only chance. Losing is not an option."

"Sometimes losing is the only way to win."

She obviously has never been inside of a casino.

I look at her, though, wondering what kind of stupid brainwaves are going through her head. I take her bottle away from her and take another sip of the balsamic vinegar, suddenly wishing I had some salad to pour that on.

"Caly, if you want to prove yourself to Mr. Grunt, don't bend yourself." Said a girl who bends for a living. "If they like you as an employee they'll keep you anyway." Said no smart person before. "I was never fired from a job. But because of my living arrangements where I moved from state to state, from town to town, from borough to borough, I had to work in different clubs. The hardest part is when I asked for references, my bosses were as mean as they come. It is this kind of business I'm in where people get bitter, girls get jealous, and there's so much drama. I want out. Hopefully, today my life changes. All I have with me is a chance to start and one suitcase."

"Okay, just help me get us to Hawaii, help me with Adam, and you don't have to pay me back for your ticket. It's my present."

"Thank you."

Muhammad stops at a light so suddenly I almost spill the wine on myself. I catch a glimpse of him in the mirror to warn him that I disapprove of his careless driving. Just because we made him go to JFK hardly means we need a bumpy ride. Sitting closer to him makes me notice how enormous and feathery his eyelashes are. Naked, he probably looks like that Chimpanzee picture I photoshopped. His nostrils could take fisting.

Somewhere close by, an airplane is taking off. It means we're approaching the airport. We still have an hour before the flight, thank God. Ahead of us, I see signs for each terminal and I tell our camel to drop us off at terminal five.

When we stop, I return back to my seat and shake Chloe and Natalia's shoulders. Chloe wakes up; Natalia doesn't. I pay for the cab with Natalia's credit card, tipping Muhammad 25 percent to maintain his harem together with the money to pay for the car insurance. I give Chloe my bag but her hands are full, so I employ Ruby for that task. While holding Natalia by her waist with one hand and Elizabeth with the other, I get out of the cab, noticing how the night fully swallowed New York while the lights from the terminal ahead attract the travelers like a lamp would attract moth.

An employee at the curbside check-in station greets us outside before we enter the terminal, explaining to me we could check in Ruby's bag for two extra dollars. But we don't have any tickets yet. I tell him we'll be back while in reality we could check in her bag in the terminal for free. The sliding door opens and we enter the airport. Natalia woke up, but she operates on autopilot. With eyes opening and closing she talks nonsense, coughing occasionally.

"Ruby, I need your sunglasses," I say.

"Why?"

"Why? I pay you that's why. I want you to put them on Natalia's face for disguise, because she looks drunk."

"She is."

"The security officers are not supposed to know that, Dumb Dumb."

I straighten up Natalia's sheepskin jacket a bit and wipe off the lipstick from her cheek, after which Ruby puts her sunglasses on Natalia's face.

The first thing on my list is to get our tickets and check in Ruby's bag into which I plan to stick Elizabeth as a way to transport her across the continental USA. A line at the front desk, however, seems to go all the way to Delaware. The self-service kiosks are also crowded, just not as much. I help Natalia sit down on a bench and with one finger get Chloe's attention.

"Chloe, please look after Natalia. I'll get our tickets at the kiosk."

"Okay." She sets down the tote, the pumpkin, and Anubis' case, planting her butt next to Natalia.

"Ruby," I say, "put Elizabeth in your suitcase. We will check her in."

"I don't need to check in my suitcase. It's good for overhead bin."

"It may be good for you but it's not good for me. We need to transport the fish and nobody will let her on board in that huge bottle."

"Oh." Ruby giggles and unzips her skinny suitcase, pulling out a pink sweater, which she hands to me.

"What's that for?"

"To wrap the fish. Why else?"

So practical. I'd never thought of that myself. I wonder if that's how Ruby gives away condoms during lap dances. Why? To wrap your little fish in the back room after I'm done, that's why.

Carefully, I wrap the Patrón bottle into the sweater, placing it in the middle of the suitcase, where wigs, makeup, and shoes take up all the space with no room for anything else. Like that's all she wears. Into her suitcase I throw in the Cute Mango dispenser, in case it's considered liquid.

I reach the kiosks with Natalia's credit card in hand. Choosing the shortest line, I stand behind a lady who obviously has no idea what she's doing, the touchscreen in front of her is choking with exhaustion as though saying: "Stop torturing me, dickwad." Blue jeans outline the woman's bulky behind, where her brain must be hidden. Her blonde perm reeks of bleach and unwashed hair. My hair smells, just not at all as much.

The woman is puffing like she's a train pushing a heavy load. She sighs and she cries and she talks to herself, with one hand on the screen and the other holding a cup of coffee. Leaning forward I notice an Alaskan driver's license in her hands. Why is she even here, in this terminal? Alaskan Airlines aren't here for sure. When something goes wrong on the screen, she cusses, slowly sips her java, and restarts the session. I impatiently grunt without her noticing.

"Excuse me," I say, tapping on her shoulder. She slowly turns around. "My name is Sheila Stone." Perfect last name, I suddenly think, but only after eating some weed brownies. "I'm the manager of JFK airport. This kiosk is out of order. You need to get a ticket from the front desk. Sorry for the inconvenience."

Her face features are funny: small brown eyes, saggy lips, nose shaped as a potato. If I were in advertising, I'd advise her to audition for a Pringles commercial.

"Where's your badge?" she says, looking at me distrustfully.

"I lost it. Anyway, go to the front desk."

"The line's too long at the front desk."

"Ma'am," I say in my management voice, "it's out of order. It'll take about an hour to fix it. You can come back later. As a professional and as one pretty woman to another, I can assure you we can't do anything about it."

"What's your name again?" she says.

"Ruby Sprinkles. What's your name?"

"Coochita Mamoth."

I squint with disbelief until I catch a glimpse of her name on the screen she's typed up. She ain't lying because it does say Coochita Mamoth. It explains if her parents were hippies when the naming happened, but of all the odd names, it yet beats Diva Thin Muffin Pigeen Zappa.

"Well, Coochita," I say, "please proceed toward the front desk. This kiosk is out of order."

"Ugh, manager, I'm not going anywhere."

"Well, excuse me for trying to be helpful."

Behind me, the line starts resembling a Boa constrictor: long, curvy, ready to consume anyone it gets in touch with. Farther down the hall, an even bigger line, an anaconda, is forming at the security checkpoint. We'll miss our flight at this rate, especially if I don't take action.

I instantly get a plan. Airports page customers all the time, and maybe if I page Coochita overhead, she'll leave the kiosk. With my finger, I get Ruby's attention and ask her to come to me. Ruby drags herself slowly, which makes me want to take off her wig and rip it up. While Ruby is walking I wish I had something to throw at the stupid Alaskan husky but I don't have anything on me.

"What's up?" Ruby says.

"Ruby, stay here behind this mammoth," I whisper, "to keep our spot. If she moves, whistle."

"Where are you going?"

"No time to explain."

Rushing toward the front desk, I try to cut the line like a barbarian warrior woman through the tangled bushes of wilderment. Monkeys protect their spots without letting me move, several call me names, but ever so politely I explain my emergency. "I lost my child!" Monkeys and other creatures resembling them step aside in both directions, creating a path. With *The Lion King* music in the background and a kaleidoscope of light from above, I finally reach a hungry-looking rhinoceros at the counter, her ears spiky, and a pimple for a horn.

"Excuse me," I tell her. "I lost my friend whose name is Coochita Mamoth. Coochita Mamoth, I ain't no kidding none. Could you make an overhead announcement to meet me at the front entrance? I need to deliver her back to the zoo."

The lady looks at me distrustfully, though regardless of what she thinks of me, she picks up a tiny microphone in her hands.

"Coochita Mamoth," she says, her voice heard overhead, "please meet your party at the front entrance."

"Thank you," I say and look back.

Coochita caught the bait. She picks up her suitcase, turning obediently toward the Everglades and walks far away from the check-in lines and normal people. I sneak back through the debris of the Amazon rainforest, placing myself right on Coochita's place, which Ruby held for me.

When the coast is clear, I cancel the session Coochita has attempted to start. I swipe Natalia's credit card when prompted. The kiosk thinks for a few seconds, finds our reservation, and dispenses four tickets right away. What was so damn complicated, Coochita?

I give Ruby her ticket and her driver's license back, reading again that her name is Lindsay.

"Lindsay," I say, "go check your bag at that fancy curbside check-in. It's two extra bucks, but it's worth it. The lines are too big. We'll miss our plane otherwise. Hurry up."

She stretches a smile when I call her Lindsay, but I don't understand why. She hands me the Gooseberry when I ask her, and once holding my wallet, I find two Washingtons, their face expressions mad for giving them away.

"Be lucky," I want to tell them, "you didn't end up in Lindsay's underwear as a stripper tip."

"Be lucky," they tell me, "she didn't strip after she saw the money."

With Lindsay gone, I return to the bench with Chloe and Natalia.

"Chloe, is Anubis allowed on the plane?"

"Of course, he is. If he isn't, then I'm not going."

"Have you traveled with him before?"

"Sure did. See, you just stick him under the seat and that's all there's to it."

See, see. She's such a liar. We'll get kicked out because of her black cat, and so far I dislike it. But even if she's not going I still have Lindsay to help me.

Lindsay returns, minus the suitcase. I collect Natalia and lead toward the checkpoint line, which is barely crowded than it seemed. Now we need to somehow sneak Natalia through the TSA, a task I mentally ignored while in the cab. Natalia looks drunk, but it's better than to look/to be dead.

An officer resembling a sloth is spread on a stool, working slowly on checking IDs. For the amount of money we pay, he should be able to, at least, sit up straight and work faster. Mentally I cuss him, patiently waiting as he checks a couple's passports in front of us. As I hand our IDs to him, without even giving it a measly glimpse he lets us go clear, half-asleep, half-dead.

Ahead, another sloth-looking officer (in gloves) checks our tickets, IDs, and our legs. He looks suspiciously at Natalia at first, but his expression changes significantly when I notice how his tiny black eyes light up on fire when he sees me. At first, I'm happy he's checking me out until I notice that his gaze isn't aimed at me, but through me. Intrigued, I turn my head around to learn who he's staring at: Chloe. Of course. My, what a big chest you have, Grandma. Maybe she can change her name to Chestiti. I'm sure he'd paw her if he had a chance. I turn back around and drag Natalia toward the X-rays.

Several tipsy people teeter ahead of us in line, undressing. They remove their laptops, wallets, and other precious belongings, placing the valuables in bins. The smell of feet permeates the air; someone farted too. I undress Natalia, one article of clothing at a time. I take off her Prada pumps and put them into a bin, into which I add my own shoes together with my watch. I push the bin toward the conveyor, positioning myself behind Natalia, holding her waist to support her. I let go of her and she stands for about thirty seconds by herself, until she starts leaning on me. Thirty seconds ain't enough time for her to go through the X-ray, but I'll have to get crafty.

The officer at the X-ray points at Natalia with a baton. His face is elongated, with a spike of hair and ears set up like horns. He resembles a wildebeest. I watched a documentary about them not so long ago, so I would know.

"Miss," he moos sternly and motions Natalia to move forward. I dislike him immediately.

This is my cue, I think, while I close my eyes and pray. Then slowly, as though playing bowling, I push Natalia (aka a 120-pound bowl) toward the X-ray in hopes to get a strike. She goes through the X-ray without beeping, which relieves me, but she fails to stop on time and bumps into the officer. If she were a lion, the wildebeest would stand no chance. I sprint through the X-ray immediately after her, but another officer pulls out a plastic baton.

"One at a time," he cautions me, pushing me aback. When Natalia starts leaning on the officer's shoulder, he grabs her flank before she could fall flat in front of him. He stands two feet shorter than Natalia, but he looks strong.

"Is everything okay?" he asks Natalia, looking up, almost buried in her two sisters.

"She's fine," I say loudly, projecting my voice. The second officer keeps blocking my way with his billy stick. "She's just so, so sad. See, her husband, who must be your twin, died in Honolulu. We're going to the funeral."

The fact the husband resembled the officer might have been a compliment, but the fact the imaginary husband died could potentially irritate the real guy.

"He was extraordinarily handsome," I add. The officer almost winces with pride.

"My condolences." He pries Natalia away from his chest and brings her back to me. She leans on him for support, mumbling or singing something in Russian.

"She appreciates your support," I say.

I catch Natalia by her waist with one hand while with the other I try to push the truncheon away from me, which I fail to accomplish. The other officer is way too persistent. Natalia, who smells like a barrel of cognac, doesn't help any by snoring here and there. Chloe and Lindsay must have taken a different X-ray line. Obviously, they had no problem getting in.

In the meantime, the first officer picks up the walkie-talkie he has hanging from his uniform pocket.

"I have a little situation here," Wildebeest says into the walkie-talkie. "The lady at the checkpoint is either drunk or drugged. What should I do?"

My eyes pop from disbelief. My ears wilt with disappointment. I make a promise to never watch another documentary about animals for the rest of my life. "Which may be shorter than you think," my liver insults me further.

Response from walkie-talkie comes distorted, indecipherable.

"I'll inform her," he adds, placing the walkie-talkie back on his uniform. "Miss, you have to step aside with your friend. I can't let you in. Your friend is drunk, and we're not allowed to let such people in."

"But our plane is boarding!" I almost yell. "We need to fly to Hawaii! I beseech you!"

I sound stupid, helpless, insecure. Me, sober.

"I guess you won't fly to Hawaii tonight."

My heart almost stops. Never drink Manhattans if you plan to escape from its concrete jungles is what precisely I wish to tell Natalia.

CHAPTER FOUR

Champagne Problems

Being pointed at in public is embarrassing. People either give you an apologetic nod with a closed-mouth smile or stay away from you, thinking just your presence is enough to influence their kids to be bad, turn gay, or start enjoying Justin Bieber's songs. I set Natalia on a nearby bench, sit down next to her, and try to avoid looking anybody in the eye.

What would Natalia do if she were in my shoes? She'd most definitely light up a cigarette first and then have her Russian logic take over: If she remains asleep, there will be no Hawaii. No Hawaii means no leverage on Adam. No leverage on Adam is a guillotine toward unemployment.

What else can a normal (whatever defines "normal" these days) woman do to a guy to make him change his mind? How can I convince any of these men, who suspect us of being dangerous to society, that all I need is actually fairly simple? The easiest way to a man's heart, they say, is through the stomach. Offering making him lunch would sound something only Coochita Mamoth would do.

Chloe and Ruby have both finished dressing. After the fight they've had in the cab, their dislike for each other cannot be understated. In fact, Ruby must be appalled by the cup sizes of Chloe's fake boobs while Chloe looks at

Ruby much the same way I looked at my gynecologist when she had told me I needed to go see a dentist.

Gawping at Ruby, I wonder if asking her to execute several lap dances for the officers in return for our freedom is overboard. The girls are unaware of what happened. I send a text to both, explaining our situation.

Since whatever alcohol left running through me seemed to have evaporated, I'm convinced my body starts burning fat, using oxygen as its primary energy source. I stand up and off of his badge, I learn the officer's name: Officer Cooper. He told me we were waiting for his supervisor while I make small talk and learn he was born in Austin, Texas. With teeth clenched and fingers crossed behind my back, I tell him I love George W. Bush, but that doesn't make him warm up to me. This is just like a game of poker, the game being called Texas Hold 'Em, and Cooper took it just a bit too seriously, and now the fat Texas Holds 'Us.

Ruby is chatting with another officer, flipping her hair in a flirting manner. I wonder if she'll leave for Hawaii even if the verdict comes negative. She's got nothing to lose, a ticket in her hand, bag already checked in. Chloe for sure will stay with me. But we can't stay. We need to be in Hawaii. We need to find Adam to make sure my job is safe. Maybe I can talk Chloe into taking Natalia home while I go to Honolulu by myself. Would that be a shitty thing to do since Natalia entrusted her life into my hands?

Sitting back down, I explore Natalia's face up-close and I hear her speaking without speaking: "Don't chicken, Calyssa. Chickens don't get laid, chicks do." But how can I not chicken when Cooper's concerned?

Maybe Universe is trying to send me signals as a warning something bad might happen. Maybe Cooper should be a signal to stop and turn around, go back home and pray for the best. Maybe our plane might crash when the pilot decides to snooze during the flight. Maybe Hawaii is going to be attacked by pirates while we'll be kidnapped and turned into slaves. We'll wash floors, drink rum, gas like men, and even cuss twice as much as we do now. Well, why not? I already drank red wine today and, trust me, nothing can be worse than that. Chloe and Ruby join me by the bench.

"What are we going to do?" Chloe asks.

"We need to wake her up. Then we need to do everything in our power to board that plane."

I take Ruby's sunglasses off Natalia's face and place them on top of her head. I shake her shoulder and slap her cheek. Her eyes open. She looks horrible.

"I need to take a pee," she murmurs.

"You will. Listen, we're at the airport and security officer refuses to let us go toward the gate because he thinks you're drugged. We're late, so we need to hurry up. Let's tell him you're narcoleptic, okay?"

Natalia gawks at me as though I somehow turned into a talking blunderbuss, or how I would gawk at a person who just turned into a talking blunderbuss. She probably only understood half of what I said. I whistle to get Cooper's attention. He takes his time, dragging himself like he weighs a ton.

"Now, what?" he asks, irritated.

"You see she's awake?" I say. "She didn't do drugs."

"Really," he says and interlocks his arms in front of his chest.

"Excuse me," Natalia slurs. "I have a very important meeting in Vegas. I've never done drugs, except for cocaine once in a while. I took allergy medication once and it made me loopy. I drink occasionally and on Fridays. And I need to take a pee."

"Vegas?" Cooper says. "I thought you were going to Honolulu for your husband's funeral."

"Honolulu?" Natalia says.

"Honolulu?" Chloe says.

"Honolulu!" I say.

We sound just like the Three Bears. I give them both a look as though it was part of the plan.

I turn back to Cooper. "Can we please go? She's awake. All is fixed, right?"

"Not until you talk to him." Cooper nods in the direction of a short older cop with a long white beard and spectacles, who is either a psycho or someone who likes to molest little children. He's so fat he must swing his hips left and right, maneuvering body fat. Natalia closes her eyes and falls back asleep while I try to hold her sturdy in my hands. I swiftly put the glasses back on. Officer Cooper dismisses himself while the other one takes his place.

"Excuse me," I tell the fat cop with some newly found confidence. "What seems to be the problem here?"

"Ma'am, are you under the influence of drugs?" the child molester asks Natalia instead.

Dumbstruck by his rudeness, I hide behind Natalia to avoid eye contact. I wonder why he failed to speak to Chloe first since she has the biggest chest devices. He probably can't see Ruby and doesn't want to look at my bloated face. This is why he had to speak to Natalia.

"Nope," I say, pretending to be her.

"May I see some sort of identification, please?" he says politely. I hate polite cops. With Natalia's ID in my right hand, I lift her arm above mine with the ID stuck between two fingers. He takes it promptly and explores it. Now I notice the buckle and his boots. He might have looked funny at first, but boy does he have a deep, scary voice, his Southern accent making a no-brainer I'm dealing with a psychopath. Gumbo he's had for dinner is partly scattered around the collar of his shirt, a starfish-shaped slice of okra near his badge.

"Could you please take off your glasses, ma'am?" he says with his eyes still buried in her ID. I take Natalia's head in my hand as though a puppet, turning it left and right for a no.

"You see, she's been crying all week," Chloe chimes in, "and she should better keep her glasses on. See, her uncle died. We were here for his funeral. She's very upset."

"I see," he says, giving Chloe a glance. I wonder what he sees: an attractive woman or two chest devices used for building skyscrapers. "Why aren't your lips moving, Miss Romanova?" he asks.

"She's a ventriloquist," Chloe says. "She flew from Vegas to perform this ventriloquist concert."

"I thought she was here for her uncle's funeral. I'm confused."

"We killed two birds with one stone. She never really cared about her uncle that much, see? She married him for the money. Though instead she's got the cat as an inheritance." Chloe lifts up Anubis so the officer could take a closer look at the cat.

"I'm sorry, but I can't let her board the plane. She looks drugged or drunk or whatever is wrong with her."

"She only had one drink," I say defensively, sticking out my head so he could see me. "But you have to understand how sad she is." With my hand, I make Natalia nod.

"Hold on," he says. "Let me get this straight. So she married her uncle who is now dead. And this lady said," he points at Chloe's chest, "she never cared about him that much, which means Miss Romanova ain't sad. She also said Miss Romanova is sad. So which one is it? You should put your story together."

"See, she's sad," Chloe says, "because her show wasn't that good."

"This show isn't that good either."

"You see," Chloe goes on, "she has a sore throat and she took some NyQuil. She's quite drowsy. You see?"

Chloe kicks me as a cue to cough (or so I understand). I clear up my throat as loudly as I can and cough a bit behind Natalia to make sure the officer doesn't see me, just hear me. The fibs coming out of Chloe's mouth are hard to follow, even for a liar like me with an outstanding lying history, trustworthy lying face, and thirty years of lying experience.

"And," I add, "she's narcoleptic."

"In that case, maybe madam is capable of spelling Mississippi?"

Have we been pulled over? The only word I'm capable of spelling correctly would be "vodka," but even that I may screw up, turning it into a "cocktail." I turn Natalia's head left and right for a no, thinking we're running in circles. I could sing him the alphabet song, however.

"It's my birthday today," Chloe lies. "Can you please let us go to our plane as my birthday present?"

"You can go anywhere you want. It's her who cannot board the plane."

This is when I lose my faith. Not only did we come off as drunk and stupid, but we also ain't getting on none of them planes. Tears swell up in my eyeballs. To get even with the officer, I have a strong desire—a rash—to litter. There's nothing in my bag I could throw out, no candy wraps, no receipts, not even useless retail store reward cards. I want to warn the officer if he doesn't let us go I'll go on a hunger strike or a sex strike, but he seems he won't care if I die from starvation or from lack of sex.

"How can you have a problem with her?" Ruby says. "What I mean is, look at her: She is drunk—she's beyond drunk—she's Russian. So what? Russians have been drunk for centuries, and what did she do to you? Look at her! She's fragile. It's not like she can hurt anybody. What is she going to do on that plane besides sleeping through the whole flight? What, you think she'll be able to hijack the damn plane? You're so ridiculous I pity you. Just because you haven't seen your pipette of a penis in years because of your humongous bellypop, which relieves you from doing any matrimonial duties, you stupidly aim your anger at Natalia. Way to go, sir. I hope you sleep well tonight knowing my chance of a new life is ruined because of you. Look at us! We're all drunk here. All the passengers. Just invite a few cops here with their Breathalyzers and you'll know what I mean. Who doesn't drink before flying? Show me that stupid idiot and I'll pee on him. Or her—right—shouldn't be sexist these days. It's stressful enough alone, thinking the plane will crash or collide with another plane. Natalia is better to society than most of us because she's not going to demand the stupid free juice and free chips that are full of GMO. Their food lacks nutrition. They want to kill us. If I develop cancer, I'll blame you. That's right—you! That's how it all starts because you, on your own accord, decide she's too drunk to fly. Next time I see you in my strip club I'll tell house mom who you are and don't you think I don't have powerful connections in the industry. They'll never let you in. True, by going to Hawaii, I'm planning to quit, but because of you I won't. I won't forgive you ever, ever, ever."

"Ruby, are you okay?" I say.

"I'm fine. And let me tell you something else."

"Ruby," I jerk her arm, "he said we can go."

In her rage, she failed to notice how the officer, after being blamed for cancer, just shook his head, gave us clearance to go, and vanished. Ruby, in the meantime, accumulated quite an audience around her and kept blabbing, seeking comfort in other passengers.

"This is why I never lie," she concludes, her voice back to normal: barely heard. "It scares people more."

I blink twice before Chloe helps me carry Natalia to our gate. Even though Ruby did a good job, I decide not to give her any credit, mostly because she can hardly handle cash.

To withstand the eleven-hour flight I decide to down a sleeping pill as soon as I get to my seat. The four of us enter the plane and we're greeted by two stewards in purple shirts, who smile in earnest. I show our tickets to one of them and he points toward the first class. Lindsay and Chloe go toward the economy. After noticing how crowded the economy is due to its full capacity, I salute Natalia for picking the other side of the plane. I wonder whether Noah had first class on the Ark. "This section," Noah would explain to chimpanzee Babette, "is reserved for our VIP guests, lions and whatnot." Maybe I'm a lioness then. Rawr.

One of the stewards helps Natalia to her seat after I explain to him she's narcoleptic while I stare at the other steward, trying to figure out if his butt is real or if he's trick-or-treating as Jennifer Lopez. Being a sucker for a cute butt, I stand and admire him. Women want to see a butt, I always remind guys who wear shapeless, saggy jeans. I drop my ticket before Lopez, hoping he'd pick it up for me. He bends over right away while I inconspicuously inspect his butt. Not bad at all. I come up with the following fact: his butt looks real but if I keep looking at it, I'll eat him alive. When he hands me back my ticket, smiling I trudge along the cabin, silently roaring like a lioness.

Natalia is sleeping by the window, proved by fierce Russian snoring. A thick, chubby man sits in the seat next to her. One simple glance at my ticket indicates how Little Teddy miscalculated, putting me in the next row, but not next to Natalia.

Annoyed, I tap on the stranger's shoulder. "Excuse me. Would you mind terribly if I sit here, next to my friend?"

The chubby stranger looks up, and while I'm certain he's human, he fairly resembles one. His shaggy hair might as well be an alive sheep. His chin wobbles funnily, his eyes the size of my fist. He must be the reason why folks came up with the Jingle Bells song because his bells are most totally jingling. Chubbly Wobbly opens his mouth to answer. A thick accent escapes his lips while I automatically look down in search of subtitles.

"I've no idea what you just said, sir, but could you be so kind and vacate the seat? I would like to sit with my friend over here. See the Sleeping Beauty? She's my friend."

Wobbly's face is whittled by confusion. Despite the fact I speak clearly, he doesn't seem to understand me either.

I point with my finger. "Could you sit over there while I sit over here? Please?" I propel each word with precise accuracy. Chubbly Wobbly shakes his head and shrugs while roaring I plop on my assigned seat. Natalia is passed out anyway, so there's no need for us to fly next to each other. The guy sitting next to me is reading a book without paying me much attention.

After shoving the Gooseberry under the seat in front of me, I notice how first class seats provide us with lots of extra leg room, which is an exciting fact because I can wiggle my feet, put my legs on top of the other one, and do, well, all sorts of fun stuff. I give Wobbly an imaginary middle finger, wondering why people can't just read mind. Scientists have invented everything from a light bulb to a phone that speaks to you, but we can't make an easy solution to communicate better. I decide to try and send a strong mind-message to Wobbly: "Go, finger-blast yourself." Thanks to him the plane will be tilted to the left.

A young bleached-blond stewardess kneels before me. "Would you like a complimentary choice of champagne or passion fruit juice?"

Please, I think. "Champagne, of course."

"Only one drink before we take off. We're not allowed to serve drinks until after we're up in the air." She's amused for some reason. Her nametag says: Cave. She appears dumb not only because she had the nerve to offer me the juice, but also because I can see it in her banana-shaped head where brain would logically have no room to grow. Where's my Lopez? I want him to be my stewardess.

When my champagne is served, I finish it in nothing flat. The second flute Cave allotted to herself, pouring it down her trachea while nobody but me was watching. Slacking off on a job and drinking. She resembles me.

The engines start humming while I hear Cave's voice overhead: "Captain, the passengers are all in! Let's take her to air. Dear passengers, please fasten your seatbelts and prepare for takeoff. Turn off your electronic devices until we tell you otherwise. Dinner will be served soon."

Rolling my eyes, I wonder why God wants to punish me so much. Two choices: stay awake and have dinner or fall asleep and be hungry. I'll wait for dinner because it seems I haven't eaten in a week. I fasten my seatbelt and get gum from my bag because I hate when my ears pop during a takeoff. Cave approaches me.

"Can I borrow some gum?" she says. "I forgot mine."

"Of course," I say, giving her a piece. She puts it in her mouth, devouring the flavor, which is proved by a juicy chewing sound. I guess in the caves of Nevada deserts they teach no lessons on how to chew gum without producing any sound.

"Thank you," she says. "I love watermelon."

"Well, it isn't exactly watermelon. It's strawberry and orange."

"I guess strawberry and orange create watermelon. You know, like blue and green create purple."

"Actually, blue and red create purple."

"You have no imagination, lass." She rolls her eyes and withdraws herself.

She's right: I have no imagination before the takeoff. I'm terrified, that's why. Other people must experience this feeling as well. The crash. In fact I'm so afraid of flying, I threw my *Peter Pan* book out the window at the age of ten. Another reason: Mom died on the way to the airport in a car accident, not even making it to the actual plane. Also, the word "flying" never made sense to me. F-lying. Airplane inventor laughed at her first failed attempt and said: "Who am I effing lying to? F-lying is what it should be called." That's how it started, according to Calyssa, one of the Grimm sisters.

So nothing is on my side. To make this flying experience as least painful as possible, I brought my sleeping pills with me; they will put me to sleep for the entirety of the flight. Until we're in Honolulu, no one will be able to wake me up, not even a kiss from Prince Charming. I'm going to wait until we're up in the air so I can ask for some water to chase the pills. Those pills work in fifteen minutes and I'll sleep without waking up once.

To stop freaking out about the takeoff, I close my eyes and try to imagine an enjoyableness, like an apple martini. Elizabeth comes to my mind instead, and I think of her, wondering how she's doing in the old, dirty suitcase full of Ruby's wigs and makeup. The good thing is Elizabeth has a home now, the

Patrón Silver bottle, so at least she's like the Queen of England who got lost in her Buckingham Palace.

I won't lie if I say there's horror movie score is playing on the background as we're traveling up the runway, rapidly gaining speed. Soon the plane tilts and I feel how the Earth's gravity is trying to bring us back down. My heartbeat triples. Oh man, how I hate taking off. Soon enough the plane stabilizes while I chew on the gum, holding the seat handles like a complete sissy. One minute passed, maybe two. Maybe three. Very clearly I remember my first flying experience. My mom and I were going to California to visit her friend whose name was Understanding. Mom couldn't leave me with Aunt Sarah, who was on vacation with her then-boyfriend Cheng, my cousin Christina's biological father. I was seven years old. As our speed and altitude were ascending, I saw toy cars, toy houses, and toy people through the plane's oval windows. Nothing seemed real; nothing seemed normal. I wanted to take the toys and play with them, but reality scared me: they were not toys. I remember crawling all over Mom, which annoyed her no end. I read somewhere in a legitimate magazine that fear of heights comes from fear of closed spaces—claustrophobia—another attribute of my personality. So a plane is like the double negative because of its enclosed space and such a high altitude. Hopefully dinner will be served soon, so I can go to sleep.

Someone taps my shoulder and I open my eyes. Cave. Her earrings stick out like two stalactites, long and thick, growing from the bottom of her ears, which have already been stretched to a spaghetti-like shape. My drop earrings are a family heirloom that I inherited from Mom. They are trimmed with French wire, fourteen carat gold, made out of emerald. I wonder what was the name of the stone that bequeathed Cave hers.

She avails of an empty seat ahead of me, sighing. She's either exhausted from life or has never learned how to moisturize her skin. The lines on her face are like dried rivers of the Grand Canyon.

"As one alcoholic to another, cheers." She hands me a flute of champagne and touches my glass with hers for a toast. "It's my birthday today, but I was unable to take one freaking day off in a whole year. Can you believe it? They're such pricks. I'm glad I met you, my new drinking buddy."

"Happy birthday," I say and drink the champagne, partially taking offense in being called an alcoholic on a basis that I said yes to free champagne. What kind of nonsense logic is it, anyway? If what, she offered me sugar she'd think I was obese? Such lucidity doesn't sit well with me, though in the past I've learned not to bitch about people who are in liberty to give me free drinks, and she's exactly that person. So instead I'll bitch behind her back to somebody else. "How come you couldn't take a day off?"

"Because nobody cares about us. Two people called out and once my turn came they offered me to either take the shift or start looking for another job."

"That's rude."

"No kidding. I've been working as a flying attendant for ten years already, started right after high school, but do you think I get anything? Not even a day off for my birthday. So screw them, I'm drinking." Cave finishes her flute and makes a round of refills after I catch up and finish mine. If she's twenty-eight (by my best calculation), then by forty people will start mistaking her for a totaled car trick-or-treating as a Shar Pei. She can't be younger than me. The idea of it simply sounds idiotic. Tired, exhausted, and did I mention I was talking about her face?

"And that boyfriend of mine left me because I have a mental disorder." And hair like thatch. "And because I'm barren. As if children are everything. If I ever get married, it'll be because I get married to a tree."

"Well, paper covers rock."

She smiles but looks confused. "But I have a lover in each state. That helps." Yeah, I think: Rocky in Philadelphia, Lincoln memorial in D.C., Statue of Liberty in New York—a lover in every state. What a blabbermouth she is, too. Worse than me.

"What kind of mental disorder?" I ask, interested.

"Depression. I have to be on medication all the time or I'd tie a noose and jump into it. But how can you not be depressed in such society?"

"Roger that. Why don't you quit?"

"Quit? Are you crazy? You know how hard it is to find a job with a disability like mine. God himself must have hired me here, and I'm going to keep it that way until retirement. But as a person who drinks to put myself out of my miserable life, I can tell with assurance that you have just as much misery. Tell me. Maybe I can be of help."

Cave speaks of her problems so freely, unafraid to sound more stupid than she already seems to be. I'm guilty for being naïve and vulnerable sometimes and for making mistakes and for going on a date with Moshe, but I would never, even to myself, admit those mistakes.

After I fail to respond, Cave refills the champagne into each glass, taking a deep, loud sigh. "Come on, tell me. Nobody drinks because they love their life. We drink to cope with sorrow. I noticed you came in with a drunk friend. Look at her over there. The way she smells . . . I can tell her misery is worse than mine, as though her misery is fear of anticipation."

Oh, what do you know about life, you talking rock! is what precisely I wish to shout out loud, but decide better of it.

"She's just unhappy with her . . ." I find myself lost for words at this point.

"Husband?"

"Work problems," I say. "That office rat Babette Hook is making her life miserable."

"What did she do to her?"

"Babette is miserable so she spreads rumors and wants her fired."

"I had someone at work who wanted me fired, too."

"What happened to her?"

"Her plane crashed."

She bursts out laughing, loudly and scarily, reminiscent of an old witch who's got a little boy in her pot. My heart automatically sinks.

"I'm kidding. Don't be such a sissy. Just wishful thinking," she adds sinisterly.

"Natalia is afraid to lose her job, because if she does, what would her mom say?"

"See? This is the same problem we're all having. Not being good enough. It all comes from fear of rejection is what my mom always tells me. I would never disappoint her, though. She was a flight attendant and wanted me to follow her footsteps."

"What if, let's say hypothetically, she chose that job for the money but she hates it sometimes?"

"Love or hate, a job is a job. She's lucky to have one. Have you read about the unemployment rate in our country? Even educated people cannot find a job. Nobody wants to do lower-class jobs like cleaning, delivering, servicing. Everybody wants to have an office job."

"Hers is an office job."

"Then she's an idiot to even complain."

"So what should Natalia do if her boss decides to fire her."

"Be a woman. Admit your mistakes. Play the victim. Submit. Be dumb. Nobody likes smart women. That's how I presented to my boss when I accidentally got laid in the bathroom with a customer and I'm still here. Just keep drinking and life will appear normal."

Cave suddenly sticks three small bottles of champagne in between my thighs, placing her flute in my free hand. At this moment, Lopez bypasses my seat, and Cave stands up. "I'll go pretend I'm working."

When she leaves, I transfuse the champagne from her flute into mine.

True, I'm the girl who wears suede shoes that become ruined after rain, and I'm definitely the girl who wears white and spills red wine on it—and why must it always be red wine, by the way?—but I'll never be like Cave. I'll never look as exhausted with life. Besides, there are ways to move up in my company, unlike being a stewardess where the only way up is during a takeoff. Potentially, once the war with Babette is over, I could become her, Mr. Grunt's secretary. And soon after, I could become Mr. Grunt himself, and make so much money. "You're such a sissel," I imagine Natalia say. "You keep telling yourself that," Ruby would stick her mind in the gutter. "Pretending is healthy," Chloe would disagree with Ruby. "Just keep drinking," Cave would finish, "and life will appear normal."

Soon, dinner is served. There's nothing remarkable in a turkey sandwich with a small pouch of potato chips. For dessert I serve myself dried Turkish apricots and more champagne.

A tiny screen ahead of me shows our altitude: thirty-five thousand feet (twenty-five thousand if you're Bigfoot). Our speed is over five hundred miles per hour, a kind of speed that makes my brain blow a fuse. How the hell can we go so fast? That's all I can think about every time I fly, which is quite rare. I follow a little white airplane on the screen indicating we drift somewhere near Detroit, the Rock City, where Cave was born. She just turned twenty-eight today. She should die and then make a comeback and rise from the ashes by the age of thirty.

Champagne brings me to a state of bliss. After the third serving, I'm relaxed, unafraid of flying anymore. I wiggle in my seat while getting sleeping pills out of my bag, which I place underneath the seat in front of me. I notice my neighbor, the same cute man who's reading a book. We interlock looks for a second—and he's even cuter than I remembered—but I turn away immediately as though I didn't mean to stare.

His eyes are big with thick lashes and generous brows, his hair cut short and styled to the left, he smells vaguely of cologne, but most important he has freckles. If only one other thing I like better than men is freckles on men. I could even date a horse if a horse had some. I'm not a big fan of men who read so much but a flaw only means good. It means he has good qualities, like being good in bed to substitute for such a tiny factory error as reading. At least one of his parents must have had a faulty chromosome. My perfect man will be working as a factory slave, cutting beef for food. He can't spell for his life but his tongue could do miracles in my mouth and other unmentionable parts. I'll make him dinner every night—peanut butter and jelly sandwich, the only dish I've excelled at—and for me he can juggle up an apple martini once in a while. Thinking this, I realize I've been staring at the cute guy the entire time. Embarrassed or annoyed, he turned away and by now I can only see the back of his head. What a sneaky way to keep me from falling asleep, I think, by being so extra cute.

Finally, I'm ready to release the valve, and I go to the lavatory and cuss myself for waiting this long when I start dripping. I can hold any liquor for hours, but champagne makes me flow like a river. I wonder whether I'll keep running to the bathroom every half hour, making the cute guy assume I have a UTI.

After I'm done with my lady's duties, I try to put myself together to look attractive and presentable. When that fails, I try to make myself look like human again. Alcohol has already puffed my face while my stomach got bloated. I notice how my forehead is all oily, reason why I'm undesirable or otherwise the cute guy would have talked to me.

I call Calyssa the plumber to give my face an emergency repair job. Oily skin is a pain in the neck to take care of, and I never realized this until some beauty queen handed me an oil-absorbing sheet. The fool that he was, he expected me to know how to use it. On top of that, he started making out with a guy I'd been chatting with all evening, after which I promised myself to never again dine in Chelsea, New York City's "gayborhood."

Until then I was old-fashioned and used powder to eliminate shine. But seriously though, these oil-absorbing sheets are truly fablelike, why they come at such a stiff price. My pores, God bless them, produce so much sebum I could bottle it and sell it wholesale should someone ever needed sebum. Since oily skin helps bomb my face with zits, I've tried every product on the market to target pimples, but apparently nothing works best than covering them with three layers of foundation. To remove oil, toilet seat covers are the most inexpensive method I've ever discovered; after all, they are free, even if somewhat gross. I discreetly get a seat cover and blot my face until all the shine is gone.

I also need to brush my mop but the brush, however, squirreled away. If I were sober, it would have taken me three seconds to find it. When I fumble inside of the bag, I realize it's just one big disorganized mess. I say it like it's possible to have two big disorganized messes per a handbag. One by one, I remove each item from the Gooseberry, surprising myself with the stuff I've got. A pen. A "get out of jail free" card from Monopoly. When did I play that? Now, everybody needs a 2" by 2" photo of Babette, one that I stole from our database. Her forehead is also shiny, a reflective gloss of sweaty oily skin she's no idea how to take care of. As much as I hate Babette, I decide to keep the photo in case I end up playing darts. I'd use the photo in place of the bull's eye as my only motivation to win.

The brush hides at the very bottom, tucked in the right corner next to an envelope with my paycheck I forgot to deposit. I shove the envelope deep inside and quickly brush my hair, finishing off my "emergency repair work" by putting on some lip-gloss. I look in the tiny mirror, wondering three things: Why didn't I set up a direct deposit yet? What is wrong with me? Why am I so good with chopsticks?

Without being able to do anything with my puffy face and feeling like a used one-dollar bill that's been in Ruby's bra, I return to the cabin. The cute neighbor I've spotted earlier looks up as I loudly splatter myself on my seat. My vision is vibrating, which has something to do with turbulence.

"Hi," I tell him, turning my head to the right. It isn't me speaking, really, but Blabber, my mouth. When I drink, he has a mind of his own. Drinking releases the courage that even shy people possess, and my courage is no exception. "Have you seen Cave?" Blabber asks.

"Pardon?" he says. "Cave?"

"Cave? Ah, right, Cave. What about Cave?"

"You asked if I saw a cave. Which cave?" His voice is mellifluous. His face grows cuter by the second. My confidence is boosted.

"Oh, the stewardess. I'm Calyssa, by the way." I stretch out my arm for an arm shake. The second I do it, I wonder what kind of woman, besides Caitlyn Jenner, would offer her hand for a handshake, and I mentally shame myself.

"Marcus," he says, shaking my hand.

Marcus . . . what an interesting name, I think. Whoever gave you this name was the smartest mother on Earth. Oh, and to be brutally honest, I'd be so happy to go on a date with him.

"Really?" Marcus says.

"Really what?"

"You just said you'd be happy to go on a date with me."

"I said that?"

"Yes, I'll think about it."

I put both hands on top of Blabber to keep him shut. I can't believe I just said what I thought I was thinking. What a dummy. I blink twice before letting my arms go, slowly. "Sorry, sometimes my mind cannot catch up with my mouth."

Marcus awkwardly stares at me without saying a word.

"More champagne?" Cave chimes in, breaking the silence. How I'm happy to see her for diluting the weird moment of my drunk stupidity. Cave has a tray with several jumping flutes in her hands.

"Oh," I say, "I'd love some champagne. And give one to Marcus as well. It's her birthday, let's celebrate."

"I'll bring you some cake," Cave says and leaves.

After I have a sip, I stare at Marcus the same way my coworker Jessica's Bull Terrier looked at my juicy leg when I visited her house, just ready to consume me alive. Marcus is clean-shaven, the kind of look many handsome underwear models possess, men of decent educational level, and also men who don't fart in public. One of the three criteria is fine with me, really, since I'm not that picky. Beard, mustache, or other kinky things men tend to wear on their faces is what I'm definitely not attracted to. Blame this guy, Billy, I once went out with, who showed up with grains of what looked like basmati rice stuck to his chest-length beard. I was mad, of course, but mostly because he said he wanted to lose weight and was staying off carbs.

If women wore a mustache, we'd never get away with it.

But Marcus will have no way to hide his rice from me, even if he wanted to. Trying to contain myself, I drink my champagne, watching a cake topped with freckles. If only people knew what kind of dreams I'm going to have for the next two weeks just imagining Marcus in bed with me. Alcohol is a sneaky substance, because after you've had some running through your blood, you actually want to prove people you're sober by pretending to listen and ask questions. The easiest way to spot a drunk is to go bowling with them, something, unfortunately, I'm unable to do with Marcus. Someone said alcohol makes you drunk faster at higher altitude, but I don't find that to be true. I'm perfectly normal.

"What are you reading?" Blabber shamelessly asks instead, unwilling to give up. And what does he have to lose, anyway? It's not like he can wear a hat and sunglasses like a celebrity to prevent himself from being recognized in the morning; the damage is already done and it's simply impossible to get to the point in future that is more embarrassing than the present.

Marcus tilts the book in my direction, calmly, without treating me like an intoxicated woman—with a sigh for instance or with a middle finger. "*R Is for Ricochet* by Sue Grafton. If you're into mysteries."

Oh, boy. First mystery is why we are not in bed with each other. Second, what I'm into doesn't involve any mysteries, just old-fashioned, man-on-woman, lights-off sex. Is this too much to ask?

"Do you realize you are still speaking your thoughts out loud?" Marcus says. "Or was it intentional?"

I furrow my brow. "What did I say?"

He smiles. Ah, his smile is like a new car on the lot that hasn't been depreciated yet and still costs its full price. His smile is new and exciting. Marcus puts his book on his knees. "I'm into old-fashioned, man-on-woman, lights-off sex."

"See? That's the same thought I was having. We must be soul mates." At this point I'm finally happy he's speaking my language.

Marcus bursts into a laugh. "And I feared the flight would be uneventful."

"That's why I never have any expectations. Just go with the flow."

Lopez appears out of nowhere, cutting me loose by picking up my champagne flute. "Ma'am, there have been complaints from other passengers that your voice is slightly too loud. As you can see the lights have been turned off and some passengers would like to sleep. I would appreciate if you'd comply. Much obliged."

I hate when sober people treat me like a child and use sarcasm.

"My sincere apologies," I say cheerfully. "Just think I'm dead."

Lopez shakes his head. He seems infuriated. "One more peep out of you and you'll be arrested when we get to Honolulu. Understood? We reserve the right to peace and quiet. So get peace and get quiet."

I nod in earnest but I don't mean it.

"He's creepy," I whisper after he leaves. "At first I liked him but your butt cannot alter your personality."

"Is that true?"

"Unless you're a baseball player. I don't even care about their personalities. But Lopez is mean. It's Cave's birthday and they wouldn't even treat her to a day off. Can you believe it?" I decide to spare him details of my birthday celebration that lasted a whole month.

Marcus shrugs. "So I heard when the two of you talked. She seems a bit unhinged if you ask me. Work is work, though. Sometimes you can't control it."

"Well, can you control your work?"

"Sometimes."

"What do you do then?"

He hands me his business card. His name is Marcus Truman, an architect, suite seventeen, and he works for Architects by McGill, Seed, and Black. Several phone numbers are printed on the card, along with three email addresses. The physical address, neatly printed on the back of his card, puts his office on Broadway and Fulton Street, a fancy downtown area. He reads books, and he's not working underground or in a factory, which means I need to test his tongue immediately.

"And this is mine," I say, producing an invisible business card in front of Marcus. "See how it says Calyssa Pantaleo who works as a secretary? Floor fourteen, which in reality should be floor thirteen, but thirteen is an unlucky number. Our office is on 5th Avenue and 51st Street. Shred Unread is our name."

"I think I've used you before."

"Oh, sugar, I'd remember if you used me before."

"I meant the company, not you, as in 'you' literally."

"Well, Calyssa's business card is yours." I hand him the imaginary business card, close my eyes, and lean in for a kiss. "She says she wants to kiss you."

When I open my eyes, ten seconds later, I realize Marcus is gone. He fled the cabin and into the lavatory after he heard what I said. My cheeks burst into flames. I'm so stupid. What is wrong with me?

I find a blanket underneath my seat and cover myself with it. As fast as I can—before Marcus manages to come back—I swallow the sleeping pill dry, using saliva to drive it down my esophagus. When the pill gets stuck in the middle, right underneath my lungs, I fist the area near my ribs, which kindly helps. I close my eyes and if Marcus tries to speak to me I'll pretend I'm asleep, and in fifteen minutes or less I'll be asleep for real.

When I open my eyes, there's an announcement: "Ladies and gentlemen, please keep your seatbelts on as we're preparing for landing at the Honolulu International Airport."

I slept through the entirety of the flight. Night became morning, proved by bright sunshine penetrating the cabin. At least something got penetrated! I put on a big smile and decide to keep it on throughout the weekend. Nothing, and I mean nothing can make me frown today.

Natalia punches my shoulder so hard it instantly gives me a bruise. Nothing can make me frown, except for Natalia. She stands in front of me, her Russian stature so prevalent and strong. She somehow maneuvered around Chubbly Wobbly, who's staring at me together with her.

"Hey, watch it," I say.

"What do you mean Honolulu?" she says, fully awake, no more exhausted by the toxins of alcohol. "We were supposed to be in Vegas. You better tell me now or I'll shave your pussel and teach it how to play poker."

I've never seen her eyes angrier, a contempt stare making me feel small. Her face tells me I've sat on her chair, and drunk her whiskey, and slept with her man. If I were Lupita this would be the time to pack my bags and scram into the woods, but Goldilocks Pantaleo doesn't have a parachute or she for sure would jump off the plane.

CHAPTER FIVE

So Filthy

Marcus and Chubbly are both waiting for my reply. Not to sound like a drama queen I shush her away.

"Not now, Natalia, later," I whisper. "I'm scared of the touchdown."

Partially it is true, I'm scared of the touchdown. Natalia returns to her seat. She closes her eyes and takes a deep breath, making one of those expressions men make when they're finding control in themselves not to strike a woman. She looks out the window while I turn in another direction, only to find Marcus and his concerned demeanor that reveals he heard everything Natalia said.

"What the hell?" he mouths and I just ignore. First, I want to kiss him, and now my friend wants to teach my vagina how to play poker. What only must he be thinking?

With nowhere to turn, I face the screen ahead of me, which is turned off. This morning Marcus is wearing a Yankee baseball cap, which frames his face so perfectly, portrait-worthy, that I half expect him to just sit there and wait until Jack Dawson asks to draw him in the nude. I'd pay fourteen bucks to see *that* movie. Few sprouts of scruff appear to be growing on his face, the five o'clock shadow going on full shade. By midnight it'll be full of basmati rice.

At 7:30 we land. All I need now more than food is a long, relaxing shower. Since I'm so nasty and sticky, I can hardly wait to check into our hotel and soak myself in a bathtub for three hours. In fact, I feel so filthy I might as well be rich.

My butt is numb after sitting for eleven hours so I give it a nice, relaxing massage as soon as I get up. Chubbly Wobbly watches me as though he's never seen a butt massage before. Maybe he's studying my technique, partially borrowed from Giada De Laurentiis, the Italian chef from the Cooking Channel. The way she makes cookie dough is just perfect for it: slow, gentle, with sugar on top; just omit the butter, and no heart attack.

As soon as the seatbelt light goes off, Natalia takes her red leather clutch and storms off the plane before anybody else, pushing Cave aside in such rage she's scary.

Marcus and I acknowledge each other by a nod, but after the humiliation I went through last night, I decide to stop talking to him to give Blabber a rest. Marcus stands up and I peg him at six feet one. Tall men, just like champagne, dried Turkish apricots, and fried chicken are my passion. Surely one can see where my life is going. Truth, with tall men, especially sexy black men, you feel safer and protected, unafraid to walk with him in a dark alley—heck, excited to walk with him in a dark alley—eager to get mugged so that your tall, strong boyfriend can protect you. If Marcus were mine, I'd climb him up like a Palm tree and would cling to him without letting go, occasionally coming down for an apple martini, but only if the moon was blue. Marcus waves goodbye as he exits, how I notice the worst thing about him: A wedding ring coruscates on his finger. Ah, no wonder he took to his heels as soon as I leaned in for a buss. Why does it always happen to me when it comes to finding the worst guys? Well, bye-bye Marcus. It was nice meeting you, though not really.

Before I egress the plane, I catch Cave by the hand, her hungover face perhaps a reflection of mine. She averts her baby blues in a displeased, almost angry manner.

"I'm so sorry for Natalia's language. She's really mad this morning."

Cave's skin looks as though she's been tumble-dried for days. When she finds that particle of niceness in her, she smiles again, and I swear dead skin cells start falling off her. She resembles quicksand.

"Indeed she was mad," she responds back, laughing. "It's a long flight; people get cranky. Have a fantastic time in Hawaii."

Fantastic, I repeat after her quietly, seeing how the word would taste in my mouth. What a weird word to choose. *Splendid* would do just fine.

The terminal is quite serene for an International Airport of such vastness.

I follow signs for the exit, rotating my head in circles, hoping to identify Natalia in the crowd. Sure enough, she's outside, having a cigarette.

Yawning, I spot a magazine stand, a souvenir boutique, a restaurant filled with people, and a duty-free alcohol shop. Several oversized planes peek through the tall terminal windows, which are washed to such perfection they appear missing. While waiting for Chloe and Elizabeth, I buy a cup of coffee and a breakfast sandwich from a Dunkin' Donuts stand, devouring the food with such passion as though I haven't eaten in months. Soon I'll have a bellypop like the child-molesting officer if things continue the way they are.

Chomping on the sandwich I position myself in the corner, right where I can see the upcoming traffic of passengers, most of whom follow signs for the baggage claim.

Natalia returns to the terminal while a trail of smoke follows her beautiful body, unwilling to depart her company. Her wild eyes dart in every possible direction until she locates what she was looking for, her victim, who is me. She grabs my shoulder in what could be another assault, her orbs locked with mine.

"Are we really in Honolulu?"

Sign "ALOHA, WELCOME TO HONOLULU," located behind me fails to answer her question. I almost choke on the food, coughing.

"No, we're in Disneyland. Why?"

"*Why* is the question *I'm* asking. Why are we here and not in Vegas, Calyssa?"

"They have casinos here too, you know," I say, breaking free from her strong grip.

"I don't care about casinos. I need to be in Vegas."

"Why Vegas?" I say. "I thought it would be fun to change scenery. Vegas: been there, done that. Don't you want to see rest of the country?"

"There's a hole in your face, called 'mouth.' It's for telling people if you change plans. Use it."

"Natalia, you blacked out. What, I get no credit for dragging you through the airport security? You should be thankful you're alive."

"Goddammit, Calyssa. Grow up. For once take responsibility and admit your mistakes. How many times can you defend yourself?"

"Why is everything my fault? What's so hot in Vegas all of a sudden?"

She sighs, and shakes her head in an unmistakable gesture of repugnance.

Hands collected into fists, Natalia crosses her arms in front of her chest, but keeps looking at me without answering my question.

She leaves for Dunkin' Donuts, where she purchases a cup of coffee.

Then she trots outside for a cigarette, lighting it halfway while still in the terminal. I've never seen Natalia quite like this: non-talkative, secretive, and mysterious. She speaks her mind and she hardly cares if you happen to hear her or not. She stands behind her word, for sure. She may appear mean, abrupt, and even arrogant most of the time, but never have I seen her reticent. So this one single thought gives me chills, for I don't wish to fight against her. Plus she's the one who's supposed to purchase my ticket back to New York. But she won't buy it anytime soon because her behavior suggests I set my pubic hair on fire.

Still, one thought makes no sense: What's so important in Vegas? Maybe she tracked down Lupita and wants to punish her for "eloping"? Sounds like a legit explanation, so thanks, mind.

Chloe appears in sight with the cat, the pumpkin, and the tote. I wave to get her attention. Her movements are robotic. She looks tired and cranky. Ruby—oh, I forgot about Ruby—walks right behind Chloe in a slightly different fashion. Ruby looks groomed, made up, and refreshed. Her hair is combined into a neat bun at the top. Her kinky-looking bag is hung on the left shoulder, but instead of stilettos she's wearing flip-flops that flip and flop as she drags her feet, half-mooning for the guys.

The three of us follow signs for the baggage claim. There, Ruby's pink suitcase comes second on the carousel, right after a stroller. I help her haul the skinny pink suitcase from the conveyor belt and she opens it after unlocking a teensy-weensy padlock.

Elizabeth is wrapped in a wig instead of a sweater, which doesn't surprise me after seeing the way the airport staff handles luggage, throwing it up and down carelessly. The fish swims hastily from one corner to the other, pretty much alive. At least the Patrón bottle is undamaged, thank God, and now I know why they don't call it Patrón for nothing. Anubis' gaze is fixed on Elizabeth the minute I get her out of the suitcase, his eyes like the second hand on the clock following fish in circular motions. He immediately could sense her. If they ever met in the wild the fish stood no chance against that black beast. In a cartoon, Anubis would be checking out a Giada's cookbook at this very moment, fishing out a recipe how to prepare Elizabeth Italian style.

Fish in hand, Gooseberry in right, I walk ahead of the girls toward the exit, trying to figure out what to do with Ruby. She said she'd help execute the blackmailing plan, so she can remain with us for the weekend. When the weekend is over, she either stays in Honolulu at her own free will or goes elsewhere at her own risk.

The weather outside is perfect, as Honoluluey as I imagined. So warm, in fact, it must be up in the low seventies and it would upgrade to eighty by noon. Palm trees peek from behind the building. Natalia is smoking yet another cigarette, the only filthy smoker in a mile radius. She doesn't fit into the beautiful, smoke-free Hawaii.

The four of us reunite, sober this time around, and we stand beside each other, devouring an awkward moment of silence like we're waiting for Jesus to get born.

"Natalia?" I say, uncertain, with a question mark at the end, the way Chloe says. It sounds so innocent I feel bad for myself. "You remember Ruby from last night?"

"It's Lindsay," Ruby says.

Ah, that's right. Lindsay Goldplenty. Last night must have been wilder than I remember, though what I do remember is blurred out, bleeped out, or wiped out from my memories. The producer—my brain—tries to keep it G-rated, even for my own sake.

"Of course," Natalia says, as though not to sound stupid. I know for a fact she doesn't remember Lindsay at all, simply because they never met. "Calyssa," she adds, "I need to talk to you in private."

Whatever Natalia is about to tell me is not going to be pretty. Quickly I prepare myself mentally while in the meantime I spot our bus destined toward Waikiki Beach Palace, the hotel Little Teddy ordered for us last night.

I point with my finger. "Go take a seat in that bus, and we'll join in just a second."

Chloe and Lindsay obediently do as told.

"Sorry," Natalia says when it's just her and me. "I snapped. I don't need to be in Vegas until Sunday. Today is Saturday. Because yesterday was Friday." Sounds logical. "Listen, I have a headache that would make a fish drown, so do me a favor and reserve me a ticket for Vegas. Make sure I get there tomorrow morning."

"What's in Vegas?"

"Stop," she interrupts me, turning back to Natalia I know: mean, abrupt, partially arrogant. "It's bad luck talking about something that hasn't happened yet."

Russians are very superstitious is what she told me, so I decide not to argue.

Natalia hands me her clutch—which I promptly place in the Gooseberry —and enters the bus. I'll order her that ticket if that's the last thing I do to prove to her I can be trusted, and also to prove to myself I'm capable of making amends after I mess up. I wish I could travel the way Natalia does without anything else besides her clutch, which is filled with cash and unlimited supply of credit cards.

The shuttle bus driver, with an Afro on his head, is a synonym of happiness, his positive energy recharging my mood. Natalia takes a seat with Chloe, who is familiar to her while I sit by the window seat ahead of them and push Lindsay to the aisle, putting on a seatbelt just in case the driver decides to take a nap during the ride.

Besides us four, a few crooked people sit on the bus, including Chubbly Wobbly who must be staying with us at the Waikiki Beach Palace, and some loud Europeans who blab in a tone more appropriate for a pub. The Europeans make the rest of us look bad because we're like dead fish in the sea for being quiet like that. I lift up Elizabeth to give her a smile, to acknowledge her existence. I imagine how funny it would be, if right this minute Giada were cooking something fishy on her show. How sci-fi would that be?

The driver fires up the engine and the bus moves. A pamphlet I picked up from the stack in front of the bus contains various shots of beaches and other Hawaiian Islands with description under them I read with enthusiasm. From the pictures, Hawaiian Islands look like heaven on earth and whoever created this beautiful piece of land was the real God. I also learn from the pamphlet the island where we're located is called Oahu, the "Big Pineapple," nicknamed by tourists. Great, we came from one fruit (the Big Apple) to another. Americans lack imagination. In fact, apartments in New York lack space and maybe we should rename it to the Small Apple.

"Do you have any painkillers for Natalia?" Chloe says, tapping on my shoulder. "She feels awful." I pass the Gooseberry, too tired to search for the bottle of Advil myself.

"You'll find it in the compartment. You'll see what I mean," I say.

In about seventeen minutes, we arrive at Waikiki Beach Palace. Behind me a passed out Natalia is snoring. After a futile attempt at waking her up by calling her name, I pointlessly shake her again and again to realize she's incapable of waking up. I know for sure she only drank coffee this morning, nothing stronger than that, and she smoked nothing stronger than cigarettes.

"Do you know what happened to her?" I ask Chloe. "Was she snorting something illegal?"

"Just that she had a headache," Chloe says. "I gave her the painkillers from your bag, but that's about it."

Promptly I look in the Gooseberry and note with one sharp look those pills Natalia took, unmistakably, were not painkillers at all.

"Those are sleeping pills," I tell no one in particular, annoyed just once more at my laziness and the fact that I should have just given her the painkillers myself. But it didn't even occur to me that *anyone*, let alone a thirty-year-old woman, could misread the label that is written in plain English.

"I'm sorry, Calyssa," Chloe says and flees the bus as though afraid I might slug her.

I must carry Natalia again. The good thing is I'm good at it: If she walks like Natalia, and talks like Natalia, or even quacks like Natalia, it's probably me, since I do all those things for her. I never really understood the mechanics behind how Natalia can walk during sleep, but it's magical.

Without further instructions, Lindsay exits the bus, taking the Patrón bottle from my hands. I realize one thing: It must be really bad that we're working as a team without having to explain anything to each other. When I raise Natalia, her feet won't move. I walk two extra feet, dragging Natalia behind me like a dead body, but that fails to work either. In poker this signifies Natalia is ready to fold and give up on her game.

Sometimes her Russian mind must be offsuit, completely lost in the virtual reality of drugs and vodka. As a professional gambler who makes her fortune by precisely placing bets and who nearly lives in Atlantic City where she mainly absorbs her daily caloric intake by sipping alcohol and manages to function after that, Natalia sure lost her bet to a sleeping pill that knocked her out as though she fought Muhammad Ali. This is the time where I wish I could tell her: "See how you can't even monitor your tolerance to sleeping pills? Now, who's the sissel here?" I take Natalia back to her seat while I'm fishing out a plan, which comes to me exactly thirty seconds later.

I reach the front of bus, where the driver gives me a cheerful smile. His Afro makes him appear as Diane Ross circa 1970, and I half expect him to start singing *Touch Me in the Morning*. Or just touch me *this* morning, whichever of the two comes first.

"Excuse me," I say just as cheerfully to match his look. "Can I request a wheelchair? That's for my friend who's sitting out back. She passed out, see? She can't walk on her own."

"Let me check with the front desk," he projects with excitement.

While Afro makes a phone call, I scrutinize Natalia, whose fuzzy gray jacket above the black tunic makes her resemble a knitting ball. Poor woman, I think, because of the things she must go through to have some fun.

The very first time we went to Vegas, in August—almost right after we met, followed by another outing at our bar—Natalia drank the entire weekend, and then on Monday she called me asking if I remembered what had happened the previous Friday. Like salt in water, she was just dissolved in time for three days without being willing to wake up or daring to remember what was going on with her. One inevitable thought crossed my mind several times: she either liked to feel fermented or her life was so questionable that she had to ask alcohol for answers. To this day, it's unclear to me which one of the two portraits the truth.

"Ma'am," Afro says, breaking my memories, "the wheelchair will be delivered in a few minutes."

"Thank you," I murmur.

Indeed, a few minutes later, a bellboy brings the promised wheelchair and he even assists me with positioning Natalia inside. *That's* what I call good customer service. Natalia—in the roomy wheelchair—seems out of place, much the same way as would seem a hotdog link inside a French baguette. I push the wheelchair and, exiting, thank the driver one last time. I silently give him a haircut with a chainsaw, completely aware of the fact he looks exactly like Moshe. Lindsay and Chloe stayed by the bus, and they grimace at each other, just two roosters before a cockfight. Chloe puts the pumpkin in Natalia's lap, sighing with relief.

Waikiki Beach Palace is a tallish building, beautifully decorated with Palm trees near the entrance. Once again, I can't help but notice the pleasant warmth of the air, and even the breeze is evidently polite as it slightly buffets my hair. At the entrance we're greeted by a man and a woman in nature costumes: the man has a hay belt covering his men's parts and the woman wears the same, together with a hay bra. I instantly wonder how they wash a hay bra. Their uniforms are equipped with headbands made out of red flowers, and the woman has pink strands in her hair. These two creatures put colorful flower necklaces around our necks, followed by a piña colada with a straw and a little umbrella in it, like it can get sunburned otherwise. That's our fate, the fact our abundant desire for a drink is visible even at eight o'clock in the morning. I thank the man for mine, thinking I honestly didn't expect any such greeting.

Pushing Natalia with one hand and sipping the drink with the other, I enter the lobby. From the inside, I'd use two words to describe the hotel: elegant, sophisticated, and spacious. Oh, the two words are: "Heck Yeah!"

Fresh plants with big red flowers grow in planters throughout, mosaic tile clean and simple. In the background, I hear the idle chatter of people sitting around the perimeter in clusters of two or three. Shaped like a fish spitting water, a fountain positioned in the center of the lobby, surrounded by a gaggle of kids who see their reflections in water and laugh, perhaps amused by their distorted images as though in a fun house.

I wince with pride for the hotel management, wondering who else besides me would seriously place a fountain, shaped as a spitting fish, in the middle of their hotel. Fish—symbol of sleek simplicity, an idiom for alcoholism, and the main source of food for the Japanese—right here, in the middle of the hotel lobby, fins raised in an elegant pose, mermaid-like, absolutely shamelessly spits water into the basin, where ornamental turtles sit in clusters on top of one another while a fake crab aims to catch the fish with its claw. If Mario put such a fountain in the middle of his bar, he'd probably get shut down by the PETA, or arrested for substance abuse, or whatever stupid excuse the cops would find just to remove the fountain. Hey, forget the fountain. According to my lease I'm not allowed a water bed, a water tank over five gallons, not even children who are not potty trained. Landlord is very precautions, as he put it, to preserve the expensive wood floors. (They do look good though.) But I'm surprised I have a bathroom, and seriously concerned I'll have to sneak in Elizabeth under false pretenses.

A lady at the front desk is probably in her early forties, or right about the time when we all should start lying about our age. She wears a yellow muumuu with big red flowers printed on it. She probably stole the dress from a cheap store in Chinatown somewhere—no offense—but my envy cannot be subsided that the dress sits perfectly on her fulfilled (let's call it that) body. Her name tag reads Taisha Tripps. Her hair is a chic Afro only singers like Beyoncé can get away with.

"Welcome to Waikiki Beach Palace," she says with a generous smile. "Are you checking in?"

"We have a reservation for Natalia Romanova," I say.

"Let me check on that for you." She claps on the keyboard, retrieving our reservation. "Ah, I found you. A two-bedroom suite on the eleventh floor," she says to herself while looking at the screen. "A most splendiferous view of the oceanfront available on the shore, a total steel wheel. Just a lustre of a room."

Taisha smiles and her teeth give a surreal sparkle, abundantly straight and bleached to a quality of translucency, which brings an extra shine to the lobby.

"Cats are allowed, right?" Chloe asks her, lifting the case.

"Utterly so. Pet companions are encouraged!" Taisha sings. "Oh, look at her. She looks so benevolently adorable. What kind is it?"

"She's a him. York Chocolate. Name's Anubis," Chloe says in shorthand. "His birthday is today. Any freebies he can get?"

"I apologize, but we do not have any treats for pets. If there's any conciliation, what a quite sophisticated name for a little fellow he has. I can't quite tell what color he might be."

In a stupor, Chloe watches Taisha for several seconds without a single blink, contemplating a response. "He's African-American color."

Taisha gains an exaggeratedly confused expression, as though she doesn't know what color African American would be.

"Chloe, stop lying and just say *black*," Lindsay tells her. "The cat is black, not African American."

"Black is inappropriate," Chloe whispers. "Considering, you know . . ." she trails off, nodding slightly in Taisha's direction.

"Black is fairly appropriate!" Taisha says with such excitement people reserve for when meeting a celebrity. "You said nothing aberrant here, so you know."

Chloe turns her face around, cheeks royally flushed. Lindsay finds satisfaction in the conversation, her leer buoying up onto her otherwise poker-face visage.

Taisha claps on her keyboard. "I bet you're excited to get settled right away and go see the sights."

"All I care about right now," I say, "more than anything, is to take a hot, relaxing, drain-your-boiler-long shower."

Taisha obtains that same overblown "sorry" face, followed by a long pause, during which she tilts her head to the side like she spotted a cute puppy.

"My sincere apologies, but we were having frivolous difficulties with our water pipes the past couple weeks, which led to acute difficulties, and finally a desideratum to turn off the main water pipe in the hotel had been decided upon our management staff. The matter should be fixed soon, I opine. As we speak, our plumber is going room to room, attempting to find the source of the problem."

I ogle her face with disbelief, unable to hold back a gasp of vexation. So now that my shower dream is ruined, what am I supposed to do? Looking askance at the kids, I wonder how appropriate it would look if I jumped into the fountain under a false pretense to stumble on a banana peel. But how will I find a banana and explain the soapsuds that will bubble up right after I shampoo my hair?

"Do you know when it's going to be fixed?" I ask.

"Surely no later than midafternoon. Sorry for the inconvenience," Taisha says with such unassumingness in her voice, one would think she means what she says.

However, I frown, annoyed, so annoyed in fact I want to cancel our reservation and go stay at a hotel—one of the ten hotels I spotted growing numerous stories high—across the street, where they have good plumbing. Instead, I count ten apple martinis to calm my nerves.

"Just please call our suite as soon as you know something. I'm Calyssa."

"Nice to meet you, Calyssa. I'm Taisha Tripps."

On their cue, Chloe and Lindsay go about introducing themselves as well, after which we switch attention to Natalia as though she's one of a kind. I introduce her to Taisha, who looks at the Sleeping Beauty with such contemplation, asking without asking for some kind of—any kind of really—explanation.

"Natalia has been feeling terrible lately, see?" Chloe says. "The gallery she owned downtown burned to the ground, with all the expensive art. She wasn't insured, see? Now everybody who ever knew her sues her, even her husband."

"What an execrable chain of events!" poor, deceived Taisha manages to exclaim.

"Yeah," Chloe goes on. "So if you could send some booze upstairs and some food. She really needs to keep up her strength."

"Absolutely! I'll send something right up. That's just terrible. Just terrible."

Chloe gives a look of preeminence to Lindsay, who sighs and walks away.

Taisha turns back to me. "The last thing I need from you is a credit card for the deposit and you're all set."

Taisha smiles and her white teeth give a little sparkle, as though with a sound—ding—like in tooth commercials. I hand over Natalia's American Express credit card that has already been bruised from overspending. Taisha takes the card, swiping it on her device. She hands it back to me.

"Call me down at the lobby if you have any further questions or need anything."

OUR SUITE OPENS A CLEAR VIEW OF THE BEACH. IT'S SIMPLY BUT smartly set up, with a kitchen and a kitchen island by the entrance. There's a living room area with a couch that sits against the wall, with two graphite chairs on either side hugging a glass top coffee table in the middle, an over-sized TV on the wall.

The two bedrooms are located straight across from each other, a bath-room inside each. Chloe helps me lay Natalia in the bedroom to the right. Natalia's tall physique doesn't even fit on the double bed. Since her feet are too long, I bend them and turn her sideways. I plonk the pumpkin on top of the kitchen island and fold the wheelchair by the door, gluing a mental sticky note to bring it back down. I take off the ridiculous-looking flower necklace.

Lindsay leaves Elizabeth on the coffee table, flips her phone open, and disappears in the bedroom to the left. I return to Natalia's room, where Chloe's standing by the window with the cat in her hands.

"Isn't this much better than Vegas or what?" I say.

"I like it," she says nonchalantly. I knew she wouldn't make a fuss over it.

In the bathroom, turning both handles makes the faucet fart; no water comes out. My need to shower is now multiplied by ten, as per law we only want what we don't have. That law is also a reminder it was first decided upon humanity to create people with three livers. Then God realized there was nothing else we could possibly wish for Christmas, so God left us with only one. Don't even get me started on that one.

Out of the red Prada clutch, I get a hold of Natalia's cell phone together with her wallet, longing to call Little Teddy and order Natalia a ticket to Vegas immediately. I place the clutch on the foot of the bed, by Natalia's unshaved legs, and remove the pumps off her feet. I notice her feet are twice the size of mine while covering her with a blanket.

As I step out on the lanai, I note the breathtaking view: Not only are we facing the ocean, but also the sun, the sand, and the scenery work together as a catalyst to happiness. Now I believe I'm in Hawaii, all right. Surprises me none Adam chose a paradise for his vacation, far away from New York so he could cheat on Eve guilt-free.

A square glass table divides the space between two lounge chairs. A white shaggy rug runs across the length of the lanai. Lowering myself into the left chaise chair, I put my piña colada on the table and dial the number on the back of Natalia's credit card.

I wait to be connected to the representative while I'm being baked slightly by the sun like a potato. When I'm done with this conversation, I'm off to the beach for more baking. The wind makes the rug bristles quiver.

"Thank you for calling the personal concierge. My name is Cavalier. How may I assist you today?"

His voice is full of testosterone and I suddenly forget the reason for my call. Then I remember and clear my throat. "Hi, this is Natalia calling. I need to purchase a ticket to Las Vegas, please." I'm back in my royal power tone, but I also remember to use a magic word "please," which works magic on people.

"I'll be happy to assist you. First, for security purposes, please verify your identity. What's your mother's maiden name?"

I suddenly become alive. My brain gets electrified thinking of an answer that I would never know. I try not to sound too suspicious. "Hello, Cavalier, are you here? I can barely hear you."

"I'm here—"

"Hello? Stupid reception. Hello? I'll have to call you back. I can't hear a damn Russian thing."

I hang up the phone, my heart racing and my hands shaking. They must be under the assumption Natalia's credit card has been stolen after the shenanigans last night. Natalia paid for the drinks, the four plane tickets, and the hotel. I shame myself for breaking the first rule of lying to never call an object "stupid," as in "stupid reception," because that's how you can easily spot a liar. What annoys me the most is how Natalia entrusted me with ordering her a ticket, but even that I mismanaged. When she awakes, she better call the customer service herself.

I return to the suite, feeling how the air-conditioning contrasts with the hot air outside. I slide the credit card back into the wallet and toss it on the couch in front of me as though playing rugby. In the bedroom, making eye contact with Chloe, I freeze.

"Calyssa, check this out."

Chloe cackles. Natalia's finger is deepened into a glass of water and toothpaste spread on her face. Sometimes, in such situations, I question Chloe's ability to run her humble existence: living by herself on the Upper West Side and working as an accountant for the Time Warner Cable. Not until recently I started to ponder whether she'd lied about that too. I pull Natalia's finger out of the glass.

"Please wipe the toothpaste off her face, Chlotilda," I say sternly. When she hears her full name, she listens. And she'll do as told. "What is wrong with you?"

"We always do silly things on our trips."

"This trip isn't silly. Lindsay and I have business to conclude."

"What kind of business? Who is she, anywho?"

Someone knocks on the suite door and I pause for a second wondering who that might be.

"Let's talk later," I say.

When I enter the living room area, Lindsay is halfway in the process of opening the door. Chloe bumps into me from behind. With a greeting, a handsome Asian bellboy walks in, pushing a cart full of food. The aroma churns my stomach with such vigor it'll soon turn into butter. There are all sorts of fruits and vegetables, a bottle of champagne, and even a bouquet of fresh-cut flowers set in the middle.

"There comes my free food," Chloe says excitedly, giving Lindsay a grin and an imaginary tongue.

The man rolls in the cart, parking it by the kitchen island. Every fruit imaginable, cut in chunks and slices, lies along fresh baked foodstuffs. The only fruit missing, from the look of things, is mango. Mango is not in season then, I presume.

"The food has been billed to your room," the man says.

"Wait," Chloe interjects. "It's not free?"

"No, I don't believe so. Enjoy."

He quickly withdraws.

Lindsay leers, one eyebrow raised as an arc. "Lying will not deliver free stuff to your door," she says.

Chloe disappears in the room with Natalia and closes the door behind her. Retrieving one ice cube from under the champagne bucket, Lindsay leaves for the second room after taking a banana from the cart, popping the ice cube in her mouth. Exhausted and slightly tipsy after finishing the piña colada, I ease into one of the graphite-colored chairs near the couch, taking a strudel from the food cart beforehand. The chair feels so soft, I wonder whether I'll ever manage to get up without help. It must be made out of cream cheese.

On the side table, magazines are stacked in a pile, issues of *Hawaiian Style* prevalent. As if we would otherwise forget that we're in Hawaii. On the coffee table, Elizabeth rests comfortably in her bottle while Anubis watches her from ten feet away. The coffee table is peculiar, created by a thick glass positioned on top of an old-looking suitcase. Maybe this kind of furniture is in style, but how would I know? The coffee table I purchased was from IKEA, a copy of the table my cousin Christina has in her house. It's black, rectangular, and inexpensive. Since Christina inherited the Asian gene, part of her house is decorated in Chinese Modern. This monstrosity must cost $1,000 or under $10, depending on current trends.

Calling Adam nets me nothing in terms of a response. I send him a good-morning text message, but he fails to send one back. He must be nursing a royal hangover from last night; his belly bloated to the point of being unrecognized, his head splitting. He sure loves drinking a lot. While at it, I check the missed calls log, messages, and emails. It's hard not to notice how the phone is now discharged to 53 percent. I wish I brought my charger. The email inbox contains a letter from Target, reminding me about an upcoming Halloween sale next weekend. I wonder if Target carries hay bras because I'd like to try one out and learn how to clean it. I imagine coming to work in a hay bra, so exotic and cool.

Lindsay reappears, wearing sneakers and leotard, her hair now blue, shoulder-length, with bangs. The strudel is freshly baked, I learn, biting into it.

"My friend Delight just called me," she says, crossing her arms in front of her chest. "She said she saw Ian with some girl last night. She said they kissed on the dance floor in the club. That's incredible. How could he do such a thing to me? You know what I'm saying?"

I nod, but I don't know what she's saying. "Why do you care? Unless you still love him."

"Fat chance."

"Skinny chance!" Chloe yells from Natalia's bedroom. The two of us stare in her direction for five consecutive seconds until we face each other again.

"Lexi, you left town anyway. Problem solved."

"Not Lexi, Lindsay. Gosh. Whether I left town or not is not the point. It's the matter of principle and boundaries and dignity. Ian is the living proof that men cannot be trusted. Am I right or am I right?"

Chloe exits the bedroom with a smile that couldn't possibly stretch any longer. "Getting a boyfriend is easy, but *keeping* a boyfriend is a task you can't tackle, can you?" she whispers.

"Hey, I get it," Lindsay responds. "You won. Good for you." She shifts, tears swelling up in her eyeballs. The blue wig bears a resemblance to a cartoon from a Japanese anime. What a joke. "I'm going to ditch that bum."

She flip-opens her phone and dials Ian. She puts the conversation on a speakerphone and the ringing suddenly starts. Annoyed, I look at her, wondering why she decided to involve me in her private affairs. People who speak on speakerphones or people who talk loudly or people who dance on the subway platform, they are all attention-seekers is what I just presume.

"Hello?" says Ian, who picks up on the seventh ring, his tone a hoarse *I-just-woke-up* kind.

"Ian, I'm breaking up with you."

"What? Who *is* this?"

"Lindsay."

"Leslie who?"

"Lindsay Goldplenty, that's who. I'm breaking up with you."

"Wait, who? What?"

"I'm through with you—that's what's what. You stuck your toy into someone else's bin, and I'm not playing in that playground ever again."

"Hey, calm down," he says. "What are you chinwagging about?"

"Stop searching for me, stop calling, and I hope you live your life happily with a four-inch penis."

"Yeah, well, I've got crabs. Have fun, Latoya."

He hangs up on her while her face turns a bright orange color, a mix of anger saturated with embarrassment. In fact, if her face were a cocktail, it would definitely be a Mai Tai. Lindsay removes the battery from the back of her phone, after which she eases into the second chair, tucking feet under her like a chicken ready to roost. Chloe takes the couch. Anubis wobbles lazily, jumps on the couch next to his mistress and enjoys himself by licking his paws. Meanwhile, he watches the coffee table, eyes aimed at Elizabeth as she swims in circles. It reminds me I need to determine what to feed her, the little green beast.

"He didn't respect you, Leila," Chloe says.

"It's Lindsay, hot goddammit! None of your business, Chunky."

Chloe suddenly gets off the couch. "Why are you on her side, Caly? Who is she, anyway?" She grabs Anubis in the middle of him licking his belly. "I distrust her."

"She's a friend of mine who needs help. I'm helping her."

"I wanted to help too. Why nobody listens to me?"

"Because nobody believes you anymore," Lindsay says. "Calyssa just takes you for granted at this point. Nobody takes you seriously. Everything you say is like listening to our current Republican President: There's no truth to it."

Chloe skedaddles toward the lanai without a solitary word, taking a magazine from the rack, Anubis in hands. She closes the door loudly behind, sticking her tongue out.

"I'm sorry," Lindsay says. "I didn't mean to butt in."

"Fine" is all I say.

The way Lindsay shares her thoughts out loud lacking any sort of filter makes me want to shove a sock in her mouth, tie her to a rock, and throw her off a cliff. No, you're right; no need to waste socks for nothing. I realize that drunk I act like Chloe, when lying is the only way to conduct business. Lies are so much more comforting in a way. In fact, I just lied to Chloe about

Lindsay as though I knew her, as though she's my friend. If I told her I had just met Lindsay, Chloe would otherwise make a scene and perhaps start a fight. Come to think of it, I wonder what most people prefer, be like Chloe or like Lindsay? Sometimes I wish I were Natalia, a woman of few words, but words that are sharp, that speak to the point, that make people listen regardless of where those words originate, in a country of truthfulness or in a state of complete A-lie-ska.

I wiggle myself out of the chair and determine that I want to stroll on the beach, but only *after* a shower. Taisha mentioned the plumber was walking door to door, so he might soon show up, which means I have some time to kill. The best way to kill time is with champagne and a snack, so I pick up fruits and pastries from the array of foods and crack open a bottle of champagne, pouring myself a flute-full. There's nothing more to be done at the moment. To avoid being bored, I'd clean, but I don't want to piss off the maid. Chloe remains on the lanai reading the magazine while Lindsay decides to occupy herself with yoga in the other room. On my question about how she plans to spend her day, Lindsay merely snores a response that doesn't register in my brain.

With the flute in hand, chewing on grapes, I return to Natalia's room, readily acknowledging the fact she'll get mad at me when she learns I was unable to purchase her plane ticket. She should have told me from the start why she needed to be in Vegas because then I could gauge whether it was worth the trouble in the first place.

Even though taking a shower is out of the question, I decide to change into a pair of clean panties anyway, followed by my favorite, and only, dress. Not too deep in the neckline and almost as low as ankle-length, this dress caught my attention at a street fair for Cinco de Mayo. I never regretted the thirty bucks well spent. What I do regret though is the fact I missed a chance to try corn on the cob and apple in chocolate because I was on a diet—low carb diet—on which I gained five pounds.

One article of clothing at a time, I remove the green ruffled blouse, the flats, the slacks, and change into a fresh pair of underwear, tucked in one of the compartments in the Gooseberry.

With the dress on, I turn sideways in front of the bathroom mirror. My cantilevered belly looks not dissimilar to a barrel, and I wonder how soon it'll be until people start giving up their seats for me on the subway. From this point forward, turning sideways in front of reflective objects should be prohibited. Mom must be sitting at a bar in heaven—eyes closed from embarrassment—unwilling to believe her daughter could let herself go this far. Well, Mom, send me a sign from above or something.

Like a "sign" would make me work out. Even a personal trainer failed to motivate me before.

Resembling a shot duck, tall Natalia is spread across the small bed like a giant who came down the beanstalk and assembled itself in a human's bed. I envy her perfect curves, trying to unriddle the secret behind how she keeps trim. In Vegas, she mostly eats salads, but then again she drinks like a Russian fish, so this question has remained a mystery for two months now. They say misery loves company, a precise explanation why Natalia pays for us on these trips. Natalia feels unfit in the female world since her transition from a man to a woman is fairly recent, why hanging out with me was probably a bad idea in the first place. Maybe meeting Lindsay will benefit us all, all for different reasons: Chloe can learn to tell the truth, I can learn makeup tricks, and Natalia can learn why it's mandatory to shave legs for every woman past the age of twenty-one who wants to get laid.

The sudden ring of the room telephone makes me jump. Three fast rings are followed by two seconds of silence. Who can be calling us this early at precisely nine in the morning? And why? And most importantly—who knows we're here?

I pick up on the fourth set of rings, half expecting heavy breathing and the murder's chilly voice telling me he knows what I did last summer, which is great because I don't.

"This is Calyssa?" I say with uncertainty, as though asking the murderer whether it was her name.

"Calyssa, this is Taisha Tripps with the front desk. We came across a quandary regarding your feline companion. Could you take yourself downstairs? Anubis might be in a *biggish* problem."

She stretches word "biggish" as though it contains five i's. No problem can be *this* biggish, compared, I mean, to my protuberant belly. Taking three steps out of the room, with the telephone cord stretching in the process, I eyeball the lanai where Anubis sits perfectly fine on Chloe's lap, half in the process of cleaning up his filthy self.

"What happened?"

"We may charge you a $500 fine."

My mind spells three letters: WTF. "I'll be right down."

CHAPTER SIX

The Cat's Out of the Bag

Exiting the suite, I notice a guy by the elevator with a cooler in his hands and a tote bag by his feet. He's wearing shorts and a tank top. Even from the distance, his protuberant muscles, spread across his body like illegal immigrants across the country, enchant me to follow. Before the elevator collects him, I race across the hall, then stop, and casually bypass him as the door to the elevator opens. He turns around as he steps in and smiles politely—dangerous, but beautiful Siren—holding the door for me, trying to lure me in with his cheating, beautiful song, so that he can kill me should I come closer. With my finger, charmed to the point of insanity, I point to my left as though to tell him I meant to go elsewhere while nonchalantly he wishes me to have a good day.

He's so annoyingly handsome, much handsomer than Marcus; more muscular too. Usually, muscles are not important . . . oh, who the hell am I kidding? His shorts reveal his glutes; his biceps are the size of little baby elephants, something I would know as I've been to the Bronx Zoo on several occasions. He's the man to throw you around in bed, exactly how I like 'em. A tattoo sleeve runs down his left arm. When the elevator hides him behind its doors, I wake up. If I have a fling with anyone on this mini vacation—if you let me call it that—it must be him. My quim shut its gates after it had figured I gave up trying to use it, but Siren has the passport to enter my secret island. I'll let him in even if he's dangerous, even if he's married, and even if he's impotent. Curiosity never killed the cat. It never hurts to flirt a little, I think, and take the fire steps, two at a time, to make it downstairs before him, wiping off the drool.

Down at the lobby, I hide around the corner to make sure I remain unseen and peek here and there while catching up on my breathing. The lobby is packed with people, mostly hotel guests in swimsuits and bikinis, whose goal is to hit the beach bright and early. My man comes out thirty seconds later and stops at the front desk to blab with Taisha, who greets him with such exaggerated excitement it seems as though they're best pals. Minutes drag on unmercifully, punishing me for trying to spy on a guy, but like it's my fault that I'm snoopy by nature. Fortunately, I'm attired to my finest, my dress, and even though there's nothing to do about my stomach, let alone my thighs, my confidence inflates to match our economy. To get his attention I'll even suck in my cheeks.

While my Naiad is chatting with Taisha—over five minutes now—I get further acquainted with the lobby. Its walls are painted pastel orange, the color of a pumpkin, which makes me want to carve them. Contemporary art embellishes the lobby. One painting is too modern for my taste with dots and paint of diverse colors splattered throughout. A Jeff Koon's inflated dog, in red, sits by the door to the restaurant, redolence of breakfast being served impossible to miss. Poor dogs can't get a break that even fake ones aren't allowed inside. As for the art, the inflated dog I understand, kind of, but the painting completely throws me off, mainly because such duplicitous art is deceitful compared to, let's say, Cubism. Picasso, for example, with his *Young Ladies of Avignon* that I saw in the museum of Modern Art in New York—a painting with five prostitutes, perhaps the five original strip club dancers (the original Lindsays)—is a painting worth mentioning. What made Picasso want to depict such a moment with two ladies wearing African masks, and why did he choose pastel pink? Experts speculated on what inspired Picasso; controversies followed. Ways to guess such works are numberless, infinite, and it takes years upon years of discussions while there's only one way to speculate dots or smears of paint on canvas: they are just dots or smears of paint on canvas. Everybody cheats, I presume, even artists with their lack of imagination.

In the middle of counting how many kids play by the fish fountain, I take my phone and dial Adam, as who else would remind me more of a cheater? I personally don't care or have any concrete proof, but rumor has it he's having an affair with an accountant whose name is Hera.

"Yes?" Adam picks up on the third ring.

"Adam, hi. I want to apologize for last night. I was wrong for calling you so late."

"Don't mention it. I was drinking last night so I vaguely remember our conversation, except for the part when you asked me to come in on Monday. Sorry I'm calling out. But you'll survive, right?"

"Sure, I'll pull through. How's Hawaii?"

"Hawaii is surreal it almost feels fake."

"Where in Honolulu are you staying?"

"At Ke Iki Beach, in a bungalow with some guys from Germany. Those boogers can drink."

Just like I planned: Adam will be drunk before I know it, an easy way to take off his shirt and have Lindsay give him a lap dance while the whole ordeal is paparazzied by me.

"Are you doing anything fun tonight?"

"There's a masquerade party at Ke Iki Beach," he says. "I'm planning to attend that."

"What time is the party?"

"At seven. They perform these nice hula dances I like." *Because of half-naked girls in hay bras*, I finish the sentence for him mentally. "I'm only staying for a few hours because then we might hit the casino with the guys."

In the background, I hear his toilet flush.

"What's that sound?" I say.

"Um . . . I'm at the beach. Sorry."

Right, I think, the beach. I know for a fact the beach would put down the lid.

"Well," I say, "you're busy. See you next Tuesday."

I close my eyes, mentally writing down the name of the beach, Ke Iki, and the time of the party, seven. Right away, I open a calendar on my phone—finally useful—and type all the information into it. I set up several reminders in case I forget, which is more than plausible. The battery is down to 50 percent, dangerously indicated by a battery sign exactly half full.

A masquerade party, huh? Instantly, my brain generates a new plan: As soon as Adam's drunk, I'll ask Chloe, Lindsay, or Natalia to take a picture with my digital camera while I pretend to kiss him. (I'll be wearing a mask, totally unrecognizable.) No mess, no fret, no recollection on the next day. That picture will be my leverage against him. The four German boogers get stuck in my mind and I see a quick daydream about Hamburg, a town where I consume three hamburgers with a side of an apple martini.

My man—my beautiful Siren—finally lifts his cooler and heads for the exit, his butt, like a full moon, following him. Without any time for recuperation, I race toward the front desk, eyes devoted to his muscles, mouth consecrated to Taisha.

"You called me? What happened?" I say.

"Calyssa, I'm glad you're here."

She puts a cage on the counter with a black cat inside. Seduced, fake, or dead, the cat's just sitting there silently.

"Is this Anubis?" she asks. "The cat sneaked into one of the suites. I'm afraid we may charge you a fee for the damages."

Staring at the cat, I positively know Anubis he ain't, for I just saw him playing with Chloe out on the lanai not ten minutes ago. On closer inspection, I notice a lack of fur in several spots, like the cat didn't tip well at a barbershop and they swooshed him with that kinky-looking hair clipper.

"He is missing a white spot by his collar," I say in defense. "This cat is completely black. Besides, Anubis is with Chloe upstairs on the lanai. Plus, I also have a reason to believe that Anubis is a *he* and this cat is a *she*." How I arrive at such a conclusion, I've no idea. All I know is I need to hurry up before my man disappears from sight. He already made it through the doors and turned right.

"Are you sure it's not Anubis? Then where did *this* cat come from? The lady said she was going to charge us $500 for the damages."

"Why five hundred?"

"She claims the cat pooped on her wedding gown. I even volunteered to get it cleaned for her in our laundry facility, but she wants a prompt payment by cash and a full refund of her one week's stay. My apologies for troubling you with this. The hotel will recompense."

"What are you going to do with the cat?"

"That's a whole new predicament. I'll telephone a handful of places I'm familiar with to ascertain adoption possibilities. I refuse to believe the cat sneaked into the suite by herself. How could she fit under the door? It's a cat, not a rat." Good she knows the difference.

I shrug. "Well, call me later if you need anything. I'm going to stroll on the beach." Stroll, yeah right. I'll be running like a rocket after my cute beast.

"Bye," she says, which to me sounds "bah," as though she's too lazy to say the whole word, almost sheep-like.

In the meantime, my man gets completely out of sight, so forgetting about the cat right away I run toward the exit in what—in my shape—could only be a fast walk. Outside, blinded by the sun, squinting, I circle around until my eyes finally identify my man crossing the road toward the beach. I follow him as casually and inconspicuously as I possibly can. Palm trees with a strip of land separate the road and the beach, nature and people living in such close proximity to each other. Several men with surfboards bypass me, followed by two bicyclists.

My man turns in the direction of Diamond Head, a tuff cone creature formed by volcanoes that since long have been dormant. I remember watching a documentary about it, and seeing it in person is thrilling. Maybe later, after I execute some harmless flirting, we could climb Diamond Head with the girls. Before the party starts, that is. From the scraps of the documentary, what comes to mind is that the tuff's ridgeline resembles a dorsal fin of a tuna fish, called Leahi. Ahi means tuna in their native language. Pausing, from this distance, I take a picture of the tuff, but because of the weird position of the sun, the picture ends up being dark. The phone battery drops down to 47 percent almost immediately.

My man removes his flip-flops, shoves them down the tote, and detours toward the sand. Inconspicuously, I follow. Humid Hawaiian weather makes my skin feel welcome, since typically it gets dry and flaky. Dry skin makes me itch with such vigor that people on the subway distance themselves from me by at least five feet.

On the sand, next to the water, the crisp breeze buffets my hair, messing up my already crooked mop, which hasn't been washed in what seems like a decade. This is the only time when with assurance I'd rather be a boy than a girl for the ability to have short hair or be bald altogether—whichever comes first. After I collect my strands behind my back, the wind blows them forward, as though a little guttersnipe who is out of toys to play with found me to torture. Good thing I'm not Lindsay or my dress would probably fly up in the air, doing a striptease for the tourists at Waikiki, followed by humiliating laughter at my mismatched undergarments.

There are all sorts of people on the beach, men and women, old and young, black and white. Hot Latina ladies shamelessly show off their gorgeous bodies and perfect brown skin. Next to the women, hot Latino gentlemen sunbathe. There are also kids, many many kids, and then even more kids, all generously covered in sunscreen, their screams instantly getting on my nerves. Kids are not my sip of vodka.

Following my man, I notice how sun umbrellas cover 67 percent of the sand while families and people in groups are strewn throughout the free space of the beach on blankets or boldly on the sand without anything underneath them. Games are taking place. In water, little black dots—people's heads—move around with synchronized precision. The ocean is calm and pacified, and it mirrors the cloudless blue sky. No wonder it was named the Pacific, for it stands still, calm and quiet like a wise old monk. My man keeps walking forward even farther, perhaps trying to find a quieter spot for himself, where fewer people can bother him. This is exactly what I would do.

According to my watch the time is only 9:32 A.M., which would be 3:33 P.M. in the afternoon in New York. I add an extra minute just in case (you never know). A good night's sleep on the plane was a good enough boost to energize me throughout the day.

The beach, even though almost full, will likely get even more crowded by noon, so I shouldn't stick around for too long. Not to blame anyone who came out though; the weather is just perfect for the occasion, as though Fibonacci, that famous mathematician, applied his golden ratio to this particular beach. I can imagine how my favorite goddess, Afrodite, helps Fibonacci calculate the perfect weather with the sequence of special numbers and all the formulae they must create. And yes—Afrodite is an African version of the Greek Aphrodite. In my mind, this particular goddess is responsible for the things that supposedly make life seem better: the sun, the beach, and the champagne. She's African because it gives her the dark, beautiful, blemish-free skin only black people seem to possess, together with the ability to stay looking young forever. How I envy black people. Sometimes I wish I were black, but then again, sometimes I wish I were so many things all at once. Optimist I am, there's still hope for the second liver to develop.

The smell of the ocean is quite refreshing, the air full of vitality and of a newly cleaned apartment. Heated by the sizzling sun, the white sand is perfectly unsoiled, without the occasional dead shells or dirty seaweed one might find on an East Coast beach. Since sand is also a perfect callus remover, I intentionally rub my feet on it, instantly noticing the results. Carrying my flats and my phone with one hand, I lift the bottom of my dress with the other one and divert toward the ocean without losing the guy from sight. The water—as felt by my feet—is heated to the perfect temperature, thanks to Fibonacci and Afrodite. There's not a cloud, not even a blemish in sight for as far as the eye can see.

My mysterious man keeps luring me even farther, and I follow him like a cute but creepy stalker, casually avoiding children, afraid I might step on one and make him or her cry. Though wouldn't that feel great!

Out in the sky, a plane flies by with an aerial advertisement banner clipped to its back about a local wine bar near Waikiki. Like we, Americans, are not fat enough that we need to get even fatter by checking out local wine bars. We complain and complain but do nothing about our chubby tummies, including yours truly. What I wonder is the following: since there are Internet ads, paper ads, *air* ads, how soon will it be before ads will be featured underwater? You're scuba-diving happily, minding your own business, exploring the coral reef ahead of you, taking pictures of exotic fishes only found near the coast of Honolulu, until a submarine passes by advertising a nearby seafood restaurant. At least all the sharks will be scared away.

Other than the wine bar ad, I think of how beautiful life can be just to walk on this beach every day and that for two cents—all I have left in my bank account after buying my new couch, the one purchased on credit since I had no cash to begin with—I would unblinkingly trade my life in New York to stay in this paradise. But that's what I say every time I travel anywhere with better weather than New York, and that gives me a whole new spectrum of choices.

I keep following my man, but he keeps walking and walking like he's trying to work out his glutes. I don't know about his glutes, but even my glutes are all worked up and ready to take a nap from all the outdoor activities. In New York City, people take subway, then sit on chairs all day long, take another ride back, rest on the couch, and lie down to sleep, exhausted from all the sitting. The only time we walk is when we need to go to the bathroom, though debatable. No wonder my breath is almost all sucked out of me.

Suddenly, out of fuel, the guy stops and puts the cooler on the sand, positioning himself on a blanket on which another guy welcomes him with a kiss. On the *lips!* A big juicy smooch. And then again. And again. Amazed and angered, as though someone keeps squeezing a bottle of ketchup in my face, I keep staring at the two of them with an open jaw, much the same way as I did when watching a documentary about Russian prisons (something Natalia recommended). In fact, the two men get into such heavy petting I stare without dropping my gaze, envious and stunned by their passionate exhibitionism. For all that walking, I was foolish enough to believe I deserved some loving, but instead it made me feel deceived, broken-hearted, and humiliated. It should be me on that blanket kissing him. It should be me later tonight underneath him. It should be me. Period.

My genome must have been mutilated during birth because I somehow ended up a woman. The lucky guy, the one who embraced my man is as well handsome, as well tattooed, as well heavily built on the muscle. How many guys does a woman have to go through before finding at least one who likes women? Exasperated for all the misfortunes, I keep walking straight into the serene ocean, wondering if it could lenify me. Do rich people have misfortunes, or are those solely reserved for folks who are broke?

Contemplating suicide by drowning myself, I stand knee-length in water, holding my dress in hand, wretched, until some fish bites on my ankle—as though sent by Elizabeth—trying to tell me how ironic it would be if I die before my fish does. I quickly detour toward the sand and one last time scrutinize the happy couple, two guys who are so into each other that neither must fear cheating. I dig a hole in the sand with my toe, thinking how unfair the world has become. Next thing you know men will expect us to offer anal sex on a first date. Personally, I'm not a big fan, but I wonder whether it might potentially help with constipation.

"Calyssa?"

I turn around, attempting to find the direction of the voice.

Nestled under a palm tree, just thirty degrees to my right, Marcus waves his hand at me. Great—exactly what I need—another unavailable guy to make my life completely miserable, just a final twist of a knife into my heart. If yesterday meeting him on the plane was a pleasant surprise, this morning it is a stupid coincidence. It must be a test, I think while taking several steps forward, looking at Marcus in admiration. His body is tanned to a perfect dulce de leche color; just put him in a jar and sell him, that boy made out of caramel. I'd pay $3.50 for a jar of *that*. Afrodite must be testing how good a person I am, and whether or not I would sleep with Marcus knowing he has a wife, as a simple theory of balancing the world, which states: If I do a good thing for her, the universe must do a good thing for me in return. Oh Afrodite, you know me—I'm better than that—I would never sleep with a married guy. Notwithstanding, Marcus is sizzling hot and one could cook an omelet on him.

The palm tree casts shadows on his shirtless body, much like prison cell bars would cast shadows on a shirtless inmate—a fantasy of mine if you really must know. Whose fantasy it isn't, I mean, to have a dangerous guy (with tattoos covering a good 87.5 percent of his body) to flip you around?

The buildings behind Marcus rise tall, spread out throughout the Waikiki Beach in all shapes and sizes, like the Hanging Gardens of Babylon. Someone opens a beer can so loudly, the pop echoes along the beach. There is a chain reaction of beer opening shortly after by the other beach-goers.

As I reach the blanket, Marcus stands up, a tall brunette with freckles. Can this day get any worse? He could have worked out a bit more, however, because his abs are barely outlined, as though he and the gym were never properly introduced or as though he drinks too much. Whichever came first.

"Are you here by yourself?" he says. "How's your morning going?"

"Yup, all by myself. The girls are back at the hotel, where we have no water. I decided to take a walk, think about a few things, and follow a cute butt. In the mantime, yes—mantime—I met a swooshed cat and learned about his pooping abilities. Then I learned that cute butts like men, so I'm not apparently getting laid today." I have nothing to lose at this point. That's the best part of talking to someone you're not interested in, to someone who's gay, or to someone who's married.

No filter—and sober—I sound just like Lindsay, with no evident respect for myself.

"What?" he says while a small laugh explodes from his mouth. I watch his stomach, wondering why it is connected, the laugh and abdominal muscles, wishing, in part, there were six little cubes on the stomach instead of the half a one I discern.

"Sorry, I'm a mess."

"You're fine. But you do look like you need a drink." He hands me a red solo cup that he was holding in his hands, and I take it, finishing the whole thing in one sitting—to show him he ain't dealing with an amateur here. Margarita. And refreshing too. "This beach is magnificent, isn't it?" he says. "I'm having some brunch if you're interested."

At almost ten o'clock in the morning? That's called breakfast, dummy. The answer is: of course I do, because I need some serious male attention but, somehow, the emotional part of me—my heart—tells me to run away before it could get hurt while the other part of me—hormones—keeps staring at him and wants me to join his so-called brunch. Good for me, hormones are stronger than the heart.

"Sure, I'd love to."

While Marcus makes small talk, I sit down on the blanket and notice how the ring has disappeared from his finger. Maybe the swooshed cat taught him a valuable lesson to catch more fish without the ring than with the ring. It'll never fool me, though, because I know a cheater when I see one, and every-thing about Marcus screams infidelity: the way he smiled, the way he waved. From his fingers to his biceps, I notice how incurved they look, not flabby, but halfway there, and I want to tell Marcus he needs some serious—any, really—exercising done if he wishes to be in shape. Remembering my reflec-tion in the mirror, I decide to dry up.

A half-blue, half-white cooler is located in the middle, and his slippers are placed on either side of the blanket, a notion behind which, I presume, is to simply protect the blanket from flying away. Smart ass, I think, considers everything. A bottle of SPF 30 sunscreen, near the cooler, looks bent and almost empty, streaks of pale white paste smattered all over Marcus, as he carelessly dabbled the sunscreen on himself just some time earlier. Without asking for permission, I take the bottle and massage the lotion into my arms, neck, chest, and legs, in a firm but steady circular motions, unwilling to leave myself looking as though a tube of toothpaste has just exploded on me.

"You're so precise with your lotion application process," he says.

"I'd rather die from a liver outage than from a sunburn. Once, as a child, my mom forgot to put sunscreen on me and I still haven't forgiven her for that. I forgot mine at the hotel. That's all right?" I lie, knowing perfectly well I have none at the hotel.

Marcus nods and smiles again, now from one ear to the other, revealing a pleasant sight of straight teeth. He should do a tooth commercial or something. His face is cleanly shaved with no visible sprouts in sight, just like the rest of his upper body. His chin and cheekbones are set, skin elastic, with no lines, wrinkles, or pimples. Mirror, mirror on the wall, whose legs are fairest of them all? I think Marcus'. His legs are not shaved but not a jungle either. His thighs look decent, but I'm pretty sure I can take him in a fight.

"You're funny," he says. "On the plane last night, you were kind of tipsy. The way you spoke your thoughts out loud was very much amusing. What a coincidence we meet again."

Mentally, I roll my eyes. It's not like we met in the middle of the country. I mean, we did take the *same* plane. And besides, many tourists stay at Waikiki, so us meeting up again is not a coincidence, but more like a given.

"I'm sorry," I say instead, stretching out my feet on the sand. "I've had a rough week, and I drank uncontrollably last night just to forget."

"No need to apologize. I know exactly how it goes. I started having margaritas as soon as I got to my hotel this morning, so I could forget about my week as well."

Marcus finds another red solo cup in the cooler, puts a straw in it, scoops some ice with his dirty (I presume) hand, and pulls out a bottle of premixed margarita. I suppose he could have made it from scratch. But who am I to judge if the only drink I know how to make comes from a Kool-Aid package? Unlike Mario, Marcus pours the drink without juggling the bottle. When the cup is full, he offers it to me.

"I must toss that cat out of the bag, Calyssa. I may sound drunk, but I rarely meet people who make me laugh. You seem to accomplish it so effortlessly."

"Because I'm not the woman you think I am," I say, getting a hold of the cup.

Sunlight makes his eyes appear extra blue, same as the ocean. I make a sudden decision that I can look at them all day. A couple of kids are building a sand castle just a few feet to our left, Diamond Head sitting in the distance like a wise, deaf, ancient man, who listens to our secrets but who is unable to comprehend them. In the meantime, I gulp half of my margarita from the side of the cup without touching the straw, just to show Marcus how professional I am. Margarita is sweet and sour, and quite strong, for it instantly gives me a buzz after mixing in my stomach with the champagne from earlier.

Warm with pleasant heat, I set down the cup while staring at Marcus' hand. Instead of the ring, he has a white patch of skin that was untouched by the sun. That part of his finger, I want to tell him, will definitely have fewer chances to get sunburnt in the future.

"What happened to your finger?" I point casually, as though genuinely concerned. "It's like you've been marked or something."

"Oh, that. It's from my wedding ring. I removed it this morning because it started to hurt. I think my finger got swollen. I blame it on that champagne you made me drink."

"I see. You're married," I state instead of asking.

"Was married. We got divorced in May."

My buzz goes away as fast as it came: Marcus finally turned a nice dime. This day is suddenly getting so much better, so I sit up straighter, tuck in my tummy, and suck in my cheeks, in a vain attempt to look thinner. Since Marcus is rapidly becoming more and more attractive, I must follow close behind. But I know that sneaky Afrodite, and this is still a lesson, so there must be something—anything—wrong with him, perhaps a mental sickness.

"I'm sorry to hear that," I say like I mean it. "What happened?"

"Do you really want to know?"

I nod, though honestly I don't. The only thing I'm interested in is how soon until we're having sex.

"Have you heard about a woman cheating on her husband? Well, this isn't that story. I cheated on her instead."

I knew he was a cheater. I knew Afrodite wouldn't throw in bones to a dog without fixing up some funk to go along with it. "Really," I say.

"So I'm not the man you think I am. I cheated. There's no real explanation to it except that we stopped having sex. I'm sure you, of all people, will understand." I get insulted, but not enough to leave this delicious margarita behind. Again, I made a fool of myself and I wonder whether Marcus thinks of me as a buddy who makes him laugh. "The passion we used to share was gone. Cheating was my desperate attempt to fix something that wasn't broke. I didn't care about her feelings. All I cared about was my desire. I hate myself."

"Don't be so tough on yourself."

"It's impossible; I tried. I just wish it never happened. In fact, I wish I never got married in the first place. Worst of all, she caught me in our bedroom. With twins. Who had just turned eighteen."

I half expect him to add, "Oh, and they were also guys," but instead he gets silent, waiting for me to absorb the information. To be brutally honest I'm not a fan he cheated with eighteen-year-olds but I'm sure I've done worse. (Moshe.) I realize Marcus and I have more in common than first appeared. Just like him, out of desperation, I'm technically cheating my own job by trying to acquire blackmailing material on Adam. People cheat death; otherwise, we wouldn't need doctors. People cheat high school and college exams. People cheat themselves by being in denial. Chloe cheats by lying while Lindsay cheats by being skinny to fake confidence; Natalia cheats her physical appearance by changing sex. Money don't smell, and neither does cheating.

Cheating, turns out, is a good thing.

Suddenly, I wish to slap myself in the face. Love-struck with the cute beast in front of me, my brain is justifying Marcus' actions to have him appear in a better, innocent light. *God* no. I could justify him better by telling him the real reason why I'm here, that I'm in no way any better, but I hold my horses. This is not why Afrodite made me find him; there should be more.

"Why do you keep wearing your ring?" Furring my brows, I finally say, half wanting to add, *Pour me some more of that margarita*. A polite guest I am, I pour the margarita myself.

"As a reminder I can't treat people like that. Cynthia threatened to file a restraining order so I couldn't see our daughter, Lydia, not until she's eighteen, anyway."

"You have a daughter?"

Great, I think and realize Marcus' image in front of me is getting blurry. His bad points: dad, cheater, almost alcoholic; good points: handsome, flies first class, almost alcoholic. In this particular case, the good beats the bad. For a fling, at least.

"Why so surprised?"

"I'm sorry," I say, and for once I mean it. "You're just young and it didn't even cross my mind. How old is she?"

"Thirty-three."

"I meant Lydia."

"She's five."

"And Cynthia won't let you see her? It makes no sense." *What is wrong with that psycho?* is what precisely I mean to add.

"She's punishing me by manipulating. There's nothing more I can do but hope she changes her mind." Marcus refreshes his throat with a sip of margarita, his eyes full of drunken uncertainty and sadness I've only seen homeless people and dogs going number two manage to express. "Lesson learned: never get married if you want to remain sane."

"That's a wise piece of information," I say sarcastically. "Never wanted to in the first place."

"Smart woman."

Speechless, I sip my margarita. Another airplane passes by above us, advertising a local strip club called XOXO located downtown. I imagine all the dads on the beach mentally jotting down the address of the club to check it out later. That's why all men are liars: just look at all the advertising they're getting and women are getting none.

"Tell me more about Lydia," I say. "How's she taking it?"

Marcus seems startled. "You want to hear about Lydia?"

"That's what I asked."

"Have you had kids before?"

"No, I'm not a baby person. My cousin Christina is pregnant with a baby and that's as close to one as I'll ever get."

"At first we hadn't told Lydia we broke up. Cynthia told her I have to travel for work was the reason I was never home. But kids her age catch on fast. Someone in her class suggested the idea of us splitting up and she came home, asking questions."

"So she knows."

"Yes. In the meantime, Cynthia became obsessed with revenge. She threatened to file a restraining order last week, claiming I have alcohol addiction and might hurt them both. Couldn't be further from the truth."

I decide not to roll my eyes while watching him finish his cup and pour more margarita. "Is this the only legal way?"

"She doesn't want to settle this on good terms. She's got the apartment through settlement, but that's not enough for her. I already pay alimony, child support, insurance, but she's not satisfied with that either. Half of my paycheck pays for her expenses."

"She doesn't work?"

"She wants to be a housewife. Stay home with the kids, go to social activities. She's not carrier-oriented. She comes from a wealthy family and her dad helps her with expenses whenever she asks for it."

"Did she go to college?"

"Yes, she went to Princeton. But she claims it's important for a child to have a full-time parent, especially because I work around sixty hours a week."

I silently fart, and start fanning the area to sabotage the fat man sitting near us. I'd prefer to hold it in but there's something in the drink; also, I already burped three times. "So where do you live now?"

"I moved in with my best friend in Brooklyn until I figure out what to do. Cynthia stayed in the Gramercy Park apartment I purchased six years ago."

"By the way, what will she accomplish by filing a restraining order?"

"My guess is just as good as yours: she's trying to punish me so I learn a lesson from it. And I have: I'll never get married again, that's for sure."

"So a father has no rights on a baby?" I say, squinting.

"Right, because we live in a democratic society. A woman reserves all the rights on a child."

"Sounds like she copyrighted a song. Well, that's dumb."

"I guess the Republicans would argue with this. They believe a father should have the same rights as a mother. After all, half the child is ours."

"Yes, the expenses."

"Look at how the world has changed: Just two thousand years ago, women had no rights of almost any kind, and compare that to society in the twenty-first century. Funny, right?"

Not laugh out loud funny when it comes to lack of women's rights and rape reports, but I let this one slide. Freaking men, man. "I'm sorry," I say and sigh, thinking how unfair things sometimes happen to good people. "Cynthia sounds like a complete moron."

"She's just hurt. I totally understand her."

"Well, that's pessimistic, Marcus. If you want anything in this life you must fight for it." Case in point, I'm here to fight my boss. I'm half tempted to clue him in on my plan that I came all the way to Hawaii to blackmail Adam. Marcus seems to like me anyway, and I'm sure he would find this funny, like me better, and learn a lesson on how to get things done by working hard. But pride stops me and I say, "Sometimes we only fight for things we never appreciated until they're slipping away."

"Good point."

After a short silence, I think of the swooshed cat for some reason, how miserably he sat in that cage. I suck up the rest of the margarita, which under the hot sun makes me woozy. Sun plus liquor is a hideous combination. Sun plus liquor makes you sicker. Liquor and sun, you'll figure it, hun.

I rub some sand on my legs, rubbing them slowly to exfoliate my filthy, unwashed skin.

"If it's any consolation," I say without making eye contact, "I never knew my father. My mom got knocked up when she was nineteen. He must have known she was preggo because he was courting her for a while. Though after I was born, my father never searched for me. I know they didn't stay in touch. In fact, he was an immigrant from the Middle East, though not even certain which country. But he's for sure gone, possibly dead. I'm honestly debating what's worse: being unwanted like that or being taken away, like Lydia might be taken away from you."

As though I just asked something complicated, Marcus just nods, perhaps wondering why I'm not a hot bikini model. Quickly, before I lose my momentum, I suck up my cheeks again and face him to reveal my most appealing look. He could also be thinking about my dad and himself, two correlated stories, wondering the same: Did he ever care? If Cynthia is indeed a psycho, and she definitely sounds like one, she'll make Marcus a ghost by cutting him out of pictures and deleting videos they took together. He'll be completely wiped out from existence, as though all he ever was just that: Lydia's pure imagination. Five-year-olds forget fast, blame ADD, ADHD, and other disorders kids are diagnosed with on a daily basis. I mean, what kind of kid doesn't have an attention deficit disorder?

A cheerful breeze sweeps around to mess with my hair while a sailboat in the distance crosses the ocean in slow motion, blurred by my margarita vision.

"What do you do for work?" Marcus asks. "You started last night, but somehow we got disconnected." I suddenly feel attracted to him more for asking the first-date questions.

"Sorry about that. I'm a secretary at a shredding company called Shred Unread."

"Oh, that's right."

"My direct boss, Adam, is responsible for advertisement." Since Marcus spilled the beans about his failed marriage, for the last time I wonder whether to tell him why I'm really here in Hawaii. Then again, silence is golden. The margarita is making me dizzy and I can hardly keep my eyes open, reality twisted into twirls and swirls.

"I don't think the word secretary is appropriate anymore," he says in a teasing manner. If I knew him better, I'd say this is his flirting manner as well. "How does your company operate?"

"Well, we rent a floor at this building in midtown, near Rockefeller Center. Our men come in a truck with a large bin and pick up your junk. Whatever fits in the bin is a flat fee. You can request two or more bins. Our people take it downstairs and shred it on our truck equipped with an industrial shredder while you watch. For an extra fifteen, your wife can watch too." I laugh, patting myself for being so clever.

"I don't get it."

"It's a line from *Pretty Woman*. Kit came to the hotel to pick up the cash Vivian had left for her. When Kit saw this older man she told him how much she charged per hour and added for extra cash his wife could watch." Now that I had to spell it out for him the joke doesn't even seem to be funny anymore.

"I've never seen that movie."

My phone beeps when a reminder about the Ke Iki Beach party pops up. For what reason I set up a reminder ten hours ahead beats me. "Sorry. I should be going soon. I have to get ready for a party."

"What party?"

"At Ke Iki Beach tonight. There will be some hula dance party for which I need to buy masquerade masks and whatnot." I sit up, shaming myself for the direction this day took, three margaritas off its course.

"One thing before you go," he says.

Slowly I turn my neck in his direction, finally realizing how strong his margarita mix really was, its sneaky lime camouflaging the taste of alcohol. Before I could say anything, Marcus lures me into such a smooch it must look like a breeding tie between two dogs. I lie down on the blanket and he follows. With one hand he cuffs both of my hands in a strong hold just above my head while his mouth is half inserted into mine. Unable or unwilling to undo his tight grip, I give in, partially blaming alcohol for making me such an easy target. His hand rubs my thigh, after inserting his hand under my dress. Whatever he finds there, he seems to like it, because his grip tightens around my knee. His other hand moves down my body, and his mouth finds my neck, my most sensitive spot.

Suddenly, he lets go and eyes me, his drunken face a reminder the kiss meant nothing but that it was done between two drunken people.

"You certainly kiss like a secretary, I must admit." Marcus falls back onto his blanket, guffawing at his corny joke. Teasers are the best.

"And you certainly kiss like an architect."

I lie down next to him and the two of us watch the sky and laugh. This is the kind of laugh that makes you wake up the next day and shame yourself for things you've said the night before. However, at the moment, this in particular is what I love about being tipsy, or—in this case—drunk: anything you say that is stupid sounds funny.

Two more minutes and I'll skedaddle without ever seeing this guy again. Or maybe I will. I'd suggest we have sex, but when I fall for a guy I no longer can; I'm too shy. The "easy-me" moment passed. Now I'm a respectable woman.

The sky above us is clear, just a cloudless blue blanket hanging so high up in the distance as though limitless. What a contrast to hazy New York where you first see a talking swooshed cat before you see any sky at this time of year. I close my eyes. My skin feels good being bathed in warmth of the sun. So perfect. So, in fact, perfect, I want to stay here forever. I can feel his thigh next to mine, his hand holding mine.

Two minutes later I open my eyes, which are partially covered by the shade of the palm tree. Hangover's approaching. Quickly I check my watch and learn it's a little after eleven. That means I fell asleep for about an hour. There's a feeling in my stomach indicating I may urp due to the amount of margaritas I've consumed. Geez, what my tubby has to go through these days. I sit up and imagine the bags under my eyes must resemble two of Lindsay's suitcases. And I guess the time has come to get them rolling. Marcus is lying on the blanket, stomach down, his back being baked like a perfect apple pie.

He unglues his face. "Oh, you're awake."

"I must go. Thanks for the drinks."

"Any time," he says lazily. "Can I take your phone number?"

"Why not."

I stand up and an inward force in my head makes me lose my balance for a few seconds. That's all Marcus' fault for compelling me to drink those margaritas without any food to help with digestion. I give him my full name and my phone number, which he dutifully types into his phone.

"I'll call you," he says.

Nodding, I turn a hundred and eighty degrees on my left foot like a soldier and march toward the hotel, feeling hot, sleepy, and anxious. I can sense his gaze on me, eating through my dress, drilling a hole in it. I walk forward without turning back to show him my indifferent state of mind, which is also my embarrassed state of mine. I made a fool of myself and passed out in front of him. I can't help but wonder what he must be thinking: that

I'm either a sick narcoleptic lady or simply a drunk mess. When I'm at a safe distance of a hundred feet, as sneaky as a fox, I skillfully turn, searching for Marcus in the crowd, hoping to see him one last time. Now at a distance, he appears to be a blurry golden dot as though a mirage. In fact, maybe I was so hungry for a man I made him up.

When I turn back around, I stumble. It happens so suddenly I'm unaware I fell until I'm flat on the ground, snacking on sand. This should teach me a lesson not to walk with eyes facing backward. I get up on my knees first, noting the reason for my collapse: a bright green beach ball by a volleyball net. The owners, or so I presume, appear straight across from me playing in the ocean like some idiots. I get an urge to shout something nasty and obnoxious (since they should be watching their toys), and because not just my only dress is full of grit, but also my bra, my hair, and my face. I get up and wipe off an ample amount of sand from the dress but I doubt I'm capable of doing much without a drink, a laundry machine, and a shower.

As I enter the lobby of the hotel, I head straight toward the concierge desk, praying the water pipes are back on.

"What happened to you?" Taisha says, her expression animated by eyes that double in size.

"I fell. You said you had a laundry facility here or something? This is my only dress and I was kind of planning to wear it tonight for my party. And I'm unable to even blame the cat for it, unfortunately."

But that's what cats (it seems) were created for—to be blamed for our mistakes.

"Speaking of the cat," she says, excitedly. "Guess what? The lady who claimed the cat pooped on her dress actually *brought* the cat in a bag *with* her. Can you imagine? She checked in this morning, so my manager Mr. Floorman and I rewound the footage, and we saw the cat's face through the fabric as she dragged the cat along. After the cat had damaged her dress, she pretended the cat wasn't hers, like the cat is worth nothing. But now that we know she lied, we asked her to leave our hotel and to never come back. You should have seen how Mr. Floorman ordered her to get out. I wish we could call social services on her, too. That would definitely serve her right. She was so furious and she vociferated, raising hell, saying she was going to write us bad reviews online. I'm glad you were out on the beach during that time. What a mad woman!"

"Was her name Cynthia?"

"Who?"

"Sorry. Inside joke."

"Oh. Anyway, about your dress: just take it off and bring it downstairs. I'll call the housekeeping right away; they can take care of that in less than two hours. But here's one last thing: What happened to Lindsay?"

"What do you mean?"

"Just about thirty minutes ago she came downstairs with her suitcase, and when I asked her what happened she couldn't even speak. She seemed terrified, worse than the cat. She just left and said she wasn't coming back."

I rush back to the suite to find the door ajar. Suspiciously I peek inside to find the suite quiet and peaceful, with only a slight breeze playing with the curtains (now that my hair is out of the playground zone). Chloe is chilling on the lanai, what seems like reading her book, and I walk around in circles, trying to remember where I put my cell phone. Ah, Natalia's bedroom. When I push the door to open, I'm dumbstruck by an empty bed where Natalia was passed out just a few hours ago. Maybe she's downstairs having lunch at one of the restaurants, or doing her favorite: a massage at the spa. Then I realize I'm actually holding my phone. By the foot of the bed there's a note on a plain white piece of paper, folded in half. I unfold the note right away and learn it was part of the hotel-provided notebook I previously saw on the desk with "Waikiki Palace: Hotel and Spa" printed neatly in green cursive at the very top. The rest of the note is done in blue ink, written by a two-year-old child from what I can gather from the penmanship: "Calyssa, I had to leave. Emergency came up. It was nice meeting ya'll. Thank you for the ticket and your hospitality. XOXO, Lindsay."

CHAPTER SIX

The Cat's Out of the Bag

Lindsay's phone goes straight to voicemail. I dial her number four times before remembering she removed the battery after the conversation with Ian. *Emergency came up*, my ass. Chloe must have offended her immensely while I imbibed margaritas, enjoying the Hawaiian sun. Stinging sunburn has started prickling my face and by evening I'll be lipstick red. Opting out to leave a voicemail, I walk toward the lanai with the note in my hand, first detouring to grab a pancake from the food array we've ordered earlier.

Positioning myself in front of Chloe, I block the sunlight, half the pancake already in my mouth. Crumbs of a frosted pastry are scattered all over her white tank top; instead of jeans, she's wearing Wonder Woman pajama bottoms. Unconcerned, Chloe lifts her head, a sneer visible on the side of her muzzle together with custard.

"What did you do to Lindsay? Did the two of you have a fight?"

"Cool it. You lost me. Lindsay who?"

"Read this."

When I pass the note, Chloe takes it, and I notice how her fingers are full of frosting. She examines the note without offering an apology while I shove the pancake down my throat like a real lady. Chloe folds the paper, and I snatch it.

"Well, Chloe?"

"Well, what?"

"Did you insult Lindsay?"

"Last time I saw Linda was two hours ago."

Enraged and pumped to test my feisty Jersey side—after living there for two months—I scowl, folding my hands. Anubis jumps on Chloe's thigh from the nearby chaise. He instantly gives himself a power wash by slurping on his tail with such vanity and joy I only imagine guys at the gym do while watching themselves in the mirror deadlifting two hundred pounds. Jealous of cats for their ability to bathe themselves, I wonder whether it would look suspicious if I started licking my body with my tongue.

"It's your fault," I say loudly.

"Don't blow your stack. I saw and know nothing."

"Stop lying."

"Don't jabber me. She left so she left."

"Not just left. She packed her skinny pink suitcase and took it. Taisha said she seemed upset."

Eyes buried in the book, Chloe quaffs Lindsay's wine from the cranberry juice bottle. How she put her paws on it, that is the question.

"You've made a mistake, Chlotilda."

She jumps so suddenly off the chaise I choke on the pancake. Anubis scrams back to the suite, mewing angrily. "Indeed I've made a mistake. By coming here with you."

"Why are *you* so livid?"

"Because I'm *your* friend, Pussyfish, but you're acting like *she* is."

"We're allowed to have more than one friend, Chloe."

She narrows her eyes and snap-closes the book, waving at the second empty chaise chair. "Come on, Matilda. Let's go get a muddy splash."

"Leaving solves diddly-squat. You're disappointed because the guy from that lousy website never responded, but Lindsay is unconnected to this. Making people carry your emotional baggage is wrong."

Ignoring me, Chloe silently flees the lanai. I said "diddly-squat"? There must be something utterly wrong with me. In the mirror ahead I notice her sticking out a tongue at me, so childish and so passive-aggressive. I caught her doing that on several occasions, mostly when she's incensed.

Chloe returns. "Nobody gives praise for good deeds, but when a slight error occurs, fingers start pointing. This is unfair."

"Why else would Lindsay scat?"

"I may have personal problems, true, but unlike you I accuse no one for my mistakes."

"Meaning what, I blame others for my mistakes?"

"Yes. I'm certain Babette had nothing to do with your failures at work. Your ploy required a scapegoat to avoid humiliation. Now Laura disappears, I'm peccant. Next week you're fired and Adam's liable. You never take responsibility."

"That's horseradish."

With eyes swollen from tears, Chloe leaves the suite, slamming the door shut. My baby blues stare in her direction for thirty seconds, half expecting her to return. My stiff neck reminds me of the number of surfaces it experienced lately: on the desk at work, on the plane, on the sandy towel. I need a real shower with real water and a real nap with a real pillow.

Did I really just say "horseradish"?

The air, thick with humidity and hot from the direct sun, makes me beg for air with long inhales, followed by short exhales. The dry pancake seems to have stuck in my esophagus, failing to reach my stomach due to a lack of liquid to help it along.

With my heart racing, as it always does after a fight, I claim Chloe's chair, now angrier than ever; on a scale from one to two, it's probably two. I tolerated their squabbles within the past twelve hours, but enough is enough, and three fights are my limit when it comes to disrespect. *Shredders' Weekly Magazine*—my daily source of world news—teaches its readers to remove "always" and "never" from their vocabulary, especially in a fight. "Always" and "never" are a cheap way to easily hurt a person. Now I understand why. Chloe declared I never take responsibility and the many times she thought it she kept it to herself. We need to figure out a way to converse with each other to avoid such communication gaps.

She hates confrontation, however, and I love it.

I decide to finish Lindsay's wine to calm myself down and to help the pancake finish its journey down my trachea. I unscrew the top of the bottle, taking a long sip. The hot, dry wine tastes filthy, and my entire body convulses, awakening me in a second. Also, the pancake, without moving an inch down, seems instead to have soaked up the wine, only expanding more in the gullet. In the meantime, my stomach enunciates a squeaky noise normally serving as an indication for an imminent fart, and like a real lady, I let it happen. Seriously, how Lindsay handles such nasty wine on a day-to-day basis without falling into a coma is a miracle and a legit explanation as to why she abandoned the bottle. To have us poisoned. Against implied odds she might return since she's nothing but an impecunious freeloader. Contradictorily, why would she take her skinny pink suitcase with her?

Having finished the wine, I leave the lanai to escape the damaging sun and to relax on the couch to avoid further complications of erythema solare, a fancy expression for "sunburn" I learned from *Are You Smarter than a Fifth Grader?*

When I plop on the couch, the fluffy cushions consume my behind, burying me inside. Maybe Lindsay and her skinny pink suitcase remained in the suite, eaten by this hungry piece of furniture. For thirty seconds I'm transfixed, waiting to hear a heartbeat thumping beneath, but the only thing heard is my angry stomach that wishes to be fed.

On the coffee table, the fish catches my attention by swimming to the front of the bottle. Elizabeth and I play a staring contest for a whole minute until she blinks and, as complete losers should, sinks to the bottom of the Patrón bottle. And I sink further into the couch. Like in *Princess and the Pea*, uneasiness settles in when an item underneath makes sitting uncomfortable. It's certainly not Lindsay or I'd be burning on her fire-red hair. I wiggle my bottom—part of my body where the frontal lobe of my brain must be located —to figure out what treasures are trapped under the cushions. To my surprise, my butt can feel something larger than a pea, perhaps a can of pea soup, and I wiggle again, my hands digging in hopes of finding something both valuable and important. The treasure is a TV remote control, not so much valuable and important but I flip the channels nevertheless. In no time, the heavy, partially drunken lids cover my eyes, unable and unwilling to watch a black-and-white movie starring Marilyn Monroe.

Loud thuds awaken me. The sound is not dissimilar to a hammer banging a hollow, metallic tube. Disoriented, I open my eyes and note it's noon. I apparently fell asleep. Again. My whole body aches as though I've been powerlifting for a week; name a bone, it hurts. State of sleepiness, as would state of drunkenness, makes it hard to get up, muscles wooden from failing to stretch. I decide to blame the complimentary champagne Cave pimped out for her birthday celebration. Free stuff is not always good. The banging seems to be coming from our bathroom and as a consequence my head is splitting in half.

I rub my thumbs against the eyelids, yawn, and open my eyes. When the focus clears, there's Natalia perched on a chair in front of me. She's filing her nails, legs crossed, the color of her body a stark contrast to the graphite chair. She's wrapped in a luxurious white towel as though after a shower, with another one around her head like a Turk. A layer of paint with several fixings can make such a difference: Her eyes are blue with no apparent puffiness under them, thanks to foundation. She smells strongly of lavender. The TV is on mute. The unmistakable smell of bacon is whiffed from the kitchen, the sound of an operating microwave heard in the background.

"What's that banging?" I moan.

"It's the plumber."

"Plumber? Then how come you took a shower?"

Natalia places the nail file on the coffee table, blows on her fingers, and extends her hand to an arm-length. In such a position she eyes her nails from the distance.

"I didn't take a shower. I used seltzer water from the fridge, heated it up, and gave myself a sponge bath with it. Don't try doing that yourself, though. The shit blew up in the microwave until I figured out I wanted a cold bath anyway."

"What did you use for a sponge?"

"A sponge."

I look at her askance, wondering whether her tone represents sarcasm, bitterness, or indifference. It's impossible to read her thoughts with her poker face, apparent how years of gambling trained Natalia to say things without expressing true meaning. Sure, she cries and yells, but once at the table, she becomes so focused that she's a flawless liar. Unlike Natalia, if anyone caught me gambling they'd spot me applauding myself upon receiving a good hand. I'd lose with a royal flush in front of me. No wonder my money disappears, proved by last month's trip to Atlantic City when the three of us went. Natalia for work, Chloe and me for pleasure. That's why from this point on, I only play the slots and one-dollar lottery tickets.

The microwave beeps, announcing to, I presume, Natalia the food is ready. My stomach gives a growl at the smell of bacon, though I'm getting tired of pancakes and breakfast items. Time for a real lunch.

Russian women always seem to devise a solution—a sponge bath— followed by all sorts of plans should the proceeding one fall short. However, I've yet to confess I was unable to buy her a ticket to Vegas. Sitting up, I decide to come clean, even if I'm very dirty at the moment.

"Natalia, I tried ordering your ticket, but your credit card was declined."

"Declined? What do you mean?"

The noise from the bathroom resumes.

"I called the concierge service and they started asking me security questions, so I had to hang up. I'm sorry."

"Fine. Where's the wallet now? I'll call them myself."

"Don't you have it?"

"No, I don't have it, Calyssa, because I just asked you where it was. How could I possibly have it?"

The peculiar tone of her voice reminds me I was the mastermind behind this and I ought to comply.

"The wallet's in the suite; maybe in the bedroom. Help me get up and I'll find it."

Ignoring me, Natalia disappears in the bedroom, mumbling in Russian. Elizabeth, in the meantime, does a somersault while I wonder whether she's begging for food.

Chloe walks into the suite in the middle of me standing up. There's a pouch of tortilla chips and another piña colada in her hands, book tucked under her left arm. Not ready to apologize as of yet, in a neutral tone I ask her, "Have you seen Natalia's wallet?"

She shakes her head. "I can help search."

Like the dogs of the Scotland Yard, the three of us start sniffing the premises. I backtrack my steps to the moment I walked into the suite. First I called the number on the back of the credit card. What did I do with her wallet after that? Didn't I place it next to a sleeping Natalia? True, sober I wasn't after the piña colada and as far as I could tell, only one other, sober witness was present: the fish—sobriety level to be determined later—but for obvious reasons, however, I decide to relieve her from being asked such dumb questions. Elizabeth obviously paid no attention or she would've volunteered the information five minutes ago.

Rummaging through my handbag, right after swallowing a few grapes and a square inch of cheese, I replay my encounter with Marcus. He's single, on vacation, and interested. What if I meet him sober and he ends up being a complete ass, one of those guys who only care about their work or "bros" they hang out with? What do I even know about the guy, besides he drinks margaritas, besides he's an architect, besides he was married and has a daughter due to that union? Does he know anything about me? He never asked what my favorite movie was, which happens to be *Freaky Friday* with Jamie Lee Curtis and Lindsay Lohan. What if Marcus never calls me?

Then again, Marcus cheated on his wife; reason suggests he might cheat on me should we date. However, how many mistakes are we allowed to make in a lifetime? When is it okay to finally forgive? Am I willing to accept Marcus after knowing the truth; or, more importantly, should a man get credit for opening up? Do we open a new page when we begin a relationship or start a new job? Do relationships change our personalities? And last, do we eventually return to our normal selves and repeat making the aforementioned mistakes?

Would you just hear yourself? You're asking these stupid questions, and presumptuously, at that. Like a little girl. Suddenly I realize what Chloe must feel after the online cat-loving man disappeared when she shared her pictures. Of course she took it personally, but who wouldn't? Knowing myself, I'd probably sleep around with every bottle of alcohol: Monday night I'd fall asleep with a bottle of tequila, Tuesday night with vodka, Wednesday would be rum. Somehow, in times of grief, alcohol keeps you company and unlike Marcus alcohol doesn't cheat on you. The anxiety of dating is hardly a laughing matter, something I completely forgot being busy with fighting at work or busy chatting online with still photographs of possibly fake men. Just when you think you're good enough and just when you think there are no more problems in your life, you meet a guy, and you become crazy and obsessed, you're heartbroken, and your bank account is empty after buying all the liquor you can get your hands on. How can a man have so much power over us? Really, I long to apologize to Chloe for being insensible earlier, but I decide to postpone my apology until the wallet issue is resolved.

Not finding Natalia's wallet in my bag, I scratch my dumb, empty head as though that may help me think of an answer. And it does. Because a hateful thought finds its way in, and that thought is: Lindsay stole the wallet, walking away with the Cute Mango soap dispenser in the process, as it still remained in her skinny pink suitcase as far as my memory allows.

I wake up suddenly, all buzz, together with any hunger, gone. What a perfect crime she committed, an innocent little girl who never lies. While I was at the beach, while Natalia was asleep, while Chloe was reading her tramplet book, Lindsay stole Natalia's wallet and escaped.

My genius plan was to call the cops—a task for which I called Taisha—and two policemen arrive promptly, within fifteen minutes after the initial call. As soon as I hear a knock, I volunteer to open the door, unable to avoid Natalia's scowl. Chloe decided to be left out of this and locked herself with Anubis in the bedroom to the right.

I open the door while chewing on grapes from the breakfast assemblage. Like nesting dolls, the policemen are alike, and where one is tall, skinny, and handsome, the other one is taller, skinnier, and handsomer. The first one resembles an English cucumber with a cute blond hairdo and a uniform that would make every woman like myself drool, because men in uniform are my long lifetime passion, together with my long lifetime passion for men in general. His eyes are light green, nose as a gherkin. The second cop is slightly older and he resembles the Empire State Building: he's not just tall, but *grand*. With his looks, he probably sees as many women as the Empire State Building must on a daily basis. Their limbs are not dissimilar to tree branches, long and thin and ready to be climbed up.

Gherkin and Empire take their hats off as they enter the room, a real gentleman move to impress some ladies.

"Good afternoon," the two of them say simultaneously.

"Hi," I say. "Please come in. Would you like some water?"

"No, thank you," they say in unison.

Well, good, because I suddenly realize water we ain't got. No water in the pipes and Natalia washed her body with the remaining seltzer.

The banging in the bathroom continues, making the policemen turn their heads in the direction of the sound. What the hell is he doing in there with those pipes? One would assume plumbing should be fairly simple, being we basically just upgraded to indoor plumbing not so long ago. It can't be that complicated—yet. It's not the future, where we can email our brown dumplings over the Internet at somebody we hate and the plumber is trying to fix the Wi-Fi connection.

The four of us arrange in the living room by the couch without sitting. Like it's inappropriate. Even Elizabeth climbs to the very top of her bottle so she can eavesdrop on the conversation.

"Please, tell me what happened here," Empire says. His tone is calm and proficient. He was born to be a cop.

"Her wallet was stolen," I say, pointing at Natalia. "The thief is Lindsay Goldplenty."

"What was in the wallet, ma'am?" Empire asks Natalia.

Natalia looks at him for a second like what a dumb question he asked. "Everything," she finally says and rolls her eyes.

"Could you be more specific?"

"Five credit cards, three grand in cash, ID. Everything."

I notice how Gherkin vigorously writes everything down on a notepad while Empire seems to be the boss.

"Could you describe her?"

"Skin and bone. Ugly red wig. Skinny jeans," Natalia says, annoyed, using the same tone she would use if someone asked her to describe the sun.

"Do you have a picture of her?"

Of her naked . . . I finish up for him.

"Why do you need a picture? My description wasn't enough?"

"You misunderstood why I asked that question. It's easier to find a suspect when we know what she looks like."

"I just told you what she looks like. Plus, she isn't a suspect, she's a thief."

Natalia finds a cigarette in her bra and lights it up. When I make eye contact with her, giving her a nasty look to remind her this is a non-smoking room, she loudly sighs and leaves for the lanai.

I point toward the two graphite chairs. "Sorry about Natalia. She's extra cranky today. You can understand why. Please, sit down and I'll try to answer all of your questions."

"Thanks," they say in unison again. Word "thanks" must be perhaps their most rehearsed phrase. When two people work or live as a pair, whether a married pair or otherwise, they finish up sentences for each other. My boss, Adam, is predictable to the point where I get him a cup of coffee at least fifteen minutes before he asks for it. And then he'd argue he didn't want coffee when the cup is already before him. He'd ask for it eventually anyway.

The cops ease themselves onto the chairs while I take the couch, being consumed halfway into it. I accidentally sit on the remote control and turn on the TV. If I did that with my butt, imagine what I could do with my hands? Show that to Mr. Grunt to demonstrate my proficiency. The black-and-white movie I started earlier had been replaced by an episode of *The Andy Griffith Show*. The bathroom tumult resumes, with the plumber banging on the pipes so violently you'd think he's trying to break them instead of fixing them.

"What's that noise?" Empire asks.

I give him a stare—like "what noise are you talking about?"—by squinting and raising my brow slightly. It's a boogeyman, who do you think? Doesn't everyone have a sound of a sledgehammer constantly coming out of their bathroom?

"Don't pay any attention to it. A plumber is working on the pipes."

"Okay. Do you know where Lindsay usually spends her time?"

"No clue. She was headed for Ohio at first, or at least so she said. She could have lied, you know."

"Do you know her address in Ohio?"

I shake my head.

"What else could you add that could be helpful?"

"She drinks red wine." I want to smack my head from embarrassment. *Calyssa, get your shit together.* "She's a mess, obviously. Her mom was a bitch, but what breed she failed to indicate. To be honest, this is the extent of my knowledge."

"Any friends in common who could be of help?"

"Doubt so."

"How long have you known her?"

"About a year," I lie to avoid appearing naïve. I stare at the TV, so not to look at them directly as I lie more. "We've been friends—my—for a century. She comes from a good family, but you can always find a rotten apple in a peck. I don't know what else to tell you about her besides her permanent address is a friend's couch."

"Son, did you write everything?" Empire asks Gherkin, who nods.

The cops are related. No wonder they are identical like two drops of apple martini: papa cop (the apple) and son cop (the martini). Is this what we children do, follow our parents' footsteps? If so, what does that make me? Mom died at thirty. Is it my turn now? She accomplished nothing, and neither have I.

The banging in the bathroom turns into drilling, and the three of us turn our heads, listening patiently until it stops. When I turn my head around, I notice how Elizabeth swims in circles from one side of the bottle to the other.

"Well, this is all the information we need for now. We'll look at the footage from the security cameras for her picture. If something else comes up, give us a call."

After Empire puts his hat back on, he shakes my hand like I'm some male pal down at his cop corner. Gherkin's handshake is weak, and I make a mental sticky note to talk him into doing a round of arm wrestling in the future. When the officers leave, I change into the last night's outfit and bring the dress to the lobby to get it cleaned.

On top of the counter, I notice the poor swooshed cat. That's the main reason behind why having a tiny pet (like fish) instead of something the size of a cat is more favorable. When it poops on your dress, you can just flush it down the toilet. The cat looks miserable, as though it understands its fate, which means to either be homeless or live in a cage his entire life. I have trouble deciding whichever is worse since the cat has nine lives left. If my calculation is correct and a regular person lives a century (plus/minus ten years for dying from unnatural causes like choking on fried chicken), imagine being homeless for nine hundred years? Or being imprisoned for that long?

That's what you get when you poop on someone's dress. Lesson learned: I'll never make such a dumb mistake myself.

Back in the suite, Natalia, dressed in the last night's outfit, is speaking on the phone with her credit card company. Avoiding her gaze, I slip into Chloe's room. She looks up as I enter.

"I'm sorry about earlier," I say. "You were absolutely right. I misjudged Lindsay on so many accounts. Who would've thought? She looks nothing like a thief."

"Thanks for apologizing. I'm sorry for snapping back. While I was down-stairs I checked my email, but the guy hasn't responded back. What do I do?"

"If I knew all the answers I wouldn't feel that way about Marcus."

I quickly fill her in on the shenanigans down at the beach, adding, "See? If I remained in the suite instead of being with him, none of it would happen. Men just ruin everything."

I only partially mean that, but I make it sounds like I do 102 percent.

Chloe perks up. "Do you want to lay out on the beach or climb Diamond Head?"

"I wish. I need to take a shower before I start smelling like a bag lady. After that I need to figure out what to do with Natalia. She's mad at me. And the worst of all is I don't blame her."

"She'll be fine. You know she always comes around."

"Speaking of always and never. Is it true I never take responsibility?"

"I said that to hurt you. You know I meant none of that. I won't say 'never' again. Sometimes—sometimes—you do."

Chloe leaves for the beach soon thereafter while I wonder when the plumber will finish up. Trying to content my impatience, I count people down at the beach, make an imaginable drink, and even talk to Elizabeth.

Natalia exits the bedroom. "I'll go downstairs and see if I can bum a smoke from someone. I'm completely out."

Like a dog who peed on a good carpet, I stare at her in fear, knowing perfectly well if not for me she'd be able to buy her own cigarettes because her wallet would still remain safe.

I sit down on the couch and flip the channels on TV, one after another, commercial after commercial. You'd think television companies wouldn't charge you a fortune if all you watched could be summed up in thirty seconds and involved insurance. The door to the bathroom squeaks, and I turn around to catch our plumber finally coming out. To my surprise, the plumber is a woman, her hair splayed out in all directions like she doesn't give it a hundred strokes before bed. She reaches the breakfast cart, an empty bottle of beer in hands, toolbox in the other. She helps herself to some cheese and crackers as soon as she drops the toolbox on the carpeted floor.

"Hello," I say, standing up, then cross the room to greet her.

"Freaking finally finished there," she says slowly without looking at me. Her Southern accent must be Mississippi bound. Mississippi—one word I hate when drunk. And even though I don't drive in New York, I know I would need to learn how to spell eventually. "Stop throwing toilet paper in the toilet, because that's what causes it. Put the paper in the trash can located nearby. You got that?" She looks up at the ceiling and slowly drives a piece of bacon in her mouth, as a sword-swallower would do. "Spent all day going up and down every room, trying to find a problem, and guess where I found it? In this suite."

"May I use the bathroom now?" I say.

Chewing the bacon, the plumber stares at me without moving anywhere, blocking the food cart as though she's glued to the floor, yet she manages to swing back and forth on her feet to prove she isn't.

"Wait a minute there, I'm not finished with my little story yet. I asked you a question, Yankee. Do you know the main reason behind why the pipes were clogged?" She brings her hand up and I have to squint to see what she's showing me. "A black strand of hair, just like yours. Found it in the drain, clogging it. You reckon where I'm going with it?"

I nod, prepared to be hit by a wrench from the sound of her voice. To look extra honest, I make the same puppy-eye face I used on Natalia, in case the plumber demands to run a DNA test to compare the strand of hair in her hands to mine. From her rough exterior, I gain she won't ask for a sample politely but would rather rip a few hairs from my head herself. Her penciled brows are shaped in two triangles, servicing as two roofs to her blue eyes.

"I didn't have time to take a shower yet. I just arrived here this morning and the water was already off. Thank you so much for your help though."

"You darn tootin.' You'd be tattered and feathered if you saw how much smut I clean up every day after people like you. Took me an hour and a half to fix your damn plumbing. I've been doing contract work here for twenty-five years, but nobody appreciates a good worker. Management here consists of a bunch of cheap assholes who deserve to drown in their own crap. And sho 'nuff nobody would give me a tip, even after I've been slaving in that garbage for that long."

"The best tip I could give you is you can disguise red wine in a cranberry juice bottle if you want to be discreet." *Sho 'nuff* rat Lindsay comes to mind with her ideas. The plumber's eyes are impressively big for such a minuscule face, like she has a pipe stuck up her butt and her eyes have popped out from such a surprise.

"Okay, thanks again." I smile like I mean it.

She reaches the fridge and opens it. "Nothing to drink? You gotta be kidding me. Give me a break."

I gape at her in disbelief, part-scared, part-offended. I could use my feisty Jersey side. I would smack her good and I look at Elizabeth for reassurance. Elizabeth says yes. Through her ripped jeans, however, I notice her legs big and strong, as a warning if she kicks me I'm dead meat.

"I forgot to purchase alcohol, but come back on Monday and I'm sure we'll have plenty by then." There are only so many polite ways of asking someone to leave, and I think I've used them all. I'd call Empire, but she'll possibly toss an ax at me as soon as I start dialing his number. The plumber looks at me with a grin, the same look dog-kickers possess. And then my best idea hits me. "But we have something in the freezer." I sing the word *freezer*, stressing out word *free*.

When she turns around to open the freezer, I know this is my only time to escape. I drop on all fours and crawl toward the couch next to the wall. To tell you the truth, crawling on carpeted floor is hardly the best way of getting around, and even though it's quiet, my knees heat up from friction. Passing the coffee table I keep crawling, now hidden from view by the chair. Hiding is never the best solution, but at the moment it is the only solution. I figured since the plumber lost her soberness to the beer like mother Mary to virginity, she may assume I was a mirage if I suddenly disappear. Dehydration causes mirages, I read. And drinking causes dehydration (borrowed from experience). She will have no other option but to leave the suite empty-handed. When I successfully cross the room, I hide behind the couch in a little alcove. Dusty; the maid hasn't vacuumed this area, that lazy bitch.

"Hey, where'd you go?" I hear her say.

The outside sounds are muffled. The beige carpet is lighter in color down here, as if a human shoe never touched it. The carpet bristles are soft to the touch, but in my honest opinion I still favor wood flooring. If maintained properly, as in my apartment for example, wood gives space a flare of class while the carpet can be installed anywhere. There is a penny in front of me as a pleasant surprise for my troubles, Lincoln unrecognizable from prolonged usage. Narrowing my eyes, I spot a D on the coin for Delaware mint, year 1943, reason why Lincoln at this point looks more like Barak Obama. I wish whoever dropped the penny had enough decency to drop a Benjamin or something food related. Not to be completely cheap about it (after all it's been a hard day), I snatch the penny anyway before anyone else can. Due to the curve of the couch I notice how roomy it is back here, and drop all the way on the floor, crawling underneath the couch to completely vanish out of sight. From under here, I can see the living room, the two graphite chairs in front of me, the TV set, and Elizabeth in her fancy bottle.

Black boots appear a foot before my nose. Damaged from being used inappropriately, perhaps as a hatchet, the boots would make a shoe repairman want to cry. The laces are untied, material is falling off, and I can see her socks through the holes. The shoes move left and right before they disappear from sight. The plumber checks out the lanai, the bedrooms, and returns to the living room area. Her jeans are stained with rust, a given if you happen to work with pipes. Her boots approach the coffee table and she picks up the bottle of Patrón. From underneath I see her pour some water mistaken for tequila into a shot glass, after which she sits down on the couch. What I failed to realize was how deep the couch sinks, because the plumber's butt caused it to deepen enough to press me to the floor. As a paying customer of the hotel I recognize how the situation seems somewhat abnormal. If she caught me underneath the couch, however, then *I'd* be somewhat abnormal, so I decide to bear with such embarrassment. With my nose against the carpet, I breathe in the dust, which tickles my throat. *Don't sneeze. Please, don't sneeze.*

The plumber cusses, realizing the shot of tequila was in fact water and fish pee. She places the shot glass on the coffee table and stands up while I take a mouthful of air.

Her boots leave the living room area, headed for the exit door. After the door slams, I claw out from under the couch and race toward the bathroom. I sneeze so hard that I have to clean up my brain from the walls.

I lock the door, turning on the water in the sink to block all the outside noises and to also make sure the lady fixed the plumbing. I no longer care if she comes back and learns I'm here . . . plus, what can she do, break the door? The sink, as though angry, rumbles a few times before a stream of rusty water finally comes out. Little by little, the rust clears out to undrinkable quality, but clear enough quality for a shower. I sit on the toilet lid for about a minute, now fully convinced the plumber is gone. Now I can finally take a shower at one o'clock in the afternoon.

I STRIP ALL THE WAY DOWN, EXPLORING MY FAT BODY IN THE mirror, promising myself to get on a diet when back in New York. The bathroom is laid out in white tile, granite countertop surrounding the sink where towels are folded into cylinders and placed to the right, a plugged-in hairdryer to the left.

I slide the white shower curtain, which opens up a bleached ivory claw-foot bathtub ahead with a gigantic rain showerhead above. The size of the bathtub is better described as Jacuzzi, intended for giants and such. I crank the hot water all the way up, waiting for about thirty seconds until it warms up completely. I get in, instantly forgetting any problems I had. Hot water will clean away my sins and clean my body.

There is a hotel-provided body wash on the rim of the bathtub together with a small white towel for a washcloth. I pick up the body wash and learn it smells strongly of lavender, the same bottle Natalia must have used during her sponge bath, a cooling hint of menthol as an after smell. Standing straight under the stream of water I let the water run while I soak up the washcloth. Water beats against the bathtub and immediately drains into the wide opening underneath me, with little holes here and there like a spider's web. I lather myself thoroughly, washing up the sand bits stuck to my body after the trip to the beach, scrubbing away the dirt from the plane and grime from the bar. I become less filthy with each drop of water. The washcloth becomes slimy with soap while I vigorously rub it against itself to produce more lather and give myself a second round of scrubbing. After rinsing, I feel fresh and slightly chilled, courtesy of menthol. Next, I shampoo my hair with a lavender-scented shampoo I find next to the body wash. Why all the beauty products are lavender? Now that I strongly smell of lavender, I'll attract all the Hawaiian bees and will be totally vulnerable to being busted in the butt with a sting.

I never thought a simple shower could bring such joy. What we take for granted always seems more pleasant after we fight for it. Though I doubt having to fight a tiger chained to the bathroom (or a drunken plumber) would make your morning routine any better, but you would definitely appreciate the shower more, after you dispose of the tiger's body. Maybe skipping the bar one week would make me want to propose to Mario after not seeing him for so long.

My feet feel smooth after the spa session on the beach, calluses completely removed by the Waikiki sand. My arms appear to be getting red, however, thanks to a low SPF lotion Marcus pimped me for sunscreen. Not only I'll be red, I'll be red in distinct spots where my dress failed to cover my skin, those to be arms, neck, some parts of my ankle. I just discovered another good reason to be a man: you can just sit there shirtless on the beach like Marcus, getting a nice and toasty tan all over your body without worrying about unevenness.

As I turn off the water, I slide the shower curtain to the left, and step out onto the shower rug, the color and the feel of crumbled goat cheese. I grab a clean towel hanging nearby, appreciating its soft, luscious fibers. While drying myself with the towel, a thought comes to my mind: How in the world will Natalia fly back to Vegas without her driver's license? The TSA almost made her stay in New York with her documents on her, and they will definitely make her stay in Hawaii without any.

"Natalia," I say, storming off the bathroom. "Natalia!"

"What?"

Natalia is on all fours on the floor in the kitchenette, back facing me, head in the fridge. "Where's the champagne," she says, insulted. "What kind of a hotel is this?"

"The plumber must have drunk all of it, because we ordered some with the food, and I remember I had some in the morning. This is not why I was calling you. Natalia, listen to me. How are we going to get home with your credit cards *and* your ID being gone?"

She turns around, making a face. "What's wrong with you, Caly? I lose my wallet all the time. I always have a plan B."

"Right, if we were in Vegas that would be true, but we're in Honolulu. That's Hawaii, a state from where we must take a plane. But nobody will let you on that plane without your photo documents. It's not like you just hop on a bus from Atlantic City. So what's your genius plan B?"

She unsticks her head from the fridge, pursing her lips. "You're asking me? *You* brought me here."

"Don't make it sounds like it's my fault. I thought it'd be a good idea to spice things up a little bit for our own good. Besides, you always want to do something fun. You may not remember, but you almost begged me to do something crazy when we were in Atlantic City the other week. This is what you asked for."

"That was very dumb, Caly. You better come up with something fast because I'm losing time."

She walks toward the lanai, lighting up a cigarette on the way. I follow her in quick, short steps, the towel in which I'm wrapped preventing me from walking faster. Outside, Chloe's reading *Latent Tramplet* with Anubis taking a snooze on her lap. Her face, just like mine, appears pink from the walk on the beach. The sun with its ruthless rays is as harmful as unprotected sex. Mom used to bathe me in sunscreen should we be outdoors, which we were most of the time, and now she's looking down at me from heaven wondering why I want to have old, saggy skin. The air is heated to about eighty-five degrees, the beach as an anthill with little black dots going in and out of water. We could be enjoying our time on the beach too, but instead Natalia and I are about to start another argument. Since I failed to put lotion on my skin, my face tightens and I understand what plastic surgery must feel like.

"Natalia," I say, "we will find a way to get back. Maybe we can hire a private helicopter or something. You have enough money for a helicopter, don't you?"

She looks at me as though I have a big hole in my brain. She deeply inhales the smoke from a cigarette, its end color of ocher. "What am I, made of money? And even if I were, the wallet's gone, thanks to you and your friend."

"There must be a way to get to New York without having to show your ID."

"We can go back by boat," Chloe says. "It's relatively inexpensive." Natalia and I look at her simultaneously. "That's how Ouchita got to Los Angeles without her passport."

"That's a great idea," I almost sing. "Why didn't I think of that myself? Of course, a boat. The two of you can take a boat and then you can take a train to Las Vegas and, Chloe, you can take a train or a bus from there to New York."

"Why do you say the two of us?" Natalia says.

"Well, I have a very important meeting on Monday. I *have* to take a plane to New York. If I'm out traveling the entire country I'll be fired."

"Really. That's great. I guess you got it all figured out. Chloe and I are going to travel three thousand miles like two rotten pussels, through the ocean, through the desert, and you're going to take a plane. How smart of you to first bring us here, then dump us here. I guess you consider we have no life of our own. That and the fact I could be out traveling for who-the-hell-knows how long while you take a plane. I have to be in Las Vegas tomorrow at two in the afternoon, and if I miss it, I'll never speak to you again."

"What's so important in Vegas anyway?"

She exhales the smoke slowly, unwilling to let it go. "My application has been accepted to this Ladies' Elite Gambling Society in Vegas. I've been waiting for a year for that invitation. There is a tea party with other ladies, followed by an initiation process and some gambling. If I don't make the meeting on time—they said in the email—they'll never consider me ever again."

"What society? What does this society do?"

"It's only for ladies, if you can't tell from its name. They are the cream of society. The ladies who luncheon. They play cards together, they gamble together, they're VIP at any club in Vegas and in many others throughout the U.S. The dues are high, but being there is worth the money. It's not easy to even be accepted for the interview, and I had to work hard to pull some strings. I'm going to have to lie that I have help, but by the time I'm accepted I'll hire someone again."

"Natalia, there are so many elite clubs in the country. It can't possibly be more important than me keeping my job. If I travel with you on a boat and then the train it may take a week or more, but I have to defend myself on Monday, which means I must fly. You understand, don't you?"

The sneer on her face looks almost too dangerous. She extinguishes the cigarette by placing it in Chloe's piña colada. "You're just like Lupita for leaving me like that. Or *wanting* to leave me like that. Plus, I'll be a good friend and help you avoid the same mistake she did."

Natalia walks back into the suite and I, still wrapped in a towel, walk right after her in tiny steps, like a lap dog. After Natalia lifts up the Gooseberry, she turns it upside down onto the coffee table while item after item falls down with slight, bumpy sounds. Elizabeth gets scared and swims a few circles at an accelerated rate. The content of the bag ends up on the coffee table, haphazardly scattered around. Natalia gets a hold of my wallet, flips it open, pulls something out of it, and throws the wallet back into the pile of junk I happen to carry with me in my bag. I make it to the table in three steps to learn Natalia has a hold of my ID card.

"Natalia? What are you doing?"

I catch her in the bathroom as she throws my ID card into the toilet. The ID promptly plops to the bottom as though chained by a heavy anchor. Before I can stop her, Natalia flushes the toilet, which instantly sucks my mugshot down the toilet with a slurping sound like the toilet was thirsty. What a lousy time to have water in the suite. This is as close to a real royal flush as I can get, apparently. The royal flush of the toilet. The paper-like New York state ID will travel through the plumbing without any problems, because it will probably dissolve before it reaches the ground floor, but if it gets stuck in one of the pipes and the lady-plumber sees it, she'll throw me out of the window or put me under the couch and sit on me, whichever one will come to her mind first. I blink twice before I can say anything, yet words are stuck in my throat.

"Now I guess you *have* to take the boat, princess," Natalia says, putting the toilet lid down, performing a curtsy.

Then, she places her hand in her bra to produce a New York State driver's license. She places the license before my eyes—a license that contains her photo on it where she smiles, looks happy, and still manages to look crooked like the rest of the folk on government-issued photo documents. I can even smell the nicotine breath coming from that sneaky, rotten smile.

"I told you," she adds, placing the license back inside of her bra, "I lose my wallet all the time. Double up on the IDs. Safety first."

CHAPTER EIGHT

Law of Destruction and Creation

AFTER MY ID CARD HAD GONE FISHING, I FIND THE ROOM telephone and dial Taisha at the front desk to price boats. I need to learn what our options are, being that amongst the three of us I'm left out when it comes to taking a plane. As much as I'm mad at Natalia for drowning my ID, I understand where she's coming from. I caused her more trouble than I meant to, and now I'm intended to fix all the leaky plumbing myself.

Taisha's unmistakable voice, with its sharp deepness, has a bass of E sharp in the first octave on the piano, something I learned the hard way. Taisha must have put something in her mouth right before picking up, because when she says a distorted hello, it sounds like her mouth is full of gooey peanut butter.

"Taisha, we have another little problem on our hands. Here's the thing: Since Lindsay stole Natalia's wallet, Natalia has no way of getting back to New York by plane. Are there boats we can take to Los Angeles? And how much would those be?" Of course I decide to leave out the part where the boat is actually for me to save face, because Natalia has got her driver's license on her.

"One second."

Taisha puts me on hold, leaving me with something Beethoveny playing in my ear. How soon are they going to come up with telephone holds that play nice popular music?

While I wait, I browse the room to spot creases on the bed where Natalia slept. A fake-looking ficus, a foot taller than me, is sitting in the corner with teeny green leaves spread in all directions, its trunk a collection of intertwined stems. A TV mounted to the wall is perhaps fifty inches diagonally, an unusual size if you ask me. The room looks fine otherwise, reason why I take five good shots with my phone as a reference to use for my own decorating purposes, noting how the charge on my phone has diminished to 30 percent. Why did I forget the phone charger? What is wrong with me?

When Ludwig's lively tune stops, the song *Transylvanian Lullaby* from *Young Frankenstein* replaces it. My cousin Christina used to love it as a child, listening to it every Halloween while I hated it. Its monotonous melody is soporific. I wonder why Natalia never discussed the Ladies' Elite Gambling Society. She mentioned its members are ladies who luncheon, which sounds boring to begin with. Also, anything that abbreviates into LEGS just can't be good. Maybe she's trying to prove to herself she's now American, or maybe she wants to be seen in the circle with the rich, though I never remember her complaining about our bar in East Harlem. The night we met two months ago (at the end of August), Natalia's date had dumped her for being transgender, after which she drunkenly stumbled into my bar. She bought me drinks and complained about men. The date had told Natalia she wasn't girly enough, in fact a bit "too butch" for his taste. So she hankered after a membership in a society consisting of only women to feel girly.

Taisha returns two minutes later, cutting the tune in the middle of a vibrato, just as I start enjoying this stuff. "Okay, this is what I found." I hear her tapping on the keyboard as though she's chatting with sexy army men online. "Here's some information from their website. A boat leaves at 7:30 P.M. every day. It's a big cruise ship that travels around the Hawaiian Islands before it goes to Los Angeles. It stops here to pick up loose passengers. The price is $125 per person, unless you are a student, a refugee, or in the military, which gives you $5 off."

Darn, I wish I were in school to get the discount. Or were married to some sexy army men. All of them. "Thank you," I say and hang up.

If I use my credit card, and if I cash my check from work, we'll have enough money for the trip. For Natalia, I'll purchase a ticket to Vegas, from where she could fly back home. Chloe can afford a plane ticket of her own, even though I'll offer to pay for it as means to apologize. More credit card debt. I decide to spare them details about having enough money; I must downplay it immensely. I must persuade them to attend the party under a false pretense as to "borrow" money from Adam. Then I'll clue them in on my blackmailing plan. Besides, I ain't attending some sketchy party alone. Monday meeting isn't happening, so exaction is my safety net. I'll spy on Adam at the masquerade party, get him sauced (something absolutely easy to accomplish), and snap several provocative photos. What kind of provocative photos will depend on the situation.

Chloe's reading her book out on the lanai while Natalia's smoking a cigarette next to her, a fixed gaze on her face in the direction of Diamond Head. How do I coax Natalia to attend the Ke Iki Beach party if she's a Xerox copy of a serial killer who'd rather slice me for a sandwich? Maybe being lavender-scented, like in good ol' days of wizarding, protects me from being smacked.

"Girls, I have an idea," I say. "We need money for two plane fares and one boat fare. Gee, what a coincidence. My boss is vacationing in Honolulu. He told me on the phone he'd lend me the money if we attend this masquerade party tonight. And, Natalia, I'm sorry about Lindsay. Let's hope the cops catch her."

Chloe's look of content must mean she's satisfied with winning the battle against Lindsay, and listening to my problems sure feels good. I fancy her mouthing, *Told you so.* "Sure," she adds aloud.

"I apologize for flushing your ID card," Natalia says toward the ocean. "Even though you upset me, I understand I jumped the Russian gun."

"No need to cry over a spilled drink. I appreciate your apology and I'm not mad at you. Let's get the money situation straightened out first. We'll attend the party, relax, and have fun, and I'll borrow money from Adam. Then tonight, right after the party, you, Natalia, can American-Airline it to Vegas and land in time for your interview while you, Chloe, can decide later what transportation you prefer, the plane or the boat."

"Supreme," Natalia says.

"Since it's a masquerade party, we need three masks from a party store."

"Outstanding. While out shopping, pick up champagne and cigarettes because I hate bumming fags."

"I'll be shopping on my own?"

"Yes," they say simultaneously.

I leave the lanai. First, I put myself together in front of the bathroom mirror like I'm some Lego toy: I apply makeup, eyeliner, and fix my mop. I change into a gray tee I brought with me. Then, ashamed, like a convict, with my head down, I exit the suite, unwilling to make eye contact with anybody.

Chubbly Wobbly bumps into me near the elevator without even noticing me. In his mouth sits an unlit cigarette. He wears a goatee that makes him resemble a goat. I wonder whether he'll bleat and milk his nipples or just produce some grass from his pocket and chew on it. With his mouth, he assembles together an incomprehensible sentence, spoken as clearly as would be spoken by a goat. It's a must for him to carry a TV with closed captioning on the screen. Listening to him nets me nothing.

"How nice," I say, realizing by mistake I might have agreed to be penetrated. I chew on each word, propelling it in a manner one would surmise he's deaf. "Do you by any chance have more cigarettes? My friend is out and I wonder if you could share. We have a lanai with a breathtaking view of the beach and a plethora of sunlight. Room 1112."

Sometimes I strongly believe my purpose in life was to become a real estate agent. As opposed to, I presume, a fake estate agent. Though Wobbly seems unmoved by my advertising.

"Should that help any, Natalia is pretty, single, and willing."

Wobbly smells his armpit, contemplating to go or not to go, like he was some Shakespeare. After he mumbles something under his nose, he wobbles toward our suite, knocking on the door with three distinct bumps. The elevator collects me and I'm happy to depart his company. Chubbly Wobbly smells musty, courtesy of cigarettes, a kind of future awaiting Natalia if she continues the nasty habit.

Down at the lobby, I catch Taisha heading out the door. Equipped for a date, she's dressed and perfumed, smelling like a bouquet of roses. Her outfit is no longer the shapeless muumuu but a tight blue flower sarong, her afro changed to a short hairstyle in which the part of her head is almost shaved while the other half is long. Maybe she's like Lindsay and wears her hair depending on occasion.

"Where are you off to?" I say behind her back.

When Taisha turns around, she automatically smiles when she recognizes me, revealing her bleached white teeth—ding—like in commercials. Without stopping, she continues forward. I try catching up with her, which is easier said than done. We exit outside where the same hay bra creatures greet new guests with drinks and flower necklaces. I'd snatch a piña colada but I've got no time.

"Taisha?"

"Yes?" she says, clearly annoyed. She narrows her eyes in an attempt to remember me.

"I'm Calyssa. Pantaleo? We checked in this morning."

"What's up?"

"Where are you rushing to?"

"Downtown."

"One quick question: Where can I purchase a masquerade mask?"

Taisha stops near a pink Mazda, parked less than ten feet away from the entrance under the porte-cochère. Her face shows a few working muscles responsible for thinking. Her skin glows. Her face, as though ironed, contains no wrinkles. I'm jealous of her genes because she'll remain young even at eighty-five (or maybe she's eighty-five already).

"Where can I purchase a masquerade mask?" I repeat my question.

"From the Internet," she says.

"No, I mean for tonight."

"There's a store downtown on Kapiolani and Ward. They have all sorts of shit."

"How can I get to that store?"

"A bus across the street will take you straight there."

"You said you were going downtown."

"No, I didn't."

"Yes, you did. Could you give me a ride? I hate buses."

"It's really out of my way."

"It must be close, if both places are downtown."

She growls. "It's quite far, actually."

"Well, just drop me off wherever you need to be, and I'll find my way from there."

She hesitates. "Get in the car." She manages to speak her sentences with a speed of a tongue twister.

Inside, her car is way too pink for my taste: pink leather seats, pink mats, a Hello Kitty ornament hanging from the mirror. The steering wheel is bedazzled. Taisha removes a diaper from under my seat before I ensconce myself down. She throws it on the back seat, where enough stuff is piled up for a garage sale extravaganza.

"Sorry for the mess," she says.

"That's all right," I lie, though it's definitely not all right. As a true secretary, I get insulted by her mad organizational skills.

Taisha puts the keys into the ignition and throws the gears into reverse. Suddenly, we pull back with the sound of screeching wheels. My neck cracks a bit when she switches gears and we start moving forward. She presses the accelerator in a peculiar way as though trying to swat la cucaracha. If she isn't practicing for Formula One, I don't know what she's doing. Realizing I forgot to buckle up, I retrieve the seatbelt and fasten it tight before we wreck into an upcoming car or a tree or other objects that cars tend to wreck into, including a train.

At the next street light, Taisha flips the light indicator, ready to turn. She carefully measures the distance between us and a white Mercedes coming from the right side, after which she presses the accelerator, making the car roar. We jump in front of the Mercedes. I cover my eyes to avoid seeing us crash. However, when I open my eyes next, the Mazda is now on the inter-state, passing an RV, which, when compared to us, doesn't seem to be moving. Taisha's car rambles in an abnormal way, way too abnormal if you ask me, because it sounds like we're missing wheels. Taisha maneuvers around vehicles, pushing a steady sixty-five miles per hour, as though we're chased by an angry goose. She's worse than Muhammad, I think, but she's a perfect candidate for a taxi driver.

"No speed limit in Honolulu or what?" I ask. "Why are we going so fast?"

"I only got ten minutes," she points out, justifying her careless driving.

I watch the road, eyeing a car in front of us with a child showing me her tongue through the back window, just like Chloe did earlier this morning.

"Ten minutes for what?"

"My favorite writer is doing a book signing and I want to have a book signed for Linda, Misses Lewis' daughter I babysit."

"Babysit when? On weekends?"

"No, as my full-time job."

"You have two full-time jobs?"

Taisha switches lanes to pass the car with the child and then, making the poor pink Mazda moan in protest, she brings us to a whopping eighty. If my window was open and my tongue happened to be sticking out, the wind would blow my tongue to the side of my face, like a dog's. I grab the door handle for extra safety, ever an optimist I am.

She sighs. "Taisha was right: You're so needy."

"What do you mean?"

"I'm Taisha's sister, Oaisha. Thanks, nice meeting you too. I like your hair as well, thanks for the compliment."

What a bitch.

Observing her, I wonder whether she might be lying. She's Taisha's exact copy, which only means they're twins; or that Taisha has a split personality.

"You are her sister? Why did you keep it a secret the whole time?"

"The owner of the hotel knows nothing about me substituting for Taisha when needed. And he won't know it now either. Got it?"

"Sure. But why? What's that to him?"

"Would you quit questioning? Somebody, please cut my throat. Taisha told me about you and now I know what she meant. We don't normally have drama at the hotel so it was a refresher."

Offended, I keep studying her face. Where Taisha had a sunny disposition, Oaisha's comes from a week of rain with no break in the clouds. Bossy women, for instance Natalia, seem to intimidate me easily because I suddenly feel little compared to them. My mom was the opposite, but Aunt Sarah is exactly like that.

"Drama was a last-minute gig, right after happiness called to cancel her reservation," I say sarcastically. Who does she think she is?

"Nobody comes to Honolulu—after spending twenty hours on the plane —just to lie on the beach for one day."

"Eleven hours."

"I know there's more to that missing wallet than meets the eye. You're trouble. I sniffed it the moment I saw you."

"What do you mean?"

"What do you think I mean? I was substituting for Taisha when Natalia came downstairs and told me the whole story."

"Which was what?"

"'Which was what?'" she mocks me. "Playing hard to get, fish? How is that working out for you in the real world? Natalia told me she's a professional gambler and needs to be in Vegas for a very important interview with an elite society, but she blew it because you brought her here instead."

"She did not say that."

"Yes, she did. It's none of my business, of course, but you really hurt her feelings. Wouldn't surprise me if she never speaks to you again. I definitely wouldn't. You must beg, apologize, and crawl on your knees to just be considered for forgiveness."

"It's impossible to hurt her feelings. She's as strong as a Russian tank."

"People don't respond to words; they respond to actions. You'll understand you lost a friend *only* when she stops responding to your texts. Of course, you overlooked the fact you hurt her feelings. Who wants to admit to being hurt? She hates playing the victim, and where you believe she's as strong as a tank, she's actually a very delicate person. You'd also enjoy her company *if* you listened to what she says. You're like a child: shady, lying, and conniving. Your ego seems larger than Mother Earth's. I said nothing new here, so close your mouth."

The Mazda shifts half a lane to the right in such a manner it'd make a kamikaze feel right at home. I close my mouth as told, and swallow a load of accumulated saliva, lubricating my dry throat. Today nobody seems to give me any credit so I decide to turn around and look out the window, the feeling of guilt making my ass swampy from all the sweating.

Tall buildings of downtown Honolulu slowly rise ahead, gleaming in the day's sunshine. To my right, hills take over the landscape, just occasionally hidden from view by trees and one-story houses with gray Sombrero roofs. The traffic on the interstate is light, even though Oaisha is hardly shy when it comes to speeding and maneuvering around cars without hesitation. I kind of wish Oaisha did some trick, like throw us off a bridge. Not that I really want to experience that, but I thought it could help me with constipation.

Oaisha takes the next off-ramp for Kapiolani Boulevard, and after three turns, without bumping into a train or a fence, she enters a full parking lot. Without slowing down the car to a mandatory five miles per hour, she parks in an empty slot with a luscious Monkeypod tree ahead, its branches lengthy and covered generously in thick greenery. The building ahead is a two-story stucco, modern and in good condition, though its dirty windows are hard to miss.

Oaisha brings the car to a halt, turns off the engine, and unbuckles herself. Her belt is sucked up fast with a slurping sound while the motor, growling less and less, finally comes to, what seems, a complete stop. The car hollers and shuts up for good. When I remove my seatbelt, one look to my right indicates how parking is not Oaisha's sip of vodka at all, because she parked too close to a Chevy, preventing my egress. How she has never scratched her car makes me scratch my head in wonder.

Oaisha's rush is contagious. After she exits, pulling her belly from underneath the bedazzled wheel, I follow, planning to use her door as my emergency exit. Hello Kitty dances in front of me as a goodbye. Oaisha mentioned she only had ten minutes, and according to my watch she accomplished it with three minutes to spare.

"Hurry up, I don't have all day," she impatiently says.

I find myself moving with urgency, something I'm not used to, not even when I spent years learning how to type a hundred and twenty-five words per minute, a task I handle okay even though it ends up being a gibberish abracadabra. It only helps when Adam nods in my direction and I pretend to work. I finally cross the car from my seat to Oaisha's, carefully avoiding a scary-looking stick shift, and given the chance, I try out her pink leather chair, which is still warm and quite stretchy, an inevitable outcome caused by her weight. When I shut the door upon exiting, Oaisha locks the vehicle by pressing a button on her keychain.

"The shop I was referring to is about eight blocks north," she says, pointing her finger. "Take the bus back to the hotel from there. Hello."

She breaks into a trot, speeding up to fifteen miles per hour (and that's in high heels). What a trooper, I think, imagining myself on a track in running gear, giving up after the first lap. Drinking is my cardio, not running. Oaisha disappears inside of the building while I'm thinking, *What kind of a moron says "Hello" for "Goodbye"?* When I turn around exactly a hundred and eighty degrees, ready to explore my sad fate—eight blocks of walking—I notice a sticker on the Mazda's windshield, written in bold pink lettering: BIGGEST BITCH.

No kidding.

Watching the entrance, I wonder what biggest bitches read these days. Maybe the book could teach me how to outbitch Babette. What if the writer happens to be some sort of a warlock who helps needy people by doing magic tricks, hypnosis, and illusions? Since it's only three in the afternoon, I have plenty of time to go watch him perform, and as I turn back around I march toward the building ahead, mentally washing its windows with Windex and paper towels.

INSIDE, THE BUILDING IS DONE IN WALNUT COLORS: FRAMEWORK, stairwell handles, and all visible doors. I say "visible" as though invisible doors are walnut too. They are green, of course. After I enter I find myself in a vestibule, where the receptionist is absent, missing, or nonexistent. Everyone's gone to watch the warlock perform.

A door ahead opens up to a long corridor. There's a poster with a book called *But I Wanted to Be a Clown!* written by Grace Bishop. The reading and signing are scheduled for today at 3:00 P.M. On the cover of the book, there's a crying male clown with an exaggeratedly large red Afro, dressed in a white doctor's smock, stethoscope in hands. A stretcher, a hospital, and several nurses are visible on the background. To match his red hair, his red shoes have comically large round toes with yellow polka dot sprinkled here and there. The clown wears multicolored tights, hidden halfway by the smock at the knees. This must be my lucky day because I love clowns! There will probably be a show of some sort and, excited, I decide to move along.

The walls of the corridor are painted yellow, on either side decorated with black-and-white and colored photos of people, along with blown-up extracurricular activity photos, including (but not limited to) people who play baseball, swimmers, dancers, and runners. I lost two pounds from just looking at all of the activities photos. This building is a high school judging by the way the photos are displayed. In my high school, there were also pictures of eaters and I was a substantial part of that. Actually, in reality, my favorite class was no class at all; Mom supported me, even though Aunt Sara and the Principal weren't thrilled. I scrutinize the phony smiling faces people were forced to produce for the sake of a photograph. When these people perish, we'll remember them as happy, even though at the time they might have been sick, broke, or worst of all, sober. Three main reasons why I hate photos of me are: the fact that they're "lingering" in your library for years to come, they're fattening, and they make me look bloated. Might as well just drink for the same effect with no "lingering" consequences.

The mysterious school is silent with no visible souls in sight. I say "visible" again as though somehow I could see invisible ghosts. Everyone knows I wouldn't be able to do so without an infrared light. Duh. The quietness gives the school a flare of a church. I tippy-toe to avoid disturbing the dead, but my rumbling tummy could never hide a secret. I place my hand on my stomach, tap it gently to assure it'll soon be fed as though it were a baby (I say it as though it's possible to be pregnant with something else). Oaisha walked down this corridor is what I gather from the unmistakable aroma of roses, yet it's hard to tell which way she went. Cinnamon rolls were baked here is what I gather from the lingering scent in the air. So far I haven't spotted a single reminder of my favorite holiday, Halloween. Like people in Hawaii forgot.

Ugly artwork is hung on the walls as well, along with crookedly drawn pictures of houses, people, and/or nature. The sun on such pictures is portrayed as a yellow round at the top left side with five to six sticks coming out of it. Or if a nighttime picture is presented, a half-eaten moon, like a bitten cookie, sits at the top right side, with stars sprinkled here and there all over without giving a strict definition between the earth and the sky. Laughter haunts this building.

Carpeted floor is dark beige with short, stiff hairs, vacuumed to a fare-thee-well. I pass a gymnasium, a staircase, an open door to a broom closet with various cleaning products, buckets, and mops. Where did all of the people go? Olly olly oxen free! Anyone? I keep walking and pass an empty room with several computers seen through the glass door.

Straight ahead, I notice a half-person—a stinky child—who opens a door at the end of the hallway, disappearing inside as though eaten by a black hole.

Following the progeny, I reach a set of double doors, reading the tag in small golden letters: Auditorium.

I open the doors a crack. A small stage is positioned ahead with seats going from it upward. Slightly dimmed and chilly, the auditorium consists of several rows to fit about a hundred people, most seats already occupied.

After I spot Oaisha eight rows down blabbing with a lady, I open the door wider, stepping inside as quietly as humanly possible. There's an empty seat in the top row, right by the entrance, ready to be occupied by my butt. What a lucky duck I am to get a seat right away. I sit down excited because magic and witches always thrilled me and as a child I stayed up late watching *Hocus Pocus* during the entire length of October.

Will the real warlock, please stand up.

A boy with unraveled hair next to me—who couldn't be more than eight years of age, icing spread around his mouth in a way that tells me of his sloppy eating habits—flips through a picture book, its cover the same as the poster I just saw in the hallway with the clown in a doctor's outfit. A parent next to him is talking about how she's happy their house is finally paid off. Looking around the room, other kids have similar books in their dirty hands, a copy on Oaisha's lap as well.

Like birds in the morning, adults and stinky kids chatter here and there, waiting for the warlock/clown in a white doctor's coat to appear. The auditorium resembles an amphitheater and it reminds me of my high school auditorium wherein we used to get lectures from professors about botany. Like *that* helped me get around in life. As though knowing about the X and Y chromosomes made me smarter. I bet thirty pesos if I check under the seats I'll find chewed gum fixed to the chairs underneath. Bacteria frighten me. It will be mandatory to power wash my outfit after this, next to all these unsanitary children, half of whom are probably sick with chicken pox or the flu, whichever one got to them first. Glad I'm wearing my gray tee, which I can throw out as soon as I'm back at the hotel. Kids sitting around make me wish I had hand sanitizer, but maybe this is my fate to die from an unnatural cause, like Impetigo or have my butt itch from a diaper rash.

Staring at the stage, I wonder if the show begins with a clown or a guy cutting a woman in half, who should be Babette, and the guy who's cutting her in half should be me. The same poster with the clown stands on the stage, next to a microphone and a stool.

The chatter stops when an elderly woman appears at the foot of the stage and walks toward the microphone. Woos and applause greet her, but I decide to reserve my clapping for entertainment. I hate mindless ovation. But normally I'm physically unable to clap due to an apple martini in my hands.

The woman may be elderly, but she's spry and she reaches the stool in eight seconds, after which she blows kisses to thank the audience for the warm welcome. Wait a minute; is she the warlock? I imagined a man wearing a cape, a magic wand in hands. Her mop resembles the "I-just-woke-up" hairstyle, a trend, rich and lazy people have started: it sticks out in all directions, flattened in some spots as though someone sat on it for a while. You'll find kids wear the same hairstyle as well. She taps on the microphone to check whether it works. The woos and applause stop, and even though there's a sick boy coughing, the rest of the people sit quietly. Coughing, the boy fails to cover his face, endangering us to catch a flu. As a child, nursing a flu is legit: You're allowed to cheat school by staying at home and watching TV. As an adult, your coworkers presume you're nursing a hangover, which is true at least half the times when I call out.

"Goodbye," the woman says, which makes people laugh.

Her outfit consists of white slacks and an elegant blouse, also in white. The blouse outlines her fragile exterior. Her hair is either black and white or sprinkled with salt and pepper. Maybe she escaped from being dinner to a giant.

"I'm sozzled with happiness to visit the school where I spent my childhood. It brings back great memories. This is where I tried my first booger." The kids hoot. "Let me take a moment to thank Principal Henry Ante for allowing me to start my book safari in my own school, same as with the other eight books." She waits for the applause to start and die out. The principal nods his head, but remains seated without showing himself. "If you don't know who I am, my name is Grace Bishop."

I swear she looks at me when she says that. And it's partially true, since I've no idea who she is. The writer of the book, I quickly realize as her name pops in my mind.

Her voice is serene, soothing, and professional (whatever defines that). By that I mean I find my voice professional too, though half the time when I'm on the phone doing business, I find the person I'm speaking with to repeatedly tell me to put mommy on the phone. Grace wears a turquoise necklace, which stands out against the background of her elegant white blouse. To match, she wears a turquoise bracelet and a turquoise belt. The velvet red curtains behind Grace contrast with her white clothes.

"You wanted to be an astronaut, but now you're a taxi driver. How did it happen, kids? Didn't your mom teach you from early on you can become whoever you want? Now you've matured, but your dreams changed. Well, boys and girls, girls and boys, and everyone in between, this book is about a little boy, Michael, who jumps into the future, precisely twenty years ahead, and learns he's no longer a lion tamer but a doctor. He's disappointed in himself."

What is she gabbing about? Where's my clown? Is he out of town?

"As a little girl—I'm sure by now you've figured out I'm not a boy—I wished to follow my parents' footsteps. Mom and Dad were ballet dancers, and I remember watching them dance. At eight, I joined their rehearsals, working hard to become them."

Oh, tush push. Where's my warlock? Hiding in the bush?

Grace coughs once. "Now, is there an adult in the auditorium who remembers their childhood dream?"

Principal Ante raises his hand. "Me."

"Who did you wish to be, Principal?"

"A firefighter," he shouts out, tickling the auditorium to death. Grace laughs with the rest of the folks while I sit and blankly stare at her face. I remember seeing her on a photo out in the hallway, but I forget which one.

"And what happened to that dream?" Grace asks and Principal Ante shrugs. "What I miss about being a child is the fact I could dream. I dreamed big, but this is not what my book is about. The book is about a choice we make. Michael chose to become a doctor and when you read the book, you'll learn why."

People chuckle here and there after every couple of sentences. I, however, hardly find it funny, or sad, for that matter. I place my right leg on top of left and interlock my arms in front of my chest. I want a show. I want my warlock to turn water to snow. I want elephants rolling on a ball. I want Spiderman to climb up a wall. I want servers to bring me champagne. I want Natalia to stop snorting cocaine. I want Chloe to no longer lie. I want Lindsay to slowly die.

Grace sighs. "When something old ends, something new begins. This is the Law—how I like to call it—of Destruction and Creation. One exists *because* of the other. As children we have dreams, but as adults we have choices. Everything accomplished was chosen to be accomplished. Lazy people and those in denial blame the government, their parents, or circumstances. Blaming others is easy because it makes those people feel better about themselves. Do you agree we should take responsibility?"

Kids moo a "Yes."

"Never blame others. What you choose is your choice only. Nothing happens for no reason at all. This is what this book is about."

I bring my hair forward and start combing it with the fingers of my right hand, shaped as a comb, the same way Lindsay did. Then, according to this crazy lady, Lindsay chose to be a stripper and I chose to be—wait for it—a secresitter? Our destinies brought us there, out of luck if nothing else. I wish I had an apple martini to entertain myself with or a chicken bone to throw at Grace.

"Michael travels through the world as a clown," Grace continues in her soothing voice, "and he meets these wonderful people, and he wants to be all of them. First, he wants to become a TV anchor. Nothing is wrong with that, right? Then, when he meets a pilot, guess what Michael wants to be?"

"A pilot," kids say as a group.

Grace pauses and clears her throat for eight seconds like she has a monkey stuck up there. I sit back and close my eyes. I long to leave but it seems inappropriate at such a quiet moment, inappropriate even for me.

"Nothing in this world you can't do is what I want to communicate with my book. Dream big. Imagine, you're allowed to be just anybody, from a green ninja turtle to a pepperoni-spotted CatDog. What's more important is to remain yourself." I open my eyes and lean forward. "I never became a ballerina and I don't own a tutu, but I found passion in writing. What changed? Priorities. Growing up, I found salvation in writing. But I hated myself for not following my dreams to be a ballerina because I thought I failed my parents. Mom and Dad told me dreams change, and I hope you never think you're not good enough because you failed to accomplish something. Today, my priorities have changed again to being a wife and a mother and a grandmother."

Her voice trembles in a way which tells me what she's about to say is hard for her. I put my legs on the floor, gluing them next to each other, sticking my hands in between for warmth.

"My idea of happiness shifted from skipping school to seeing my granddaughter unwrapping Christmas presents. Her happiness is now *my* happiness. That present was a doll who looks like Taylor Swift, because Agatha loves her and she wishes to be a singer too. The feeling of unconditional love is the feeling of a new beginning. Moms and dads are the most significant people in your life. Family makes you feel important."

Grace puts her right palm on her cheek, a pose, smart people came up with to fake thinking. She mumbles something indecipherable away from the microphone. With my right hand collected into a fist, I put it under my chin for support, setting my left arm across my chest to support the elbow of the right hand.

Lectures are the same reason I never attend theater: boring. Actors, just like Grace, always ramble monologues without making fun of each other, the way they would in a zany clownade. I hope Taylor Swift isn't offended by being called a singer. I mean, being called a singer is an insult to a singer. Nina Simone, for example, wasn't just a singer, but she was a vocalist, a piano player, and an entertainer. When I do karaoke I'm a singer. Actually, it's when I sing is what constitutes an insult to other singers and to anybody who's able to hear. I close my eyes and lean backward, listening to her voice, its rhythm, its grace, its soothing quality reminding me of Mom's.

"Thank you, Charlie," Grace says and I open my eyes, for a hot second wondering where I am, completely disoriented. "Charlie's was the last question. It's already four o'clock and this is all the time allotted. I'll be in Principal Ante's office signing books and taking photos. Hello!"

Besides Oaisha, now I know another moron who says "Hello" for "Goodbye." What does she mean by four o'clock? I just came here and it was only three o'clock. My watch shows 4:08. That means, of course, Calyssa Pantaleo fell asleep again, shamelessly, her body with its sore parts rumbling no better than Oaisha's car.

Grace waves her hands for a goodbye. In the meantime, during applause, I get up as quietly as possible, leaving auditorium on my tippy-toes. I expected magic tricks, lion tamers, and clowns juggling bottles of margaritas up in the air. For reasons unknown, I become extremely irritated until I realize it's because of Grace when she said: "Moms and dads are the most significant people in your life. Family makes you feel important." Her words echo in my brain. Hooey, I say.

If moms and dads were so important, I would've had at least one of them from the very beginning. When people start propagandizing about importance of family, I long to jump on the ceiling and booby-trap my ears with cotton balls. I'll never know what Mom thinks of me and whether or not she's proud. I want to feel like I'm good enough. I want to be a person who's more than a secretary. But since Mom doesn't care, I don't care either.

Stupid Grace Bishop, I keep thinking while walking down the corridor. "Family makes you important." So now that I don't have a family, what am I, unimportant? Walking, one by one I remove the black-and-white framed photographs from the wall, and one by one down they fall, glass shattering all over the carpeted floor. Vandalism was never my passion, but I can't help it. If I had a sharpie, I'd detour to the bathroom to leave extra presents.

Just as I thought, Grace Bishop appears on a colored photograph. She's much younger, with blond hair, dressed in a white dress. Her eyes are see-through gray. I lift up the frame, turn it upside down, and retrieve the picture from its back. Why I do this, I've no idea, but I must please the force from above that is using my body like a marionette's.

Close to 5:00, with three masquerade masks, two bottles of champagne, a pack of cigarettes, a pouch of dried Turkish apricots, and a Frappuccino, I take the bus back to the hotel. Public transportation is something I've dislike since childhood, yet living in New York forces you to use it. Summertime is when you're surrounded by sweaty people, cramped in one subway car, and not only men are gross who clip their nails here and there, but women are gross as well, fixing their makeup like they couldn't do it at home. Here I am though, the only person on the bus for the entirety of the ride. Honolulu must be all about driving, just like the rest of the states. I like it.

I have cooled off from the weird wrath I experienced an hour ago, and taking Grace's picture in my hands, I note the elegance with which she carries herself. She's like a chopped bush with all the fat trimmed. Without blinking once, I produce my phone and order her book from the Internet. With two-day delivery, I should receive it by Tuesday. For $5.99, the book is a bargain, why I order a second copy for my cousin Christina, sighing at the fact my phone is about to die.

I stop at the lobby to collect my dress, and it no longer has wrinkles, ironed to perfection. Taisha (or Oaisha) greets me, the swooshed cat gone.

Upstairs, I find Chloe napping on a graphite chair, curled into a ball resembling Anubis, who is cuddled next to her. She's wearing a pair of pajama pants and a plain white tee. Elizabeth seems to be taking a nap as well.

Natalia is nowhere to be found. Her clutch is gone too, but nothing else with it. I put the shopping bags down and check the two bedrooms and bathrooms but she's definitely gone. For all I know, she might be taking a stroll down at the beach.

Out on the lanai, I breathe in the fresh Hawaiian air as I jump on a chaise. The sun is halfway across the sky toward its sleeping lair. In two hours I'll be trying to attain my leverage on Adam and my fate will be known then. Truthfully, I'm terrified.

Since there's plenty of time before seven o'clock, I decide to take another shower in case the pipes go out again.

After the shower, I smell extra lavender. I fix my hair by pulling it away from my face into a high ponytail, and I do bubble braids with a ribbon I find in the Gooseberry. I do four bands, puffing each one with the hairbrush until they're puffy enough. Also, I put on a new layer of foundation, eyeliner, mascara, lip-gloss, and finish by applying shimmer to my body, which sparkles when exposed to light. I notice how the bottle of shimmer is almost empty, as I only had an ounce of it with me. I put on my dress.

Natalia hasn't returned by the time I'm ready, so I dial her number. She doesn't pick up. Where could she possibly go, especially with Chubbly Wobbly? I come out to the living room and wake up Chloe. The cat scrams at the sight of me.

"Do you know where Natalia went?"

"She left with the dude," Chloe says and yawns.

"What dude?"

"The one with a goatee."

"Did she say where?"

"Nope. She said she called you, then the two of them left right after."

I check my phone to see a call from Natalia is registered at 3:10 P.M., which I somehow missed. The battery on my phone is at 10 percent, minutes before it shuts off. I'm such a dupe for forgetting the charger. Hopefully, Natalia returns soon; otherwise, she won't be able to contact me and vice versa.

"If she doesn't come back on time, we'll have to attend the party without her, just you and me," I say. "Go get ready."

"I'm ready. I already took a shower." She sits up straight and yawns again. Her face is slightly unraveled, like an unmade bed.

I sit down on the second chair, sinking two feet down immediately. "Okay then, listen. Here's my plan: When I find Adam, I need to make sure he's drunk, so then you can take a picture of him and me kissing. That's how I get my leverage."

"Wait, why are we doing this?"

"To get the money from him," I lie. "Could you do that?"

"Okay. Whatever."

I fish out my digital camera and show Chloe how to operate it. Then, the two of us finish a bottle of champagne in nothing flat. Chloe locks Anubis in Natalia's bedroom while I place the Patrón bottle on top of the kitchen island (in case Anubis manages to escape from the bedroom and gets hungry). This way while she's up there, he won't eat her alive.

Chloe models the three masquerade masks, but hates them all. I know this because she takes off the last mask and makes a face.

"I hate them all."

"Chloe, you must wear one of them. It's a masquerade party."

"I know what I'll do." She picks up the twenty-pound pumpkin and plops it on the kitchen counter. "I'll make my own mask."

"Nuh-oh. We don't have time for that."

"Then I'm not going."

Quickly I note the time: 5:55. We must leave by 6:30 at the latest to arrive by seven. Also, I've no idea how long it takes to get to Ke Iki Beach, but Adam said something about a casino afterward. I'll have to be swift about finding him before he goes there.

Professional pumpkin carver I am, I empty the seeds and scrape off as much flesh from the insides of the pumpkin as humanly possible. I cut out a generic face: two triangles for eyes, an oval for a nose, a wide rectangle with teeth for a mouth. I cut out a big round off the top of the pumpkin for extra oxygen. Chloe tries it on in the bathroom, after which she exits wearing it, her short platinum hair styled into a Mohawk. She's attired in a one-piece denim jumpsuit on top of the white tee, Crocs on her feet. She looks like an idiot.

"I love it!" she exclaims, her voice hollow under the pumpkin.

I hide the extra bottle of champagne in the Gooseberry, planning to pregame while en route. Who knows how long it takes to find Adam, and I'm unwilling to spend any more cash on drinks. Chloe picks up her *Latent Tramplet* book, foolishly presuming she'll have time to read it during the party. The suite receives a beautiful hue from the setting sun, the sky a palette of colors, mostly magenta and warm yellow.

"What did you do today while I was gone?" I ask her.

"Nothing. Read. I used a computer in the office area and checked my messages again, but the guy still hasn't responded."

"Listen, it's his loss if he never replies."

"Oh, who are you kidding? He thinks I'm ugly."

"Maybe it's you who thinks you're ugly? After all, we are our worst judges. 'Nothing in this world you can't do,'" I say, quoting Grace. "Maybe in reality you're not ready for a serious relationship. You have a good job as an accountant and you live by yourself. There's so much pressure."

She takes off the pumpkin and hangs her head low. "I need to confess something. Actually, I don't live alone."

"Roommates?"

"No, I live with my mom. Yes, I'm thirty, and I live with my mother. I'm so ashamed to admit it. And I don't have a job as an accountant, or as anyone. I'm unemployed. For a long time now. And to be brutally honest, I want to attend my high school reunion so badly, but nobody will remember me."

"Chloe, you didn't have to lie. I would understand."

"Somehow I doubt that. You're so professional, and you always make fun of unemployed people living with their parents. I sometimes feel intimidated by you. I love our friendship; it's why I never said anything. I look up to you, but now I feel absolutely under-appreciated. It's my fault, of course, not yours. The guy never responded, and for the same reason, nobody will chew the fat with me at the reunion."

"Why tell me now? What happened?"

"It hurts to admit, but Lindsay was right when she said nobody believed me anymore because of my lying. Maybe it's time to set the record straight and only tell the truth."

"Okay. Why did you pack a whole tote and asked to stay at my place? It has nothing to do with Pocket. Am I right?"

"No, Paxton isn't involved. I had a fight with Mom. She's been driving me crazy. I started volunteering at a shelter for homeless pets, the only place that would accept me. Other volunteers were great and they found owners for the homeless pets so fast; I was getting behind. So when I couldn't find an owner for a pet, I brought that pet home: first Anubis, then more cats, a dog, parakeets, fish. They loved me at the shelter for my fake 'ability' to persuade owners while in reality I was hoarding the pets at my place. I loved the attention and praise I received. It got to the point when there were over eleven cats, two dogs, and five cages of buzzing parakeets. Mom blew up, and we had a big argument on Thursday. She gave me an ultimatum. I must return the pets or find another place to live. Instead, I ran away without knowing what to do. I'm so depressed."

Chloe takes a step forward and embraces me. She squeezes me so hard my blood flow stops. Now everything falls into place. This is why Chloe was snappy at Lindsay because she was jealous of her free lifestyle; Chloe was all tied up and responsible for a menagerie of pets, including Anubis.

In such a position, I say, "Listen, I know what you should do. What you're doing for those pets is great, but you must set your priorities. Return them and explain the situation to your boss. You're a wonderful person but you need to believe in yourself. I'm sure your apartment is too small for all those cats and dogs. I can help you with a résumé if you wish and you'll find a job in no time. I promise; I kick ass at résumés and job interviews. My boss Adam hired me on the spot. He's the man: just show him a little leg, some cleavage, and you've got the job. Now, however, we need to hurry up or then there will be two unemployed women in Honolulu."

"Okay."

Chloe replaces the pumpkin while I dial Taisha. "Taisha, advise me on how to get to Ke Iki Beach."

"Who's this?"

"Calyssa Pantaleo, from 1112."

"Oh."

"Oh, what? How can I get there?"

"What's there?"

"A party we need to attend, but Chloe and I have no idea where it's located or how much time it takes to get there."

"Truth be told, and truth I'll say, today, my dear is your lucky day."

"Huh?"

"I promise, dear, I swear, my sister will take you there."

"Taisha, are you drunk?" I wonder if she just decided to make fun of me.

"No time for questions; it's not far. My sister will take you in her car."

Never again with that monster, the biggest bitch Oaisha. "Taisha, thanks for the offer and I appreciate it, but I prefer a taxi."

"It'll be thirty minutes; take it or leave it."

"I don't have thirty minutes."

"I can believe it."

"Don't you guys have cabs in Hawaii?"

"The cabs we have, you foolish dork, but this is Honolulu, not New York. Should I get one? Will you wait? I'll call them to find out the rate."

"No, I'll go with your sister. I'll be downstairs in two."

I hang up, mad at being called a foolish dork. The hotel staff is starting to piss me off. However, when people offer you free things, they have a little advantage, in which case she can call me anything she wishes. In the morning, right after we check out, I'll give her a piece of my mind.

ON THE WAY DOWNSTAIRS, I TELL CHLOE THE TRUTH BEHIND why we came to Hawaii to make her feel better knowing she isn't the only liar here, and then I quickly explain to her my witty blackmailing plan. She moos in response but says nothing. I've noticed her do that when she's deeply upset but unwilling to communicate.

Downstairs, Oaisha is standing by the door. She changed her rose dress to a miniskirt and a leopard-print tight blouse, heels on her feet making her appear super tall. She intimidated me earlier but now I'm horrified. Oaisha, however, smiles, and I know there must be something she wants from me.

Otherwise, why give me a free ride if she talked down to me just a few hours ago?

When the three of us exit the building, I notice how the air is chilled to a perfect seventy-five degrees. Oaisha's car is now parked farther, unlike earlier. Chloe and I follow her. No longer in a hurry, Oaisha whistles a tune, and I want to kick her in the butt to hurry her up. But I decide to hold my horses. Chloe refused to take the pumpkin off her head and the hotel guests stare at her, pointing their dirty fingers. I keep hearing "Look, look," intertwined with laughter.

Oaisha finds her car, yet another vehicle: an old red Volvo. The model and the year are hard to pinpoint because it must have been made two centuries back. The rust settled on the doors, the trunk doesn't seem to close, and all four tires are mismatched. The sticker along the front says, "Parteeey!!!"

"Whose car is it?" I ask her.

"Mine."

"What happened to the pink Mazda?"

"The Mazda is my sister's."

"Ah." Then Taisha is the one with a love for pink and Hello Kitty.

The sisters may look alike, but they have nothing in common whatsoever: cheerful Taisha, gruesome Oaisha.

I take the front seat while Chloe is forced to sit in the back. I don't believe in back seats, much like I don't believe in ice cream in winter and eating an apple without the word martini attached to it. Unlike in the Mazda, the back seat of the Volvo is clear of junk, but Chloe has to lie down on the seat in order to fit the oversized pumpkin, as sure as hell the ceiling of the Volvo is way too low. The car smells like French fries, and at that thought, my stomach growls loudly, indicating hunger.

A couple of goals are already set for tonight: not to get too drunk, not to make a fool of myself, and most importantly—not to pass out, something I've been doing a lot lately. To seal the deal I pop open the second bottle of champagne and take a big sip. If Oaisha minds, she fails to indicate.

The mask on my lap reminds me that soon I'll perform the most important task of my life, and if all goes smoothly—which it will—then for sure the job is secured under my belt. Speaking of the belt, I place mine into the retractor, but it seems flimsy, especially after I try pulling on the belt and it jumps back at me.

"Oh, it doesn't work," Oaisha laughs. "Just hold the handle of your car door. This is what I do." With her right hand, she switches gears and holds the wheel while with the left she holds the car door. Great, just what I wanted —to die.

Oaisha pulls the car in reverse, and I grab the handle tightly, knowing perfectly well she'll speed up like a maniac again. Instead, for the next five minutes, we're going twenty-two miles per hour, and I nervously check my watch. Oaisha keeps close to the berm on the right side of the road, a lane designated for sixteen-year-olds with a learner's permit and/or pussels (how Natalia would say).

"Oaisha, can you explain to me why you're driving like a little old lady when this afternoon you almost killed us?" Not only we'll be late for the party, but we'll arrive after Adam has already left.

Oaisha clears her throat, checking the rearview mirror for traffic. "Technically, my name is Caisha. I'm Oaisha's sister."

Turning my neck slowly, bones creaking heavily on the background, I give her a stare. "Caisha? That's impossible."

"Why?"

"You look exactly like Taisha and Oaisha."

"We're triplets."

Doing some fifth grade math, I realize their names are Taisha, Oaisha, and Caisha. And not only are they triplets who look exactly alike, the three sisters act as one entity.

"Then why do you keep it a secret and act as one person?"

"Don't laugh," she says, laughing; I hate when people trick me this way. "There are ample occasions when we need to appear in several places at once. Since childhood we have covered for each other. We hate it advertised because then we can't fool people, but Oaisha and Taisha told me you're worse than us. I see no harm in telling you."

"What do you mean worse than you?"

"True, we're pretty messed up for operating as one person, but you're messed up too. Someone wreaked havoc at the school today where Oaisha's favorite author, Grace Bishop, was doing Q and A. Oaisha told me she heard someone snoring five rows up, and it turned out to be you."

"It couldn't possibly be me. Baloney."

"She took a snapshot and sent it to me. It was you, for sure."

"So I was there. So what?"

"For some reason, all the photographs ended up on the floor in the hallway, glass scattered everywhere. We did a little calculation and we know it's you, hurricane Calyssa. Why did you do that?"

I shrug because the answer to that question is unclear even to me. "I'm sorry," I say, finally unwilling to deny anything. "Something or someone was using my body."

What did I do that was so bad? Anyone could make a mistake and end up in Honolulu instead of Vegas. And anyone could "lose" their driver's license in a hotel bathroom. And who didn't end up throwing anger tantrums at a book-signing event? How could I possibly be worse than three lying identical triplets?

"See? That's what I mean, Calyssa. You even have ghosts haunting you. I don't judge, no worries."

"That's probably the case: ghosts. But wait. Your names. There seems to be a pattern, but I'm lost."

"Our Granddaddy, bless his generous heart, loved gambling so much that he changed his last name to Tripps, original last name being forgotten in the process. Tripps is a name for a dice game he was addicted to, also called Bender's Delight, which is a synonym for binge drinking as well. Granddaddy had the most peculiar sense of humor. Anyway, our father—inspired by Granddaddy—got addicted to . . . let's say rather was fond of . . . gambling just as much, and as soon as our umbilical cords were cut and clamped, we were named after Tournament of Champions or TOC, something he thought he'd made up, but which is now an official tournament in Vegas. He said life was a gamble. Sometimes, even if you know your craft, you may still lose."

That statement makes me think: life is a gamble. Meeting people and making friends is basically gambling too then. Sometimes, it's pure luck. It was luck meeting Chloe and Natalia, and then there was a big loss when Lindsay entered my life.

This sad, sad story, however, makes me think of Natalia, and I wonder whether or not she'll name her boys Buck, Jack, or Chip; and her girls Pat, River, or Variance. By my calculation, the TOC trio was assembled the following way: Taisha was named after "Tournament" and Caisha was named after "Champions; then Oaisha was named after "of"—no wonder she's pissed off!

"Our parents," she continues, "couldn't recognize who was who. On multiple occasions, our parents would confuse me with my sisters. The three of us were having fun with this. We wouldn't change our hairstyles, dress absolutely the same, play the same games, listen to the same music, and watch the same TV shows. At the end of the day, no one—including us—could find a single difference among the three of us."

"I can definitively tell the difference by at least two of you: how you drive." I watch the speedometer, learning another sad story: we're barely making twenty-three miles per hour. "But I don't understand. You're all so different. How could people not recognize who is who?"

"Because people are ignorant and because we're triplets. Most people can't tell the difference between bleach blond Hollywood bombshells or tell the difference between Asian people or black people. The majority of folks can hardly recognize themselves." She shrugs and clears her throat. "We went to college as one person—because our parents could only afford one of us—while the other two were doing what they liked best. I loved philosophy and parties, so I went to all the social events; Taisha loved English, Shakespeare, and poetry, and she would take that; Oaisha, the most rebellious of us all, loved bad boys and books, so she signed up for book clubs, and, as a kid, she snuck out on dates while the other two rotated rooms when our parents did the usual rounds of goodnights. They never knew Oaisha was gone."

"It makes sense you love parties. This is why Taisha insisted on you driving us. You wanted to attend the party at Ke Iki Beach, didn't you?"

"Yes. Sorry, if she wasn't clear about that."

"Of course, you're more than welcome to join us." I decide to spare her details about my wicked plan, even though she already thinks I'm crazy. I wouldn't give her pleasure to confirm her discovery.

"Thanks. I have a mask too. It's in the trunk. I wore it for Halloween last year. Anyway, the three of us ran into a problem with all that hiding. Somehow, last year, we ended up dating a set of triplets as well. How bizarre does it sound?"

"I don't know. Very?"

"Their names are Bisujaksha, Kunjabihari, and Mrigankamouli, all named after their Indian lords. One of them was named after Lord Vishnu, second after Lord Krishna, and the last after Lord Shiva. Even before we met for the first time, we were lost at who was who, but now, after all this time, we're completely lost."

"How?" I say. Somehow, half the champagne bottle has evaporated. It must be hotter in the car than I thought and I cork the bottle to prevent it from drying out. Chloe's snore is heard in the background. In her pumpkin mask, seen through the rearview mirror, she resembles a scarecrow.

"How? One time Taisha needed to work so she asked me to go out with her guy, Kunjabihari, and when I went out with him I liked him, so I asked Taisha if she could instead date my guy, Mrigankamouli, but who was, in fact, Bisujaksha. Bisujaksha went out with Taisha when Oaisha had to do a presentation, and then Oaisha went out with the third brother, but who was the first brother I first went out with, and by then we didn't know which one of the three he was. So we were dating all three brothers simultaneously, in rotation, without knowing who was who, and who slept with who."

"I just imagine you for Christmas. That's a full house for sure."

"Right? So one night, we finally decided to figure it out, when the six of us met. Man, was it complicated. The three brothers told us they also had no idea who dated who. We realized it was impossible to track who was whose girlfriend because it became so complicated. Nobody knows how we got lost. We divided the brothers among the three of us, and I'm seeing Mrigankamouli at the moment. I suspect he's actually Bisujaksha. It's confusing. As of today, we kind of all lost ourselves. How silly is that?"

When Caisha finishes the story, the drain of my brain gets clogged, and I watch the champagne being evaporated while I try to call Calyssa the plumber. Instead, a scary thought comes to my mind.

"You know what?" I say. "I can relate to that. In my twenties I traveled the states, trying to find a place that fits. During that process, I kept losing myself more and more."

"What do you mean?"

"For instance, I distinctly remember in California, much like my girlfriends, after we watched a documentary about processed food, I became a vegetarian Calyssa. Not for long, thank God. Then I'd read a book on anatomy—which was in Orlando, Florida—and anatomy would be all I talked about for a year to come. When I dated a guy who was in AA, I became a non-drinking, good Calyssa. Thank God not for long, either. The worst twenty-four hours of my life. Now, after moving to New York, I'm career-obsessed Calyssa, running around the office, trying to please all the executives. But in retrospect, whenever I started something new, it somehow seemed like the most important decision I ever made. The real Calyssa disappears and is replaced by whichever trend I'm addicted to."

"What kind of Calyssa is that, the real Calyssa?"

I give it a thought, but produce no answer. I simply don't know anymore.

"Calyssa, we lose ourselves sometimes and it's okay. We're simple but diverse human beings with complex, not primitive, mindsets, and we always demand more from ourselves. Each generation becomes more sophisticated than the one before. But personally, from what I understand, I think it's a New York thing."

"What is?"

"Honey, I met New Yorkers when substituting for Taisha, and I learned in a city of such a size, people either get stripped off from layers of lies or are completely in denial. People with busy schedules never have time for faking in a city like New York, and they order take out for dinner, they do online dating, and they hire housekeepers because they have no time for any of that."

"What's your point?" I say.

"See, on an island like Oahu, simply because there's nothing to do, we search for entertainment. People whose lives run slowly lie to themselves. I'm telling you, even though Hawaii is indeed a paradise, it becomes boring after a while. We cook at home, we go on an awkward first date, we clean our own house just to occupy ourselves with *something*. We fake things. We invent things. Maybe the city is making you understand who you really *aren't* instead of making you *lose* yourself. The city is making you understand that you were in reality not a vegetarian Calyssa, nor that you liked anatomy."

"I still don't get it."

"The point is: whoever you really are, you'll soon be stripped to that bare layer, and only *you* will know what to do with it and what color to paint it. Then you can fake it, make it, or take it."

I watch her, wondering what this woman does in her free time. She told me she liked philosophy. Was that philosophy too when she mentioned stripping to the bare layer or was it simply something only Lindsay would do?

Her point, however, cannot get any clearer. It cannot be misinterpreted. She possibly described me to my truest: Maybe I'm becoming a real Calyssa who could easily blackmail her boss and who fights with monkeys at her office. The singular thought of such a Calyssa terrifies me.

"But then again," I argue, "each time when I'm this Calyssa or that Calyssa, why does it feel like it is the most important decision I've ever made?"

"The same happens, possibly, when people get married. After spending a certain amount of time in solitude, we want a relationship. We start dating, and in a moment of complete lust when things are new and unfamiliar, when we wait for a terrifying moment of that first kiss, we get married. Not only because this person we meet is the best thing that happened to us, but because we're in love.

"The next day when we wake up married, we realize it wasn't a fairytale we dreamed of, so we file for a divorce. Still, the man and the woman—or the man and the man, or the woman and the woman, whoever—don't understand why they got married in the first place. Because if such a universal answer existed, marriages would remain intact.

"And there you go: another riddle from God to have us occupied. Personally, I believe the answer to everything is quite simple, but we intentionally twist it, for we, humans, dislike simple ideas. They're all in our heads: the problems. Our insecurities are something we made up in our brain by mimicking other people, by watching TV, or by reading books. We expect more from our lives because the twenty-first century demands it. Nobody dreams of the Cinderella story anymore, because no woman wants to sit at home and wait for her husband. We want a challenge. But the questions we ask ourselves and the answers to those questions are within us. Creating problems is a big part of human imagination. We won't see bad unless there's good. So unless you find grief, how will you know what constitutes happiness?"

Grace Bishop said the exact same thing. Caisha must have read her books as well, just like her sister Oaisha.

"Like the Law of Destruction and Creation?" I ask.

"Bingo. Quoting Picasso: 'Every act of creation is first an act of destruction.' Catastrophes cause evolution. Emotional bottom is when you experience an emotional catastrophe; when you fail your goals. But it also can be a physical disaster: after an ice age that killed the dinosaurs, the human race began. It's really fascinating."

I stop listening. Maybe destruction—a catastrophe—is exactly what Chloe needed. It will break her to pieces, so she can rebuild herself anew.

Picasso couldn't be more correct, I think.

In Grace's book, the boy didn't know who he wanted to be until he became it. Can we change our fate or do we wait for a catastrophe to come along and give us a push?

On that thought, Caisha slows her hag and we enter a parking lot.

CHAPTER NINE

Queen of Denial

At 7:15, we arrive at Ke Iki Beach, proved by a sign near the entrance saying: "YOU ARRIVED AT KE IKI BEACH." Parking is unavailable. It births a conclusion that the party's crowded, meaning it will be that much harder to find Adam. After five minutes of circling, we finally claim a spot between two jeeps, papa jeep and mama jeep respectively. My hand's throbbing since it clutched the door handle for the entirety of the ride as a seatbelt substitute.

Before exiting the car, I affix my masquerade mask. From the three purchased, I assert ownership of the butterfly one: black body (designed to sit on a nose) and green wings (for cheekbones and eyes). For such a gorgeous mask fifteen bucks seemed almost immaterial. Caisha fumbles in the trunk of her jalopy until she obtains a mask covering half a face, gold with imitation diamonds all around—perhaps bedazzled by Oaisha—its edges curved in a contemporary fashion.

Chloe removes the pumpkin and gets a hold of the champagne bottle (half of it, anyway) and finishes it in nothing flat. She replaces the pumpkin back on. What I learned in the course of my thirty-year-old life is that nobody drinks because they're having a gay ol' time. Lemonade will suffice happy people and assholes. Chloe's upset about the guy who never replied back and alcohol will help her lift those heavy emotions off her chest. The best way to fall in love with someone is after a drink or two, when emotions are heightened, when confidence represses introversion, and when you're amorous enough for copulation. Deals are made under the influence, no doubt: just think of how Alaska was sold for seven million. No one was sober there, I'll tell you that much. Under the influence you become clairvoyant. The night Chloe and I met at our bar, she was depressed and beer shooed that depression away, turning her into Wonder Woman. Today, I believe I learned why she was depressed in the first place, because she lives with her mother. She spoke truth earlier: I make fun of people who live with their family, even though I just recently moved out from Aunt Sarah's house. Now that I know the truth, I'll try to avoid making hurtful remarks. Chloe, however, is predictable. When she's quiet, just like her cat, she's deeply upset and she won't say a word until things resolve.

Natalia, mysterious as she appears, leads an unquestionably lonely life of a gambler, drinking because she's unsuitable for the sober society. She desperately wishes to fit into the women's world, why she applied for LEGS, the ladies-only club. Being rich made her distrust people whenever the many gold-diggers were ready to kiss ass for her money. Having met me, Natalia's drunken and my drunken world collided and we became best friends—almost sisters—in a course of two months, but now I broke that trust. I wonder whether she'll ever confide in me, or speak to me, again.

Rat Lindsay drinks because she's homeless and alcohol makes you carefree. Alcohol tricks you into believing Earth is your home, proved by the drunken destitute people roaming the streets of New York, Lindsay's future unless she finds a "respectable" job. For her "respect" must be present in some materialistic form while for me "respect" always came from within. With the money she'd stolen, she'd probably bought a ticket to Omaha before Natalia could cancel the credit cards. With the three grand in cash, Lindsay will lease an apartment and construct her life from scratch just as she dreamed.

As for me, the idea of a photoshopped Babette didn't come on a dry stomach. The couch was bought drunkenly on impulse, not that I regret. In fact, all my major purchases were acquired when I was inebriated: the dress I'm wearing, the cracked phone, the masquerade masks. All my crazy ideas seemed to have evolved after a couple of apple martinis. An idea behind coming to Hawaii or getting blackmail on Adam doubtfully came from being sober. Drunk people spend money without worrying about their financial assets. Usually during a night out, I will spend a hundred dollars easy, which includes the 2:00 A.M. pizza and 4:00 A.M. McDonald's. Sober people are parsimonious, as perfectly proved by my cousin Christina who hasn't made a purchase since 1999, when she needed a pair of clean panties. If she wears something new—the peach or the maroon—it means somebody donated it to her. So in order for me to do what I intend to do, I need to wet my whistle for courage. It's been hanging on my chest dry all afternoon.

We take a concrete road, guided by a sign for dummies: "BEACH THIS WAY," complete with an arrow. At the corner, before I toss the empty bottle into a trash can, I lick the rim for extra drops of champagne. There should be a sign that reads "ADAM THIS WAY" together with an arrow to make my life easier, but alas, there's none. Somehow, all of the street lamps have been turned off, and we walk toward the chatter audible somewhere ahead in the pitch darkness. Caisha leads after telling me she knows the area.

Together with the fresh smell of the ocean, a light breeze sneaks in a whiff of ham and grilled pineapple, reminding me to feed the beast that is my stomach. Through palm trees to my left, occasional flames are seen, flickering in the distance, which must belong to the BBQ where the food smell comes from. One broken street lamp twinkles eerily, making the walk as pleasant as it would be at three in the morning in a sketchy Bronx alley. Palm trees seem threatening in the dark, ready to attack us with their coconut grenades. This is what I'll drink then, a Blue Hawaiian—a drink made with rum and cream of coconut—to avoid such coconuts falling on me as per theory of world balance. See, I have a choice: to consume coconuts with my mouth or have them fall on my head; I choose the former. Chloe defended herself well with the pumpkin, but even she is vulnerable of being knocked out should a coconut tree drop a grenade into the opening on top, which I cut out for extra oxygen.

After several turns and two false alarms when I presumed coconuts were to attack us, we step onto the sand. The blackness of the Pacific Ocean stretches ahead for as far as you're willing or unwilling to imagine. Wooden torches illuminate the area, each located five to six feet apart from the next. Torches are the only source of light, and this part of the island would be completely dark due to a lack of other illuminating devices, including the moon. Maybe the moon is on vacation, tired of making light for dummies who get lost in the jungle or other places where people tend to get lost. On the beach, dance music comes from two oversized speakers by an elevated stage and I come up with the following conclusion: Wanna hear, don't stay near. Wanna be deaf, come closer. Doesn't rhyme but not a crime. It suddenly reminds me of a certain conversation with Taisha when she called me a foolish dork.

"Caisha, why was Taisha rhyming today when I called her?"

"Taisha rhymes when she's super excited. She got a raise today and she couldn't hold it to herself. She asked me to come in to substitute for her so she could put herself together. But can you imagine that nobody asked her how she's able to work 24/7 without sleep? I mean with the three of us being there around the clock. Her boss is ridiculous. The three of us rotate between this job, babysitting, and occasional cashiering at a grocery store. Taisha makes more money than any of us so we pick up as many shifts as possible at Waikiki Beach Palace."

Great, now I need two more Calyssas to prove Mr. Grunt how good I am. Since such a ludicrous idea is out of the question, now for sure I need to get blackmail on Adam or I'm history. If only I looked Asian like my cousin Christina, I'd send her to substitute for me to smooth things out. She's a great negotiator and men are always smitten with her.

People in masquerade masks are shoaling around, and I wonder if I'll ever be able to find Adam in this mess. Bypassing all the strangers in masks leaves me feeling awkward, as though I'm visiting uncle Santa for Christmas, who wrapped all these men for me as presents. If I had time I'd unwrap them one by one, but for now they can just go lie under my tree. Female question: how to get a male's attention without, of course, making a man think I want male attention? This is a challenge. Chloe is getting plenty of attention in her mask. The way people stare at her you'd imagine they'd never seen a pumpkin before.

Since Adam failed to place a sign on himself together with an arrow, the first good clue is to check the bar, where he'd usually be dangling around like a Christmas ornament. Plus, I'm thirsty for a Blue Hawaiian so I will go and check both items off my list.

The bar is located near the stage with three bartenders working behind the counter, all of them wearing white masquerade masks. Their shirtless bodies are certified with abs as though stamped for quality control. Marcus would never get a job here due to his bloated stomach. It should be fairly easy to spot Adam, a schmuck with a belly, but apparently quite a few of those linger around the beach to prevent me from making my quest easy. Maybe like Jehovah's witnesses go door-to-door, I can go mask-to-mask until I find Adam, and even if it takes longer it's the safest bet. One thing though stops me: I'm too sober, therefore chicken for something so bold.

At the bar, I carefully study patrons who lack bellies. What a sneaky way to live your life without a belly. Your description blends in with the other folks. "It's that guy with a belly who stole the dildo," the store attendant would tell the police who would catch the thief immediately. Neither one of the patrons, I presume, needed a dildo so they're all skinny.

I sit down on a stool, eyes on the bartenders. What a tricky life to live with abs, so even if your face resembles the swooshed cat's people still admire you. The bartenders must have jumped out of some adult magazine for ladies, but unfortunately instead of underwear they wear shorts. Adam will need to attend the gym for the next fifty years to be this presentable. Moving in rhythm with the music, the bartenders dance crookedly a fact that is hardly their best quality. "Shaking drinks is what you probably do best, not shaking your body" is what I want to tell them.

One of the bartenders heads over my way and I drill him with my eyes, ready to hang him on my wall as decoration. Maybe that's how cannibalism started: a woman with too many hormones to release jumped on a bartender and then you know what happened . . . she ate him alive.

"What can I get for you?"

"Blue Hawaiian, please."

"Anything for you?" he asks Caisha, and she orders a gin tonic.

"And I'll have an IPA," Chloe tells the bartender through her pumpkin headpiece. "And a shot of whiskey."

The drinks arrive in less than a minute; I try mine to realize how fresh it tastes. I wonder, though, who came up with such a weird name "Blue Hawaiian." There must be an answer in Chloe's *Latent Tramplet* book, which she thankfully left in the car. The explanation is quite simple: "And since pimp Kainuku was upset and was feeling blue, he decided to call the drink after himself."

Caisha tries her drink, almost fainting from pleasure, or so it sounds like. "I'll get us this round," she says and pays the tab. "Oh, man. This is a great party."

During the course of my Blue Hawaiian, the bartender gets cuter and cuter. Why do they have to be so sexist and place male bartenders instead of female bartenders? Not that I complain but I thought it wouldn't hurt to bitch a little bit anyway. I get my bartender's attention and motion for him to come closer. I want to see if he knows Adam. After all, Adam has been here for a week, and he makes friends easily, especially at his sanctuary, the bar.

"What can I get for you?" he repeats, smiling. Damn, if only you knew what you could get for me.

"Do you know a guy whose name is Adam Klutz?"

"What does he look like?"

"He's about two hundred and fifty pounds with man boobs for which he wears a bra."

"Could you be more specific?"

"His hair is smeared with some highlights and styled up."

"What else?"

"He wears glasses and has a triple chin."

"Hm."

"He's a foot shorter than any guy you know. Have you seen him?"

"I doubt I have, ma'am."

"Well, in that case, while you're here," I say, getting a dollar bill out of my wallet. I get up from the chair, arms aimed at his shorts. Oh, no, I did! I shove the bill in his shorts, feeling his smooth body, which he shaved for the occasion. Before my frisky hands could reach any farther, he backs out.

"Thanks," I say, making my way back to the chair. I guess one-dollar bill is hardly a proper way to get a male's attention without that certain male discovering my shifty plan.

In the meantime, the dance music gradually fades out to a complete stop, bringing the beach back to its normal state, where you can hear water splattering somewhere out in the ocean, where you can hear an idle chatter of the cute bartender with a blonde I suddenly hate, and where you can hear the same uneasy grumbling of my stomach from not getting enough food. There is a garnish station in front of me with olives; lime, lemon, and orange slices; maraschino cherries; whole mint leaves; apple wedges, pineapple chunks, and whole strawberries. I lean forward and covertly get a handful of orange slices, seven strawberries, and about five olives. I sit back down, unseen from what I can tell.

Laying the goodies beside my Blue Hawaiian, I take a bite of the fresh strawberry, its sweetness refreshing after eating junk food for the past thirty hours. Liar. For the past thirty years. The elevated stage gets lit by an LED projector lamp so big it was probably used as a device to call Batman and Robin when people of Gotham were in trouble. A couple of greasy-haired musicians are sitting on the stage smoking while drums, guitars, and other kinky-looking instruments are spread around them like Ebola virus in Africa. A woman is placed in the middle of the stage, perhaps for decoration purposes only. No touching, please. She's wearing a mask like the rest of us, only hers looks painted on. Her tapa skirt is green grass, which makes me want to mow her, and her brassiere is made out of two coconut shells. All I can think of is: how do you wash a coconut bra? Can you tumble dry it? One thing is learned though during this trip is that in Hawaii women's bras are bizarre.

"Aloha, guests," she says in a portable microphone that's fixed on her face. Her voice is multiplied in the speakers, which creates a slight echo.

Everyone turns toward the stage, giving her full undivided attention. I'm pretty sure you can hand wash a coconut bra. Does she have underwear shaped as a pineapple, I wonder? And most importantly, is it edible?

"My name is Nalu. I'll be your MC this evening. Thank you for coming to Ke Iki Beach to attend our weekly hula party. I promise we'll have a fantastic time tonight. We have presents, drink tickets, entertainment, and a lot of dancing until we drop. The theme this evening is Masquerade Ball, and I think you did a marvelous job dressing up for the occasion. It's a mystery when it comes to how masquerade started, so let me tell you *my* version of the story in the following hula dance. First, I need a male volunteer from the audience to play Caesar. How about you, sir?"

She points with her entire hand toward a guy who's standing near the stage. I think one finger would do just fine. The guy turns his head three times to make sure Nalu means him. *Yes, dummy, she's pointing at you*, I want to tell him. Nalu claps her hands and the audience follows, creating applauding *cheer-him-on* sound. As for me, I'll clap when I see entertainment. The guy climbs up on the stage using the steps built-in to the left. Caesar, my ass. He looks more like a crooked version of Caesar salad in those tan cargo shorts and the Hawaiian-style shirt. I always imagined Caesar to be taller, dressed in an outfit with a cape, and carry a sword. Nalu keeps moving her hand in a "come-here" motion, as though if she stopped he'd turn around and walk back. When he stands right by her, Nalu picks up a cordless microphone from the floor, placing it before the guy's mouth. The floor must be as disgusting as it looks, containing perhaps three pounds of bacteria, and now it all transferred to the microphone. Damn, I wish I had some hand sanitizer after today's shenanigans.

"What's your name?" she says while her voice echoes as though trying to run away from her (for a good reason).

"Marcus," he says.

His voice is unmistakable. It's Marcus Truman.

During my beach trip I told him I'd be attending the party, but he's here of his own free will. Hey, it's a free country, after all. Or at least that's how we want it to be one day. My attention is caught instantly, and I eye him, noting that a masquerade mask and a new outfit makes him unrecognizable. Nalu is a hobbit to compare, maybe five feet two, maximum. Now my task is getting harder: How in the world will I find Adam if a mask makes such an immense difference?

"Okay, Marcus," Nalu says. "Stand right here." She motions him to stay on the left side of the stage. "Dear guests, I also need a second, a female volunteer to play Cleopatra."

If yesterday on the plane meeting Marcus was a pleasant surprise, this morning was a stupid coincidence, tonight it must be fate.

Without blinking once, I place my drink and the Gooseberry on the counter, dub Chloe's shot of whiskey, and raise both hands (to double the chance to be volunteered). I'm almost like Katniss Everdeen, though in a better outfit. If one thing I need more than finding a belly is to find someone to smooch. Plus, after all, Marcus came here to hang out with me or at least that's what I trick my mind into thinking.

"That was fast," Nalu says in the microphone, noticing me. "Come on up on stage."

She invites me on the stage, fingers on her hand opening up and closing into a fist. She's so annoying that if I were Katniss I'd shoot an arrow at that bitch. At the bar several crooked guys clap, creating a poor imitation of applause while Caisha whistles and that alone is enough to put me in the mood. I stand up and saunter toward the stage without tripping, for once. The projector lamp is nitid, true, but also a wonderful heater, giving me an idea to acquire one for winter. The whiskey heats up my throat to the mandatory three hundred and twenty-five degrees, almost ready to bake turkey. Mixed in my stomach with champagne and the Blue Hawaiian, the shot gives me a great buzz and a great desire to flirt. Want a tan? Get an LED lamp. Wanna be frisky? Dub some whiskey.

Nalu keeps motioning me forward until I stand one foot away from her.

Pointing the same dirty microphone near my mouth, she looks at me. "What's your name?"

"Calyssa."

Marcus' body shifts, and I'm 99.9 percent sure he recognizes my dress and my name. I wish I could see what expression is hidden underneath his mask: surprise or joy? Majority of people must be watching the stage, but the blinding lamp prevents me from seeing them.

"Calyssa, you stay right here on my left side. Now I want everyone to divide as well. Men to your left and women to the right. I want you to have a partner ahead of you."

The crowd, as though sheep grazing out in a field, moves in two different directions, and it takes about a minute for goats to go to one side and sheep to go to the other. Marcus waves his hand at me and I smile in return.

"Marcus," Nalu says, "repeat after Kainuku."

A man enters the stage (a hippy-looking fellow) while I suddenly remember that "Kainuku" was the pimp's name from Chloe's book. Kainuku's parents must have really hated their child for awarding him with such an outcast name.

"And you, Calyssa," she adds, "repeat after me. Everyone else, repeat after us while I chant this beautiful love story and dance this beautiful dance."

The musicians start playing a soft melody with percussions and a guitar. This sort of music is good for sleeping, I want to tell them, not for dancing. Nalu's hands and hips swing to the left and right, in hula dance motions. I repeat after her, realizing that dancing is barely my strong point, amongst the others.

Kainuku kneels down on the stage, followed by Marcus. Two dirty men, I think. Only Nalu's voice is heard at his point, music just barely decipherable.

"Caesar, the sovereign ruler of the Egyptian empire, sat on the throne, celebrating his victory," Nalu half-speaks, half-sings. "Cleopatra, the Queen of the Nile, lost her country and traveled on her royal ship, preparing to fight back."

Nalu places her arms up, flipping the palms outward like people do in the Egyptian hieroglyphs. I repeat after her crookedly. In such a position, she swings her body left and right, trying to balance on the imaginary sea waves.

"Cleopatra visited Caesar," she adds, moving toward Kainuku in a wiggly motion, and I move toward Marcus in a wiggly motion. She stops two feet away from Kainuku.

"But Cleopatra was unable to enter her own palace." Kainuki extends his arms while Nalu moves back where she stood before, in the same wiggly motion, putting her hands up the way you'd suspect she was caught by the police and heard the word *freeze*. Her hips sure can move in that grass skirt. I also realize that wiggling is barely my strong point as I repeat the steps after her. Nalu puts her arms down, placing her hands on her hips while moving her body in circles. I place my hands on my fat hips too, repeating the dance moves. Nalu does a little wave with her fingers while her hands go up and then down.

"Desperate and outrageous, rancor and bitter, Cleopatra put on her finest dress and asked her royal servants to roll her into a carpet."

Nalu twirls around two times. *Girl,* I want to tell her, *that's not how you get rolled into a carpet,* but it has to do for now. So I twirl. Maybe it's the heat from the lamp, or maybe it's the whiskey, but I almost lose my balance.

"Cleopatra is delivered as a present for Caesar; she's rolled out into his hands."

Nalu jumps toward Kainuku and twirls twice before she kneels down next to him, their eyes aimed at each other, their foreheads touching, their lips apart. Kainuku takes her hands into his, a cue for me to tumble "out of the carpet" straight into Marcus' hands. Momentarily, I get chills and my heart skips a beat but I'm not planning to chicken this time or pass out. I repeat the steps after Nalu, kneel next to Marcus, and have him take my hands into his. His eyes express joy, maybe some surprise too, and I wonder what Cleopatra felt when she was held by Caesar. Perhaps, Caesar had a better body. And warmer hands. He clutches me strongly, however, unwilling to let me go. True, even if he came all the way to Ke Iki *only* to see me, he hadn't planned on dancing with me on stage, now had he? I certainly didn't.

Nalu looks at Kainuku straight in the eye for about fifteen seconds and I look at Marcus. By now the music is hardly heard or maybe it's just me as I only hear my own heartbeat, part being stage-frightened, part excited, fully constipated.

"Cleopatra said, 'Oh, Mighty Caesar, kill me now or return my Empire back to me.' To which Caesar replied, 'It certainly takes some courage, Queen of the Nile. Your valor helps you achieve your goals.' He offered her wine from his chalice, a gesture of respect. They locked in a kiss."

Oh, no, she did! From the corner of my eye, I watch as she presses her lips against Kainuku's. Moving my lips forward, I give Marcus such a smooch, I'm sure the suction is heard all the way back at Waikiki Beach. Nalu turns around and places herself completely in Kainuku's hands, letting him spoon her. I follow.

"They embraced all night. And the night after that. It was only the matter of time before they became lovers and the Egypt was saved . . . But the war was way from being over, for alas, they got separated."

Nalu rises and positions herself in the middle of the stage. She moves her arms left and right in relaxed, slow motions, like she's pushing something aside. I repeat after her, pretending I'm pushing aside salesmen at the mall. Then I push Babette off a cliff. It's really a fun dance!

The music gets faster.

"Caesar was murdered; fear was brought." Nalu raps and the musicians rap with her, creating a choir effect. "The Romans wanted freedom; they wanted Cleo dead."

The percussions get louder; the beat gets faster. I can sense danger in that rhythm. Maybe it's the drink, but I think I must've become more attractive; otherwise, why would Marcus keep smiling at me? Kainuku lies flat down on the dirty stage, and Marcus follows. Nalu raises her hands, all fingers out and bent as though she's impersonating Frankenstein.

"The Queen of the Nile was locked in a cage by the Romans to be carried around the continent as entertainment and proof that freedom had arrived."

Ah, it wasn't Frankenstein, it was the cage she was holding. Then, as though voguing, Nalu flattens her hands, then with palms facing outwards she extends her hands to the left and right, front and back. She's touching the walls of Cleopatra's cage. Nalu sits down on the floor in a lotus position while I look at her, thinking, *Of course she sits on the dirty floor since she has pineapple underwear.*

I repeat after that slattern anyway. Nalu moves her hands the way traffic control policemen do, in all directions, touching the walls of the invisible cage.

The music slows down.

"This meant more than shame," she says slower. "This meant worse than death." She pauses and lets the music play. "On August 12, 30 B.C., an asp was brought to Cleopatra in a basket of figs by her loyal servants, by the people who still loved her, by the Egyptians."

As though putting a mink stole around her neck, Nalu crisscrosses her hands around collarbone. Kainuku soars up and makes his hand move crazily in all directions. Maybe he's imitating an asp, but unlikely believable, so you know. Marcus repeats after him, also crookedly.

"It was believed," Nalu says, hanging her head low, "such a death by an asp would bring her immortality."

Kainuku's asp moves toward Nalu and touches her neck. Nalu lifts her head, looks at Kainuku, and swing her head in circles. Marcus stands startled for a second, but then moves closer to me and touches my neck with his crooked asp. The touch gives me goose bumps, for I'm instantly all goosey and bumpy.

"The asp bit her; the venom slew her." Nalu places herself on the floor, head resting on her left hand, with the right hand next to her heart. Oh, shoot, I think, following her and feeling all the bacteria crawling on me. Like a dead carcass, Nalu remains on the floor, and Kainuku lies on top of her. Marcus kneels down, and moves closer and closer, repeating the steps. My heart beats louder and louder. And then, the weight of his body touches mine. I may be a carcass, but I'm under Marcus! And that's without taking me out to dinner or having him buy me drinks. His eyes penetrate mine, and I wish I was penetrated in other spots as well. Damn that whiskey! I wish I could place my hand on his back and move him closer, but because I'm "dead" now he'll think I'm lazy in bed. Which is only partially true. The drums go a little louder: boom pa pa boom boom, boom pa pa boom boom. The musicians start humming, as though singing mourning hymn in a choir.

Kainuku lifts up Nalu while she, like a dead flower, keeps leaning to the side. He puts her down. Her hands meet above her head while Kainuku sits down on the floor and puts his palms together in a praying mantis position. He looks at Nalu as she moves her hips left and right, and her palms, joined together, go left and right, as though smoke going up to the sky.

"She died for Egypt to be remembered as the prettiest woman of her time. Cleopatra anchored to heaven; she reunited with Caesar."

Kainuku stands up and embraces Nalu from behind. He takes her arms in his. He brings them around her chest. Marcus presses his body against mine and I suddenly think: This is what romance is about. Two people so in love with each other they reunite in heaven. And they did so without exchanging messages online.

"And to this day—she is the one and the only—Queen of the Nile."

Nalu turns around to face Kainuku and puts her palms in front of him while he presses his palms against hers. I turn around to face Marcus to notice a spark in his eye. He ignited himself like a grill. It's totally fine if he grills *me*. His hands are now hot to the touch, the thermal effect of alcohol. His palm would probably fit two of mine. His fingers are long and beautiful, good for playing piano and for cleaning beer bottles.

"Rolling into the carpet was the start of a masquerade tradition. Cleopatra veiled herself to be someone else to achieve her goals. That's why masquerade symbolizes strength, happiness, and immortality; it's what we're celebrating tonight."

The music stops, but the musicians keep *ah-ahing* for extra ten seconds. When it's obvious the dance is over, the sheep and the goats start applauding, even whistling. Nalu and Kainuku turn to face the audience and bow, holding their hands together. Marcus and I follow their example, bowing here and there. The dance couldn't have lasted for more than five minutes, but for some reason it feels longer. Since I haven't used my bowing muscles in so long, I suddenly get a cramp in my neck amongst the other body parts, thinking I should have curtsied instead.

"Thank you, dear guests," Nalu says. "Now that you know how the masquerade tradition was born—at least according to me—let the party resume and I'll be back shortly with more hula dances, games, and prizes." If she's giving away coconut bras, I'm totally staying! "In the meantime, there are two-dollar shots at the bar for the next ten minutes."

Dance music restarts, making the stage shake like a Chihuahua would. If I were deaf, I'd think it was a nonstop earthquake trembling under my feet. Nalu approaches me and gives me a hug. From the corner of my eye, I notice that Kainuku and Marcus shake hands.

"You were wonderful," she half-screams, half-says, fully obnoxious. "Thanks for your help. Here, take these three drink tickets. And you also get a pass to the VIP lounge."

She gets the tickets out of her . . . um . . . coconut bra.

"No, thank you," I also half-scream, half-say. "I'm actually looking for someone. Do you by any chance know a guy named Adam Klutz?"

"Adam? Of course I know Adam. Who doesn't? He's kind of cute, but such a hot mess."

Cute, maybe; hot, no; mess, yes.

"Do you know where I can find him?"

"Probably at the VIP lounge, sloshed by now."

"Sounds like him. In that case, I may need that pass for the VIP lounge."

I snatch the pass and drink tickets from her hands before she manages to take them away.

"I have two friends with me. Can they also get VIP passes, please?"

"Sure." She hands me two extra passes out of her coconut bra. "The bungalows are located right behind you. House number one. And if I were you, I'd forget about Adam and focus more on Caesar."

Maybe Nalu is right. Maybe it's the whiskey. Maybe it's the dance. I'm drunk or infatuated all the same. Alcohol and love always go hand in hand. But drinking is not a choice, it's a lifestyle. I look at Caesar, his handsome smile. I wish to be with him for a while. In New York I may type and file, but tonight I'm Queen of the Nile.

Taisha, I presume, isn't the only one who likes to rhyme when she's happy.

FROM THE STAGE TO THE BUNGALOWS, ALL THE WAY, ARM IN ARM, Marcus and I walk, talking. Almost like the law of gravity, after dirty dancing —and that was some dirty dancing for sure—both dancers collide into a party of one, much like Marcus and I did. Chloe and Caisha follow behind but their voices are overpowered by the loud beach music.

Outside of bungalow one, people in masks smoke pot, a disgusting smell, if you ask me. Chloe bakes delicious pot brownies, but this is plain insulting. The moon reappeared.

The entrance is blocked by a guy big enough to weigh four hundred pounds, who collects $35 a pop before he lets a patron inside. Doing a quick calculation in my head, I realize I just won us a hundred and five dollars for the three VIP tickets, none of which has cash value, plus three drink tickets (ditto). The bouncer gets a hold of my pass and rips its right side off, stamping my upper hand with black ink stating VIP. I would've done a better job with a sharpie. I get offended he fails to ask for my ID—since he thinks I look over twenty-one—but I decide not to bitch too much.

Inside the bungalow, people in masks are gathered with drinks in their hands. I search for a heavy man named Adam, though several guys easily fit his description. On second inspection, none of the fatties are him, because one is bald, the second is black, and the third is five decades older than the man in question. DJ is spinning Hawaiian tunes. (It's hard to explain what Hawaiian tunes exactly mean, but you just know it when you hear it.) A section with a lit neon VIP sign is set up near the bar, where another bouncer guards the entrance like a watch dog.

After showing the bouncer our fancy stamps, we descend downstairs. The VIP lounge is indeed VIP-like, or so I presume (since I'm hardly a VIP lounge type girl). The music here is dance while a disco ball spins around, reflecting multicolored lights. I act very VIP-ey: chin up, shoulders back, chest forward. Even though instead of a martini I get another Blue Hawaiian, I still feel classy. A classic member of LEDS: Ladies' Elite Drinking Society. The bartender takes my drink ticket and I tip him a dollar.

The room is spacious. The dance floor is half full and on either side of it there is a bar. Several entryways lead to private booths (for smooching, I presume), seats made out of pleated straw, basically patio furniture employed for inside usage. Five crooked guys hang around here and there, but none with a belly. Adam will be here soon, so I'll just wait.

In a little alcove, in one of the corridors, I find an empty booth. I assemble myself on a free chair in front of a small octagon table, in a spot where I can watch the dance floor. Marcus sits next to me, taking my hand into his. At the bar he orders a beer, and I know for a fact sober he ain't seem. Chloe and Caisha sit across from us with a gin tonic and another bottled beer for Chloe. The lounge must be located underneath the building, closer to the opposite side of the world—Japan—with a great quantity of rich Japanese men roaming the perimeter. For some unidentified reason oriental men hit on me often, but I feel strange going out with guys who enjoy practicing Kung Fu past the age of eleven.

Everyone takes off their masks except for Chloe, who apparently fell in love with her pumpkin. My face is sweaty and most likely red.

"I love the VIP lounge," Caisha says. "I'll come back here next time."

"You're welcome," I say.

"I loved the hula dance too," Caisha adds. "The guy I danced with was skinny, but not that it matters. I had to lift him up instead of him lifting me. What a great story, too. Although, Chloe, why did you move to the side with the men?"

"What's the difference?" Chloe says.

"No difference. You were dancing with the girl though. Didn't you want to dance with a hot guy?"

"Everyone wore masks anyway. As though you could see if only chicks danced on your half, you know. Come on, Matilda, let's walk around and see what else they've got here." Chloe stands up and walks away.

"Did I offend her?" Caisha asks me. "Oh my God, I didn't mean to. I didn't know she was a . . . a . . ."

I shake my head. "She's been weird today. But she's not a . . . a . . . She loves men. The guy she likes never replied back to her and she's upset about that."

"I'll go talk to her." Caisha picks up her drink. "Who's Matilda?"

"Figure it out on your own."

Marcus and I are left alone now. "Well, here we are. Caesar and Cleopatra in a new millennium with drinks. Cheers," he says.

I lift up my drink to touch his beer bottle. At the same time, a guy in a black uniform stops by our booth and puts a tray full of food on our table. Before I could protest and tell him we didn't order any food, he says something indecipherable, but I'm too tired to ask him to repeat himself. He leaves just as fast as he appears. I look at the goodies on the tray: shrimp hors d'oeuvres, ham and pineapple canapés, mango salsa with tortilla chips. Free? Maybe those are the perks of the VIP lounge is what the waiter was trying to explain to me. Hunger manipulates my hands, making them take a chip and dip it into the salsa, then take one canapé, and one shrimp appetizer, shoving everything in my mouth all at once.

"Can I say something?" Marcus squeezes my hand. "I came to the party, hoping to hang out with you, Calyssa."

"Oh?" I say with my mouth full.

"You're very interesting and funny. I like that."

An old saying states that a man likes a woman who reminds him of his mother. I wonder which part of me reminds Marcus of Mrs. Truman: Is she also a fatass? Does she like apple martinis? Does she like drinking in general? Does she also heartily believe we'd survive with one kidney if we could implant a second liver in its place? Maybe she's a mess . . . and passes out when she drinks.

I shrug, unsure what to answer to that, except, "I like you, too."

"Can I take you out to dinner when we're back in New York?"

"Maybe. But I'm a hard fish to fry."

"I got a set of nice skillets. I'm a good cook."

Mentally I laugh, but I decide to skip opening my mouth due to its full capacity. Sarcastic guys turn me on, however, and I smile at Marcus to show him I appreciated the joke. I finally swallow the food and have my drink clean my palate, ready for the next bite of the shrimp.

Marcus leans forward for a kiss—definitely sober he ain't—closer and closer he aims. I'm just numb, sitting here like a statue, waiting for tourists to paw me with their playful hands. Unlike me, he fails to miss me or fall face up in my Blue Hawaiian, but as a good sniper his lips go after mine and shoot— our lips meet. He tastes like beer and his lips are soft. His hands are gentle as he caresses my arm. I usually kiss with my eyes closed, but in this case, I keep them open to be sure this is for real and not just another hallucination of mine. The kiss lasts for less than five seconds, stopped by both of us suddenly sitting apart like something awkward has happened. That's twice tonight and counting! Odd though, in front of the crowd we did it so shamelessly, and right now we're like two teenagers sitting apart after a kiss. Luckily, I have food on the table to occupy my mouth with (to prevent further kissing) and to also ensure that Chloe and Caisha don't feel obligated to stay at a safe distance so I can spend this time with Marcus. He lives in New York, so it's not like I'll never see him again. After the two of us spend the night together —I'm planning on it—he'll either think I'm cheap and won't want to see me again or he will realize he hasn't been a loyal peach anyway and ask me for a date. But I'm sure we'll continue our kissing session later once my cunning plan is completed.

While I watch the dance floor for Adam, Marcus leans in for another kiss and I back off. What if I miss Adam while kissing Marcus and then what?

"I have an idea," I say. "Let's take a picture of us." He watches me crookedly. "To lock this legendary night forever, Caesar?"

"Fine, Queen of the Nile. I'll always do as you say."

I get the phone out of the Gooseberry and sit so close to Marcus my thigh touches his. The good thing is my thighs are twice smaller than his. That's what I like about being in the company of bigger guys—you feel petite. Without trying to offend anyone, I must say soon I may end up looking like Caisha if I keep eating like a pig. Turning on the camera application, I put the phone as far in the distance as my arm allows, saying, "Cheese." His hand travels down my back, pausing shortly near the waist before it descends down my thigh, which he squeezes a couple of times in a manner that upstages my masseuse Mei Fun. And he did it without a hot stone. I lock a look of happiness on my face, left cheek next to his right cheek. From the alcohol, his cheek is flushed with warmth. In such a dumb pose, the phone adds a flash, which makes me squint involuntarily, and the phone clicks loudly, taking a picture. I look at the photo we took, realizing how horrible I look. Even the shimmer failed to help me look like a normal person, my eyes puffy thanks to the alcohol I've consumed. Dehydration left me with black circles while my greasy forehead resembles fingertips after eating cheese pizza. No, it's not full of red pepper flakes and oregano; my oily skin is acting up again. I could always photoshop the picture by adjusting exposure or by converting it to a black-and-white one, which will remove blemishes and any visible oil. The cracked screen fades out and completely shuts down on me.

As I put the dead phone inside my bag, I notice a belly crossing the room, a belly that belongs to a short man following it. Here's the trick I learned the hard way: no one is shorter or bellier than Adam, so it must be him, hidden under his masquerade mask. His shirt is imprinted with ugly flowers, with matching shorts, and a pair of sandals.

"Excuse me," I tell Marcus, standing up. "I need to go to the ladies' room. I'll be right back."

That's the best reason you could come up with, dummy? I think, but have no time to shame myself. This is it, the moment I was dreading and, ironically, waiting for at the same time. I spot Chloe by the bar, Caisha at the other end talking to a biggish guy. I grab Chloe's arm, pulling her aside. In the meantime, I watch the belly guy sit in a booth at the far end of the lounge. I shoot a look at Marcus whose attention is occupied by his phone. Good. I don't want his involvement because he could ruin everything. At the moment, he must be checking his mail, text messages, and social networks, perhaps searching for my social network profile by using my phone number. I'm going to kill two birds with one stone: I'll get my leverage on Adam and I'll be making out all night long with Marcus.

"What's wrong?" Chloe says.

"You see that guy over there?" I point. "I think it's Adam."

"You think or you're sure?"

"I think. You have the camera, right?"

"Yes."

I put my masquerade mask back on. "This is what we'll do: I'll come closer to him, casually, take off his mask, and if it's indeed Adam, I'll pretend to kiss him or I'll even try to take his shirt off. Take as many pictures as you can."

"What if it's not him?"

"I'll apologize and move on. People are drunk anyway, so nobody will care." Chloe gives me a look of disapproval. "Listen, he's a guy and having a woman climb on top of him is like Christmas for someone his size."

Without explaining anything further, empowered by the two Blue Hawaiians, I tootle toward the man and take off his mask. Adam. He looks startled. My brain blows a fuse because it happens too fast and too unexpectedly. Somewhere, unconsciously, I wished to find someone else, so I could just go back to chat with Marcus for the rest of the evening. Adam's eyes are like two Ping-Pong balls in search of a rocket. He's *beyond* wasted. Per-fect!

In my mask, he'll never recognize me and from the look of it, I doubt he'd even recognize his own wife Eve. From here, Marcus' table is behind us and out of sight, which brings me to the following conclusion: if he's out of sight for me, I should be out of sight for him.

"Hello, sexy," I say in a deep voice, and bite my tongue to never again repeat these two words together when Adam is concerned.

"Hello to you too, gorgeous ass," he says as he smacks his hands against my rump.

I force his head in the direction of the camera and lean his face against my breasts, my left hand pressing it to stay in place. As quickly as I can, I unbutton Adam's shirt with the other free hand. He escapes my hold and gets eye-leveled with me.

"Don't move or I'll leave," I say, trying to sound sexy, imitating Marilyn Monroe singing *Happy Birthday Mr. President*.

Arms still working on his shirt, I move his face toward the camera. On the photo, he should look satisfied, as though he's enjoying himself. He should be smiling so that he couldn't deny he had been raped (which essentially what this is). The flash of the camera overpowers the disco light, its clicking loud. The fatso doesn't seem to care.

Suddenly, gigolo Adam takes my head into his fleshy paws and forces a kiss on me, his lips against mine. I try to back off, but his hold is strong. He pushes me toward the bench, his tongue searching for mine in penetrating motions while I pointlessly try to scream. These pathetic sounds resemble pleas of a slaughtered cow. He flips me around so I'm on my back, with him on top of me, the entire two hundred and fifty pounds of fat. Now I can stop wondering why Eve is so skinny: Adam flattens her every time they have sex. I would say "make love," but from what I'm experiencing love it ain't.

With the elephant on top of me, I whine to notify Chloe she should intervene. Peripherally I see her and wave my arms in a way of asking for help. Instead, Chloe gives me the thumbs up. We're not hitchhiking, bitch!

My mouth is blocked by Adam's fleshy cheek, his tongue licking my face like a pup. He reeks of coconut rum. At this point, enough time has elapsed for Chloe to take several good pictures, and I'm thinking of how to escape from under the sumo wrestler. Adam kisses my neck by sucking it, which will doubtfully leave me without a hickey. What bothers me, he doesn't even know who I am. I could be anyone. I could be underage! I could have crabs and/or cold sore. I wish I had both to teach him a lesson.

Before I can escape the love scene unnoticed, I see Marcus watching the show from the other side of the bar. I instantly wonder what he must be thinking. He must be juggling conclusions like crazy. I need to explain everything to him now without lying, which is never easy to do.

"Hello, Eve!" I loudly say. Like a missile, Adam gets off me and turns around, searching for his wife. I crawl under the table and run into the darkness of the corridor where I'm unseen. Adam turns his head back but miscalculates and falls on the floor, knocking his drink off the table on himself. I hide behind the curtain and run for the hills toward Marcus.

"Is everything okay?" he says, taking me into his hands. My heart is pumping adrenalin and I feel as accomplished as I would after punching Babette in the jaw.

"That man was so drunk," I tell him and add in a speedy manner, "that he just grabbed me and started kissing me." I wipe my neck from Adam's drool and take a deep breath.

"I'm gonna punch that son of a bitch in the face."

"No need to, Rocky. See, he's drunk, and he doesn't know what he's doing."

"It doesn't matter, Calyssa. He's a jerk and he needs to learn his lesson." Marcus moves forward and I have to hold him in my hands to stop him. One thing I don't need tonight is a fight between him and my boss because that will go south fast.

"He thought I was his wife, see, because he called me Eve. That must be his wife's name. Let's don't make a scene. I'm having such a good time."

"I sensed he was drunk," Marcus says, getting calmer. "Your friend wasn't helping you at all. She was taking pictures. Did you see that?"

"She's a photographer, see? She likes to take pictures of random things." With all that "see, see" I sound like Chloe. My heart, however, keeps racing. I got my leverage *and* I got my man. From the corner of my eye, I notice how Adam sits on the bench, and as though after a dream wherein he was penetrated by four German Boogers, he seems confused.

Marcus gains a distrustful expression. It *might* have happened for real: A drunken guy jumps on a bypassing girl like a lion jumps on a bypassing deer. A real story stolen from the jungle is what this is. Plus, why do I defend myself as though I did something immoral? I guess I just liked the way Marcus kissed, that sexy beast.

"Let's just get out of here," I say. Might as well leave the crime scene unnoticed. I take Marcus' hand and lead him toward the exit, where I stop and wave to get Chloe's attention. Like a maestro at a concert, I move my finger indicating for her to find Caisha, moving my hand toward the exit to indicate we're leaving.

My face gets itchy and I scratch it as soon as I remove the mask. My forehead is sweaty like I just sprinted at ten miles per hour, jumped through a hula-hoop, and ate sixty hot dogs under one minute. A drunken man stumbles on me, making me drop the mask. Without an apology, he proceeds toward the bar. I purse my lips, but before I can pick it up, another guy accidentally kicks it while I watch it being passed around the dance floor as though a puck during ice hockey. Whatever. I no longer care anyway; we're out of here.

I notice how four guys surround Adam, and one of them slaps his face with a side of his palm. I assume the guys are the German Boogers who drink too much, the only friends who can tolerate such a heathen. Two of them lift up Adam, each holding one arm, and carry him in the direction of the stairs, slowly passing us. To escape being recognized, I turn my head around and whistle, pretending to search for Caisha.

"Calyssa," I hear Marcus say behind me. "What are you doing?"

Adam awakens. "Calyssa?"

I cover my face with palms, knowing perfectly well this is the end.

"Calyssa, is that you?" Adam says.

Shit! He isn't as drunk as I thought.

"What are you doing here?" he adds.

I turn around sheepishly and notice how Adam sways toward me, longed to give me a hug with his arms wide open. I take a step back, moving away, but he trips and falls on my chest, which flattens my titties. From the floor, I watch Marcus, hoping he rescues me. But, dread the luck. Adam's shirt is wet due to the drink he spilled earlier and it stinks of coconut rum and Coke.

"Come on, get up, buddy," one of the Boogers tells Adam with a strong German accent and pulls the elephant away from my chest (which I touch right away to make sure my breasts are still there). Thankfully, they are.

"I'm sorry, Miss," the same Booger says. "He's very drunk."

"No kidding?"

The Boogers pull Adam away toward the door, two on one side of him, two on the other. Adam loudly cusses, repeating my full name and my position in the company while the Boogers treat him like a child, agreeing with him as though he's hallucinating, which seems to pacify him. Marcus, in the meantime, shakes his head. His eyes no longer express confusion or anger, but they express something else.

"So you know him, Calyssa Pantaleo? Secretary at the shredding company," Marcus says, mocking Adam.

I say in my tongue twister manner, "Listen. I know it sounds strange to you, but let me explain. I might as well come clean. Okay, I *do* know him. Whatever he mumbled is true. He's my boss, Adam Klutz, and I came to Hawaii to get leverage on him."

"What leverage?"

"I'm here to get blackmail on him. Ha ha. This is funny, right?"

"What blackmail?"

"To keep my job. I needed to take pictures of him kissing another girl so I could blackmail him later to protect me from Mr. Grunt. I'll explain everything. Let's leave and go someplace quieter."

"You know what? This story is sketchy. First he's a complete stranger, now an employer. What's next? He's your husband you fell in love with over again? This is crazy. Whatever is going on between the two of you doesn't involve me. All I wanted was the truth. Though clearly you are doubtfully the one telling it."

He starts for the staircase and I follow after him like a tail would after a cat.

"Leave me alone," he says. "You're nuts."

"You're jumping to conclusions. Let me explain."

"Liar, liar, pants on fire."

That sentence takes me aback. I watch him, hurt and startled. True, I might have neglected to mention a couple of things, but I wasn't a liar. Was I? Maybe one little lie, but so what?

"Cheater, cheater," I yell after him before he could reach the first step, "pants on . . ." Damn it. "Doesn't rhyme, but it's okay." Great, now I fail to produce a decent rhyme to humiliate him. "You may be hot, but so is . . ." Marcus disappears, making it upstairs before I can finish my sentence. "So is Elizabeth. Yes, and she's a fish. So what if you left, you fancy architect? See if I care. And if you haven't noticed, you smart aleck you, I'm not wearing pants, so how can I be on fire? I'm wearing a freaking dress!"

A bypassing Japanese gentleman gives me a pitiful stare. An anguished woman yelling at the man who left her drunken ass. "What are you staring at?" I tell him. "Yeah, that's right, you skinny asshole. The show is over. He left me, so what? He doesn't deserve me and neither do you. You think you're smart, wearing that Asian mask of yours, but can you fix this phone?" Quickly I recover my phone from the Gooseberry, so he can see the crack on the screen. "No, you can't. Because you're also a cheater, a liar, and probably not even a man, so take off your glasses and pull that cord back in your ass."

The gentleman swiftly disappears while I shut up, finally realizing what I'm saying. I was dumped, and this is what dumping does to a girl. Dumping to a girl who can't even take a dump because she's constipated. Rejection is a strong feeling. To make it stop, you must take the anger out on someone else, and the gentleman was it.

Marcus found himself on the opposite side of cheating, and what he saw made him realize how Cynthia really felt. It was a superior two-second romance. Two seconds are enough for all romances to last anyhow. Stupid infatuation, I think. That's why drinking is tricky as you fall for a cute smile or for a beautiful dress while in reality you know nothing of that person, who can be a sociopath or worse, a teetotaler. You like him today and he's gone tomorrow while he'll crush your heart and stick you with the check (if he's crafty enough; Moshe being a good example).

Chloe reaches me and hands me back the camera. At least I have my leverage, something to prolong my work, to prove I'm unwilling to quit. With the anger circling through my body's pipes, revenge is the only way to pacify me. I'll send the blackmail photos to Adam tomorrow as an ultimatum. Since I'm unable to fly due to my ID traveling through the Hawaiian plumbing, Adam must protect me when I'm back at work, whenever that might be. To feel better, I divert my attention to food, and at our table I shove three tortilla chips full of mango salsa in my mouth, finish the drink, and return to the exit.

"Where's Caisha?" I ask Chloe.

"She's with a guy over there."

"Go and get 'er!" The mean command escapes Blabber by itself. I can't control him anymore. "We're out of here."

I push the on/off button on the camera. The screen lights up with a merry sound, opening a preview. I play the slideshow counting how many photos Chloe took. Ten. Instead of Adam and me kissing, however, there are two blurry dots not kissing. Diluted. Out of focus. My mouth automatically opens from disbelief: the camera contains not a single photo of Adam that looks acceptable enough for leverage. Adam is unrecognizable in the dark shots.

PLAN B IS TO FOLLOW ADAM AND THE BOOGERS WHILE THERE'S still time. Obviously Adam knows I'm here—or thinks he knows I'm here—so I'll lie I came to Hawaii to visit a friend. When he blacks out, I'll remove his clothes, snap a bunch of photos, and leave. He wouldn't want Mr. Grunt and the entire office to see his nudes. Anger suggests sending them anyway, to everyone, but I must be smarter than a fifth grader.

By pulling her arm, I unglue Caisha from a handsome guy she's chatting with near the bar, and in my "Peter Piper picked a peck of pickled peppers" manner (like I normally talk), I come clean. I also reveal my leverage plan and the fact that time's running out. If she's mad I interrupted her conversation, she says nothing.

Outside, I spot a drunken Adam and the Boogers immediately. The Germans carry him because Adam's unable to walk on his own. The same thing I do when Natalia drinks, but at least she's lightweight and she normally sleepwalks.

The guys round the corner toward the parking lot. Where would they be going at 9:00 P.M., a time when nothing is yet opened or is already closed? They arrange Adam on the back seat of a black BMW while I suddenly imagine the Germans to be Italians, and not the Boogers but the Sopranos. What if they plan to kill Adam by stripping him down and dumping him somewhere in the Pacific, reason why they let him drink freely? All they need is to tie a rock on Adam's foot and drop him off a pier, which to me sounds like a perfect crime because the body wouldn't be found for the longest time (if ever). Us following them will only make the matters worse, especially after they sense we're on their tail. In the end, four corpses will be discovered instead of one. I drop the claptrap idea when I remember that back at the VIP lounge one of the Boogers spoke German. (They're not Italian at least.) Even if they're mobsters, Germans don't frighten me with their sexy booger accents. To get scared, I must hear a rough twang and see a pistol and/or a cigar.

Their BMW is parked five rows ahead of us. We get in the Volvo as well and wait patiently, watching what they'll do next. Caisha mentions she's excited to snoop again as it reminds her of the way she was following her ex-boyfriend who ended up cheating on her with a Japanese tourist girl.

Chloe still hasn't said a word.

In the meantime, I clutch the door handle and notice how the stars punctured the silky black sky, scattered around a full moon. What I need, however, is Adam's full moon, taken by my camera for my blackmailing purposes. For his ass, I'll probably have to do a panorama shot to make it fit in.

"Let's follow them wherever they're going," I say quietly, as though the Boogers might hear me all the way in their BMW.

"Where are they going?" Caisha whispers and puts on lip-gloss. It's dark in the car and her eyes sparkle, reflecting the light from the moon.

I shrug. "It'll be a surprise."

The BMW exits the lot. Caisha turns the keys in the ignition, but the Volvo won't start. The car rumbles in a peculiar manner. It reminds me of when someone who needs to sneeze but can't. Three tries, followed by nothingness. You just want to smack the vehicle in the head and say, "Come on, sneeze already!" Caisha plays with the ignition, her keychain jiggling the extra keys she's hooked together with the car's.

"That's funny," Caisha says, trying to start the motor while I'm as damn sure there's nothing funny about that. If we lose the Boogers from sight then that's the end of it, brother. "It happens sometimes. We just need to give her a little push. Come out, keep the door open, and get her rolling. When you hear her roar, jump in."

"Oh, great."

We both exit (me with an exaggerated sigh, Caisha with an embarrassed smile) and start pushing. The parking lot is hilly, and so far we are going downhill. Caisha helps me push the car for thirty seconds and jumps behind the steering wheel while I keep pushing until I hear the motor sneeze, fart, and start. I jump in and close the door behind me, clutching the handle for my own safety.

"Come on, baby," Caisha tells the car and presses on the accelerator, "we need to behave tonight." She switches gears in such a weird way, I fly forward and almost hit the windshield, but my "seatbelt" (my arm holding the door handle) saves me.

The Boogers carefully exit the parking lot with music blasting from their car like they're four pimps. We follow them religiously. Caisha's buggy is loud and exhausted, ready to be retired into an impound lot forever. I bet if I were the Boogers, I'd most likely suspect a tail after hearing suspicious farts coming from the rear of the Volvo. Our headlights appear to be turned off.

"Do you want to kill us?" I say.

"What?"

"The headlights are off."

"Oh, that."

"Don't tell me they're broken too. Listen, Caisha, if there's anything else is broken in this car, maybe it's best we call a cab."

"They work. The guys will know we're following them if the lights are on. Wait until we come out of the parking lot. Ever watched any cop shows? That's what they do."

If she drives this way—illegally—we'll meet those cops in person. However, when we turn toward a dirt road, she flips on the lights. The BMW is all but gone.

"Let's hurry," I say.

Caisha speeds up until BMW's taillights are visible in the distance. I sigh, relieved, because for a second I thought we lost them in this darkness. As we get closer, I notice a passed-out Adam showing his head through the back window, and I swear their car is unbalanced with all the weight now concentrated in the rear.

The Boogers turn right at the next intersection and Caisha, without losing them from sight, does the same. The road we take is split into two lanes: one is designated for us while the other for traffic on the opposite side. The Boogers speed up, and we catch up with them a minute later. Our motor grumbles to indicate it's ready to fall off while my fat cheeks jiggle when we go over dips. By all means, I like to drive in a sloppy jalopy resembling a Flintstone's car, so don't take me wrong. Okay, I exaggerate. Flintstone's car was much better.

A van bypasses us on the opposite side of the road with a swishing sound. I catch a sight of our speedometer: fifteen miles per hour. The surroundings are pitch-black, and somehow the atmosphere in the car feels intimate, for I get slightly aroused. I wish there was a man to kiss.

If it weren't for the headlights, we'd probably get lost. The celestial objects aren't bright enough. More cars bypass on the opposite side and each car seems closer and closer, as though about to smash into us. I clutch the door handle harder.

In ten minutes of driving in fear, we finally enter the highway, headed downtown, proved by a road sign that says: "DOWNTOWN." I hope my mop remained my natural color without turning gray, and after trying to catch my reflection in the mirror while jumping up and down, I learn it's still black (but it does look like a mop).

The Boogers, as though on a German autobahn, speed up, making a wonderful example of don'ts of the road. In their defense, the highway traffic is light, with only five crooked cars visible, distanced by good half a mile from one another. For the most parts, all lanes are ours to use and Caisha, the designated driver, speeds up, making sure to utilize all lanes for her pleasure, perhaps longed to get arrested.

"I had a drink with the lawyer," she says. "I already had a DUI once. Let's not blow it tonight."

Giving her a dirty look, I don't appreciate her choice of words. Don't blow *what* tonight: the situation, the Breathalyzer, both? It's good she confessed about having a drink, which at least explains why she drives so carelessly. True, I don't even have a driver's license, but I'm positive zigzagging is hardly a proper way to navigate a car.

After I check my "seatbelt" once again for assurance my fingers are still locked in place, I grab the underneath of my seat with my left hand for extra support. Like that's going to help me survive if a truck runs into us.

"I'm lightweight," she adds, "so one drink is more than enough."

Lightweight? I love delusional women; we are a dying breed.

It only takes five minutes for the Boogers to speed out of sight, and that's with an empty road ahead. Caisha presses the accelerator but her hag is all washed up, with the speedometer staying at a constant thirty-mile mark.

"Do you see them?" I say.

"No, they must be way ahead of us."

"Well, could you speed her up a bit more?"

"I'll see what I can do."

And I see what she can do. We make thirty-one, thirty-two, thirty-two still, down to thirty, and then up to thirty-five, our highest roaring point. It's hardly a racing car, I get it, but thirty-five can't possibly be the car's limit. We move so slowly, a man with a baby in a stroller passes us by, doing—what it seems like—his evening jog.

"We're not going to find them at this speed," I say.

"What do you want me to do?"

"Push, girl, push is what I want you to do."

"I *am* pushing. But it's not a rocket, you know. She'll get mad at us if we push her too far."

I roll my eyes, wondering what kind of a person considers her car a person who can get mad. Police sirens are vaguely heard and I learn they're coming from the opposite side of the highway. Looking for an explanation, I spot a bunch of cars smashed into one another in a pileup, courtesy of drinking-and-driving, I presume. Our side of the highway is empty, on the other hand. Buses, trucks, and minivans bypass us in adjacent lanes while our motor is not only suspiciously noisy, but I think Caisha was right when she said the hag might get mad. The Volvo throws expletives at me like a stevedore. The car then shakes, making me jump on my seat.

Ever hopeful, I keep searching for any signs of the BMW, but in about three minutes of the wild goose chase, I think we finally lose the Boogers when there's a guy on a bicycle speeds up ahead and disappears from sight. I guess I learned it the hard way that the Boogers really know how to drive. I also learned it the hard way that the guy on the bicycle is actually really cute.

New plan: because I'm most positive we'll fail to catch up, I need to guess where Adam would go on his last night out. I come up with at least five places, but all of them are bars. Also, I don't scratch the idea of them heading to some fancy restaurant since Adam has to sustain his image as the fattest man in Hawaii. Last, he is *addicted* to gambling.

Casino—I suddenly think—is where they're going! When we talked on the phone earlier this morning, he mentioned something about a casino. What a dope I've been for forgetting about it.

"Caisha, are there any casinos nearby?"

"Yes, why? Are you trying to tell me you want to gamble?"

"Don't be silly. Not me, Adam does. I was thinking since we'll never catch up with them we need to think ahead of where they might end up."

"Smart. I know of a casino located just minutes away."

"Perfect. Let's go there."

We take the next off-ramp, after which we turn left onto a busy street. Cars are parked along the berm and Caisha slows her hag while I'm on the lookout for a parked BMW. After three turns, we end up on another street, but no BMW is parked anywhere in sight. By now I'll recognize their car everywhere, having stared at it for the past thirty minutes driving behind it.

We enter, what appears to be, a mini mall with a movie theater, shops, restaurants, bars, and one drug store tucked at the very corner. Maybe that's the order of life: you watch a movie, shop, eat, drink, and visit a drug store looking for a frozen dinner to curb that drunk, 3:00 A.M. appetite. Don't ask how I know.

The parking lot is busy, and Caisha maneuvers around cars from one row to the next while I devote my attention to the task at hand: searching for Adam, the four German Boogers, or the BMW, whichever appears first.

Disconnected from the mini mall buildings, the casino, called Anakoni's, is set up on its own, one block farther. There's an oversized sign on top of the entrance: a neon $100 chip; no BMW seen in the casino's parking lot.

The night crowd consists of younger people, dressed in standard Hawaiian outfits: skirts, shorts, and sandals. Several girls in dresses like mine and fancy boys in suits cross the parking lot ahead of us, so we wait patiently until they're out of sight. We circle around the mini mall twice, but the Boogers have vanished from the face of the Earth. Being alive still beats the idea of being drowned somewhere in the Pacific, but I'm hardly pacified, I'm angered.

If tonight ends without that leverage on Adam, for which I traveled all the way to Hawaii, tomorrow I'm as good as drowned in the Pacific anyway.

Caisha gives the parking lot a few more circles and exits to an adjacent street; no BMW there either. The Boogers took Adam someplace else. I could take a wild guess, but my brain is drained. The cute bicycle guy came here to gamble; his bicycle chained to a street lamp as proof. What a cool bike, too. When Caisha offers me a closed-mouth smile as means to say, "They're not here," I realize this is the reality.

Cleopatra was Queen of the Nile, the prettiest, smartest, richest woman of her time. But my stubbornness to give up, my unwillingness to break, my relentless to stop make me a perfect candidate to be named Queen of Denial. Until the very end, I denied a possibility all could go to hell. And it did. There's nothing more to deny at this point. I'm so ashamed of myself I want to cry. I'm sober, without leverage, without my ID. I traveled all the way to Hawaii—ruining everything else in the process—and all for nothing.

CHAPTER TEN

Stripped

Caisha pulls into a parking lot across from the casino while I sit and stare out the window, fishing out a plan. In casinos smoking is allowed, drinking is encouraged, and gambling is mandatory. Why people are so eager to toss away their money so easily? Simple: the rash. Natalia explained to me how gambling recharges her adrenaline levels. A meek thought of hitting the jackpot is worth the nerves. Several hoary ladies enter the casino, followed by an octogenarian gentleman smoking a cigar, his suit completely white as though he's about to get married. As a virgin. A guy by the entrance is talking on the phone, gesturing maniacally with his free hand. I get my phone out of the bag to call Adam, but my phone is dead, and, of course, I don't know his cell phone number by heart if I were to borrow Caisha's to call him.

The building adjacent to the casino appears to be a club with a blue neon sign XOXO above the door. The sign occasionally blinks, but not in any particular timed manner you'd hope for. Letters fade and light up whenever they wish. The club was advertised on one of those aerial ads clipped behind a plane above Waikiki Beach: "A place where gentlemen can always relax." On the ad there was a lady with the biggest melons for her breasts, her lips sucking on a maraschino cherry with such joy and enthusiasm you'd suspect she just had two apple martinis right before the shoot. For free.

A casino and a strip club next door to each other are possibly heaven on earth for the gentlemen. Adam and the Boogers are excluded from being called gentlemen, as otherwise they'd come here.

Moving clockwise, red neon hearts encircle the XOXO sign. Each heart gets its own spotlight before the next heart steps in, putting the former in the dark, much like the stripper girls in the club who fight for attention. The hearts fade out completely, blink two times as a group, and repeat their circle dance, lighting up and turning off one by one. The sign sits there, as would a fat Joe, enjoying the view of the booty.

Resembling the woman on the plane ad, the girls who hang around outside of the strip club (1) look alike and (2) create a melon valley: double-D melons, triple-D melons, and even quadruple-D melons. All those melons make me hungry for a snack, so I dig a pouch of dried Turkish apricots out of the Gooseberry.

The name of the club is odd, I think, slowly chewing on the apricots. People rarely use XOXO in their everyday life, being it must be written or you'd sound like a moron trying to speak it aloud. However, I guess that's what girls do in such an environment, they X and O all night long (and repeat twice). This is the second time in twenty-four hours someone used it on me and I wonder who it was.

I fumble in my bag. Once I find Lindsay's note, I read it again. The last two words are: "XOXO, Lindsay."

I almost choke on an apricot from such a surprise.

She's a stripper; where else would she go? Why was I stupid enough not to think of this earlier? Lindsay saw the aerial ad from the hotel, stole Natalia's wallet, and came here to blend in with other double-D melons. If not for the money, for the environment. A strip club is familiar and non-threatening. She'll find a hookup there and spend the night with him, someplace where she can wait out until the three of us leave Honolulu.

Lindsay may even decide to stay on the island since she has no obligations to be anywhere else. The beauty of living life with no strings attached is that it matters the least where you start a new career, here in Hawaii or there in Omaha. She's got nothing: no job, no home, no boyfriend. She's got nothing but Ian's crabs, Natalia's wallet, and my desire to "find her, shave her crotch, and drown her in the Hudson." Suggested by Natalia, this is exactly what I'm planning to do to Lindsay once I find that red-wigged mess. Especially since I lost Adam, I have nowhere to be, so I can devote my time and the accumulated anger to ripping off her face and smacking her hair. I'm so nervous and excited I can't even think straight: ripping off her hair and smacking her face is what precisely I wanted to say.

"Caisha, your sisters must have told you about Lindsay who stole Natalia's wallet, right? I believe Lindsay is working at XOXO. I can just feel it."

"How can you tell?"

"She's a stripper and in front of us is a strip club. I'm going to go in there, find her, and show that Florida-born, Ebola-infected, STD-full brat a piece of my Jersey mind."

"Look at you! So spunky!"

"This is nothing. Wait until you hear a murder report in the news tomorrow morning. If you see a dead layabout anywhere within your vision vicinity, don't worry too much, it'll just be her."

Caisha laughs, foolishly thinking it was a joke. "You go find that wallet stealer."

"I'm on it."

"I'm sorry we didn't find Adam."

"I'm sorry too, but one drink at a time. I'll talk to him as soon as my phone is charged. Finding Lindsay will make me much happier."

Caisha gives me one of those apologetic looks that don't require any words, as plain as a spare tire on her belly: the one where her eyes stay relatively neutral, head tilted, lips sucked into her mouth. The look you give to a starving child begging for money while tightly holding your purse.

"Let God help you, Calyssa."

"God, at this point, can't help me; an apple martini, however, could. Anyway, go home. It's very late and you didn't sign up as our chauffeur. Thank you for your help."

"You're welcome. I had a blast. By the first way, Waikiki Beach Palace is nearby, just a ten-minute cab ride. By the second way: you're wild, dude."

She gives me a hug, smooching the air near my ear in her own version of XOXO while I give her mine by tapping her back and sighing deeply. Caisha —even though a terrible driver but a sweet, innocent person—evaluated me with absolute absurdity: dude, an improper term for a lady; wild, complete underestimation.

"Good luck," she adds. "I sincerely do hope you keep your job."

"Me too. Hope you figure out your love triangle with the Indian boys."

"I probably won't see you again."

"And I *will* see you in the morning at the front desk. One of you."

"Bitch," she says, smiling.

After exiting the Volvo, I open the back door and realize Chloe's asleep. The hollow echo answers back after I knock on the pumpkin as a means to wake her up. She mumbles something indecipherable while getting out. Her denim jumpsuit looks fairly inappropriate compared to the outfits the ladies and gentlemen are wearing as they enter the strip club, but it has to do for now.

In the meantime, I notice a thick slice of pizza in the window of a takeout pizza joint, where I plan to stop by for a snack before venturing to the club. Caisha drives off with her hag rambling, a bumper sticker on the back of the car saying: "Student Driving—Watch Out."

Shocker.

I watch her disappear from sight, take Chloe's hand, and guide us into the pizza parlor where I order a thick, juicy Hawaiian slice with pineapple cut into handsome chunks and ham looking real fresh. Chloe orders a slice of pepperoni pizza. We claim a table by the window and I assemble pepper flakes, Parmesan cheese, and garlic powder near me. Other than us, there is a funny-looking guy with a mustache sitting in the corner, slurping on Coke.

Chloe removes the pumpkin from her head. Her face is red and sweaty, being it sat inside the hot mask like pork ribs in the oven. She tosses the carved pumpkin into a trash can while the eighteen-year-old worker boys watch us in a peculiar way. Not to flatter myself, but maybe they find us beautiful. I'm afraid to look in my compact so I decide to take their word for it. One of them delivers our slices in two minutes while I sit and stare at the club entrance, wondering how to sneak inside without my ID, as sure as hell the bouncer asks for it from what I can see.

"What are we doing?" Chloe says, placing *Latent Tramplet* in front of her. The girl on the cover is a copy of the melon girls. The book read: " . . . not yet a tramp, but a tramplet."

"See that club over there?" I point, shamelessly shoving the Hawaiian slice all the way in my mouth, like a real lady. Pineapple and ham—what a great combination. "I think Lindsay might be working there."

"What makes you think so?"

"Snooper's instinct."

I keep watching the bouncer and the line of people trying to get in. Fairly attractive lads come in alone while a group of hookers dangle nearby, looking for clientele. The bouncer checks an ID, swipes it on his ID scanner, and then opens the door to let the patron inside. In lack of any other appropriate name, I call him

Sesame, since he opens the door to everyone. Hip-hop music is playing in the club and since I've never been to a strip club before I wonder if that's normal. What if I try to wheedle Sesame somehow to have him let me in without my ID? I realize it was a good idea until he turns down a couple of underage boys who look older than me. Great, even with a fake ID I would stand no chance against that beast.

I say, "That bouncer will never let me in without my ID. What should I do?"

"I have an idea from the book, but I doubt you're going to like it." Chloe opens *Latent Tramplet* and after flipping pages, she stops in one spot, mumbling something indecipherable as she reads.

"What's the idea?" I say, sifting more Parmesan cheese on my slice.

"Okay, there: 'Ouchita played sick and fell down on the ground in front of the club. The evil Praetorian kneeled down, wondering if the tramplet was alive. Ouchita pulled out a boomerang and said: *Gotcha, you bitch,* and threw the weapon in the air. The boomerang flew high up and returned, hitting the Praetorian on his booby head. He dropped unconscious on the pavement. Ouchita ran into the club. Toward her dream. After her man. *That's what you do,* Ouchita thought, squeezing the toothpaste into her mouth for fresher breath, *when you lose your passport.*'" Chloe closes the book. "Pretty clever, isn't it?"

"It won't work," I say and swallow the last bite.

"Why not?"

I roll my eyes. "I don't have a boomerang."

"We can make you one. The book teaches how."

"Chloe, focus. Even if I had a boomerang, with my luck, it wouldn't hit him, it'd hit me instead, and possibly not just once."

"Oh, I know. Maybe I could distract him and show him my breasts while you sneak in."

"Chloe, those girls in front of the club are enough for him. He doesn't seem to care."

Once outside, the humid, clean-smelling air helps resume the motor of my brain. After contemplating for a straight minute, my cerebrum produces a genius plan to loiter by the entrance and sneak in when Sesame turns away. Fiddle faddle. Nobody enters the club without his permission. I bet thirty pesos he used to work for a state prison because he looks as sly and suspicious as he's buff and unfriendly. Just a damn WWE wrestler. His uniform consists of a black suit with a white shirt, too formal for my taste.

I yawn while observing some stripper girls, stripper women, and older stripper ladies, all three generation of females hanging out shamelessly together, dressed in—under normal circumstances—inappropriate clothes.

Middle-aged hookerish lady, who's been smoking nearby, throws the cigarette and clicks her heels toward the entrance.

"I need to see house mom for the job. Is she here? I'm Destiny, love," she tells him. Her voice belongs to her mouth for sure, but its depth must belong to an eighty-year-old heroin addict who somehow stayed alive.

Her triple-D melons to Sesame, like water to me: nothing. Sesame examines her outfit, assembled with a mini (almost non-existent) denim skirt and a pink halter-top. Her skin is yellow from the cigarettes and her knees connect two sharpened pencils with red erasers at the bottom (the pink stiletto pumps). She's a copy of Lindsay, but twice the age, twice the swag, and diminished to such a fragile exterior as a contradictory proof not everyone gains weight when older. She's that woman who gets her shit done one way or another.

"Upstairs," Sesame says. "Ask for Cassidy."

He speaks with a rough Middle Eastern accent in a way real mobsters do, or at least what I could pick up from watching *Mob Wives*. He stamps Destiny's hand with a black XOXO mark and opens the door for her. Sesame dismissed asking for her ID, which brings me to a conclusion that strippers don't get carded regardless of their age.

That's interesting to know. All I need is to pretend I'm a dancer applying for a job.

I grab Chloe's hand, and explaining my plan on the way, I guide us around the corner where I take off my dress, instantly feeling like a cheap hooker. The good thing is I'm wearing the expensive panties or I'd look like a *tacky* cheap hooker. I shove the dress in my handbag and hand it to Chloe.

Without the dress on, goose bumps attack my skin, the hairs on my arms rising as though alarmed, ready to support me in the time of crisis. Human bodies are smart, protecting us with such reflexes as goose bumps, sneezing, coughing, accelerated heartbeat, and runny nose. Runny nose is obvious, it cleans out the bacteria, but goose bumps is an unnecessary condition with no other purpose but to make you realize how stupid you are for stripping on the street, especially if you lack a beach body.

I eye the entrance from around the corner, embarrassed, waiting until other patrons enter the club, and when the coast is clear, I start running in my undergarments and ballet flats, Chloe following behind. Up close, Sesame's nose seems broken, his previously black eye a shade of pastel purple, perhaps a given should you work as a security guard, a job where you deal with drunken people on daily basis. Drunk people equal trouble; hence, fights are inevitable.

Sesame is rugged, weathered, and bullshit-proof after years of experience dealing with all sorts of lying assholes trying to get in/get out of prison/club. Standing in such close proximity, I suddenly forget what the triple-D melon hooker named Destiny told him earlier, so I interpret it as such: "We need to see house mama. It's work related. We have an interview and whatnot, if you can't see by the way I look. I'm Chyna Fierce and this is my friend, Bambi. She doesn't have a last name, sugar."

Not quite triple-D melon talk but it has to do for now. I realize I forfeited the first rule of lying: be brief. I also realize I picked the worst two stripper names ever invented, making us sound like two drag queens, another given after an excessive marathon of *RuPaul's Drag Race,* reruns of which was back-to-back last week.

Sesame examines me, perhaps thinking that I couldn't for a century get a job here, even if I could make tacos with my vagina, especially not with a name like Chyna Fierce. Though never could I possibly be worse than the pencil-legged Destiny whose hand he stamped just a few minutes before.

"Interview?" Sesame says. "Since when they have interviews?"

"With a name like Chyna, do you think I know anything about . . . anything?" I purse my lips and blow in some air, trying to imitate Destiny. "I'm dumb as they come, honey. You can probably see through my head. See? No brains there."

I need to appear easy to talk to and stupid to resemble Lindsay. Lowering my face, I start curling my hair over my finger, after which I put the split ends in my mouth, batting my lashes from that sensual "stripper" angle.

"She's applying too?" He points at Chloe, who looks more like a lesbian farmer named Sarah-Belle McDonald than a stripper named Bambi.

"Yes, I am, jarhead," Chloe says in her defense. "You got a problem with that?"

I kick her and loudly clear my throat. After all, we need to get in, not the opposite. "She's usually the secret weapon, and she only comes out when the night is slow and the management decides to pull out the big guns. She's *that* good."

"Okay. You'll find Cassidy upstairs."

Without asking for any identification, Sesame, with a smear on his face, imprints me with a black XOXO above the previous VIP stamp, opening the door for me. Music wakes me up as I step into an antechamber and freeze, unsure of myself whether to proceed through the second set of doors. I wait for Chloe, who enters six seconds after, bumping into me from behind.

"Well, this was easy," I say sarcastically.

"I'm sure boomerang would be faster, though."

Trying not to look at anybody directly to avoid being mistaken for a stripper, I cover the top portion of my face with a palm and imagine being a customer, even though I'm half-naked (or half-dressed, depending on your optimistic/pessimistic personality). It happens in reality: a lesbian with her partner comes in for a bachelorette party, with one of them missing outerwear. Destiny found Cassidy, because she's nowhere in sight. I head toward the bar to get a drink.

Even though a strip club is a new environment to me, I realize I'd be stupid to misinterpret where I am; this is definitely not a freaking McDonald's. Rich and horny-looking lads are hanging around, most of them in suits and with vodka martinis in hands. Adam, in his flowery Hawaiian outfit, would never fit in.

Three melons pirouette on the stage, two sway on top of the bar, and one's walking around with Jell-O shots. They are in shape, pretty, and quite comfortable being braless. Lindsay is none of them.

As though in an imaginary grocery store, the melons belong into the same produce section with other girls whose breasts resemble small Idaho potatoes, sticky carrots, and even hanging bananas. On the stage, a brunette is flawlessly working a pole with confidence that comes after years of practice. When she finishes, her place is taken by an Asian girl, who jumps on the same pole with such gusto she probably has a pogo stick for her shoes. If all there was to it as to jump on a pogo stick or a trampoline—braless or otherwise—I'd apply for a job for sure. Holding Chloe's hand, I lead in the direction of the bar. So far, attention is brought only to the braless girls, yet guys manage to paw me as I pass by.

At the bar, I order a shot of Patrón. Unlike the bartenders at Ke Iki Beach, bartenders at XOXO wear tuxedos as though showing abs is inappropriate. Chloe orders a shot of whiskey and chomps down a piece of lime for a snack. Imagining the tart lime on my tongue, I make a face, down the shot, and pull out my debit card.

"Do you know a girl named Lindsay?" I ask the bartender. He looks so professional that if I were to fake a wedding I'd ask him to be my husband. But then again, why would I want to fake a wedding? While I counted pros and cons for a fake marriage, I missed his reply.

"What was that?" I ask.

"Describe her," he says, snatching the debit card from my hands with the same boldness I reserve before stepping into the New York City subway, ready to fight for a seat.

"She's twenty-five, my height, looks like a dirty hoe. If she's here, she probably applied for a job tonight."

"There are a bunch of girls applying for a job *every* night. Since this is the only strip club downtown, we're swamped with customers and always need girls. But I doubt you can find anybody here. The club is huge. There are two more areas—upstairs and downstairs—with a bar in each."

"Okay. Help me find Cassidy. She must know for sure."

"Check in the management office through the door behind you." He points his bony finger on a rusty metal door with "Do Not Enter" printed on it.

"Chloe, I'll be right back. I guess I'm going to have to find Cassidy. She must know every girl who applies for a job here. You sit here and watch the stage. If you see Lindsay, whistle."

With the Gooseberry in hands, I swim my way through the people toward the door, which is easier said than done. Why would you want to come to a club where you need lubrication in order to move around? Unless, of course, you have business to conclude with house mama. A fat, nasty man, in his late forties, grabs my butt before I reach the door, and I collect all of my patience not to smack him in his collarbone; though I should have seen it coming my way, being almost naked and all. He gets a hold of my arm unceremoniously. He must have spotted me the minute I walked in because his clutch seems carefully calculated. His two upper teeth, the only two left, pop out as he attains a smile. I pull my arm, but the fatso wouldn't budge while his free hand grabs my muffin top.

"Dance with daddy, gorgeous," he whispers in my ear. His voice is funky, so is his breath.

I try to free myself from daddy's grip. No dice. If pulling away fails, the next best way to deal with drunken men—I learned the hard way—is to tell them you'll be right back. They believe you, and in the meantime, you can leave without being followed.

"Daddy's name is Basil. What's yours, princess?"

"Cilantro. You're cute. I'll be right back."

"Where are you going, hotstuff? How much do you charge?"

"I need to change my panties: These are too clean. I charge $50."

He smacks my ass once more and blows a kiss in the air. "Woof. Hotness. Daddy will be waiting."

Basil eyes me the entire time while I maneuver around all the patrons. I look back once, winking. I open the door with my hip and enter a long, empty, narrow hallway lined with closed doors on either side of the wall. I stop in my tracks to deeply breath out. What I've just experienced unfortunately cannot be undone, and distorted images might haunt me for months to come. How could people be so clueless? "Woof? Hotness?" What is he thinking?

The music volume diminishes when the door shuts. As in any basement or city sewer system, pipes line the ceiling and hum of something electrical—perhaps a mechanical room—heard through an unmarked door to my left. Also, it beats me why the creeper thinks I have a fantasy to kiss my father, but being called "daddy" is such a turnoff. Though it's only fair: the club must have both, mama Cassidy and daddy Basil.

With the bag over my shoulder, I proceed forward, checking doors as I go. All locked. The hallway is lit by several plain light bulbs sticking down from the ceiling on long cords. The light bulbs can't be more than forty watts each, barely illuminating the corridor. Some flicker eerily, giving the space the same friendly atmosphere as would a mental asylum.

The hallway curves right and ends with a wooden staircase leading up. When I reach the first step, the chilliness and dampness of the hallway award me with goose bumps. I retrieve the dress from the Gooseberry and shrug into it, instantly feeling warmer and more expensive, upgrading my imaginary rate from $50 to $299 (plus tax). To be honest, sleeping for money never occurred to me until tonight. Is $50 undercharging? Is $299 overcharging?

Holding the balustrade, I move up while broken steps creak under me, bound to collapse during the next few sunsets. The wooden steps must be swept, mopped, and waxed, let alone fixed, sanded, and replaced by an elevator. The walls are painted bright yellow. Coats of paint peel off, revealing white plaster underneath. This part of the building hasn't been maintained well from what I can tell. Strong cigarette odor lingers in the air. Should I see the smoker in charge I'll cough passive-aggressively in their face, even if just to be a bitch, courtesy of my hostile mood. I'm ready for a fight. Finding Lindsay would be such a revelation.

Once upstairs, there's human chatter, laughter, and clinking of glasses ahead. With the newly-found enthusiasm, I skip toward the noises. The lighting upstairs is provided by several lamps screwed to the wall, Japanese paper lanterns pimped for lampshades with an occasional hole in each. The wooden floor is now hidden under a volcanic (ash-colored) carpet, with stains of red wine, smell of dog pee, and a bounce of a freshly-carved baseball bat. The stage at Ke Iki Beach was squeaky-clean comparing to this.

"Bob was here" is written on the half-white, half-yellow wall, as though "Bob wasn't here" would make much difference. Lindsay decided to spare details of her whereabouts on the wall, unlike Bob, who was a probable exhibitionist. Who isn't in a strip club, however? The good thing is I can even smell the perfume Lindsay—the dirty redheaded hoe—was wearing. It means she was here sometime tonight. The music from downstairs is absolutely unheard up here; all the dancers need peace and quiet to unwind, meditate, or read the newest issue of *Hooker Weekly*.

The voices lead me to a set of double doors and I peek through. The spacious room opens a view of braless ladies, who chat and giggle without paying me any attention. I immediately spot two redheads in a group of blondes, but after careful consideration, I realize Lindsay is neither one of them. Mirrors surround the room like in a funhouse, a barre positioned along the perimeter. Several carrots are stretching their legs on the barre, warming up before their dance on the poles downstairs. Several vanity chests are occupied by melons and Idaho potatoes, in front of which they're applying makeup. Even from the far, wide streaks of black eyeliner are discernible in their reflections, a trademark of XOXO, judging from this group and the group of girls working downstairs.

I ease my head out of the room. Behind me another corridor reveals several doors on either side of the wall. One door turns out to be a bathroom, and I quickly avail myself of the facilities before continuing my search. The bathroom is empty, but shockingly clean and generously stocked with toilet paper, paper towels, and soap.

I exit the bathroom and check the other three doors: one called "Inventory" is locked, so is the one called "Auditions" together with the third, called "Office." There could be a hidden entrance because the club looked longer and deeper from downstairs. That's where Cassidy keeps the dirty money the club earns, piled up in one-hundred-dollar bills, stored in safes full of diamonds, stocks, and guns.

The "Inventory" door opens. A handsome Latino fellow in a tuxedo emerges with a box full of liquor bottles, after which he hurriedly descends downstairs without noticing me at first. He allows one quick glimpse of his big brown eyes under the perfect brows. God is the judge of how much I'd like to be squeezed by him. God is also the judge of how much I'd like to put my hands on those keys to the "Inventory" door—the liquor heaven—riches far exceeding the value of gold and joy of Disney World roller coaster rides. I try the door just in case, but the bastard locked it.

At the end of the corridor one last door remains. Before I try it, I turn around, waiting for the fellow to return and kiss me after he realizes how beautiful I am, my confidence assisted by the shot of Patrón cruising through my veins. I strike an innocent pose, one where I pretend to resemble a lost tourist: eyes wide open, lips slightly pursed into an oval, head tilted while trying to read a map. Coincidentally, this is also a face for eavesdropping on scuttlebutts in our work's bathroom stall. How do you think I know all the news and stay in the loop? One time this "tourist face" snatched me a date when a New Yorker offered me directions to the M&M's World store on Times Square. I lied, of course, because I knew exactly where the store was located. The man, the prince, was the most attractive man I had ever met —in shape, model-like, clean-shaven—and he stole my heart with his handsome, polished look; he also stole my wallet, but I didn't realize that until he said he needed to be on his way and I was next in line with three pounds of candy.

Obviously, I learned my lesson not to trust skinny guys for directions when it comes to chocolate.

The Latino never returns. The only way to receive male attention tonight is to dance with Basil, but only after he lays himself on top of thick slices of mozzarella and tomato and pours a generous drizzle of balsamic vinegar on himself. Gosh, I'm hungry again, pizza being a prelude to my never-ending hunger.

The door in front of me is unmarked and is open a crack. I knock but hear no response. Once painted pink, the door now has a rough multicolored exterior, due to wear and tear, shoe marks, and partially because someone left ax marks on it. I knock again and slightly push the door to open, which cheerfully cheeps in response.

"Hello?" I say toward the dimmed room.

"Come in," a woman says.

I compose myself slightly and walk in. A woman of unidentified age sits at a desk ahead. She must be a sister of Medusa with her hair curly and spread out in all possible directions, much the same way as you'd expect a palm tree to appear. I step farther into the room, leaving the door ajar behind me. A desk lamp, shaped as a starfish, serves as the only source of light, leaving acidic glow on the woman's face.

"Are you applying for a job?" she asks sourly in an unmistakable British accent. If I were to ask her whether she's from London, she'd probably throw the starfish at me in an anger tantrum and tell me she's not British but Australian. Don't ask me how I know. "Auditions are over."

"Actually, I'm searching for a girl named Lindsay. Last seen, she wore a red wig, black stilettos, and denim shorts. She's twenty-five if a day, about my height, skinny."

"A dozens girls would match such a description, but none of them named Lindsay, love." Her voice is like a bottomless cavern: hollow and with an echo in its wake. The last person who called me "love" cheated on me with a curvy Latina chick. That explained the mystery behind why his apartment was always so clean.

Medusa studies me for ten seconds, head lowered, eyes patiently watching me. She stands up. Under her tight leather dress, she must be wearing a corset tied around her waist, a waist that can hardly be ten inches around. It's a miracle she can breathe. I also wonder if she likes to be tied up for her S&M fantasies as well.

"You're hired, though. Your body's perfect," she says, which makes me smile involuntarily. Maybe my muffin top is getting less visible now that I fasted for about an hour.

"Thank you."

"Yes, full figures are quite in season."

My smile fades just as fast. Medusas and mangoes are not in season then, I presume.

"What's your name, love? I'm Cassidy, house mom."

Ah, I think, house *mom*, not house *mama* (as I told Sesame). The latter sounds like a maid in a bathhouse for European immigrants.

"I'm Calyssa." *Love*, I silently add.

"I'll be gobsmacked." Cassidy reaches me gracefully, moving her body wavelike, as would an eel. "Brilliant name, love. I've never heard of such a name before."

"Thank you."

"Until earlier this evening, that is."

"What do you mean?"

"Another Calyssa applied for a job. Are you two related?"

That's impossible because my name is unique. Unless, of course, Lindsay stole my name and introduced herself as Calyssa. Medusa loops around me twice like I'm a diamond ring in Tiffany's window. Also, thinking that people are related because they have the same name sounds idiotic, because what kind of mom, besides Kim Kardashian with her North West baby, would name two sisters Calyssa?

"Calyssa is a sole name for a sole girl," she says. "Add makeup and eyeliner and you'll shine, love."

"Well, where's the Calyssa you were talking about?"

"She's changing. She's as gorgeous as you are, and I hired her on the spot. Sit down. Get comfortable."

She bossily points at a chair near her desk, so I oblige and get comfortable as told. She jumps back into her swivel chair. Up close, her eyes are the size of two big lemons, outlined with thick black eyeliner, and her lips are blood red, outlined with a lip pencil. The starfish lamp gives a gleam to her eye. Her skin looks elastic, as though transplanted from recycled water bottles.

"House fee is a scarce $100," Cassidy says. Not even a wrinkle on her face, just a pale complexion of fat-free sour cream. What the hell is wrong with this woman? "Plus 10 percent from lap dances. The rest is yours. Isn't it a scrummy deal? Our competitor, the King's Lounge on Kawaiahao Street, charges twice more. Their girls are thin and breastless and butt-ugly. What a cock-up place, love. You have quite a potential in my club." She touches my breasts and winks. "Just as I thought." Cassidy takes a sip from a whiskey glass, ice cubes tinkling against the walls.

"I'm just looking for that girl Lindsay and I'm out of here."

"Bollocks! You cannot skive off working tonight. You don't want to have a kerfuffle with Cassidy, love."

She makes a weird face expression: lemons pop out, brows angle, lips purse. What will she do, undress and chain me to a pole against my will? From under the table, she fishes out a bottle of liquor and fills up a shot glass. With two fingers, she pushes it forward. Diamond rings cover her hands. Her $100 house fee may seem scarce, but it goes a long way in providing her with the bling. At the end of the table, near a dead plant, Cassidy leaves my drink alone and picks up hers. The desk is piled with documents, binder clips, notebooks, paperback novels, and manila envelopes. As a professional secretary, I wish to smack her in the face for the mess.

"Drink," she orders. "Helps you relax."

"Fine." I take the shot glass in hand, quickly breath out, and empty it dry without grimacing. The liquor sails down smoothly while Cassidy's lemons return to their sockets, replaced by a satisfied face; she's used to ordering girls around, for sure. I place the shot glass next to the plant.

"I knew you'd love this. It's the expensive whiskey, not the piss we sell at the bar. Goes down your throat easily, doesn't it? Wait for the aftertaste."

My throat burns slightly, as though pepper was added to the alcohol. Taste of honey persists on my tongue.

"What is it?"

"It's imported from Scotland. All I care about is it tastes good and costs $500 per bottle. A Scottish girl introduced me to it. Gorgeous body. I fired her after she slept with a guest. Okay, back to business. Rule number one: No sleeping with customers. Make them admire you. Make them return for more. Make them treasure you."

"Cassidy, I'm not a stripper. I'm here for Lindsay."

"We'll see about that. And not a 'stripper,' love, but 'exotic performer.' Helps when you do your taxes. Take another shot."

Don't have to ask me twice, *love*. Cassidy pours more whiskey and I drink it immediately. Earlier chilliness is now replaced by heat. One more nip and I'll strip. Two more and I'm on the floor, working the poles shamelessly, with or without a pogo stick.

"Rule number two: No drinking with customers. You can have two drinks upstairs in the stretch room if you need to loosen up; that's why I call it rule number two: two drinks, maximum. Easy to remember."

Cassidy leans back and lights up a cigarette. She takes a drag, exhales, and flips the imaginary ash on the floor. No wonder she carpeted the club gray: to hide the cigarette ashes. Sneaky. I quickly browse around the room for paintings, inside each might be hidden a safe. No, Cassidy's smarter than that. The room—her office, for sure—is also carpeted, with several burn marks and one imprinted triangle resembling an iron being left for too long.

"Sorry, Calyssa, I'm so rude. Would you like a fag?" I shake my head in the negative and cough passive-aggressively just as I wanted, even though it makes me a bitch. "Okay then. Rule number three—"

A cell phone interrupts her, as it starts ringing somewhere on the desk. Hard to say where, since her desk is disorganized. Cassidy straightens and places the cigarette into an ashtray without extinguishing it. In an orderly manner she picks up manila envelopes, finds the phone, and examines the caller ID with a smile I reserve for a bite of a 4:00 A.M. cheeseburger from McDonald's.

"I ought to answer this, love. Our investor pulled out, and another one is interested. It shan't take long. Stay here."

Her face obtains a business look and she lifts up the smoky cigarette off the ashtray. Then, she lifts up the ringing phone and heads for the exit, her leather boots leaving nothing but silent steps in their wake. "Hello, love," she says and closes the door behind her.

What a bossy woman. I automatically follow her with my eyes to say a silent goodbye, wondering whether I'll find Lindsay before Cassidy returns. A clock, shaped like an octopus, is hung on the wall, something borrowed from *Sponge Bob Square Pants*, for sure. What a depressing office this is, compared to mine with its floor-to-ceiling windows and plethora of sunshine. Knowing —without any blackmail on Adam—that Mr. Grunt may fire me, I miss my cubicle already, mostly for our free bagel Tuesdays, my idea for which Babette will probably take credit.

A skinny pink suitcase rests in the corner, a flaming red wig on top. It must be Lindsay's. I fly up immediately, galloping toward the suitcase, knowing perfectly well Natalia's wallet is inside. Joy carries my body. I haven't experienced this much happiness since my first orgasm.

A teeny padlock keeps the suitcase secure. I land on the floor and wiggle the padlock forcefully, but the sucker won't budge. Turning the dial back and forth helps none. What three numbers did stupid Lindsay choose for the padlock combination without forgetting them? Above me, the octopus clock strikes twelve, its eight limbs turning clockwise with each strike, a fun to watch affair, even though creepy. Besides, is it midnight already? Maybe her suitcase will turn into a pumpkin and I'll carve it.

Carve it! A sharp object will carve the padlock out.

On Cassidy's desk I search for a knife, a pair of scissors, or a staple remover. Cassidy needs an assistant to stay organized, i.e., I'm disqualified for the job. Her laptop is unplugged, topped with correspondence, magazines, and an empty flask. Bottles of pills and vitamins are scattered under notepads and issues of *Vogue*. A Mason jar near the plant is full of pens, pencils, and paper clips. When the door squeaks, I hightail back to my chair and face the door, ready to greet Cassidy. Instead, in walks Lindsay.

Absolutely perplexed, she freezes, lips slowly separating for a jaw drop. Her attire consists of a black lace camisole top, denim booty shorts, and black stiletto pumps. Her black wig imitates my hair color, style, and length. In fact, she looks not dissimilar to the selfies I take, on which I manage to fake a thinner face.

"Calyssa? What are you doing here?"

"Chopping wood. What are *you* doing here, love?" I mimic Cassidy and stand up. "I thought you'd be in Omaha with all the money you stole, you little STD-full scumbag."

"What are you talking about? What money?"

"After you left, Natalia's wallet went missing. I'm sure you can guess who took it, love."

"Wait a minute. You think I took it?"

"Well, finally a smart reply."

"You have a drinking problem, Caly." Cheeks rosy, perhaps from the shame of being caught, she smashes the door to close and proceeds toward Cassidy's desk, her butt smiling at me from underneath the shorts. "You put the wallet on the couch and then Chloe sat on it with her ass. I laughed at how clumsy she was without noticing the wallet while sitting on it. When she stood up, the wallet was gone. Maybe her butt cheeks ate it. Seriously though, do I look like a thief?"

"Yes, you look like an example of how to properly dress as a thief. Prove you don't have her wallet."

"How can I prove I don't have something if I don't have it? You make no sense. Check my suitcase if you wish, but you won't find it there."

"What a tricky little bitch. You hid the wallet elsewhere and played me like a Barbie doll."

Lindsay lifts Cassidy's glass of whiskey. The starfish lamp flickers, the octopus' ticking heard in the quietness of the room.

"I didn't steal the damn wallet."

"You're lying. You stole the wallet and you stole my name. Don't look so surprised because Cassidy told me she hired someone named Calyssa and it wasn't me." Though, technically, it was me as well.

"I didn't *steal* your name, but used it because it's beautiful and because I like you, or at least *liked* you. Now you're freaking me out. My stage name is Chastity and I wasn't hired with that name at the other strip club. With Calyssa I got hired immediately. Call it dumb luck or a dumb coincidence."

"Or just dumb. *Oh, help me get to the airport. Oh, perhaps you could buy me a ticket and I'll pay you back. Oh, look at the lonely Benjamins in the Prada wallet. Oh, let me take the cash and flee.*"

"I see your problem." She puts the drink down and starts playing with her hair, a sneer of dominance on her face. "You distrust people. No wonder you're acting this way."

"Hogwash."

"You blame others for your own mistakes."

"That's absurd."

"Because blaming others is easier. You failed your job, you failed your friends, you failed yourself. Just admit it. Admit and accept the hot damned truth."

"What truth?"

"You tricked Natalia into coming to Hawaii, for one. You planned to blackmail your boss, two, it's why you came to Hawaii in the first place. Are you completely dissatisfied with the results?"

"None of your business."

"Whatever you have happening in your life is not my concern. If you want a suggestion: lying to yourself is step one to becoming delusional with your goals."

"No need for your hot advice."

"You still don't believe me, do you? Think about it for one damn second without jumping to your unreasonable conclusions. Why would I steal her wallet?"

"You're homeless. You need money."

"I make $500 a night. That's—what?—$6,000 per week? Which is about thirty grand a month. You think I need money?"

"Okay, let's not get carried away with your first grade math. Everybody needs money if you haven't noticed how the world works. Never mind. The cops will deal with you."

Lindsay interlocks her arms in front of her chest. "Fine. Then the cops will find the wallet under the cushions and I'll take the last laugh."

"You're embarrassed, I understand. Let me make a deal with you: You return the wallet and I'll be on my way."

"Calyssa, you're pushing limits here. I don't have the damn wallet."

"If you're telling the truth, why did you leave in the middle of the day without so much as to try talking to me first?"

"I called you. Pick up your phone once in a while."

"I didn't see your call, you little idiot. Why did you leave?"

"Because of Natalia!" Her voice trembles in fear. "She . . ."

My stomach squeezes uneasily. "She what?"

"You should have warned me about her."

"Warned about what?" I say impatiently.

"What the hell is she? Is she a man or is she a woman?"

That's a question I was unprepared to answer. Hands shaking slightly, Lindsay adds three fingers of whiskey to her glass. I ask some for myself with a nod toward the shot glass. We ease into our assigned chairs, me in mine, her in Cassidy's, and wet our whistles accordingly.

"Lindsay, she's not a man and not yet a woman. She's transgender. She was born as a man with all the works of a man and their emotional insecurities, but she's trying hard to be a woman."

"You should've warned me."

"Yes, great. *Lindsay, meet Natalia, who looks like a woman, but she has a dick. Are we still on for dinner?*"

"I mean you could've given me a hint."

"By what? Having you paw her crotch?"

"Calyssa! I saw her balls when she woke up. She peed standing up. You know how scary that looks when you come unprepared? I thought you were all freaks." Lindsay lowers the volume of her voice, her face a color of a White Russian. "Are you a tranny, too?"

"No! I'm at least 90 percent woman, born and raised."

"Gee."

"Listen. Natalia plans to cut off her penis, but apparently, from a psychological point of view, she's terrified. She's still one of the girls, you know."

"I'm sorry I left. I panicked. No wonder Natalia has enough foundation on her to build a skyscraper. She must've had a nose job done. Breasts, too. And I bet cheekbones as well. I should've guessed it all along, but I was creeped out."

"Why were you creeped out?"

"Just last Thursday I watched reruns of *The X-Files*, and there was this episode about a female serial killer. She was caught on camera in the morning exiting the building as a man, but nobody knew she was female until the very end. She dressed as a man, that's why. Creepy, right? Then, a day later, you bought me a ticket that costs a bunch and on Saturday there's a man dressed as a woman right in front of me. What would you do?"

This conversation took the turn toward unanticipated. "I would probably jump to conclusions."

"And that's exactly what I did. I thought the three of you were going to murder me."

"What makes you think we aren't?" Her eyes show fear and her muscles get tense. "I'm kidding."

I start laughing awkwardly, and Lindsay joins five seconds later. She then breathes out and stands up, though she looks unstable on her feet. She proceeds toward a vanity chest where makeup, mascara, lipsticks, headpieces, and wigs are haphazardly spread throughout, creating a mess mirroring Cassidy's desk. Lindsay settles on a stool in front, powder brush in hand, and after checking her reflection closer, with gentle strokes, she applies powder on her pale cheeks.

I study her. "So you want to tell me the entire time the wallet has been under the cushions?"

"Positive about that."

"Natalia—so I believe—left for Vegas because she thought she had no other options. I feel like a moron. She'll never speak to me again and I can't blame her."

"Natalia will be fine. Listen, up until now I thought you came here to murder me. There are so many exciting emotions running through my head now. Like, we could still be friends. I decided to stay in Honolulu and work for Cassidy. The clientele is great. But if you come here or I come there, here we come, there we come, everywhere we come, come." The last sentence she sings in tunes of *Old MacDonald Had a Farm*, but for what reason beats me. She starts laughing with her signature laugh: no sound. That's how, I suppose, I'll forever remember her.

"What about wanting to start over and quit exotic dancing? You feel disrespected as a stripper. Where did those feeling go?"

"Oh, please. With the money I earned today, I can stay at Caesars Palace for a week. So what if I have little respect? This is a brand-new me. I love myself."

The door squeaks and a man enters the room. Built as a wrestler, his face is dried up and swollen, thick mustache attached above his lips. The two of us suddenly shut up. The man's jaw is pushed all the way down to his collarbone because of a cigar as thick as my ankle in his mouth. In a brown suit with a rose in his upper pocket, he looks rich, sixty-seven years of smoking and hard labor of killing men for debt.

"Are you girls new?" he mumbles through his cigar in a voice that must belong to a pirate robbing a ship. "I've never seen you before. I'm the co-owner of the club, Wolfgang." He speaks with a Jersey accent. I would know; I lived there for two months once.

He puffs, releasing the smoke from his nose. There must be a gun affixed to his belt, and I know for sure he operates illegally when it comes to . . . everything. You mess up his coffee order: "Sir, but you did order a skim no-whip Grande latte." One look from this man and (1) you're fired; (2) you're dead; (3) both.

"Yes, we're new," Lindsay says cheerfully, getting up. "This is my first night at the club. I was just hired by Cassidy."

"Please to meet you."

"Nice to meet you, sir." Lindsay knows how to suck up to the right people. Suddenly, so energized.

They both take a step forward. His eyes are crossed and his pupils are pinpointed toward the schnozzle, a scar on his cheek the size of my palm. Wolfgang takes the cigar in his hands to shake off the ash.

"What about you?" he asks me. "You're also new?"

"I'm off today but, yes, I'm new."

"Nice progress. Cassidy finally hires girls who exercise," he tells Lindsay. "You look like you exercise."

"Yessir, most of the time."

"What about you?" He turns his head in my direction.

I just shake my head in the negative and shrug, wondering whether in a perfect world drinking is considered an exercise. "'I used to jog, but the ice cubes kept falling out of my glass,'" I say, quoting Mom's favorite rock singer, David Lee Roth. The scar on his cheek stretches out as he puts the cigar back in his mouth.

"I see." He turns to Lindsay, checking her out from top to bottom. "Yes, what's with all the skinny girls? I wanna see some booty, man. You know what I mean? Nice legs, toned arms. You have nice legs. Are you a runner?"

"Yes. I used to do track in high school and now I mostly do five to ten miles every other day."

"I can tell. You have runner's legs." He bends over to touch her calf. He's probably used to paw all the girls in the club; co-owner's perks.

"Thank you, sir."

"Don't call me sir, call me Wolf."

He inhales the smoke and it escapes through his nostrils. He removes the cigar and tries to laughs. Instead, deep-sounding coughs are heard. "Your legs are crooked at the calf."

"Crooked?"

"Yes. Put your legs together."

Uncertain, Lindsay follows the order while Wolfgang patiently watches.

"See over here? Your legs are supposed to touch at the ankle, at the calf, at the knee, and at the thigh, making three openings in total. Your legs only connect at the ankle and at the thigh, making a big round in between."

Lindsay studies her legs, turns toward the vanity chest mirror and stares at them from the distance. "There's nothing to be done about that. They naturally grew this way."

"Cancer starts growing naturally. Cigarettes start as a plant, but they kill you. Alcohol is mostly made out of wheat, which is food."

Now he speaks my language!

"Do you wear proper footwear when you run? Looking at your heel, I can tell you're a supinator and you need a support shoe. My friend operates a running store downtown on Nuuanu Avenue. You should see him before your legs go bandy. The store is called Running Store Downtown. Mention my name for a 25 percent discount."

"No, thank you. My shoes were bought at a running store. And my legs are not crooked because I run. They're crooked from birth."

"As you say, yet it's a small road from *crooked legs* to people start singing wheels on the bus go round and round. It was nice meeting you, girls, but I need to find Cassidy. She's elsewhere, I gather. See you at them poles."

Wolfgang leaves the room, closing the door behind him. The cigar smoke opts to stay in, however. I get up from the chair unsure what to say, my legs weak as they're driving my body under the influence. I hate people who give advice, even those whose knowledge seems legit. Let Lindsay run. Let her legs turn into a wheel. Who cares? Do dentists imagine fixing every crooked tooth they see? Or do hairdressers, on the way to work, want to cut that crooked mop? Possibly. Especially since all I cared about since walking into Cassidy's office was to clean up her desk.

Lindsay's emotionless face reflects in the vanity chest mirror, her eyes aimed at mine, asking for reassurance that what he said was untrue. Avoiding her, I study her body instead, and note her muscular legs: a bit crooked, yes, but not that bad. I'd hump her.

Suddenly, she jumps toward her suitcase like a horny dog on a bitch, unlocks the padlock, and unzips it. She starts throwing items from the vanity chest with abrupt, quick gestures inside.

"What are you doing?"

"Screw him! *Crooked legs.* Who does he think he is?"

"The co-owner of the club."

"That was a rhetorical question, Calyssa."

"You lost me."

"Rhetorical questions don't need answering."

"Then why did you ask?"

"It doesn't matter. I'm not staying here another minute."

When she clears the table, it creates a pile in the bag while Lindsay presses the suitcase with her butt and groans, trying to zip it.

"I'm off to New York to seek stability. I wanted respect, but clearly nobody will offer it up for grabs. I need a place to call home, where I can recoup after being humiliated. But you know what? I won't tolerate any more insults. Money is money, but first comes dignity."

"This is the same thought I was having, but about Cassidy's whiskey. Money is money, but whiskey is bought with money, so first comes the money."

"You know a crazy thing is I wish I were Chloe. She'd definitely tell him off. She may be chunky and childish, but not rude. If I meet her again, I'll apologize for the way I behaved. I'm all alone because nobody wants to date a stripper. I'll return to New York, start saving, rent an apartment, and get a legitimate job. I'm leaving straight for the airport."

Tears collect in Lindsay's eyes. Visible, real tears. Her fake confidence ran into the woods after the wolves and had been replaced with the truth she feared to admit. Covering her face with both palms, she sobs. I reach her and place a hand on her shoulder for some comfort, which she seems to appreciate.

"Well," I say, grabbing my bag, "I better go too, before Cassidy chains me to a pole downstairs and puts me to work. Besides, Chloe's waiting for me."

Lindsay nods, wiping her face with a Washington she retrieves from her bra.

"One last thing," I say, stopping by the door. "It's not because you're a stripper. Your self-esteem should come from within, not from a silly belief strippers are not thought of highly. You can be respected and honored selling water for profit or donate sperm, though impossible for you. Natalia did it to survive the first year in the states. Anyway, look at us. People will buy anything so long as it's labeled healthy or low fat. You're healthy and you're *definitely* low fat. Trust me, you'll do fine. Just lie once in a while. It won't make you less human. This is not how I wanted this to come out, but it has to do for now. You know, whiskey talk. And, by the way, for tax purposes, call yourself an exotic dancer."

"I got it, no worries. Thanks. Let's stay in touch?" She stands up from her suitcase to give me a hug.

"Sure. Take care of yourself." *And put some clothes on,* I silently add, picking up the Cute Mango dispenser from her suitcase on the way out.

CHLOE'S ASLEEP ON HER STOOL. FIVE SHOT GLASSES SURROUND her, along with lime peel and three uneaten maraschino cherries on a napkin. Papa Basil is occupied by a lap dance. I pay the tab and take Chloe's arm while men fluff me as though I'm a pillow at Bed Bath & Beyond. Chloe breaks from my grip and corkscrews forward. She swings her head in the rhythm with the music and I push her from behind. Chloe mumbles something indecipherable, perhaps talking cat. That's the theory I came up with: All the cat ladies learn to speak cat, so when they're home alone they have a companion to discuss the current affairs with. Same goes for the dog lovers. As for me, I'll soon be sucking in my cheeks and lick the bottle of Patrón from the inside.

Chloe overdrank, for sure, because her coordination and motor skills are now of a toddler, just ready to fall on her butt any second. She leans left, then right. I grab her denim onesie at the waist, but that helps none in terms navigating her.

Outside, there are no cabs near the club. Chloe breathes heavily, inhaling the chilly night air. Suddenly, she starts running. She swims through a line of guys toward the corner and I rush after her. She leans on all four like a dog, releasing any food and drink her stomach held hostage. In movies, characters in such situations normally ask: "Are you okay?" Which happens to be question number one on my "dumb list." Obviously, she's not okay. Instead, I sit on the edge of the sidewalk and tap her back. Chloe wipes her mouth with a hand, her face red. In the dark ocean she created, I spot pepperoni pieces she failed to chew, and I almost vomit myself.

"Did you find Lindsay?" Chloe asks, her voice croaky from dehydration. She reeks of lime and tequila, a smell I love, but only if it comes from my own mouth.

"Yes, but she isn't a thief."

"Huh?" She faces me, looking pretty much like a crumbled piece of paper.

"Let me tell you everything tomorrow."

"I knew it."

"Knew what?"

"You went to hustle yourself back there."

"What?"

"To get the money for our trip back."

"No!" I say, insulted. "*God*, no. Let's go back to the hotel and I'll explain my plan in the morning when you sober up."

She nods but opts to say nothing. I help her stand up while browsing around at the same time. There are yellow cars (presumably cabs) idle ahead of us, and we cross the street hand-in-hand. The street has odor strong enough to kill flu virus, so I breathe through my mouth.

"Smells like a dead cat," Chloe says.

"How distinctive of you."

"Do you guys have five bucks?" she asks a walking-by couple. They ignore.

"Chloe, what are you doing?" I whisper, tugging on her arm.

"I'm getting us money for the trip."

"By begging? Are you crazy?"

I pull her away from the couple, who just snigger and walk away. She breaks free from my hold. Without looking at me or speaking, Chloe crosses her arms in front of her chest to keep herself warm. The yellow cabs were a mirage (maybe I'm drunker than I thought) because up close they're regular cars. The source for the visual illusion is the light from the street lamps, reflected on them with a yellow tint. A bus stop behind us contains no other passengers. Moreover, which bus to take? Does the public transit still run this late or do we have to wait until six in the morning?

Chloe talks to every bypassing stranger, begging for money. I hurry to grab her arm to explain the money is under the cushions, but a bum blocks our path with a shopping cart full of black garbage bags. The bum looks ancient as though the original pharaoh from Cleopatra's era, or Cave's husband from our era. He's in charge of the dead cat smell Chloe was talking about earlier. He's dressed in several layers of clothing despite it's not that cold. A puppy runs across the street looking for the bathroom, and it finds it on the bum's leg.

"Excuse me," I say, trying to maneuver around him and the dog.

He moves his cart, preventing me from walking forward. "Hey, you bitch," he says. His voice is of someone who led a rough life. Maybe he was the one who caught Moby Dick. Maybe Moby bit off his, um, dick. "*I* beg here."

"Me, bitch?" I say, trying to make sure I heard him right. I breathe through my mouth. "Whatcha call that dog peeing on you?"

"It's Ralph. He's my dog so he can pee anywhere he wants. He's marking our territory. It's from Punchbowl to Cooke. Get out of my corner."

"What are we in Hookerville dividing corners?" Chloe says.

"You sluts must respect and learn the rules," he says. The remaining teeth are either stained or gone. The golden ones he probably pawned. "Either leave or I'll call the cops."

That totally wakes me up. Ralph, a German shepherd, moves his tail, sniffs ground, and reaches me. I lift my leg just in case.

"I beg where I want to," Chloe says. "It's a free country. Got it? Beat it. Forget it."

"You're disgraceful," he says. "Ralph, bite these assholes."

But Ralph sees a cat and starts chasing it.

"You know what's disgraceful?" Chloe says. "To carry your belongings with you in a shopping cart."

"Fine," he says. "I bet ten bucks I make more money than you in five minutes."

"Ignore him, Chloe," I tell her, grabbing her hand. "Let's go to the hotel."

"Yeah," he mocks me, "go to your swanky hotel, bitch."

Chloe dislodges her hand from mine, unbuttons the denim onesie, and before I know it, off goes her bra. Her pushes the suit down, stomps it with both feet, and leaves it on the pavement. There she stands, the way her mom birthed her, plus a thong. She swings her hips, and in par her breasts swing too. She's now Bambi, the stripper. The few muffins she stored in the middle of her belly don't look all that bad.

"Let's see who makes more money," she says, breathing hard.

I rush to cover her body with my arms but she breaks free. People who loiter nearby stop to watch the show like they've never seen a real stripper before—and they still haven't.

"Get dressed, whoretown," the bum says. "The world is horrible as is."

Chloe sings a tune and continues to shake her booty. The bum mumbles something under his nose, a flask now visible in hands. I decide to wait for Chloe to calm down; after all, how long can she dance like this in the cold?

Somewhere in the distance, vaguely, so vaguely, a police beacon visualizes. It's nearing. Closer. A black-and-white appears in sight and stops near a trash can. Out comes Empire, ready to save us from the bum. A breath of relief escapes my mouth. Empire is taller and handsomer than before, his guns protruding, his eyes piercing. His wife is so damn lucky. That shrew. I give a superior look to the bum, like, *now let's see who's got the cops on their side* and almost tap my chest, but decide to high-five myself instead. Someone must have called them when they saw the bum loitering nearby, begging for money in such a hop district, talking R-rated language to the pretty ladies.

"Well, hello again," I tell Empire in a flirty voice.

"What are you doing here?"

"Learning tips on how to be homeless."

"What?"

"Sorry, my humor. Hard to explain."

"Ma'am, you have to put on your clothes," Empire tells Chloe. "Or I'll have to arrest you."

That was unexpected. I chicken when word "arrested" is concerned. Arrested I don't want us to be, especially not tonight. The bum, however, gives me a superior look, like, *bitch, told you.* He taps his chest. Chloe ignores Empire and, instead, she twirks, twirls, almost makes a split, and shakes her body, performing a burlesque routine. During her robotic movements, where she slows down and her fingers stiffen, several people pull out their phones to film, which no doubt will end up on YouTube. While I get an idea.

"We're filming a movie here," I tell Empire. "I'm directing the picture."

Empire squints with disbelief, obviously for good reason. "A picture? Really?" His voice softens. "What's the name of the picture?"

"*Latent Tramplet*," I say without thinking, remembering one title that I'll never forget, mostly due to the boomerang. Empire looks at me in a peculiar way, perhaps thinking whether he can trust me.

"Do you have a permit to film?"

"Yes, of course. Now, get out of here. How can we work while you're interrupting?" That was wrong. What am I doing?

"May I see the permit? And where are the cameras?"

"Well, they're hidden. You see that one?" I point at a camera above us near the street light.

"Ma'am, this is a patrol camera to watch the traffic."

Chloe and the bum, in the meantime, get into some sort of a verbal argument, which ends up with Chloe spitting in his face. Empire and I turn around, mesmerized by what two complete strangers can be arguing about. It takes less than five seconds before the argument gets physical, when Chloe and the bum push each other. Gherkin appears in front of us and helps Empire separate Chloe and the bum: Gherkin holds the bum; Empire holds Chloe. I, for some reason, still have my leg up in the air, so I slowly put it down. The bum keeps using inappropriate (even for me) language while Chloe keeps dancing in front of him, topless in a thong.

"Ma'am, you have to put on your clothes. Now!" Empire repeats strictly. Rawr. Give it to me baby, rough and stern. "Public nudity is illegal. And," he says, pointing his finger at me as I was about to defend her, "not a pip out of you or you'll go to jail too."

I thought we were friends!

"Maybe you've got some money for me, Mr. Cop," Chloe says sensually. Batting her lashes, she spanks her ass and swings her hips left and right. When she positions her arms behind her neck, I get slightly aroused. "'Desperate and outrageous, rancor and bitter, Cleopatra put on her finest dress and asked her royal servants to roll her into a carpet.'"

Without any further instructions or warnings, Empire handcuffs Chloe, for she fails to follow his orders and/or common sense. I pick up her clothes from the ground, following the three of them toward the car.

The bum is left alone on his own. He'll never get arrested because without a proper gas mask, a wetsuit, and thick gloves, the mission is impossible since he smells like a dead cat.

Before we leave, I tell the bum: "Do me a favor and never take the New York City subway."

He ignores my comment, foolishly thinking I was joking. In the car, Chloe keeps reciting the Cleopatra story. Time is 1:30 A.M.

At a precinct, they take Chloe away without arresting me. I sit on a waiting bench pondering an upcoming turnaround: Will they let her go or what? We've never been arrested before, unless Chloe lied to me and had been. Sitting here at the cop station churns my stomach from fear. Or all the food I failed to consume. I'll never live in Hawaii. People are weird around here.

With my handbag on my lap, I do calf raises, a sign of how nervous I am. A calf raise is an exercise I learned after buying three personal training classes with Angus. That was his name. I finished two and a half classes with him and quit after I learned he was married. Waste of my money. "And those stretches you gave me mean nothing to you?" I wanted to shout while doing the elliptical, chewing on the protein bar he pimped me 30 percent off.

The perimeter of the precinct is the size of my bathroom; air stuffed, unlike my belly. The lighting is dimmed. This depressing picture makes me wonder what my taxes pay for. I retrieve a pouch of dried Turkish apricots from the Gooseberry and snack while studying the surroundings. The walls are painted mousy brown. Ahead, there's a barred window and a red door wherein Chloe was taken next to it. Behind the barred window, a heavyset lady-cop laughs, watching a movie or a TV series on a smartphone without paying me much attention.

Empire emerges from the red door and heads toward me. I'll never forgive him for failing to fulfill my fantasy, in which he handcuffs me and interrogates me in a small room until he learns my lips are sealed, so he just rips off his cop outfit and starts doing nasty things to me. The rest is just a Disney movie: we lived happily ever after. Of course, in my fantasy, the handcuffs are fuzzy and pink.

"Are we all good?" I say, standing up.

"All bad. We booked her."

"But she's not a plane!"

"She'll have to spend two nights in jail. That's what you get for public nudity."

"If I promise we leave Honolulu right away, could you pretend this never happened?"

He shakes his head. "You have the option to bail her out."

"How much?"

"Two grand." My pupils turn into dollar signs. He notices the dollar signs because he clears his throat. "I assure you this is a typical amount."

Before I can protest, I suddenly—almost immediately—realize Natalia mentioned she had had over $3,000 in her wallet, and the wallet is hidden under the cushions at the hotel, enough for the bail. Knowing Chloe's fragile interior, I presume she won't tolerate real criminals she's sharing the cage with. Of course, she'll pay back the amount owed, but that's out of my jurisdiction.

"I've got the money," I tell Empire and exit the precinct.

Five taxicabs idle near the police station. *That's* where they hang out. I quickly hail one, and the entire ride to the hotel I keep wondering whether Lindsay could have lied about the wallet just to throw me off her scent. Once I discovered her "office," Lindsay put on a show and escaped to Omaha, *if* her story about Omaha was real in the first place.

In the suite, I gallop toward the living room and swiftly pull out the cushions. I inspect the couch as carefully as I can. Lindsay lied. The wallet is not here.

CHAPTER ELEVEN

Choices

In the bathroom, splashing cold water on my eyes to wake up, I notice how my face a copy of the swooshed cat's: a mixture of hurt pride after being accused of robbing a bank, and a sad, miserable expression of being caught spending the stolen money. On useless items, like soda, bottled water, and other non-alcoholic beverages. Sleep-deprived and cranky, I watch the scary reflection in front of me, where a pair of swollen, dehydrated cheeks meets a pair of tired, puffy bags under my eyes. Looking like this, I must return to the precinct to learn my options when it comes to bailing out Chloe, with or without money. Under normal circumstances, I'd prefer to opt out of dealing with cops, but the circumstances are definitely abnormal.

Eureka! I'll introduce myself as a psychologist, telling the cops Ms. Tenderfoot is my abnormal client who suffers from a psychological undressing disorder, from a gene mutation on the sixteenth chromosome, a disease most celebrities suffer from. Nobody wants to be responsible for a mental breakdown, meaning the cops may free her.

I rummage through Chloe's tote bag until I find a Wonder Woman scarf. I tie it around my face and head to completely eliminate the upcoming hang-over look: pillow lines, puffy bumps, and narrow red eyes. In the scarf I'm Arabian, my dark eyes bigger and prettier. My body, however, resembles

Caisha's rattletrap, partially exhausted, partially falling apart. If there's any truth to how long human's intestines run, then there's truth to mine being filled to their full capacity: five feet of food, a legit explanation for heartburn, a strange sensation in my lower back, and unusual gassiness.

Before I leave the suite, I check on the pets. Anubis has found a cozy spot on the bed, curled up like a tiny black ball on the bleached Egyptians sheets. On the kitchen island, Elizabeth does a somersault upon seeing me, her mouth sucking on the bottle in what could only be a food-begging plea. Her tail fin flares up the way a peacock's would, and she starts performing a fish dance, tapping her way from one side of the bottle to the other. Her front fins open and close like a Flamenco fan. She sinks to the bottom and scavenges for food. She foolishly believes I show up and—bam—she gets fed. Not with me, Elizabeth. Tomorrow I'll make a quick stop at a pet store and buy fish pellets, but in the meantime, I don't worry about her. Starving is good, makes you appreciate food better. Homeless people eat rarely and they'll gladly consume a cow's tripe, medium-rare spoiled food, and drink anything that burns while rich spoiled vegetarians, say, would hardly touch a delicious slice of pepperoni pizza or a medium-rare steak. So before Elizabeth becomes a picky brat, I'll teach her to eat the first thing she sees. Who knows, maybe in a few months I'll have a drinking buddy too?

I turn off the lights and take the elevator downstairs. Moon moved halfway across the sky. The air is damp as it fills my lungs with rich saturation, along with the smell of the Pacific Ocean and grilled food. I spot the same Japanese cabbie who drove me from the precinct and flag him down. After I ask him to return to the police station, he gives me such a stare as though I asked him to get naked and make love to me, which I'd never do on an empty stomach. Even though my face is in disguise, he must recognize my dress and the Gooseberry, perhaps wondering what kind of business I'm trying to conclude going back and forth. The cabbie's mugshot with his name is posted behind Plexiglas. Junko Murakami. A gold earring sits in his ear, his eyes smart but tired.

When we start moving, I wonder where my life is taking me. I wanted to blackmail my boss. Two thousand years ago this would never happen, mostly because women were prohibited from working and, sadly, prohibited from drinking too. Knowing myself for thirty years, back then I'd run an under-ground moonshine cartel, if not so much for drinking but for a way to pay off the first couch, made out of sober-toothed tiger's fluffy skin. And yes, *sober*-toothed, so that we're clear who's the drunk one in this relationship.

Chloe's phone rings inside of my bag, dinging a merry chorus of *I Love*

Lucy for the ringtone (her favorite TV show). The phone number comes blocked, which is candy for a snooper like me. If there's one thing more exciting than fried chicken—almost a contradiction in itself—is a blocked number of an unknown origin. To answer, I stick the phone underneath the scarf next to my ear for hands-free conversation. I saw how other Arabian women do just that, without having to waste battery on Bluetooth.

"Hello."

"Chloe? Is that you? I haven't heard your voice in years."

"Yes?"

"This is Amanda Gellar. Oh, my God. I can't believe I'm speaking to you. Do you remember me? My mother was the math teacher; she's now retired and lives in Santa Monica, California. Stunning house."

"Um."

"I'm the blond girl who helped you with your math homework, and you helped me babysit my little sister Greta. My father was a doctor, Robert Gellar; he passed away a few years back."

"Oh."

"How great! Listen, your mom gave me your cell phone number. She said it was okay to call you. Dear, I was cleaning out the attic and found my high school box with my cheerleader uniform. I'm looking at the pictures now. We look unbelievable: so young, skinny, and stunning. Brandon looks exactly the same in his uniform, so strong and handsome. Who knew I'd marry my high school sweetheart? Chloe, I haven't talked to you in years, dear. How are you? Do you still live in the city?"

"Right."

"I know I've been out of touch, but with three tykes and a husband there's no time for social life. Tommy turns eight tomorrow and we're planning a big birthday party with some neighborhood kids. And we signed up Leila for kindergarten. She's such a pretty girl. Oh, and Craig is almost two. I can't believe Brandon agreed to take care of them for the entire week. We bought a big van and a DVD player. On the road kids usually watch movies, which is nice. They don't fight at least. How about you? Are you seeing anybody?"

Oh, Aunt Geez. I was unaware anybody was a worse chatterbox than Blabber, my mouth. The cabbie eavesdrops on the conversation, occasionally making eye contact through the rearview mirror. He's definitely smart. I presume the waves of his brain are trying to come up with new ways to drive a car, his thoughts reflected in the sleepy pupils.

"Sure," I say.

"Oh, that's great. Listen, the reason I'm calling is because I wanted to ask whether or not you're going to the high school reunion next week. I received the invitation and cried remembering our good ol' times."

"Well."

"Listen, dear, I'm definitely going this year. Brandon and I live in Rhode Island and I hardly ever get to enjoy the city anymore. Next week Brandon and the kids are going to visit their grandparents in upstate New York and I have a week—the whole week—to do whatever I wish. I've made a reservation at the Plaza until Thursday. Do you want to get together on Monday and have dinner? Then on Tuesday, you can be my date for the reunion. What do you say?"

That means whatever Chloe was afraid of is untrue. I become energized and pick up the phone in my hands.

"Yes, hot dammit, Mandy, I love you. I mean, thanks for the invite. I'll call you as soon as I'm in New York and we'll schedule something up. Text me your cell phone number and I'll text you back when I'm free. I'm kind of cuffed up at the moment."

"Cuffed up?"

"I mean tied up. Okay, later."

I hang up quickly, thinking of how much happiness it will bring Chloe once she finds out Amanda called, and not only she remembers her but is very excited to see her. All I have to do now is to make sure Chloe is jail-free or she'll never make it to the reunion on time. In the meantime, we pull out in front of the precinct, and I pay ten bucks for the ride.

Taking a deep breath, I step inside the building, where the same heavyset lady-cop sits behind the barred window straight ahead. Up close, the cop's lips are squished, as though locked in a kissing position. Her greasy forehead is a likely indication she's been working a long shift and, believe me, testing her to find out whether she's cranky or not is hardly in my plans. The room is otherwise empty, maybe even eerily too quiet.

The lady cop interrupts the movie on her phone to give me a death stare. Bored, she returns her eyes toward the phone screen. Meanwhile, I'm thinking of a clear way to express what happened, which is unclear even to me. I unwrap the scarf from my mouth just enough to talk and say, "Chloe Tenderfoot got arrested last night and I'm here to bail her out immediately."

"Two grand," she says without making eye contact.

"I know. But here's the thing: I'm Chloe's psychologist, see, and I'm afraid she'll have a mental breakdown. Her personality is unstable and she's sick with this rare African King Quads disease. It makes her scratch a lot, which is why she undressed. Then a homeless person started attacking us. It's all his fault, really. Can you please release her? I swear I'll keep her out of trouble."

"Two grand." She creates a peace sign with one hand, suggesting "two," while scratching her chipmunk cheek with the other.

"I don't have any money on me, but I definitely have enough money in stocks, bonds, and in my checking account. My father owns a hotel chain. I can hook you up if you need to stay the night. Mention my name when booking. The chain is called . . . *Hilstin*."

"No money? Go suck Donnie."

"Wait. I know how you feel. I'm tired too. I woke up at eight o'clock in the morning and the day just suddenly became so weird after a stripper stole my friend's wallet. I have an idea. How about I pay with a check? You accept checks, right?"

"Sure."

"Then, I'll write you a check. How silly of me not to think of it sooner." There's not enough money in my *Hilstin* checking account, but the cops won't know it—foolish chaps—until several days later when the check bounces. Chloe was arrested unfairly, so I'll play the same game. And if worst comes to worst, which it will, I'll avow the check was forgery. I'll even fake my signature.

The lady cop hands me a bailout form and a pen. I claim a bench and crookedly write down all the requested information, turning in the sheet together with a $2,000 check, signature falsified. Good thing I carry my checkbook in the Gooseberry. The lady cop studies the form with pursed lips for eleven seconds, distrust gleaming in her eye.

When she finally stands up, she walks toward a filing cabinet located at the far end. I see her clearly now: her hair is long and greasy like a bowl of lo mein noodles while her body resembles a glazy donut, and not just glazy but lazy. Although I want to tell her to hurry up, I decide to dry up in case she has a temperament of a bull. One thing I'm unprepared for this morning is to fight a tank, even though it sounds like fun. I also notice how long her feet run. She'll never need to rent skis when she goes to Aspen for the winter break. What a lucky woman, I think, saving all this money on ski equipment. Her boots must be size twenty-two and probably made to order. I now understand where the legend of Bigfoot comes from, and if only there was a cash prize for this creature I'd shoot her in nothing flat.

"How do you spell *Chloe*?" she yells from the far end of her office. How to spell it? Did she go to school or what? *Chloe* is spelled E-L-I-Z-A-B-E-T-H. "Should I look under a *k* or under a *c*?"

Under an "i" for an "idiot," I wish to yell out. She's either stupid or very good at pretending.

"C," I say and spell the whole name. "Last name *Tenderfoot*. See under a *t*." I spell that as well. If she wants me to remind her the order of the alphabet, I'll even sing her the alphabet song if needed. But she needs to hurry the hell up.

Bigfoot finds a manila folder and skis back. She hands me the application Chloe filled out last night after they brought her in.

"Okay," she says, "now I need your driver's license."

"Great. Are we going out? Why?"

"To make a photocopy for verification purposes."

"Well, it's my check."

"Your driver's license, ma'am."

"Do I look like I own a car? I'm a New Yorker."

"What about other forms of identification?"

"Nope."

"Passport? Visa from Saudi Arabia?"

Mentally, rolling my eyes, I shake my head.

"Then sorry." She throws the check at me and closes the window with a clang.

I knock on the Plexiglas partition. "Excuse me?"

She opens the window. "You got your driver's license?"

"No, but I can prove it's my check. Tell me the address on it and I'll tell you it's true. I mean, I can tell you the address on the check so you can compare. If the check was falsified, then how in the world would I know the address on it?"

"Never mind the address. I need your driver's license. Do you understand plain English?" She created a megaphone with her hand as though I'm hard of hearing. "No driver's license, then visit your bank and bring cash."

After getting a "get out of jail free" card from the Gooseberry, I knock again.

"What?"

"Do you take these?"

She takes the card in her hands. "A 'get out of jail free' card?"

"Well, what else are they for?"

"From Monopoly? Get outta here."

Upset, I return to the bench and put one leg on top of the other, the classy gal I am. (Still dressed in the last night's outfit, dirty, a bit hungover, with a scarf over my head.) One description cancels off the other: If I didn't sit in a classy pose, I'd look like I belong here, and this way I, at least, try to stand out.

While fishing out a plan how to bail Chloe out, I find *Latent Tramplet* in my bag, ultimately wondering who published this trashy book. On the flap it states it was a company based in New York, so it must be legit, legitimacy level to be determined later. Chloe left off almost at the very end, marking it by folding the edge of page 233. I flip through the content quickly without paying attention to details. My eyes stop on the following sentence: "Happiness was a choice, Ouchita thought. Abortion was a choice too. Becoming the tramp was a choice; unfortunate choice. The only choice she hadn't made in her life was to be born. Life's like poker, she thought. You have a choice to place your bets, or cash out. Far ahead you will see the light or the darkness. You'll be very rich or poor. You'll have a family or remain alone. Our choices determine our lives. Even the least successful people could turn their life for the better, forget the past, step into the future. Even the most successful people could miscalculate, lose their empires, die without a single person by their side. That was the game of life. That was the dark side of life. That was the beautiful side of life. *You don't have to do this*, she thought. *Just turn around, you sexy lady. Go back.* But Ouchita took a step forward. And then one more. That was one little step for her, one giant leap for tramplets everywhere. The choice was hers."

I turn the page and it appears to be last: "This could be her first real job. Or she could return to being a tramplet. She knocked on the door instead. Someone called her in. The interview was about to start. She knew it was the only choice." Underneath it read: "To be continued."

There is book two to it? I reread the last page once again. Maybe this book is onto something: choices. Which liquor to buy, which drink to consume, and what excuse to use to call out from work are important questions.

And the classic question: Am I good enough?

Chloe's choice to get naked put her in jail. My choice to help brought me here. Was everything that happened in my life a choice? Meeting Marcus wasn't a choice, but dancing with him definitely was. Coming to Honolulu for Adam was a choice—bad choice—but losing him most likely wasn't. At least wasn't on a conscious level. The subconscious level can do its own thing, but it's hardly my problem.

What does it all mean?

It was my choice to photoshop Babette's picture on a chimpanzee, but it wasn't Babette's choice to get born that way. It's not my fault. I didn't choose to fight with her; she did.

Instead of contemplating about Mr. Grunt, Adam, or Babette, I read the application Chloe filled out last night, thinking that my penmanship looks good comparing to hers. Under occupation, she indicated she works as the Secretary of State, which me, Hillary Clinton, and the rest of the folk know for a fact is a lie. She put imaginary Matilda as an emergency contact.

I open my eyes at 6:30 A.M. Somehow I snoozed for a couple of hours here at the police station. After I get up, I take several steps toward the barred window where Bigfoot watches another movie. Speaking with her will net me nothing. Upon returning to the bench, I now know it's impossible to bail someone without cash. The only other idea is to set the building ablaze and flee with Chloe once the walls are ruined. A slight possibility still persists I'll be sent to prison for arson. Besides, Hawaii isn't the wild west of the 1800s where the jail walls were made of timber.

An Arab-looking gentleman enters the precinct and reaches the barred window. He knocks on the partition and starts speaking with such heavy accent I must cup a hand to my ear to eavesdrop on the conversation. I've got nothing better to do. I casually stroll forward, whistling a tune. As though watching an Arabian soap opera, I kind of understand what the gentleman wants: His wife (or one of his wives) was locked up in the last episode of the show last night—she tried to bribe a policeman (since when is it illegal?)—and he wants to bail her out. Bigfoot gives him the same bailout form and a pen. After he fills out the form, he pulls out a bundle of money so thick my eyes ding like two cash registers.

I dawdle nearby and pretend to read the bulletin board on the wall. A picture of Bigfoot is placed on the board as a coworker of the month. Big deal, I think. I was chosen a coworker of the month last month and guess what happened? Maybe Tall and Ugly is on the verge of being fired.

Bigfoot counts the money, stamping PAID on the document with an oversized stamper. I watch her through the glass, wondering where she came from, the Sasquatch village or the town of Yeti. She takes the receiver in her hands and dials a number. "Bail came for Sabrina Llama. Release her immediately. Copy? Later, Mark."

Mark is such a provincial name. If I were to have kids (God forbid), I'd never name them something this simple. I imagine Mark's parents picking up his name before he was born, thinking of different combinations before coming up with this. The wife said: "This marks three weeks of us hanging out. Let's call the baby Mark, so to *mark* this big date?" Her fifteen-year-old boyfriend nodded and kept playing his video game.

In eleven minutes, Sabrina Llama is escorted out by Gherkin, and I notice how Sabrina's face is also hidden behind a scarf. I untie the scarf from my face right away or Sabrina will think I'm her sister, or worse, one of the wives.

When the couple leaves the precinct, I have an idea to hit the Arab-looking gentleman on the head, take the dough, and pay for the bail. One thing—being too sober—stops me. I return to the barred window while simultaneously wrapping the scarf around my face.

"My husband should have paid for Chloe Tenderfoot," I say. "Sorry for misunderstanding earlier. See, I called him and he stopped by, but I think he was given a wrong girl."

"Your husband?" Bigfoot says.

"Yes, Mr. Llama is my husband. I'm his wife number three. Chloe is four, and the girl who was just released belongs to the sheik."

"Get the hell out of here. Just bring the cash and we'll get over this, savvy?"

"How about these?" I take off my earrings and present it on my palm. "These beautiful drop earrings are a family heirloom, trimmed with French wire, fourteen karat gold. They're worth a lot."

She creates a megaphone with her palms. "I'm not a jeweler. For all I care these are worth five pennies."

I scowl, but she breaks eye contact before she sees it. Right now I'd give anything to be allowed to punch the bitch in the greasy jaw. Bigfoot taps the back of her head with her left palm, four times total. Her other hand touches her eyes. Surprised and interested, I keep watching, as I have no clue what's going on. Soon, something falls out of her eye, but I can't see what, and she leans down to pick it off the floor. A contact lens. She taps her head once again until the other lens falls out. One by one, she places the contact lenses into a case and puts on a pair of small glasses. They don't match her bulky exterior. Bigfoot picks up the phone receiver off the base. "Mark, Shwella come to work yet? You gotta be kidding me, kiddo. When she finally gets her ass to work, tell her I left. I'm tired of covering for her. It's eight. My shift is over. I know the rules, but I have a child at home whose dad needs to leave for work. Blame Shwella if something goes wrong. Later."

She bangs down the receiver. The phone gives a little squeal; the same way as would a piglet as soon as you start running after it. Painful experi-ence, don't ask how that happened. I give Bigfoot a fake smile, foolishly hoping she'll change her mind after seeing my sunny disposition. Instead, she stands up and skis toward the door behind her, leaving the area unattended. She grabs a set of keys and a black shoulder bag from a hook. I remember spotting a brown Toyota parked right out front before I entered the precinct, which must be her car. I should've keyed it. When she exits, the door locks automatically after her. The phone signals an upcoming call, but after six profound rings, it stops. Folders and papers are scattered around the desk, disorganized since Bigfoot is ignorant about filing things properly. Small wonder evidence, together with other important information, is lost in such fishy precincts, where hired cops are Empires, Gherkins, and Sasquatches.

Two minutes after Bigfoot's departure, the reception area remains neglected. Behind me nothing but an empty room. Chloe's manila folder and the PAID stamp chill side by side, like two lovers at Waikiki Beach. *They Belong Together*, Mariah Carey would sing. A plan is automatically created in my head. A genius one. No wonder I'm so good with chopsticks. If I reach through the small window and stamp PAID on Chloe's papers, then when Shwella comes into work, she'll think the bail was posted. She'll call Mark and free Chloe. How smart is that?

I spin my head in circles, looking for hidden cameras and cop coworkers. Could I, should I, would I? The choice I must make. No hidden cameras are seen anywhere, either that or they were properly hidden. No cops in sight. Nothing stopped Ouchita, nothing will stop me.

Without giving it another measly second, I sneak my arms along with my head through the window portion. The stamp is farther from the window than I anticipated. Now that I'm Arabic, my perception of things is multiplied by seven, or by whatever number needed for an even combination for a good wife count. With my hand, I reach farther and farther, moaning slightly, but moaning, if anybody was interested, helps none. Maybe I should soap myself in the bathroom to make myself slippery. I have the Cute Mango soap with me in the Gooseberry. I notice the stamp is placed on one of the documents, and I start pulling the document by the edge. I pull it, and inch by inch it moves closer. Finally, I grab the stamp in my hand.

I sigh with relief. I stamp Chloe's papers, praying to God I did it on the right spot. I throw the stamp back where it stood, groan from pleasure the mission is accomplished.

In front of me, a key is being inserted into the door Bigfoot used for exiting. Quickly I pull myself backward only to hit my head on the metal frame. Wishing I was soaped and drunk, I try to get out, but my head is stuck in the window. It's like the law of losers: you can get in, but you can never get out.

In enters another woman cop, a petite and frail one, and she stares at me in a peculiar way. Shit.

Anyone else care to get arrested to make it a wholesome threesome?

"What are you doing?" she says, bobbing her body toward me.

I think fast, for there must be an explanation. "I lost my family heirloom earring somewhere on the floor. It was given to me by my mother, to her by her mother, to her by her mother."

"Why didn't you tell anyone, dear? What you're doing isn't going to get your earring back. This window is too small."

Like I'm unaware it's too small. I notice how nature awarded the woman with a look of a duck with her higher lip way longer than the lower lip. I always liked ducks; it's the geese that are bitches.

"Are you Shwella?" I ask. Like Cinderella, I'm just trying to make friends with the animals.

"Who told you that name?"

"The mean woman who worked the night shift. She talked the nastiest things about you. She was nasty to me too. When I asked her about my earring, she gave me the middle finger and left for home instead."

"That was Babe, and it does sound like her. She doesn't like anybody. She recently remarried and her husband has a three-year-old child from the previous marriage. The moppet gets on Babe's nerves and she gets on everybody else's nerves. My name is Kayla. She calls me Shwella when she's mad at me."

"Her name was Babe? No wonder. Just no wonder. That little piglet."

"Let me see if I can find your earring, dear."

"Okay."

How could an imaginary earring possibly fall through the window is beyond me, but I'll let Kayla do the work on the logic. She kneels, searching for the invisible earring. Up close, she's a prettier version of the Ugly Duckling. I wonder if she'll speak or quack. As it happens, the Ugly Duckling was my favorite character in the story and apparently for a good reason.

"Oh, dear, my eyesight is not what it's used to be. I can't see a darn thing. Oh, boy, this should be swept. Just look at the dirty floor. Oh, no. Babe dropped her hot dog again. I told her the mustard is bad for her stomach. She's got gastritis, you know."

"It was diamond," I say. "Maybe Babe the pig stole it."

"She would, dear." Kayla searches for thirty more seconds, mumbling under hear breath before she gets up and meets my gaze. Her blue eyes appear double in size behind the heart-shaped glasses, her white hair collected in a neat bun. "Or you must have dropped it elsewhere because I don't see it. Stay put; I'll try to get you out."

Yeah, I think, *stay put,* like I was going anyplace. Kayla leaves the reception area, eating the hot dog she found. When she rounds the corner, she grabs my hips and yanks. Her hands tickle me and what escapes my lips next is a nervous laugh. After several attempts, she finally pulls me through the window. I almost fall, but manage to balance myself right on time. Kayla, however, doesn't get so lucky.

I help her get up, and while holding her fragile hand in mine, I shake it. Hers is full of relish. "I'm Calyssa Pantaleo. Nice to meet you. I came here to bail my friend. Even though I paid the money, see, Babe left home because her shift was over."

"She's impossible. She always does this. Was she blabbing about her baby the entire time?"

"Oh, yes. That son of hers is pretty much doomed."

"It's a daughter, dear."

The skeptical way she said it left me unnerved. "Well, then no wonder she hates her. She calls her Mark."

"No kidding."

"That's why she was furious with me. Can you finish the bailout process? My friend will go crazy otherwise. I'm her psychologist, you know."

"Let me see, dear." She returns to the reception area and claims Babe's chair. Kayla picks up the paper I stamped. "Your friend is Lucas Gonzalez?"

Shoot—I stamped the wrong paper.

"No," I almost yell at her. "My friend's name is Chloe Tenderfoot. The document next to it. Babe stamped the wrong paper on purpose."

Kayla examines Chloe's paper carefully and laughs, perhaps telling herself a little goose joke. She lifts her head. "Babe is such a bleep." She says *bleep* in high pitch, as though she were on TV and was bleeped out by producers for cursing. "She messes everything up." Kayla picks up the phone. "Mark, bail came for Chloe Tenderfoot. Please release her immediately."

My heart drops and I murmur, "Thank you," finally relieved.

She stamps PAID on Chloe's document with the most delicious sound I've ever heard—bam! Chloe is now free.

ACCORDING TO MY WATCH IT'S CLOSE TO NINE IN THE MORNING, the least favorite time for someone who normally works nine to five. Or someone who is supposed to work nine to five, that is.

As soon as Chloe is escorted through the red door, she reaches for a hug. Kayla gives me a thumbs-up while I pat Chloe on her shoulder. Chloe's short platinum hair is splayed out carelessly in all directions, her eyes blood red, tired, and dehydrated from the drinks she consumed. Her fake lashes vanished and the fake tan is slightly diminished, thanks to the fear of jail, which brought the pale look to her face. Her denim onesie is stained with several dirt spots, perhaps from the time she dropped the jumpsuit on the ground in an attempt to earn money for the trip back. She needs to brush her teeth, but I'm not about to go ahead and tell her that. I'm patiently waiting to tell her about Mandy. My plan is to get us a table at a diner, get her fed and comfortable, and then proceed with the good news. Chloe and I exchange good-mornings and nice-to-see-yous, and exit the building.

Promising another hot beach day, the sun is gingerly on its way up, only occasionally hidden by a bleached cloud against the stark blue sky. People who paid sweat and tears for their vacations will enjoy sunbathing at the beach while we'll be waiting by some pier in hopes to return home by boat.

Straight ahead, a diner appears with a neon sign BREAKFAST, about a hundred feet away. "B" is hardly visible, "A" is fully covered in mud, "T" is nonexistent. BREAKFAST is my type of place, where food costs under ten bucks and service entails no or a small 15-percent tip.

We cross Kinau Street and turn right on Pensacola. Traffic is lively, and I wonder if these are the people who wake up at a crack of dawn to attend Sunday church sermons. A bypassing pedestrian, a woman pushing a stroller with a little tot inside, gives us such a stare—to a dame with a Wonder Woman scarf across her face and to a woman in a blue denim onesie—as though to indicate we look about as good as a pair of dead defrosted hens after escaping the freezer and trying to learn how to lay eggs again. Together with the finger, I give her a death stare, one Babette used on me: mouth as an O, wide nostrils, eyes popped open. The face scares her away, and she quickly withdraws from sight.

The smell of bacon is whiffed from BREAKFAST, a rail car style diner. Out of the three outside tables, two are already occupied by uniformed cops, third leaning on one side in an attempt to indicate its service time is up. Through the window, seven patrons are seen in booths throughout the perimeter, also cops. As we take the leaning table, I wonder if the joint is always crawling with cops due to its proximity to the precinct. On the table there are two empty glasses, one stained with a fresh red lipstick print, and in the middle there is a basket with bottles of mustard and ketchup, salt and pepper shakers, and napkins held by a large binder clip. My chair is unstable, with a high back for support, the cushion dotted with several cigarette burns. A full ashtray on our and the other two tables indicate patrons are permitted to smoke, but gladly none do. That's why Natalia is so skinny and cops are fat, because cigarettes, I heard, keep your tubby slim. The cuisine in such establishments is usually American: bacon and eggs; burgers; overdone steaks with mashed potatoes resembling soup; donuts; sugar and cream with a tiny splash of coffee; soda drinks; and an assortment of fruit juices high in calories. The foodstuffs are devoid of nutritional value but packed with flavor, additives, and cholesterol. Most importantly, the food is cheap—so yes, please. On our neighbors' table I spy a pancake tower with syrup, blueberries, powdered sugar, and whipped cream; his partner is having sausage with three eggs sunny side up. They both curiously study me when I count how many sausage links are served with the meal, and I count four, not counting the ones he's consumed.

A gothic waitress, who looks like she shops at Hot Topic, stops by our table with two menus. Against the black hair, her white face stands out like a screenshot from a black-and-white movie. The menus are thick, the way they're supposed to be in diners of such magnitude. When she puts the menus in front of us, the table shakes, almost breaking from the weight. The waitress takes an unused water pitcher from our neighbors' table and fills up our glasses.

"I think these are someone else's glasses," I say.

"What's new," she says without saying hi. Her voice is yippity-yappety as of a lap dog. "Our Sunday special is three-dollar hash browns, bacon, and two eggs any style."

"Oh, I'll have that doggy style," Chloe says, giggling. I give her a raised eyebrow. "Fine," she adds. "Scrambled will do."

"Poached for me," I say, opening the menu. The first thing that pops up is that they serve brunch drinks on weekends. What a nice diner I found. "And a Bellini, please."

"Alcohol is only served after twelve," the waitress says. Her ears are flappy, like she magically transformed from pug to human. Up close, I notice gauge earrings in her earlobes, so big my hand would fit through.

"Can you make an exception?" I say. After being stuck in the window for five minutes and after being looked at as a defrosted hen, this conversation can't continue until drinks are present.

Pug shakes her head for a no. Her pupil-less eyes are icy cold, colored mauve. The hoop nose ring almost touches her upper lip.

"Sorry," she yaps. "It's against our rules."

"What if I tip you, say, 50 percent?"

"Coming right up."

Pug takes back the menus and disappears inside the diner while I bark up an order in her wake to bring us fresh glasses. Rollerblades on her feet are black, decorated with graffiti. Does she know shoes would do just fine? She rolls back out within three minutes with a tray in her hands containing two steaming plates to contrast with the chilled air. A Bellini is on the tray as well, two tall glasses, one chipped at the very top. Tattoos go up and down Pug's arms: dragons, skeletons, crosses. I just imagine her at sixty with skin sagging and tattoos transforming to something inscrutable.

When Pug leaves, I have a sip of my drink before I say, "This was great, last night, but let us not do that again. Okay? I was afraid they'd never let you out."

Chloe places a forkful of food in her mouth. "I love scrambled eggs."

"Chlotilda." I love using her full name because it shows I mean business, and I even put one leg on top of another, business-like, very high-class hooker I am. "Tell me what happened."

"They scrambled them."

"Never mind that. What happened to you?"

"Nothing happened. They put me in a slammer," she says with her mouthful.

"I know that much. What happened to you while I was away at the club? You had five shot glasses near you. You're not a drinker."

"I'm just stressed." She sighs and splits a strip of bacon, licking her fingers right after. "I'm embarrassed. One: I live with my mom. Two: the reunion. Three: something else. Snowball effect."

"What else?"

"I thought you were judging me when you left me alone at the club as though you were embarrassed by me."

I gulp half of my drink. Fizzy. Yummy in my tummy. "I was not embarrassed by you and I never judge."

"Oh, please, you're the queen of judge. This is who you are: a girl with high standards during the day who meets a girl from AA at night."

Ouch. I put the drink down, almost offended. Having a drinking problem is different from having people point it out in your face. "Ridiculous."

"I heard you talking to Christina on the phone last week," she goes on, "and how you were making fun of some girl from work because she's ugly. You judge all the time. You nickname people. Sometimes when you're drunk, you even say it in their face without understanding that it may hurt them emotionally. Remember the first night you met me what you called me?"

"No."

"Tons of Fun."

"What's so bad about thinking you were fun?"

"If you called me Lots of Fun, yes, but Tons of Fun refers to fat people."

"Are you still freaking out because the guy never replied to you online?"

"No, I had a breakthrough in jail. This is my bottom. I thought about my life and about the choices I've made. First, I need to tell you the truth about how I feel. I value our friendship and the fact I can be myself with you. I accept you for who you are: a good person who sometimes drinks too much. What I've noticed is that you've changed. Maybe it's because of your job, but you make it appear as though you're better than other people."

"Fiddle faddle."

"Let me finish. I believe us girls must stick together. Remember what you called Natalia the first night you met her? Tranny Mess. You wanted her to audition for *RuPaul's Drag Race*. You are just so out of line, Caly. If she knew the premise of the show she'd stab you with her Russian heels."

"If you want me to apologize, just say so."

"I want you to understand that you have to accept people for who they are. Natalia had it rough: She immigrated and now she's transforming into a woman. Give her a break. She's not your ticket to Honolulu. Apologize to her and she'll forgive you. I met this great lady in jail, Susie, and I told her everything. We talked. She thinks you judge others because, secretly, you judge yourself. You failed to climb to the top, but you pretend like you have while you thrash people emotionally in the process. Babette, for example. Susie thinks you're jealous of Babette, and I agree."

"Jealous?" I scratch my forehead. "Why's that?"

"Because she will get you fired, and you can't even fight back. You judge her and you judge me. Finally, you even judge your pregnant cousin Christina."

That really fries my chicken; steam shoots off my nose. "Right, I judge you because I'm on the verge of getting fired, because Babette has bad breath, and because Christina refuses to leave the house to have a drink with me."

"Caly, no sarcasm necessary. Christina is pregnant; that's why she can't have a drink with you. Pregnant with your niece or nephew. What is it, by the way?"

"Beats me. She refuses to do the sonogram. She's all about natural pregnancy. Sonogram is too hot for her munchkin."

"You're scared to even visit them. You recently moved out and made it on your own, but Christina still lives with your aunt. Has Christina failed? What are *you* afraid of?"

"I wanna make Mom proud."

What? Did I just say that? I turn around, waiting for the background laughter heard on a sitcom. I tap Blabber as though he were a weave. Next thing I know, heat rushes to my face, and my hands tremble. Bellini must be responsible for this. "Chloe, people won't take me seriously unless I remain living alone. I want to sit in my apartment and imagine her being happy when she sees her daughter is all grown up."

"What about Lindsay? She lives on her own. Why don't you take her seriously?"

"She doesn't know how to save, she's a stripper, and she's a thief."

"What about Natalia? She lives on her own and makes a ton of money. Why don't you take *her* seriously?"

"How can you take anybody who drinks so much seriously?"

Chloe points at the Bellini. "Can't argue with you there. Again, you're jealous Lindsay made it on her own with so little. You're jealous Natalia is transforming into a woman and makes big bucks, and even though she drinks and smokes, she never gossips or talks behind people's backs. You think I'm weird, but you wish you lived with Aunt Sarah and Christina without feeling ashamed."

I guess this means we're having a real conversation. In the past, our gabfests normally involved my work and her imaginary escapades, involving "see, see." Chloe breaks eye contact. She does this when the following is either hard to say or a lie. She forks her hash browns, divides them in half, mashes them without eating, and sighs deeply as though preparing to weep.

"There's something I haven't told you yet, Caly. It's very important."

"Place it on a scale from one to two."

"Two."

Oh, great. She's going to tell me she's pregnant. Otherwise, why bring up Christina and lead to such a melodramatic exit? My ears go up like Dumbo's, waiting for "see, see." I suddenly wish we had a hearty conversation such as this in our bar. Unfamiliar surroundings make me weary, and I come unprepared to what I should do or say next. I wish she didn't look this damn ridiculous, so I could at least pretend to feel sorry for her imaginary story.

She puts her fork down. "I told you my daddy died from a heart attack, right? It runs in the family. Younger, I never paid any attention to it, but now that I'm thirty I'm worried about these things. I was doing a checkup, and

Dr. Thomson told me my blood pressure was 140 by 90. It's higher than a year prior."

"Is it bad?"

"Yes, indeed. It's called hypertension. It causes hardening and thickening of the arteries and can cause a heart attack or a stroke. Dr. Thomson prescribed me beta-blockers to reduce the heart workload, told me to lose weight, and advised me to eat healthier. He said I needed to start taking care of myself, which, I must admit, I haven't been very good at doing."

"When was this?"

"A month ago. I thought volunteering and looking after the pets would help me take care of myself better, but again I failed. I don't know what to do. I'm going to die. No wonder nobody replies back and nobody will remember me at the reunion if I went."

Chloe hides her eyes in her palms and starts sobbing.

I reach across the table and put my palm on hers. "I'm sorry, Chloe. I had no idea. I kept blabbing all this time about myself, Babette, and Mr. Grunt, when people have real problems."

Chloe shifts in her chair, readjusting a clasp on her onesie. "It doesn't mean you don't have real problems. I need to get a hold on myself and start exercising. I was jealous of that brat, Lindsay. She has no fat anywhere on her body. I understand what Susie meant when she told me you were jealous of Babette. It happens when we want something we don't have."

Ignoring the comment I clear my throat. "Seriously, you want to be like Lindsay?"

"Not like her, but you know what I'm saying? She's young, independent, and works. Compare to this chick: thirty, lives with mom, heart problems. Who would you rather date?"

As though a hard question has been asked, we stop talking and dip into our thoughts. Caisha mentioned problems only exist in our imagination. Chloe piles problems on top of one another, layering them like a cake so that a prior problem seems less important compared to the next. Having heart problems is hereditary, meaning it's a gamble Chloe has almost no control over. Preventing heart problems, however, is a choice and a lifestyle change that she could tackle. Instead, she'd rather dwell on the current failures to avoid fixing what could be fixed.

What also interests me is the fact that we want to be someone we're not, because the unknown is more appealing. Lindsay wants to be like Chloe and, in return, Chloe wants to be like Lindsay. Natalia wants to be a woman, and once she's a woman, I bet $100 she'll want to be a man. If life took a magic turn, as in my favorite movie, *Freaky Friday,* and we could switch bodies, they'd all sing another tune. Somehow we never appreciate what we have unless we lose it.

Suddenly, I realize I forgot to tell Chloe about Amanda Gellar, who called and invited Chloe to the reunion. Would that help fix her heart problems? Pug rolls by and I ask her to bring us the check. By now my breakfast is finished and I top it with the Bellini, which gives me a slight buzz, just slight enough to last maybe an hour.

"Chloe, there's something I have to tell you, too."

"You also want to be the first lady who steps on the moon? Or become so rich you could open your own Chinese restaurant and have Christina work for you?"

"What are you on? No. This morning you received a call from a woman named Mandy."

"Who?"

"Amanda Gellar. You went to high school together. She wants to be your date on Tuesday night for the reunion."

"Oh, Calyssa. You'd love to have Christina work for you. You could boss her around like you boss other people."

"I'm serious."

"Do you think I should dye my hair red?"

"Chlotilda, stop. Here, call her. She already texted her phone number. She's staying at the Plaza, that rich scamp, whoever she is."

Chloe's eyes start moving left and right with excitement. She takes her phone and reads Amanda's message, received back at the precinct. Mandy sent information about where to meet on Monday for dinner, together with her telephone number.

"I can't believe it."

"Well, you better."

"Calyssa, I need to go back to New York immediately. I bought a blue dress and bedazzled it with sapphire. I planned to wear it to the reunion if I ever decided to go. And just now I decided to go."

"Attagirl. We agreed to travel by boat together, but I think you should take a plane."

"Are you sure? I don't mind flying by myself, you know. Don't worry about me. Okay, Mandy said dinner is early Monday. I need to go to the airport right away."

"Like when?"

"Now."

"What about your clothes?"

"Can you bring the tote on your way back? Thanks. Oh, and Anubis. We don't have time to pack and pick him up."

Melodramatically I roll my eyes and sigh. She's leaving Anubis with me, with the woman who can't keep a cactus alive. "Fine," I say. "Your choice." What I meant to add was: if I didn't kill the fish, it doesn't mean the cat is any safer.

Chloe puts her plate on top of mine like the two plates need to be making love in front of us.

"Here," she says, "I'm officially on a diet. And let's hurry up."

I finish her plate faster than mine and pay for our breakfast, tipping the Pug exactly 50 percent as I promised. The bill comes to sixteen bucks and I make it twenty-four total. The tip should be enough for a new tattoo.

Chloe's positive disposition is contagious and she expresses it by imagining what might happen at the reunion: She'll walk in, meet a handsome guy, and run away at midnight, losing a shoe. She flies up from her seat and runs toward the road where she hails a cab. I can hardly catch up. While in the cab, she calls the airport ahead of time, inquiring about flights to JFK. Several flights leave this morning. At the Honolulu International Airport, we get into a stand-by line, hoping that one of the tickets will be available for purchase. In about five minutes of waiting, a last minute cancelation is made, which costs only $490 with a layover at LAX. She'll arrive in New York Monday morning. Since Honolulu is six hours behind, it's mid-afternoon in New York already. With the layover, total travel time is less than eighteen hours. Chloe buys the ticket without giving it another thought.

"Can I have your key?" she asks.

"What?"

"The key to your apartment."

"Why? Aren't you going home?"

"In case Amanda wants to see how I live, I want to show her I live on my own. Please?"

"More lying?"

"Please, Calyssa?"

"I don't have a spare key."

"No worries. I'll come give them back, just call me."

"My phone is off."

"Then I'll stay at your place and keep your TV company. Please?"

Lindsay said I distrust people, and this is the main reason for my hesitation. To prove Lindsay wrong, I give Chloe the keys to my apartment and explain how to get to Astoria by subway. She gives me a long hug while I tell her not to deadbolt the apartment door, so I can use a credit card to open it, if needed. She gives me a confused, disapproving look—about the lack of security, I presume—but I swear she prances on the way to the security checkpoint with only her wallet in hand. That's what Natalia calls "traveling on the go."

"Wish me good luck!" she says without uncertainty in her voice.

"Good luck."

AT THE HOTEL, I USE A COMPUTER IN THE BUSINESS CENTER TO type up an email to Adam, telling him I'm sick and unsure when I'll be in. I also request to be paid for my sick time. Since I'm going to have to call out "sick" this week, I might as well get paid for it. Last I checked, I had at least three days' worth of sick time accumulated. The fact of being late for work is one thing—slow subway, crowds of people, hangover (so not everything is entirely my fault)—but I never took a single sick day off or a personal one for that matter.

When I enter the suite, Anubis senses me and starts mewing hungrily from the bedroom. I imagine how annoying it must be to take care of that needy cat. Fish is better: just stick her in a Patrón bottle and she never makes a fuss and/or never complains. Elizabeth must be fed at some point, but it's number eleven on my to-do list. Chloe explained there's some canned cat food in the mini-fridge she brought with her from New York, and there's a can of Gourmet Sliced Tuna I'm supposed to purchase. When did cats stop drinking plain ol' milk and started eating gourmet food? Come to think of it, the cats may be eating better than kids in Africa. Before I feed the beast, I decide to take a hot, relaxing shower, which, in fact, is really hot, and really relaxing. After the shower, I pack the hotel soap and shampoo into my handbag. Since the items are already paid for, I might as well take advantage of the situation.

I exit the bathroom as the telephone rings. I stop in my tracks and notice time. 11:05 A.M.

"Hello?" I pick up on the fourth ring.

"Calyssa? It's Natalia."

"Natalia? Natalia? Where are you?"

"I'm in Vegas. I tried calling you but your phone's turned off."

"It's out of charge. Vegas? You're in Vegas? How did you get the room's phone number?"

"I called the front desk and they transferred me."

"How? How did you get to Vegas?"

"I found my wallet inside the couch yesterday. It must have fallen through the cushions."

My eyes pop open. "Must have fallen? Must have fallen? Natalia, was it such a bother to tell me you found the wallet? I almost got arrested trying to get it back. Arrested."

"Answer your phone once in a while. Again, I tried calling you."

"Well, it's turned off," I say louder. "You could have written a note or something. A note. Or something."

"You don't need to repeat everything twice. I hear you just fine. I could have done a lot of things, but I was running out of time," she says calmly. "Listen, I'm sorry I got mad at your yesterday. Now that I'm here and my meeting is about to start I wanted to tell you I'm not mad at you anymore. Calyssa, are you listening to me?"

"Yes, I am," I snap.

"I was going to bet a hundred bucks I heard you snore. Glad I didn't bet. Anyway, sorry I flushed your ID last night. I hope you get home without any trouble. And again, I'm sorry. I'm sorry. Without any trouble."

"I'm fine. Thanks for asking."

"Listen, the reason I'm calling, the reason I'm calling is because I'm so nervous I need you to wish me luck. Wish me luck."

I get so mad that she's imitating me I want to take a grape and throw it so hard at the receiver to have it magically travel through the tubing and smack her in the ear, maybe her mouth. But then I know better: there are no grapes left. She's trying to relax by being humorous. They say laughter is the best medicine. Besides, if Natalia—one of the strongest people I know—needs affirmation from me, she must really be nervous.

"Good luck."

"Thank you. I just saw a few of these ladies and I feel intimidated. After the tea meeting, we're supposed to go gambling. I'll call you later. And charge your phone for Russian God's sake. Is everything all right with you?"

I rewind my brain videotape: car chase, strippers, arrest, Bigfoot, and Chloe leaving me to travel by myself, and now the missing wallet appears out of nowhere. "Yes."

"Good. I left you $300 in the nightstand. Top drawer. Bye. Gotta run."

She hangs up. In the background, I heard ladies' voices. Ladies who gamble. Ladies' Elite Gambling Society, aka LEGS. There were words like "dear" and "scintillating," the two most endearing but impersonal words I ever heard. When people call you "dear," it means they have no idea what your actual name is. Aunt Sarah calls people "hun" when she doesn't remember a name. Christina asks for their email address and hopes it contains their first name in the body before the "at sign."

I keep holding the receiver, stupefied. Then I replace it. Well, this at least proves one thing: Lindsay is innocent. I close my eyes, thinking what an ass I was for blaming her. She's definitely superior now, being right, but my hands start shaking all the same. If Natalia told me she'd found the wallet, everything would be different. But there's no point in carousing a nonexistent apple martini.

Elizabeth sits in one corner of the bottle like a philosopher, wondering if she'll ever get fed. The kitchen island, I notice, is a perfect place for the fish. She's a queen who's atop of her throne, watching us slaves hustling around her palace. In the bedroom, I find the three Benjamins Natalia was talking about and put them promptly in my bra. At least there's some payment for my wretchedness.

At 11:20, I decide to feed the black beast. But first I detour toward the lanai and plop myself on a chaise. The sun is high up in the afternoon sky, not a cloud in sight. The ocean stretches as far the horizon without any islands visible ahead, its blue color mirroring the sky. The same shade were Marcus' eyes when he kissed me there yesterday. I remain motionless for five minutes straight and return to the suite, wondering what Marcus is up to. I find his business card, wondering where on Broadway his office might be located. According to my brain, his office is by City Hall, near Wall Street, Brooklyn Bridge, and 9/11 sight.

In the kitchenette, I flip a switch on a coffee maker, placing a stale, pre-grounded coffee bag inside. While the coffee is brewing, I get a fancy-looking white plate from the kitchen cabinet and scoop the cat's food into it, trying not to vomit from the way it stinks. I place the plate on the floor together with a bowl of water to keep the cat from choking during breakfast. Anubis smells the food distrustfully as though I could have poisoned it. He rounds the plate, sniffing the content from every possible angle. He starts eating as soon as he feels the food is safe, and his tail goes up like an antenna. He must be catching some cat-news from the outer space. Like in *Planet of the Apes*, I wonder whether some coo-coo cat-lady named Felinity Shedeverywhere is writing a book about a planet of the cats right as we speak, something with a catchy name like *Sodomize Bitchy Canines*, describing the nature of cat life I would never care to know about. The coffeemaker produces a distinct noise, pushing the last bits of water through the beans with a harsh sound to let me know the nastiness is ready. I pour myself a cup and add two packets of sugar, automatically adding a double chin to my face. The coffee tastes disgusting but refreshing, and it instantly kills my Bellini buzz.

Since there's no packing to do and with thirty minutes before checkout, I decide to sit down on the couch and relax. I put the coffee mug on the side table and turn on the TV. Some local news channel promises a nice, sunny day ahead without any traffic or earthquakes. I flip through channels, hoping to catch something worthwhile, one of those *how-to-do* shows, where I can learn all the things needed in life, starting with how to cook, how to do home décor, or how to trim my bush. Garden bush, that is. After about eleven flips, I discover my favorite Discovery Channel and decide to stick with it. Documentaries are my passion, so I resume drinking my coffee and enjoy the picturesque clips. The documentary shows water splashing against a piece of land that is Hawaii.

"The beautiful Hawaiian Islands," an invisible commentator says, "consist of lava and water, two incompatible materials that bring life to this planet. It took millions of years before Hawaii became what it is today. Hawaii's active volcanoes erupt lava that ruins everything in its wake. The Pacific Ocean cools it down, creating land. The volcanic deposits, rich in minerals—nitrates, nitrogen, potassium, and other important sulfides and acids—develop the highest quality agricultural soil. This phenomenon makes Hawaii a land of creation that's also a land of destruction."

I learned it the hard way it was a land of destruction; no need for a documentary to remind me of that. On TV, lava and water merge, and within ten seconds (thousands of years our time) trees start growing on top of the lava-water mixture.

Just like lava and water, my mom and my dad were two incompatible forces who created me and disappeared while I'm a bush growing from such a natural abnormality. Pubic bush, that is. There's no creation without destruction. That's a fact. If everything in this world comprises this theory of incompatibility, in a year or two Elizabeth will marry Anubis somewhere in Vegas (where it is perhaps allowed) and leave Chloe and me with thirty little catfishes.

Anubis jumps on my lap and tries to lick my face; his breath is worth than Babette's. I push him away a couple of times until his butt flower is leveled with my eyes. He stares at Elizabeth and moves his tail much the same way as would a cowboy trying to lasso a bull. One thing I can be sure of is that as much as he tries, he can't reach the fish. She's so high up on the kitchen island, she's invincible. I push the cat aside, but he won't budge.

The laxatives in the coffee make my tummy produce a prelude to the "Violin Concerto in A Minor," which I, at first, listen to without paying much attention to it. Then something boils inside of me and begs to come out. I run toward the bathroom, pushing the cat aside. After three constipated days, my bowels decided to release me.

Ten minutes into my private affair, there's a smashing sound of glass against tile. I assume Anubis knocked my coffee mug from the side table. However, the sound is so loud and disturbing that I doubt a mug would create anything quite like it, especially since the suite is carpeted. Worried that the beast might have hurt himself, I finish up and wash my hands with lavender-scented soap. In the living room, I find the plumber-lady, who looks as confused as I am. She's wearing a maid's outfit.

"Is everything okay in here?" she demands.

"Yes, why?"

"I was vacuuming the carpet in the hallway and heard the noise in your suite. I had to make sure everything is good here. Last night, this couple was fighting a floor down; a man hit her with a frying pan. Her teeth were all over the place and now I'm paranoid. What happened?"

I shrug. "Beats me. I was in the bathroom, um, taking a shower, and heard glass breaking. I have a cat in here so I assume he's responsible."

"Oh, the cat. He ran through the entrance door as soon as I got here. He was terrified."

"He escaped?"

"Yup."

I notice the Patrón bottle is missing from the kitchen island. One eye after another looks down toward the kitchen floor, and the first eye sees tile while the second sees the Patrón bottle, cracked into thirty thousand pieces. Elizabeth is jumping on her fishy side, trying to stay alive.

In haste, I run toward the kitchenette, looking for a deep dish to stick the fish into. There are forks, knives, flat plates, cookware, a strainer. Rummaging through the kitchen cabinets, I realize, either due to panic or lack of intelligence, there's no acceptable fish bowl. Instead, at the bar, I grab a martini glass and fill two-third of it with water, hardly worried about what temperature it should be. Elizabeth is a fish, let her figure out her own temperature. As gentle as I can, with both hands, I pick up my fish off the floor—while she keeps jumping and flipping—and drop her into the martini glass. She dives in, fins raised. As though after a marathon, Elizabeth is out of breath and hyped up, racing the perimeter of the glass with the speed of shark. This is what happens when your world is shaken: you wonder whether you're going to make it through the day or end up dead, other problems now suddenly unimportant.

In my peripheral vision, I notice how the maid leaves the suite. I put the martini glass on the kitchen island and in my best impersonation of Ursula yet, I try to assure the fish everything will be to be okay, that she will survive, blah, blah, blah. Being a caring parent is exhausting. If I knew what French fries are to fish, I'd deep-fry some. I wonder how Anubis could reach the top of the island, which is a good four feet high. He must have raced, jumped on a stool, grabbed the edge of the island, pulled himself up, and climbed. It proves there's not always creation after destruction. All it takes is one lousy cat to bring you down with a clattering hullabaloo.

I keep watching the fish, wondering whether she's acting normal or strange by doing weird backflips, somersaults, and other acrobatic activities I haven't noticed her perform before. Elizabeth floats to the top, plops promptly to the bottom. She circles the glass clockwise, stops, then circles it counterclockwise. The water feels cold to the touch and, due to chlorine, the water is cloudy. For a second, I'm worried about chlorine, but if the fall failed to kill the fish, chemicals would probably fail just as much. She's a terminator, an indestructible creature made out of steel: the only pet that can survive with a clumsy girl like me. She might as well be a toy. Taking three steps back, I look at the mess on the floor: shattered glass, water, fish poop.

When Elizabeth is safe, my mind retracts to the cat. Will I ever be able to find him? In the meantime, the maid returns, in hand a tall broom and a dustpan on a tall stick to match. I would punch her for letting Anubis escape, but she looks too strong to be punched. Her previously uncombed hair is hidden under a bandana. Suddenly, she starts picking up the little sparkling pieces of shattered glass into the dustpan.

"I swear, dear, the couple from last night seemed innocent. Nobody knew he would do such a thing to her. You can only imagine the expression I made when I saw the woman; she was crying but had no teeth. I winced. He's now in jail, of course, and she's in the hospital. Honeymooners, my tight ass. If I only knew what the fight was about . . ."

I stop listening to her. Does she have any idea she and I had a conversation yesterday, right here in this suite, and she wanted a tip? She was obviously inebriated and today she's sober. Maybe the maid is the plumber's sister, as there seems to be a certain number of twins and triplets in Hawaii and looka-like papas and sons, that it would surprise me not the maid was someone's relative. But I decide to block her voice from my mind, thoughts finally aligning to my current affairs.

I come up with the following conclusion: we're located inside of a hotel —barely a monumental thought. But how can a cat escape the building if all the doors are locked? That's a monumental thought. I've never heard of a cat taking an elevator by himself. And in the second place, why should I even care if Anubis escapes? Why am I supposed to be in charge of the cat? If Chloe were smart enough to bring him along, none of this would have happened in the first place. One thing I'm sure of: I refuse to pay if he poops on someone's dress.

I exit the suite to find Anubis licking his clandestine parts by the door. He's completely satisfied, as though his balls are the prize for the mess he's made. The war of the animal kingdom is what this is. Anubis probably got scared when the bottle broke and when the maid walked in he escaped; otherwise, he'd be chewing my fish as a dessert. I get his carrying case from the living room and put him inside for the time being to prevent him from doing such a trick again.

I find plastic wrap in the kitchenette and put some over the rim of the martini glass to avert spilling. That, I guess, concludes my business in the suite. The maid leaves while I place the Gooseberry over my shoulder, Chloe's tote on the other.

Giving the room one last quick sweep with my eyes, I wonder what it all means. I made such a fool of myself in Honolulu. All for nothing. There will be days of travel and, who knows, by the time I'm back in New York harbor I may not have a job. A gust of wind escapes the lanai, tickling the curtain. It soon reaches me, as though pushing me out of the suite. *Fine, Honolulu,* I think, *I was leaving anyway; no need to be nasty about it.* Cat in my left hand, fish in right, with two bags on each shoulder, I leave the suite.

DOWNSTAIRS, THE FISH FOUNTAIN IS CARELESSLY SPITTING water while kids are carelessly spilling it. The lobby chatter is discernible; people scattered around in clusters, idly talking about today's business. Near the front desk, I notice the swooshed cat is gone. The plumber in the plumber's uniform—the same one from yesterday—is chatting with Taisha, who is all smiling like she won a million dollars. Turns out the maid and the plumber are relatives, and no wonder they are such opposites: a scared blabbermouth and a capricious bitch soliciting tips.

"I found this ID in the plumbing," she says rudely. "Anybody by name Pantaleo is staying at the hotel?"

That's me! She found my ID in the pipes.

"Hm, let me see." Tasha claps on her keyboard while giving me a nod to acknowledge my presence with eyes telling me to keep my distance from the plumber beast.

"If I find that scalawag I'll tear her freaking head off," the plumber says while I turn my face sideway to avoid being caught.

"Nope. Possibly, a prior reservation. I'll hold on to it."

"Okay, then I'll go take a break. Need to finish Anna Karenina for my class tonight. Hate that stupid bitch."

The plumber turns and withdraws from view, a beer visible in her back pocket.

"Is that my ID?" I say excitedly as soon as the plumber is out of sight.

"Yes, but it's completely ruined."

Taisha hands the ID card, and I take it promptly. The mugshot is washed off: my long hair now short and curly the way Mom wore it, first name gone. Last name remains with half of my address in Astoria. My crooked signature is wiped but birthday is intact. It looks miserable, let alone smells foul. The ID is definitely illegitimate for air travel.

"Great," I say. "Still, the boat."

She carefully smiles. "I promise I won't even ask you how it ended up in our plumbing. You can still buy alcohol with it: the birthdate is safe."

Mentally rolling my eyes, I put the ID into Anubis' carrying case to let him play with it. "Thank you. Where's the cat?" The swooshed cat, that is.

"I took him home. I want to teach her how to talk. She already says 'mama' and 'mew.' I can't imagine other words being much more difficult. I named her Caisha, after my sister. She's going to love that."

Yeah, she'll love it until Caisha sees what kind of cat was named after her. Tasha hands me a receipt with total charges that will be posted on Natalia's credit card. I agree to the charges—without noticing the total amount for fear of going into shock—and sign.

"Well, if that's all, I better get going."

"Thanks for taking my sister out last night. She said you're nuts. In a good way."

I politely smile. "Well, with a fish in a martini glass, I guess I must be nuts at some point."

"I won't charge you for the glass, by the way."

"Thank you."

I don't know why, but Taisha seems like a close relative by now. Maybe it's because I spent the whole day with "her," or at least with women who resembled her. I wish I could gossip about yesterday shenanigans and tell her I found Lindsay, after which we got arrested. But I decide against it. Taisha turns her head sideways, her eyes widen, and she shakes her head as though a maraca. Nothing rattles inside. She circles the desk and gives me a hug, her teeth sparkling.

"Taisha, before I forget. Tell me how to get to the pier."

"Oh, right," she picks up a pamphlet off the table. "I found this brochure for you. There's a boat leaving in about five hours. Just find Honolulu Harbor downtown, and ask someone which berth is assigned to the ship going to Los Angeles. You can buy your ticket there." She offers me the booklet and I promptly hide it in the Gooseberry.

"Well," I say, "I appreciate your help. Since there's so much time left, I need to purchase a new container for the fish. Any pet shop recommendations?"

She shakes her head. "Nope. Sorry, Calyssa."

"That's fine. Thanks for your help anyway."

"Sure. Would you like a complimentary piña colada?"

My eyes pop open in surprise.

How dare she?

Who does she think I am?

I exit the hotel, sipping a refreshing piña colada, thinking Taisha should know better than asking stupid questions. I love how they pour the drink in a plastic cup so that when I'm done, I can just toss it.

A pet shop is my priority: fish food, a better tank, few plants or decorations as presents for the caused trauma. Should I stop by a bar and get Elizabeth another fancy bottle of tequila? I think better of it and stick with the former plan.

Once outside, I freeze in a stupor. The promised Honolulu weather didn't cheat, and the air is a solid seventy-five degrees, with occasional gusts of wind picking up and dying right after. Tourists in sunglasses go in and out of the hotel, some happy, some with neutral face expressions, some quarreling over the price they paid for brunch or as much as my big ears can understand.

A mongoose—I learned there are no squirrels in Hawaii—with a bird in its mouth, looks around, waiting for a good time to cross the street. Its fur coat is gray, expensive-looking, perhaps stolen, and there's a shiny gleam to it under the hot sun. The mongoose carefully calculates the distance between cars and hops across, diving straight into the bushes near me. Even though it resembles a squirrel, it eats birds and their eggs. The mongoose scares a fiery skipper, resting nearby. A yellow-billed cardinal is hanging out in the shrubs, its red coat a stark comparison to the greenery.

Giant palm trees cast shadows several feet long. In one such shadow, a lizard is spread in its full length, maybe seven inches across, its tail curved to one side like a cinnamon roll. All these exotic animals are such a nice break to dirty New York City pigeons, squirrels, and cockroaches. But New York is home, and it's time for me to leave the paradise.

The shuttle bus idles near the entrance, its motor running, proved by a continuous stream of exhaust fumes sneaking up into the sky. The driver was helpful yesterday so I'm sure he'll gladly drop me off at a pet shop. I knock on the bus doors and the same driver from before (with the Afro hairdo) appears when the doors fly open.

"Can you take me to a fish store? Rev 'er up!"

"I only go to the airport and back. Do I look like I drive people around like a taxi?"

"Would you make an exception?"

"I said airport and back. If you need to get to the airport, then get in; otherwise, you need to get yourself another ride."

"I'll complain to the front desk."

"You can complain to whoever you want, lady. I only go to the airport and back."

Lady, yet. Lady happens to be one of the most impersonal words you can tell to a woman with a drink and two pets in her hand. Asshole maybe, but not a lady.

I step off the bus, wondering why the tourists occupying the few bus seats look at me the way they do. Maybe it's my hair. Spinning my head like a beacon light, I spot a yellow taxi cab parked near the hotel with a driver inside. Look, how lucky I am. I knock on the window to get the driver's attention, and he puts the newspaper away, opening his window a crack. He's the same Japanese driver who drove me twice last night. There shouldn't be any problem with him. Even though he looks very smart, I know he's a nice person inside.

"Remember me from last night? I need to get to a fish store," I say. "Take me?"

I learned once at a training in retail that if you want people to agree or at least not receive a rejection, you need to ask a question that sounds like a statement. Never say, "Can you take me?" Say, "Take me." After the failure with Afro, I need to learn from my mistakes.

The driver furrows brows. "Fish store? You mean supermarket?"

"I mean a pet store." Dumbass. Like he fails to see I have two pets in both hands.

"No drink in car!"

"Sorry, not gonna happen."

He sighs and closes the window while I keep wondering why everyone is so cranky this morning. Not like I asked him to go back to the precinct. And there's no way I'm throwing this perfectly full, delicious drink in the trash.

I decide to walk on foot and detour toward the sidewalk. Plastic wrap was such a great idea because I happen to tilt the martini glass a couple of times, mostly due to trying to multitask drinking my cocktail. Really, fish stands no chance. I don't know why I even bother trying. I should just toss her in the bushes and call it a day. Elizabeth stays still at the bottom without moving, and as much as I'm tempted to get rid of her, she's an alive creature. But she can be my guest to commit suicide.

Ahead, a jogger runs my way, a handsome boy in his early twenties, music player in hands, headphones on. Runners are common in New York, especially during warm months. For some reason, even if a runner isn't cute, he's cute. Something about the sporty look, which means he's healthy. And if you're into the theory of Natural Selection, it states: we usually pick the healthiest mate, probably why nobody picks me. Another answer—according to a trustworthy source, *Queens Weekly*—is because humans love movement, which is why we like to watch sports, action movies, and have to look at our phone every five minutes, even if we just checked it. Human eye will even find movement in a still picture. It explains why we drink: because then still pictures move by themselves. I flag the runner down and ask him for directions to a fish store instead.

His breathing is fast while sunscreen, in streaks, is running down his face. "Any. Particular. Fish. Store?" he says, gulping air after each word. How many fish stores does he know? What a geek!

"Any."

"I. Only. Know. One."

I roll my eyes, wondering why he asked for specifics. "Give."

He takes a deep breath, focusing his vision on Anubis and Elizabeth. "Go straight ahead, turn right at that streetlight and keep going. At the very end, there's a shopping plaza."

"Thank you."

The boy runs along, puffing while I follow his directions. Out in the sun, my neck starts itching, courtesy of yesterday's sunburn. Now I'll really resemble a redneck. I pick up my speed before all is left of me is a rotisserie roast. The heat activates my sweat glands, my armpits perspiring with fresh odor, my back damp.

The shopping plaza the boy was talking about is five minutes away, complete with a liquor store, a Chinese restaurant, a bank of unknown origin, a fish store, and an ice cream parlor. Beautiful Hawaiian weather turned out to be perfect for the beach, not for fish store shenanigans. For twelve o'clock in the afternoon on Sunday, everything seems to be closed due to an almost empty parking lot. Aside from me, the plaza is deserted, which is quite scary at first. The second thought makes me feel better: What have I got to lose? No cash, no jewelry, no expensive clothing. Even my phone would barely make the cut for muggers, being it's out of charge and without an actual charger. If anyone wants to mug me, they run a risk of getting in jail for stealing the Gooseberry with a paycheck I need to deposit and a picture of oily-faced Babette, a naughty cat, a piña colada full of spit, and an already pre-stolen fish.

I detour to the ice cream parlor, but the shop is actually closed, so is the liquor store; don't ask me how I know. The pet store has a sign "cash only" on the entrance. I step into the bank to withdraw the money, but the ATM tells me there's a $2.25 fee for each transaction. I suddenly recall the $300 Natalia left me, which I stuck in my bra. I turn around to avoid being caught on camera as I withdraw the cash from the First National Boobs Trust and Fund.

Inside the fish store, I almost groan with pleasure, having felt the wonders of a cold AC working its magic. By the time I'm out of here, I'll be all but dry. The fish store is what I always imagined one to be: divided in sections for every imaginable pet, even mice. Who and why wants to have a rat in their home when we spend so much time and energy getting rid of them in New York City? Annoying birds chirp all the way out back, where a grooming salon for dogs is located. Should I ever become a parent, my kids will have a mobile pet, one of those fake animals a smartphone application can produce, or a Pillow Pet—whichever is cheaper. There's no way I'm dealing with the real shit.

To my right, several fish tanks filled with water line the whole side of the wall. The fish tanks must be about fifteen to twenty gallons each and they're crawling with fish. Without exaggeration, there are a million little fishes in each tank. I purposely lift up the martini glass to show Elizabeth how the working class lives.

Just like at the plaza, the store is dead, and that's why the workers, all four of them, are eyeing me like I'm a rare monkey with an overly exaggerated red ass. There's no way I look like an outsider with two pets occupying each hand.

The smell is a confused mixture of poop, pee, dog hair, human cologne, and cat food. Several turtles are chilling in a large tank underneath a heat lamp. A cricket jumps out of nowhere and hides just as fast. Alive crickets are sold as food, according to the display ahead, yet one was able to get away. The freedom will net the jail-breaker the following fate: being stepped on, hit by a car, on eaten by a pigeon.

There's an aisle full of lizards in the middle of the store, each tank with a thermometer gauging perfect temperature for them, alive crickets hiding in corners. One such fat lizard is having lunch, a cricket leg sticking out of its mouth while the lizard is chewing lazily without looking excited. If Anubis weren't such a sissy when the bottle broke, I'd find Elizabeth much the same way, sticking out of his mouth.

One of the salespeople crosses ways with me near the fish tanks. His hair is long and I'd confuse him for a girl if he lost the beard and his Adam's apple. I've always been someone who likes to shop on her own but in this case, however, I decide to stick with help, because fish is a new territory for me.

"Do you need help?" chewing gum, he asks me, refusing to meet my gaze. He must have been drinking the night before. That's the only reason I would not make eye contact and chew gum all at once. I follow his gaze, which is aimed at my fish. Maybe he's talking to Elizabeth, foolishly thinking I'm her pet and she's shopping for herself instead.

"I need a new container for the fish. Her container broke and this martini glass is hardly cutting it."

"You need a container for a better fish?"

"Better fish?" Is he being fresh or am I hearing things?

"No, beta fish."

"Beats me. Alpha, beta, maybe gamma. I was never into physics or the fraternities." He makes eye contact, a surprised look on his face. "Well?" I continue. "You work here. How can I tell which fish is mine? Possibly a 'phi' since it's closer to a fish. Got it? But don't tell me she's a 'theta' because that's just one ugly name."

"Ma'am, it's beta with double *t*. B-E-T-T-A." He spells out. "These are all the bettas we have," he says, pointing to a stand with individual containers filled with water and one fish inside each. "And this is not a *she*, it's a *he*. Female bettas are smaller than males, and we seldom sell them for that reason. You have a delta tail male. One of those."

He picks up a container with an ugly colored fish—mauve—(or something along the lines) and the fish, in fact, might be Elizabeth's twin, priced at twelve bucks.

"You want to tell me my Elizabeth is a male?" I say.

"I'm afraid so. If you're looking for a female fish, we can find something from a salt-water aquarium for you. You can always get a dog. But those are usually bitches." He laughs awkwardly and clears his throat. "Sorry, inside joke."

But I stop listening to him. My last girlfriend just swam away from me while still being in my hands. Astonished, I look at her—him—as though he cheated on me with a goldfish and forgot to invite me to their wedding. They say we don't choose family and I didn't choose her, but I was taking care of her as though she were my relative. Yes, I know, I don't have any female friends left with me, and I didn't need a fish to remind me of that.

CHAPTER TWELVE

Who's Mr. Periwinkle?

After several days of travel, I finally arrive home at 6:30 A.M. on Friday, October 13. Not exactly three strikes of heels, but the *Titanic* and the *Orient Express* worked just as fine. On the *Titanic*, I realized I can apparently get seasick, and partially allergic to the ship's captain and their fried octopus special. On the *Orient Express*, I learned the hard way that the lack of clean air caused me to eat excessively, and according to their bathroom mirror—any mirror—I gained a third chin. Not much fun when you didn't know you had the second one to begin with.

I have one and a half hours to get ready and be out the door for work, even though I'm not only exhausted from a four-day trip but also ready to collapse. I sent an email to Adam on Sunday morning from a computer at Waikiki Beach Palace, telling him I was sick with flu, but later on the trip, I realized nobody seemed to carry a charger similar to mine and I was unable to charge my phone to check for a response. It has been four workdays. I missed my meeting with Mr. Grunt. I am terrified.

I exit the subway on 46th Street, a station located three blocks away from my building. Clouds stretch above Astoria like dirty black pantyhose. Rain will downpour any minute now. The temperature is tolerable, maybe fifty-five, maybe less. Broadway is empty, with occasional umbrella-carrying pedestrian passing by, giving me a look of—from what I could sense—pity, due to perhaps my greasy hair and a "Wide Open" print tee I had to purchase bypassing Nevada. Even a homeless person upon seeing me at Penn Station offered me a dollar, which I'm planning to break into quarters and use as laundry money.

Stoops are full of carved pumpkins. Many windows are decorated with Halloween things: witches, webs, bats. Black and orange colors dominate. These are the common pastel colors of New York in fall, and they're depressing if nothing else. Smells of pumpkin pies and apple cider are strong, coming from a bakery on the corner of my street. They won't open for another thirty minutes, so I'll grab something on the way to work.

I quickly sort through the accumulated mail as I enter my building. The foyer is a little square, perhaps eight by eight with mailboxes on either side. There's a corkboard with my landlord's and superintendent's contact information hidden behind Plexiglas. Since Leonard, the mailman, leaves correspondence on top of our mailboxes, not inside of them (after he lost his key two weeks ago), I don't need a mail key anymore. Nothing of interest, when I sort through the letters I've received. One letter looks suspicious, addressed to Laura Dubbs. She apparently used to live in my apartment, number seventeen, and I open the letter regardless. It turns out to be a pre-approved credit card application should the times get rough, with a guaranteed $1,500 in credit line limit. If the offer was for me, I'd apply without thinking. The trip across the country—without a driver's license or a passport, if wasn't painful enough—cost me over $600, closing in on my credit card limit by a spare $90. I deposited the joke that was my paycheck while waiting for a bus in Los Angeles. Most of the paycheck money will pay for some (but not all) bills, buy me a monthly MetroCard, and then I'm broke again.

When I climb all the way to the fourth floor, crawling at the end like a centipede, I'm completely out of breath. In one of the four apartments located on my floor, a dog begins to bark with such vigor you'd think the dog's spotted a burglar. As far as I know, the tenants are prohibited from having pets, and once the landlord becomes aware of the dog, someone's in big trouble. Feeling pity for the dog and its owner, I ain't got no time for. A black-and-white Lurch greets me with a hideous grin. Being a huge fan of *The Addams Family,* I couldn't resist hanging Lurch's full-size cutout—found on the street last year—on my door. Compared to his angry look, the "Welcome" mat seems ironic and out of place.

I instructed Chloe not to deadbolt the door, but she did it anyway. I ring my doorbell, which spits out an angry buzz. Twelve times during the trip I regretted giving my keys to Chloe. What if she's not home? Getting a locksmith this early on would make me lose my cool. After waiting for what seems like an unnatural amount of time, I ring again. Impatience sets in and I press the doorbell without letting it go.

Barking continues. I place my ear to the door, trying to pick up any noise coming from my apartment. I hear movement inside. I can swear the barking is coming from my apartment though I know it can't be true. Chloe unlocks the deadbolt and opens the door as much as the burglar-proof chain permits. Her platinum blonde hair is sporting dark roots while little spikes make her a copy of a hedgehog. Upon seeing me, she closes the door, unhooks the chain, and lets me in. Her nightgown is a tutu and a strapless bra, revealing a tattoo I never knew she had: the Pisces sign on her right shoulder. She's only half awake and her face scores several sleep lines.

I walk in, put the Gooseberry and the tote down, and try not to freak out. In view are birdcages in the living room, three cats watching the birds, and a Rottweiler (in a medium-size crate in the bedroom, the reason for the earlier barking). The stench is reminiscent of the pet store where I purchased the new tank for the fish. It looks as though Chloe has completely moved in: books are scattered everywhere, clothes are strewn in each corner, and dishes are piled up above the sink. Bottles of honey sit on top of an overgrowing trash can. I need to teach her about recycling. Little tiles on the kitchen floor are sticky, spots of dirt visible on their light-gray pattern.

Chloe takes Anubis' case from my hands, clumsily returns to the bedroom, and slides the door to close. Counting apple martinis to calm myself down, I put Elizabeth on a floating shelf in the living room. Yes, for the time being I decided to stick with the name Elizabeth. The cats eye her (and, yes—the fish is still a she). I plug my phone in to charge, after which I detour to the bathroom, longing to take a hot shower.

My tiny bathroom consists of a toilet in the corner, a small sink with a medicine cabinet above it, and a bathtub, which I separate with a green shower curtain. I literally have to walk sideways until I reach the bathtub. I slide the curtain.

Inside the bathtub, a buttload of fish are swimming in circles, the tub filled to its full capacity with water. A lobster is chilling at the very bottom, its claws tied with rubber bands. One fish is floating belly up while another fish is nibbling on the stiff. From the corner of the bathtub, I grab my shampoo and conditioner and go to the bathroom sink, which is full of more fish.

Angry enough to make a child cry, I return to the kitchen and vigorously scrub the dishes in the kitchen sink, placing the clean ones in a dish rack above the fridge. Like normal human beings who learned how to order food online, I spot several pizza boxes Chloe ordered during the week. The trash hasn't been taken out. She finished the alcohol I kept in the freezer in my flask, and now empty it sits on the counter, attracting dust. I fill it up and put it back in the freezer. She turned my apartment into a zoo is what I realize while washing a mug I never knew I had. In fifteen minutes, when the sink is clear of dishes, I spend ten minutes washing my face and hair, occasionally scrubbing under my armpits.

Chloe listened to her mama and removed the pets from her apartment—only to bring them over here. Loving and rescuing animals is a good thing, I realize, so long as I'm not involved. Just the past twelve minutes inside made me want to jump out of the window if only I didn't live so damn high up.

Mad, dirty, and unshowered, I enter my bedroom for clothes. The dog resumes barking as I slide the door to open. Chloe hides her head under a pillow. Anubis, free from his cage, watches the dog, amused by the fact the Rottweiler is locked up without being able to do anything. If cats knew how to show a middle finger, Anubis would do just that. There's a stain on my green Jennifer Lopez sheets, upon seeing which my jaw drops. A pepperoni slice is glued to one of the pillows. If only there was time, I'd kick Chloe out of bed and do laundry in the new 24-hour Laundromat across the street. But counting apple martinis, I slowly breathe in and slowly breathe out.

In the closet, I find a white blouse and a knee-length black skirt, hose and black dress shoes, an ensemble that will scream business-business, what is needed to impress Mr. Grunt. Even though I can't take a shower, I grab a pair of clean underwear and a fresh bra. I change in the living room, feeling somewhat weird with all these pets watching me. The beautiful wood floor is scratched in several spots by cat claws, from the look of things. I grab half a walnut from a special bag of walnuts I keep for fixing wood, and rub the piece into the scratches, making some completely disappear. Luckily, the wired feeling of anticipation is rushing through my veins and I can't sit still anyway.

Next I fold Chloe's clothes, stack the books in three neat piles, dust the TV. An hour left. I mop the kitchen floor and empty the trash bags, carefully removing any bottles suitable for recycling and placing them in appropriate bins: plastic and glass in one, paper in another. I fold the pizza boxes and stick them with the rest of the paper. I tie up all the bags and put new ones into bins. Forty more minutes.

In the kitchen sink, I extra brush my teeth, extra floss my teeth, extra rinse with mouthwash; everything this morning must be extra-extra. I'll even leave a little extra early, in case the M line is going to be extra late. Mr. Grunt has to know how good I am, so he can fire Babette instead.

In the bathroom, I turn on the light, realizing promptly I look a mess. The healthy Hawaiian glow left my cheeks, bloodshot eyes are halfway hidden under heavy lids, and brows need some serious mowing. After I layer my face with makeup, I pointlessly poke myself with a mascara wand, clumps of the products gluing lashes into three to four big lashes per eye. With a toothpick, I separate the eyelashes, but the outcome is hardly impressive. When the lashes get dry, I use the eyelash curler, which helps with hiding droopy lids and makes my eyes pop.

Blow-drying my hair, I notice something I wasn't expecting, besides the triple chin, that is: puffiness under my eyes makes me look not dissimilar to a blowfish. There is a saying: pet owners resemble their pets—Elizabeth, in my case—but Mr. Grunt can't see me looking this way. I could potentially wrap my face in a scarf, but I decide to scratch that idea for the time being. Instead, I find a cucumber in the fridge, cut two slices from it, and lie down on my new couch, putting a slice over each eye. I read somewhere in a magazine this cucumber routine will help revive fresh-looking skin under your eyes, and even though the cucumber is cold, it's rejuvenating.

The couch feels comfortable, but I feel far from being relaxed. The birds chirp and the cats mew, the dog barks and the fish splatter. Chloe and I have a lot to discuss after I'm back from work. Adam will probably make me stay late to catch up on work, but flu is flu, I'll tell him, not like I could come in sick.

On his question why I never responded to any emails or called, presumably he asks that, I'll tell him my phone was stolen and my Internet was cut off for nonpayment. Maybe my story will inspire him to give me a raise. Tonight, I'm definitely not going out for drinks, even though going to a bar would be the most appropriate thing to do after the crazy week I've had. Instead, I'll make Chloe bring the animals back to where they belong and catch up on my sleep.

Lying down, I realize the couch was worth every borrowed-in-credit penny. Its soft cushions are heaven after a week of rough living. The cucumber feels soothing. I can tackle this day.

"Caly."

I remove the cucumber slices away from my face and open my eyes. The dog's no longer barking. Chloe, already dressed and groomed, taps my shoulder slightly, as though afraid she might hurt me.

"I made you breakfast," she says excitedly, pointing at the black lacquered coffee table purchased at IKEA. There's a plate with French toast, scrambled eggs, and a mug of black coffee. The plate is steamy and so is the coffee, both apparently freshly made. She's fast, I think, since I've only lain here for less than a minute. Digital wall clock in front of me shows time: 10:30. I overslept! It's too late to call out now. I jump off the couch, after which I grab my handbag, unplug the charger from my phone, shove the phone in my bag, and hurry out of the apartment right away, jumping down three steps at a time. I overslept by three hours. What a dummy. If Chloe woke me up, none of this would happen.

Outside, the earlier gloominess turned into nighttime darkness without a single break in the clouds. The street to the train station is blocked off with traffic cones and yellow tape, preventing pedestrians from walking in that direction. Several heavy men jackhammer the cement along the berm of the road while dust makes it hard to breathe. I pull the blouse over my mouth and nose. What are they doing here? One thing is clear I can't reach the nearest train station. Quickly, I dash into the opposite direction toward the next station located on Steinway Street. The station is farther, but I have no choice. This area of the neighborhood is crowded, people roaming the streets in all possible directions. I must speed up and maneuver around. Slow people annoy me, which is why I never go to Times Square often.

A block away from Steinway Street, a broken traffic light has created a confused array of honking cars and hollering pedestrians. A lady in a green traffic uniform holds a STOP sign in her hand. With the whistle in her mouth, she motions for cars to continue. Oh, lord, as though I wasn't late enough. In my section of the sidewalk, a good number of people accumulate and we all wait for our turn. The traffic lady turns the STOP sign and whistles, allowing us to cross the street. I swim through the crowd, curve the corner, and run for the subway station.

The train, as expected, is delayed. "Ladies and gentleman," an automated voice announces, "because of construction, Manhattan-bound R trains—between Roosevelt Avenue and 34th Street-Herald Square—are rerouted via the F line. For a Manhattan-bound E train, please take a Queens-bound local train to Roosevelt Avenue and transfer to a Manhattan-bound express train. We apologize for any inconvenience." That means once I get off the train, I'll need to walk five extra blocks. On the opposite track, an R train arrives, picking up passengers who were waiting on the platform. Anger makes me scream out loud.

The platform quickly fills up with new passengers carrying wet umbrellas. The first thought is I forgot mine. I fight back tears, feeling like a complete moron. If I knew anything about *anything*, I'd turn around and tell Adam I'm still sick but should recover by Monday. Since I'm already here and since I've wasted all this time getting ready and waiting for the train, I might as well attempt going to work. The train will come soon. Another train approaches the opposite side, an M train. An announcement tells us there's a Manhattan-bound train two stops away. At 11:05, it finally arrives.

To infuriate me even further, the subway car is so crowded I think by mistake I enter into a relationship with a guy in a suit who stands an inch away from me. He's reading a book with his arm holding the railing above his head. He's tall and handsome while my short and fat body is pressed against his. Should I kiss him? Will he propose after this? He's kind of young for me, but he smells better than Cute Mango. When he first entered the train, he kept watching me, probably because I look so pretty and professional, but when the train started moving, he lost interest and began reading. I learned it the hard way never to trust men who read.

One stop to Manhattan, on Roosevelt Island, the train halts. Two minutes pass by, but the car doors are left open while new passengers keep trying to squeeze in. An overhead announcement comes distorted, but because of a mumbling Latina next to me, I miss it. Passengers start looking at each other, trying to find the one person with a satisfied look who understood the conductor. In a couple of minutes, I hear another overhead click and cup my ear. "Ladies and gentlemen, we apologize for the inconvenience, but due to an ongoing investigation at Lexington Avenue and 63rd Street Station, this train will be going back to Queens. You can transfer to a Manhattan-bound E train at Roosevelt Avenue or take the tram."

Roosevelt Island—a narrow piece of land that runs between Manhattan and Queens—has only one subway line and a tram that goes above water. Having fear of heights is the main and the only reason why I've never taken the tram. Going back to Queens is out of the question since I'm halfway to work, so I flee the train with the many others and follow the exit signs. On the platform, half the passengers dip into their phones without paying any attention to the surroundings and walk in such positions with necks bent, slowing the whole procession. The train leaves back to Queens, and the passengers who've also exited are waiting for their turn to enter the escalator. The tram's capacity can't be more than a hundred people. The platform is packed with at least four hundred, and I'm creating a plan to start running as soon as I'm outside to outsmart the others. It's past 11:30, an hour since I left Queens. Roosevelt Island doesn't have a bridge directly to Manhattan; otherwise, I'd take a cab regardless of its price.

The escalator looks long and exhausting. By unwritten rule of New York, you always walk on the right side of stairs, streets, and platforms. On an escalator going up, the right side is for standing while the left side is reserved for impatient passengers who need to walk up. Both sides of this escalator, however, are occupied, and nobody is walking up, creating no suitable paths to swim through. Next to the escalator runs a staircase, devoid of people because no one wants to walk. Like a complete loser, I take the stairs. Soon I realize it was a bad idea as with each next step it gets harder and harder. Halfway through, my calves remind me I ain't no Wonder Woman; they start to hurt in an unfamiliar way. My energy stores are depleted and, simultaneously while walking, I open a pouch of dried Turkish apricots, shoving three in my mouth like a real lady.

The last three steps are the hardest, but finally, I make it upstairs. Cutting through the line of people, I exit outside and run toward the tram terminal. Light drizzle supervises my jog as I round the corner. Fog has risen up from the East River, making Manhattan buildings appear as though they're hanging in the sky. The damp air is cold. At the terminal, I swipe my Metro-Card and go through a turnstile. Me and a woman with a young son are the last people allowed on board before the operator shuts the doors and makes us ascend. Finally, we're going places!

Turning away from the window, I open my phone for the first time in a week. Unread emails start to pop in. Natalia called and left a voicemail. Lindsay sent five text messages, in one of them asking what are my plans for tonight. I know what my plans are, and meeting Lindsay ain't one of them. An assortment of emails makes me freak out when over a hundred unread messages invade my phone. I'm not crazy, but I can't deal with anything unread or undone, and this mess is killing me. There are three different mailboxes synced with my phone: personal email, spam email for store offers, and even work email. Sometimes I wonder what people did without all these handy tools to multitask; open different browsers on their laptops and log in into each individual email one at a time? I put the phone away and wait patiently until we dock.

Heavy rain sizzles the street as I exit the tram in Manhattan. Queens is hidden from view by fog and rain, Ed Koch Bridge only partially visible while the other half is consumed by the bad weather abyss. Across the street from the terminal there's a corner store that sells umbrellas, but I learn they don't accept credit cards and I have no cash on me. Luckily I catch a cab, which takes me down to my office, conveniently located near Rockefeller Center. When I exit the cab, a homeless and hungry woman blocks my way. She holds a sign written in sharpie on a pizza box "HOMELESS AND HUNGRY" is how I know she's homeless and hungry. Her hair is coal-black, braided into dreadlocks, halfway hidden under a green pashmina. Within three seconds, I know I need to hurry up because if I get fired, I might as well join her with a similar sign; she'll probably kick my ass for using her corner so I'll be forced to beg on Times Square. To avoid being homeless and hungry is why precisely I need to keep my job.

I enter my office building and deposit myself inside. Noon. Well, right on time for lunch.

I'm either paranoid or everybody in the lobby is studying me as though I have a tattoo of a one-legged prostitute's anus who's sick with hepatitis C and who's been on probation for over a year and whose parents are immigrants from France (or at least how I'd react to anybody with such an elaborate tattoo). The building management has decided to decorate the lobby for upcoming Halloween. There's candy, fake eyeballs, plastic pumpkins, link garlands, tassel garlands, and black cat cutouts resembling Anubis. Several boxes marked "Halloween" are stacked on top of one another. The person responsible for decor is working on a garland, trying to hang it across the lobby. If only I had time, I'd help him.

I show my badge to the security guy, who I like to make fun of, and he looks at me askew, not quite directly in my eye but from an angle as though embarrassed. I take the elevator to the thirteenth floor and note how the elevator walls appear cold and metallic. People in the elevator are also cold and metallic. They give me such a stare that I wonder whether Babette has something to do with it. Maybe she spread rumors about me, and she had a whole week to feed lies to all the hungry employees.

When the elevator doors open on my floor, I step out slowly, trying to get my bearings. Shred Unread—the name of our company—is written straight ahead. By "unread," we mean we shred documents without reading them; as oppose to, I guess, other agencies who apparently might. Our logo is a tree with an X mark over it. Underneath, in smaller letters, our credo appears: "Please, cut trees; they cause heart disease. The more trees are cut, financially we'll worry not. Paper is good, it brings us food. Not inspired? Oops. You're fired." Mr. Grunt came up with it all by himself.

I round the corner. People are cramped in their cubicles working. Sounds of printing, typing, and low-humming voices are heard throughout. Everything seems distant and unfamiliar. Nobody even notices me as though I'm invisible. What did I expect, a red carpet event called "CALYSSA IS BACK" along with drinks and hors d'oeuvres? Well, no red carpet event needed;

drinks and hors d'oeuvres would do just fine. I'm glad I decided against wearing a coconut bra—which I purchased at the Honolulu Harbor—because nobody would stop to ask about it anyway.

A meeting is taking place in a conference room, but people there seem unfamiliar. The kitchen is empty of employees, and even though I long to get a snack, first I need to be at my desk to blend in with the rest of the working class. In a smaller conference room, a lady from HR is interviewing a man in his mid-thirties, who, on closer inspection, could easily pass for late twenties, even though my gut tells me he must be in his early forties. That's how tricky men are, man. The two of them give me a stare, as though wondering why this crazy lady is peeping with both palms pressed against the glass. So I continue along.

My HR friend, Jessica, is nowhere in the periphery. So far, no one has noticed me, which is better than having them holler my name and shame me for being late. One ugly, fake plant we keep for whatever reason has never been dusted. Near the restrooms, our truck driver, Tyron, is chatting with Bob, our mailman. Our company owns twelve trucks with built-in industrial shredders, which we send to various offices, where our drivers/agents shred on sight in front of our clients to keep it "unread." Those shredders are powerful, man, and can easily guzzle ninety gallons of paper in less than five minutes. My job is to ensure Adam misses no meetings, and most of the time I end up answering his emails when he's dealing with marketing or advertising professionals, who come here on a regular basis.

To my surprise, my cubicle is occupied by a blonde I've never seen before, who's blabbing on my phone as though she were me. Her hair is collected into a light bulb, secured with bobby pins and an oversized butterfly hair clip. She chose slacks and a cardigan as her attire, underneath which her boobs not only visible but whisper, "Touch me, I'm free." An imitation fur coat rests on the back of my swivel chair. She must be a temp substituting for me. Knowing Adam, it comes as no surprise he's picked this breast monster. She's jotting something down with my fancy pen on my fancy notepad, both won for being a coworker of the month. I'm so pissed! I rip the phone off her ear and slam it down the base. She looks up and shrieks upon seeing me as though I resemble a one-legged prostitute who's sick with hepatitis C and who's been on probation for over a year and whose parents are immigrants from France. Her glowing face and wrinkle-free skin tell me she's recently graduated college, so she *must* be stupid.

"Okay, Barbie doll, time to go," I say. I wanted to use the f-word but figured she'd understand its implication.

"Who are *you*?" Her voice is high-pitched and annoying. What a sassy little bitch.

"I'm Adam Klutz's secretary. Bye-bye."

"Not until he tells me so."

"Fine."

After positioning my bag on the desk, I grab the swivel chair and roll her out of the cubicle. I swiftly push her toward the empty kitchen. She attempts to stop the chair with her shoes, foolishly believing she's stronger than me. After a workout at the subway station, I could even box a kangaroo. She stands no chance against the animal that woke within me. *She* should be the homeless and hungry person begging on the street, not me. Besides, she's young and can live with her parents without feeling like a failure. Somehow she maneuvers to stands up, revealing her real height: six full feet. In heels, she's a foot taller than me. I could box a kangaroo, yes, but I doubt I could fight *this* beast. We look at each other without saying a word, my heart beating, her hands trembling. I don't blink in case we're playing wink murder. Her lips smooch into a face people reserve for crying and her eyes budge. She quickly disappears from view, picking up her imitation fur coat off the chair first.

I return the chair to my cubicle and jump into it, swiveling two rounds to congratulate my victory. I dial Adam right away and he picks up on the second ring.

"Hey, Adam, it's me. I'm back at my desk with no flu."

"Calyssa," he whispers, "where the fuck have you been? You never responded to my email."

"My Internet was cut off."

"And you couldn't call?"

"My phone was stolen."

"You were summoned to see Mr. Grunt ASAP. Jessica and Babette are already there. You copy?"

"What's going on?"

"Meet me in front of his office immediately."

Adam slams the receiver against the base. I *knew* he would come along to speak up for me. Why have I ever doubted him? He has a wife, Eve, and maybe in me he sees her, and how difficult it'd be on her if she were in my shoes and was summoned to Mr. Grunt's office. This company is man-made (read between the lines) and women are vulnerable against the company's bigwigs. What concerns me is why Mr. Grunt requested to see both Jessica *and* Babette.

The unsettling feeling of fear prickles my stomach and I get hungry. I need to unwind fast with laughter since vodka is unavailable. Damn, should've brought my flask! Under a pile of papers, I find a picture of the photoshopped Babette. It acts like a catalyst to happiness, for I instantly transform into a different person. With a sharpie, I give her a thicker mustache and write "looking to mate" underneath. Oversleeping and the subway misfortunes have left my mind as though never happened. Now all energized, I stand up and rush toward Mr. Grunt's office, noticing Babette's absence from her cubicle. Her desk is way too organized for my taste. Her knockoff Gucci sits as a substitute in her chair, and I'm sure the fake bag is a better worker than is Babette anyway.

Adam's pacing back and forth near Mr. Grunt's office, arms crossed. I hand him the photoshopped Babette, but he dismisses the gesture. I place Babette in my bra, folding the paper four times.

Adam has no time for jokes. I realize this right after he says, "Calyssa, I don't have time for jokes."

"Sorry."

"What are those circles under your eyes?" He points his dirty finger in my face. "What . . . what happened to you? Did you happen to catch a bus and it dragged you ten blocks?"

I can't be looking *that* bad. Taking my phone out, I turn on the front camera, but instead of me, there's a witch in the screen. What I see will leave disturbed images for years to come. The cucumber had been left for way too long because it gave me two distinct circles that are reddened near the edges, not dissimilar to the way a raccoon looks. My greasy hair resembles a mop that has been cleaning bathhouse toilets since the mid-'70s. My mascara is running in streaks and my lipstick is smudged. Who the *hell* is this savage?

"Let's go," Adam says, grabbing my bicep.

"Not looking like this!"

Before I know it, Adam opens the door, shoves me inside, and steps in after me.

Mr. Grunt looks up rapidly, his eyes of a sneaky asp with no traceable eyelids. He's gleaming. Jessica's sitting on a chair before him and turns around together with Babette, who grins and whose breath fumes reach me right away. Damn, flossing or brushing won't help; she needs to get rid of her entire face. The centipede on her forehead moves as she produces a happy face.

"Pantaleo," Mr. Grunt says politely. "I'm glad you're here. We were just discussing you, dear. Please, sit down. Klutz, please join us too, so I can talk to all of you."

His desk is heavy, expensive, and old-fashioned, its solid and polished look drawing a fine line between him and the rest of the staff. A rich Persian carpet surrounds his desk, mostly peach with some black splattered throughout. In the corner, on a brown leather chair, purrs a Persian cat, his white fat aristocratic face pointed toward the windows in front of him. He's too cool to look at us. He has better things to do. From what I heard, his name is Prince Alcott, who has—I'm sure—never gone hungry for more than two hours, been dropped, or been carried in a condom like had been Elizabeth.

I claim a chair next to Jessica while Adam stands behind because no more chairs are available. Jessica's pale face shows no signs of life. Mr. Grunt is a known energy sucker, according to rumors. My hands fall on my lap, heavy with invisible handcuffs. Ain't getting no raise today, that's for damn sure.

Mr. Grunt grunts. "Give me a minute to finish, and I'll devote myself to you. As I was saying," he says to Babette, "this is unacceptable. Hooks, we must have professionals in our office. 'Please, cut trees; they cause heart disease—'"

"'Not inspired? Oops. You're fired!'" says Babette and laughs at my expense.

"Goodily-goodsy-good, Hooks." His voice is absolutely flat, without any sort of highs and lows normal humans tend to have. He turns to Jessica. "Hirezy, return at three to finish this conversation." He turns to me. A cold, cold man. "The rest of you can run along. I want to talk to Pantaleo one-on-one."

Did he say "one-on-one" or "Juan-on-Juan?" Because if the latter, it sounds like a perfect title for a gay *Kama Sutra*.

Jessica's face is emotionless, eyes as reflective as a mirror. She ain't getting no raise today either. She and Babette stand up simultaneously, leaving the office one after another. Their departure is done in such silence; rain shmopping is heard against the two windows located behind Mr. Grunt. A fire truck passes by, its siren loud and angry against the quiet, rainy New York. Fires are ironic on an overcast day. A six-foot-tall coo-coo clock, next to a fat bookshelf, strikes once, indicating 12:30. I shiver from the dampness. Prince Alcott begins licking himself, and I hope with all my heart he chokes on a hairball.

"Klutz, you too may leave." Mr. Grunt says. His eyes devour me, even though he talks to Adam.

"Can I stay?" Adam asks.

Attaboy! I knew he was going to help me fight.

"Wonderful." Mr. Grunt keeps staring straight into my cucumber eyes. "Let be it, then. Pantaleo, question."

He pauses. Now I get it when people call him Grunt—because his nose is shaped as an electrical outlet, resembling a pig. I've never seen him up close before. His hair is shaped like whole wheat elbow pasta: curly and brown in color. Whole wheat pasta is an offense to Italians everywhere.

"If I understand correctly," Mr. Grunt says, "when you applied for this job, Jessica Hirezy was in charge of the hiring process. Is that correct?"

I nod, unable to produce words.

"Hooks, by accident, came across your application. She found your résumé, which I have before me. Should I keep going?"

From my peripheral vision, I notice how Adam gives me a confused look while I can't take my eyes off my application in front of me.

"For starters, you might want to answer this: To have an interview with Shred Unread, you must have an Associate's degree. How come you, Pantaleo, without an Associate's degree, could get on with the interview?"

Well, what kind of a stupid question is that? I have friends in the HR. I knew I should've brought my flask along.

"Maybe Klutz could answer my question because *he* was the one who overlooked that fact."

I scrutinize him while he speaks. His mouth is wide and split, and his eyes are the size of a pea: a perfect combination for a split-pea soup. Split-pea is something I'd never eat, even if the soup contained $300 on the bottom of the plate. Maybe then, and then only. Adam produces no response but keeps staring at me with an open mouth.

"Or let me read your résumé out loud. Maybe that could help you refresh your memories. You indicate the following people as your references: George Clooney, Arnold Schwarzenegger, Barack Obama, and Pussyman Periwinkle at 212-555-9087. I called them all. The feedback was *extraordinary*. Barack Obama *praised* you. He said you were like a collectible penny: cheap-looking, but expensive if you know its real value. Who's Mr. Periwinkle? The gentleman never answered his phone. It appears the three fives are special because telephones with such combinations are not in service. Does that ring a bell?"

There's only one answer to a question like that. "It's falsified." My dry voice is unrecognizable. "Hooks must have swapped my résumé for someone else's." I like addressing to Babette as Hooks—I sound so badass.

He sneers. "I guess everything is possible. May I read your past experiences out loud for Klutz? Bob's Piizeria with two i's and one z, Broadway Fir —with an i—Boutique, Starvation Army, Three Virgins—a music store, Pantaleo Fried Chicken, Big Hoe Chinese Restaurant . . ." He pauses. "Apparently, most of these places are fictitious, with the exception of the Starvation Army, of course. But even if those places existed, how could you—without any kind of experience—even imagine applying for a job here? Hirezy vowed you had a great personality and were a great worker, which is what we need in this company. I still don't understand why she spoke of you so highly when it's obvious to me you're a slacker. Tell me, Pantaleo, how is it possible that a smart, young, beautiful woman like yourself could type such bullshit—excuse my French—on a résumé? Klutz, anything to add in her defense?"

He turns to Adam, handing over my résumé. Adam takes the paper in his hands for inspection and clears his throat. "On the day when Pantaleo applied for the job, sir, Hirezy mentioned the résumé was excellent and that Pantaleo had an Associate's degree. I held the interview without double-checking. HR is responsible for this, sir. Moreover, it's Hirezy's fault."

Releasing a snorting chuckle, Mr. Grunt's eyes and mouth move up and down. I can't believe my ears. Instead of defending me, he's trying to save himself by blaming Jessica. Yes, I was wrong writing that bullshit—excuse my English-sounding French—but who *doesn't* make mistakes? (The answer is: the dead.) I thought Adam would say how good of a secretary I am, or who the hell needs a degree or experience when I've excelled in this position better than anyone else would have.

"Klutz, I assumed the fault was on the other foot. Hirezy and I will have another kiki about it later today. Let's paraphrase what I meant to say. According to rules and regulations, along with your own judgment, experience, and expertise working with her, Calyssa Pantaleo is *incompetent* to work in this company and, therefore, should be fired. Is that correct?"

"Yes."

Any kind of confidence I've had escapes me. I'm all alone. What should I write on a pizza box—to make me sound authentic—once I start begging on Times Square?

"Elaborate if you wish, Klutz."

"Sir, Calyssa is not even on time most days. She leaves early. She takes her time at lunch, and regularly I find myself thinking she's indeed incompetent. I catch her reading news articles on her computer while eating donuts. I've proposed to have external sites blocked, except for work-related sites. You'll receive the meeting minutes later today once I type them up. By myself."

Now I really need to fart, but it would only make me look like an asshole.

So I try hard to keep it in. The back of Adam's shirt is damp, even though he's wearing an undershirt. I fight back tears. What a liar. Last time Adam and I interacted in the office, he told me I was the best secretary he had ever had. He then grabbed my ass, but I managed to run away. Babette saw it. Adam could get fired for sexual assault—if I had Babette in cahoots—but I'm not petty to rat him out, or dumb enough to befriend Babette.

Mr. Grunt snorts. "Thank you, Klutz. Now I want to talk to Pantaleo. Alone." He whispers the last word. His voice is deep, creepy, kinky-sounding. Prince Alcott keeps purring, completely satisfied with his owner's sinister nature.

Adam rockets up and scoots out the door. Mr. Grunt watches me with his sneaky eyes, drilling a hole in my face. His shoulders are narrow, his head oversized.

"Where are you from, Pantaleo?"

"Staten Island."

"Interesting."

He closes his eyes and scratches his head. Minute passes, maybe two. Anything else I've got to lose? "Look, I'm really tired of this. If you want to fire me, fire me."

He grins. "Calyssa Pantaleo. Coworker of the month. Scared, you're even more adorable. Imagine, you, bringing all this fuss into the office. You're quite a trophy."

I squint, wondering if he's for real. He puts his hands under the desk and opens a drawer where he finds a bottle of rum. After he unscrews the top, he gives it a big gulp. He has rabbit teeth with the two upper ones bigger and longer than the rest, with a hole in between.

"I'm sorry our conversation started in an uncomfortable way," he hisses, "but it doubtfully will leave you unsatisfied. You can get fired, or you can stay and work as *my* secretary."

"You must be kidding."

"No, I must *not*. Whatever I just told you was untrue. All of it."

"I don't copy that."

"Bear with me. See, the older we get, the slimmer is the chance for us to move up. You're then stuck in an entry-level job before retirement, and you make minimum wage. You'll have to swallow your pride and be ready to know your place. Get ready to get humiliated. See, I saw my parents go through that, and that's what motivated me to create Shred Unread. Young people are ambitious! So I hired *you* instead. You have nowhere to go. Admit it, Pantaleo. You'll be surprised to know *I* hired you, not Adam. I read your ridiculous résumé and knew at once you have nowhere to go unless I provide the job. You showed passion, and, let's admit it, you're hot. You'll get big here. This is why I want you to be my secretary. It comes with a raise and praise."

I squint, wondering where the camera is hidden. Soon, the curtain will open and all these cameramen will jump out and scream, "You've just been *Punk'd!*" Please let it be Marcus Truman behind the curtain: the hot, sexy beast of a man who I keep imagining having sex with for the entire week. Reality, however, doesn't work this way. What Mr. Grunt has said registers in my brain, but somehow I can't comprehend this on an empty stomach. I'm familiar with practical jokes—almost an expert—but this one sounds a lot like not a joke.

"What do you say, Pantaleo? You can trust me. Say the word and you're hired."

"I'll have to think about it."

"Twelve-percent raise, plus two weeks of paid vacation. You can't turn that down."

"No one can."

"Wonderful."

My heart starts pounding hard upon hearing I'm getting a 12-percent raise. Let's say it's true, can I really do it? Babette will move down as Adam's secretary, and *I'll* be the new Babette: the ears and the eyes of the company.

Something's bothering me, though, and I can't seem to understand what it is.

"Mr. Petticoat, is that true you once wanted to be a poet?"

"Unquestionably. But what we want and what we need are two unrelated things. I'm realistic when approaching life while remaining a poet requires steel optimism."

"Isn't that the point? This is what some people call 'the gamble of life.'"

"I chose practicality versus the unknown. Gambling, on the other hand, never appealed to me the way it does to others. Luck is blind, but a carefully calculated risk is worth the struggle. Going nowhere was not an option I considered, so I invested my fortune in Shred Unread. I can guarantee I never complained."

Now I remember what was bothered me—it comes in a flash. "Mr. Petticoat, with all due respect, what did you mean when you said I would go nowhere unless you hired me?"

"I used to be like you. Always tried to find something better: a better place to live, a better place to work, a better woman. Life doesn't work that way."

"Why not?"

"I thought I was too good for so many places, but in the end, I found myself at a loss. What I realized was that sometimes you have to accept you're defeated to start your emotional breakdown. With destruction comes creation. People take risks at emotional cul-de-sacs."

"Not sure I understand what you're trying to say."

"Being faced with a wall gives you no other choice but to turn around and start over. Once you're down that pit, you grow new strengths to climb out of it and learn to be better. Before I hired you, you were in that pit. And today you already moved up once. Soon, you'll take Adam's place. You have to stay with the company if you wish to grow. My retirement is right around the corner. Guess I'll need to start looking for a replacement soon. Who will it be? Interesting. Don't you wanna be me, Pantaleo? Be in charge of this amazing shredding company? Because I'm telling you: you might be just the next hot thing who's sitting in my chair."

A dumb smile involuntarily stretches on my face. This is surreal. Even with cucumber eyes, I'm the best. "Wow."

"Wow is right. Now since that's settled, can we talk about something else? New position, new responsibilities."

"I assumed so."

"I don't know how to phrase this without sounding like a pedophile, but I'll give you some time to think about it. Adam is married. Why would you want to mess with that?"

"Pardon?"

His skin is dry and flaky, shedding faster than his cat's. He appears to be studying me. "Oh, come on," he hisses. "I know you sleep around. Secretly, I've always wanted to bend you over right on my desk. You are the prettiest woman I know. If we were characters in a movie, we'd be making out right now."

In my movie, he'd be shot at the very beginning. Mr. Grunt stands up and takes off his jacket, revealing a green shirt. He slithers around the desk, untying his tie as he goes, after which he unbuttons his shirt. I'm paralyzed, unable to move as though the chair I'm sitting on is enchanted. I realize what's going on when he reveals his bare chest on which he grows his own Central Park bushes. His hairy body wakes me up from my state of enchantment. He bends over and touches my neck with his lips, consequently biting it. Felt that, I instantly back off, dragging the chair along the Persian carpet.

"Are you nuts?" I say, getting up. "If someone told you I sleep around, those are rumors."

"Adam told me so himself. Give me a break, Calyssa. Anyone this pretty must be a slut, and there's nothing wrong with it."

He glides toward me. I walk away and round the desk while he follows. How could anyone be this hairy? Unbelievable. We meander around the desk while he licks his lips with a long tongue of his. After picking up the rum bottle, he takes another swig.

"I'll sue if you come any closer," I say. "Why don't you sleep with Babette Hooks for your fantasies?"

"You *know* why. She's an ugly bitch."

"You can hire a prostitute. I know one named Lindsay. She gives great lap dances too. I'll email you her number."

He hisses out a laugh and stops. "Well, well, well. Calyssa Pantaleo. If I knew you'd play an unattainable virgin, I'd invite you for a date first. But from what I heard you act like a cheap hooker. That's such a turn on. I love submissive women. I love your tits."

Cheap hooker? Just because I have cucumber eyes hardly means I'm a hooker. I would agree to be called a tramplet for some of the things I do, an asshole, and even a lady, but *this* spills my apple martini. He slowly moseys toward me and I patiently wait until his face "design" is within reach. I smack his cheek, watching as his scales fall off. He touches his face and yaps while two steps back, I take. The anger in his eye is unmistakable—I woke the beast —and he makes a leap forward, fist out ready to whack my face. Instead, he plummets down, face flat.

I hear a snap. "Shit" is the only acceptable word that leaves his mouth, followed by all sort of expletives. He whines. He's in pain. I notice the reason for the fall: one of his shoes is untied and he tripped on its lace. Didn't mama teach him to tie his shoes? Prince Alcott jumps off the chair with an indifferent look on his face and proceeds toward the accident with his tail up. Cussing, Mr. Grunt pulls out a handkerchief to wipe off blood running from his nose. High altitudes cause nosebleeds, so maybe he should rent an office on a lower floor. But I decide to keep my advice to myself.

Raise or no raise, this is the end of my journey at Shred Unread. Back in Honolulu, at the club XOXO, Wolfgang humiliated Lindsay by telling her she had crooked legs. Now I understand how she felt.

"For the record," I say, "even if I slept with all the men, I'd never sleep with you, you stupid pig. You're nasty, miserable, and disgusting, and those are your good qualities. And you know what? I quit."

"Screw you," he yells from the floor. "You'll never find a job in New York

City with your stupid attitude. Now get the hell out of my office, you ugly bitch. And forget about that unemployment insurance." So dramatic.

Just two seconds ago, I was the prettiest woman he knew.

He howls several sentences containing only cuss words, hopefully separated by commas in his mind. His voice is loud, angry, and different. I'm not a dummy—I want to tell him—I kind of figured he's mad; no need to yell. Blood keeps running down his face as he tries to get up. Quickly, I trot toward the door and turn the handle, pulling it open. Babette falls under my feet, being that she sat there listening the entire time. I step over her, wishing a second later to have kicked her in the knee.

At my desk, I pack in haste. Into the Gooseberry, I throw my fancy pen (fancy, because it was designed by some astronaut). The pen can be used upside down, under water, and even on the moon. I pack my fancy notepad, which probably can also be used upside down, under water, and on the moon. Not that I've tried or needed to. Since both items were won as a prize for being a coworker of the month in September, I'm taking them home. Neither Adam nor Jessica is seen within the vicinity. I leave my badge on the table; it's no longer needed.

On the way to the elevator, I catch Babette's gaze in my direction. She won. At least dealing with her breath is out of my jurisdiction. If she were the Roman Empire, I'm now lying under her, absolutely vulnerable to be destroyed. However, I exit before she's able to swing a sword into my heart. Talk about being dramatic!

Outside, it's raining cats and fish, but did I take my umbrella? Of course not. Because I'm an idiot. And I didn't steal one either, even though a bunch of them sat in the umbrella bucket downstairs. Water is running down my face, but I'm unsure whether these are *my* tears or *Mother Earth's*. I walk toward the subway, completely soaking wet, and my fancy (now ruined) shoes squeak under me with every step like a mouse caught in a mousetrap. Hopefully, I'll rust and die on the street. On second thought, even if I could rust, my face produces enough oil to lubricate me if needed, yet unlike the Tin Can Man, I still have a heart. But it's overwhelmed with a lot of different emotions. The worst is this: If Jessica gets fired because of me, I'll purchase a gun and shoot myself somewhere in the bushes near Dover, Delaware. Another emotion I fail to stomach—on an empty stomach—is embarrassment: How can Mom *ever* be proud of me?

. . .

Taking a different subway line, the Q train, I return to my apartment groggy, thoroughly wet, and bedazzled with anger. In the vestibule, a package addressed to me sits on the floor. The package contains the two books by Grace Bishop I ordered last week. As soon as I walk into my apartment, without saying a word, I enter my bedroom to pack a suitcase. Chloe's spread on the couch, stuffing herself with cookies. Anubis purrs nearby, and they're watching an episode of *I Love Lucy*, her favorite TV show. The apartment has remained in the exact state of despair. If I stay in this mess another minute, with Chloe's stuff piled up like the Pyramid of Cheops, expect a big fight. I need some quality time on Staten Island with Christina and Aunt Sarah, where I can expect a good meal, a hot shower, and a free full bar.

"I'll be gone this weekend," I say sternly from the bedroom. "By the time I'm back on Monday, please take the animals where they belong. Especially the fish."

Chloe ignores, a passive-aggressive way of not saying no. Sticking my head out of the bedroom, I notice her crying, eyes covered with palms. I drop a pair of jeans, exit the bedroom, and sit next to her.

"Chloe, what's the matter?"

She sits up, picking up her cat. "It's my high school reunion."

"What about it?"

"Amanda Gellar made a big mistake. She was trying to reach Chloé Davenport from my class. That's Chloé with a diacritic at the end."

"With a what at the end?"

"Letter *e* with a stress on it. You know what I mean?" I nod without understanding what I'm agreeing to. "When we met for dinner Amanda was obsessively impolite. She said: 'Ugh, it's you I called? What's wrong with you? Nobody would ever want to call *you*.'"

"Oh no, she better don't!"

"She was the mean girl in school, that's why I was so surprised she asked me to dinner."

"I'm sorry it's my fault. She didn't ask for your last name or details, and I didn't elaborate."

"Trust me, it's not your fault. Unwilling to let Amanda bring me down— since I'd purchased a dress for the reunion anywho—I decided to go. At the venue, as I started talking to people, I learned everybody was married or had a child at home. And I just stood there, like a stupid idiot who still lives with her mom and who doesn't even have a job. This was when I realized the jail didn't seem that bad compared to reality. This is the reality, Caly. Of course nobody wants to date this fat mess."

I take her hand in mine and squeeze it. The reunion was Chloe's emotional bottom, an anchor sinking her, the same anchor that shut down Lindsay and made her realize and accept the truth. This is why Chloe brought all the animals here because she wanted to feel better about herself. Since she's not a drinker, unlike the rest of the world and normal people, she cures her emotional pain with cookies, favorite TV shows, and saving others. Each gets her own.

"I had no idea," I say. "I'd never set you up for this."

"It helps to talk," she says, wiping tears. "Thank you. I invited my friend Sam for later. Is that okay? I really need some company, now more than ever, and you said you were leaving for the weekend."

I nod, wondering if Sam is real or imaginary. "Of course it's okay. I understand how you feel. Probably. I quit my job today and it doesn't feel good." I fill her in, sparing the details about my résumé. "I'm going to stay with Christina and Aunt Sarah for a day or two on Staten Island, perhaps for more. I keep a set of spare keys at their house and I'll use them when I'm back; you keep my copy. Whenever you decide to leave, the door auto-locks. Just leave the keys on the kitchen counter."

"Okay."

I follow Chloe's gaze toward the TV set, where Lucy gets sick on the Staten Island Ferry, the place where I'm headed next. We chat for another thirty minutes about nothing in particular, I pack and then leave with a suitcase in one hand and Elizabeth in the other hand.

While waiting for the ferry, I fetch a one-dollar lottery ticket from my bag, leftover from a week back when I first bought it. Reluctant to lose anything else, I put it back, knowing perfectly well this ticket can't possibly bring me a promised jackpot of $5,000.

Crossing the Upper Bay, I notice a woman sitting in front of me. The beehive on top of her head is purple and her sweater is purple. Purple nail polish and a purple phone case. Even though her shoes are lacquered black, there are purple laces in them, untied. Why would you have laces in the first place if all you do is trip on them? Someone loves the damn purple, though. Mr. Periwinkle may be imaginary, but at least I happen to meet Mrs. Periwinkle in person. Her jeans are the color of jeans, as perhaps jeans rarely come in purple. I instantly imagine her purple bedroom and her poor pet: a purple-colored pooch. She's flipping through pictures on her phone and I, being an enthusiast to sneak, snoop, gossip, and eavesdrop, can't help but sit and mind someone else's business. Her photos are mostly of sunsets and flowers.

I realize the psycho, at least, has something she loves. What about me? Do I have a favorite color? "No" is my answer after I give it a thought. How pathetic is that? She likes sunsets and what do I like? Fried chicken? Pictures on my phone seldom go beyond pretty liquor bottles, so what am I, a drunkard lady? How embarrassing must that sound, especially for a woman who's thirty. Mom must be dying of shame up in heaven, hiding from other souls to prevent being pointed at.

After seeing what I'm wearing, I realize I'm just as funky as the purple lady: wet, hair's a mess. There's a fish in my hands, a half-torn plain black suitcase, cucumber circles under my eyes. A person sitting behind perhaps scrutinizes me the same way I scrutinize the purple woman. Discreetly I turn around. A guy in his twenties is reading a book called *How to Shoot People.* My eyes pop open: Even terrorists are shameless now.

"Hey," I say to him angrily. "The nerve you have reading something so stupid. You should be in jail, you ass. Isn't war enough for you? No, because you don't care about society. Why do you want to shoot people?"

Hitler unglues his eyes from the book. "Because I'm a filmmaker? Read the title, bitch."

The title reads: *How to Shoot People.* Under the title, a subtitle is added in smaller letters: *a Manual for Filmmakers.* I suddenly get the wordplay and feel guilty for making a scene. Two adjacent passengers are waiting for my response.

"You should be ashamed of yourself, young man. All you care is film while there are homeless and hungry people roaming the streets of New York."

By "hungry people," I, of course, meant me.

Humiliated, I get up and, without turning back, take the staircase one level up. What a dumb title, in any event.

I think I'm officially done.

The Statue of Liberty appears in front of me: a symbol of freedom all immigrants saw the first time their ships docked at Ellis Island. They hoped for the best; their futures were plain-water question marks. For some reason Grace Bishop comes to mind with her book's title: *But I Wanted to Be a Clown!* It sounded dumb at first, but now I get it. All the mistakes made in my life were *chosen* by me. I chose to be "the clown," and luck and misfortune aren't to blame. But, luck and misfortune can suck it.

New York City is far behind me. Tall downtown skyscrapers turn into a peculiar sight: so many commercial buildings, so many personal ruins. I ran away from all the visible problems: sissy bosses and horny snakes; the invisibles remain: everything I've built in my life collapsed and/or burned to the ground. *Calyssa, get your shit together; why so dramatic?* I tell myself.

The ferry arrives in thirty minutes, and I step onto Staten Island, relieved I'll never have to deal with pointless drama and horrifying breaths. This is it —the future—and a new start with its own question mark, but can I transform it into an exclamation point?

Feeling like my life took an absolutely wrong turn, I decide to get it over with and scratch off the lottery ticket. I can't believe my eyes when I win $20!

I'm *not* done.

I'm *far* from being done!

I feel superiority rushing in my blood. Adrenaline pumps me with energy. Even after the crappy week I had, even after the job I lost, even after the humiliating conversation I had with the asshole film director, I smile. Smile in days, or what seems like months. I hold the winning ticket like a relic in my hands, proof of God's message: after rain comes sunshine. As confirmation, some sunshine is peeking through some breaks in the clouds while a light drizzle washes away my grief.

I wait at the bus stop, munching on dried Turkish apricots. A seagull rips the lottery ticket away from my hands, mistaking it for an apricot. All I can do is gasp—exasperatedly—causing people to stare. And I let them laugh at me.

No—*now* I'm done.

CHAPTER THIRTEEN

Spooky Friday

THE FERRY TERMINAL AND MY DESTINATION ARE SEPARATED BY A twenty-minute bus ride. The bus is one of those linked by an accordion in the middle that produces strange sounds at sharp turns. I sit at the very back, away from people. As the bus starts moving, I notice how much the Staten Island changes when it rains. I can barely recognize anything. Elizabeth doesn't seem to mind the rain at all.

I identify the house from far with its newly installed white fence, a blue spruce tree, and an old, broken Cherokee jeep, as a red ornament dangling nearby. Carved into a smiley face by Christina, a pumpkin greets me near the front porch. I reach the portico, put the suitcase down, and shake off excess rain from my umbrella. I knock as hard as I can due to a broken doorbell. When Christina dated Josh—the baby daddy—things used to be fixed around the house. Now both Christina and Aunt Sarah, two women incapable of changing a light bulb or drive a nail with a hammer, wait until someone offers to help. In thirty seconds, Christina opens the door as wide as the burglar-proof chain permits.

"I need some emergency fries," I say.

"Jesus, Caly. Can you knock gentler next time? You scared the hell out of me and the baby."

I hope she meant she was scared because of the loud knock, not because I look like a spooky ghost with cucumber eyes. She closes the door to unzip the chain and again opens it to let me in. She gives me a hug, like a dog sniffing me as though I were another dog's booty.

"Caly, you smell horrible. I can't stand it."

"Thanks."

"Come in."

I do. From the Gooseberry I pull out the Cute Mango soap dispenser and place it in her hands. Christina's wearing a green silk kimono, my present for her thirtieth birthday three years ago.

"My, you're growing," I say.

She takes the dispenser with a worried expression on her face. "I'm not growing, I'm pregnant. What's *your* excuse for growing? Overeating? What's this?"

"It's your belated birthday present."

"Thanks for wrapping it. Did you steal it or what?"

Ignoring her snarky comment—mostly because she's right—I watch her, mesmerized by the belly, wondering how a tiny baby can transform your body in such a way. Just a few months back she was twice thinner.

"You look horrible," she says. "And your hair smells like hair."

"What is it supposed to smell like, feet?"

"It's supposed to smell like shampoo. Are you okay? You look like a beautiful guitar after an ax struck. Twice."

I roll my eyes at her. She sure knows how to make you feel better about yourself. "Can you please make me some emergency fries?"

She ignores, pointing at Elizabeth. "What's this tank? Fries in the freezer. Help yourself."

"It's my fish, a present from Chloe and Matilda."

"Oh, Jesus Christ."

Christina picks up the tank from my hands and moves the fish around, which must be giving Elizabeth a woozy feeling. The plastic (for Elizabeth's sake) half-gallon tank bought in Hawaii is a rectangular container with a green lid and a handle on top. Since the tank was expensive ($20), I distrustfully watch how she handles the fish with her clumsy hands. I'm ready to save Elizabeth, lest Christina drops the container or cracks it by accident. She hands it back to me and waddles toward the couch, mumbling insults under her nose.

The house is unsurprisingly decorated with Halloween junk because Halloween is Christina's favorite holiday, same as me. Without fail, every year she spends days to prepare the house to appear haunted. Spider webs, witches, and other junk make me feel right at home. The entire atmosphere is frightening, and knowing Christina, a big creepy spider will be waiting for me as soon as I reach the couch. The amount of candy in this house makes my cavities wet their pants.

First, so not to waste any time making my emergency fries, I preheat the oven to four hundred degrees and return to the living room. Three out of four walls (fourth is floor-to-ceiling glass doors to the outside porch) are embellished with murals: a gray-colored graveyard, one with the Halloween essentials (skeletons, skulls, black cats), and the classic—an orange sun with a black tree, bats, an owl, and evil-looking pumpkins.

"I'm going to stay for a few days. I need to recoup."

"Good. What happened to you? You look miserable."

"Thanks."

"I'm serious. If you lie you had a fantastic time in Vegas just to make me feel bad about myself, trust me, you look like nothing fantastic about you."

Where do I even start? Gauchely, down I sit on the carpeted floor, near a black coffee table, right across from Christina, who claimed the couch.

I sigh. "I'll tell you about it tomorrow. I'm too exhausted to explain now."

"Don't explain anything. Sum it up in one sentence."

"I'm no Twitter."

"You're no a lot of things."

"Fine. I was fired today, sort of, then I got hired again, then I got promoted, then I quit."

When Christina fails to respond, I make a face. She squints. "Caly, your story sounds normal to me. You got promoted, and then you quit. That's the way to do it. Attagirl."

"No sarcasm necessary."

She picks up a cup of tea off the coffee table and slurps it like she never learned manners. Her skin glows. Even without makeup, she looks great. Her hair shines and it's blacker than mine, a puffy bun collected on top with chopsticks. Barely could she be any more Asian than that.

"Good for you," she says.

"How so?"

"I told you to quit that job. They treated you as though you're worth nothing. You need to find a place where you're appreciated and respected."

"I was appreciated and respected."

"Stop being in denial. The only reason you stayed there was because of the money."

"That's untrue."

"Oh, right, sorry. And free donuts." I ignore her comment and lean back, using my hands for support. "Caly, living alone made no one an adult. Your *head* makes you an adult. Why are you trying to connect two unrelated things? I don't live by myself."

"Because you can't afford it."

"I make a ton of money at the restaurant. Money is not important."

"Said no smart person before."

"Caly, I stay here because I'm preggo. And Mom needs me. She's blessed with having a talented child like me."

I roll my eyes, wondering how many times I did that ever since I walked in just five minutes ago. "Yes, your ability to use chopsticks as a versatile device impressed millions."

"So why did you quit, anyway?" she says. "Did you find another job or what?"

"Nope. I'll start looking on Monday."

"Then you're right on time to ask the dead about your future."

"Ask the dead? What are you gabbing about?" I say, squinting.

"Today is Friday the thirteenth, hello? Do you remember anything? Medium Chucky is coming over at ten; we're having a séance."

As kids, séances were our favorite thing to do. "Thanks, but I'll skip. I have nobody to talk to."

"Why?"

"I have no dead friends? Why else?" I say, picking up on the warm oven smell. Just a few more minutes.

"Use your imagination. You can speak to anybody. I'm planning to contact Baba Vanga, a Russian prophet. She died in the nineties. She made prophecies until year 3,000."

"Yes, and Santa Clause is real."

"Where's your sense of adventure? Since when did you become so boring?"

"Well, can't you get it? I'm upset. Besides, who sets up séances at your age? You have a baby inside of you. There must be other things to worry about. What are you now, in the eighth month?"

"Almost ninth, hello?" She picks up knitting needles and yarn from the side table. "I'm knitting a scarf for myself," she adds, switching gears.

"Never mind about the scarf. You haven't even done a sonogram, but a séance is necessary."

"I refuse to do a sonogram. It's unnatural, you know. Ask Chucky, she'll tell you."

"You're absolutely irresponsible. You're unaware of you own baby's sex."

"It has nothing to do with being responsible. I want to be surprised."

"You *will* be surprised, all right. What do you tell people when they ask you whether it's a boy or a girl?"

"Frankly, I haven't yet met a nosy person like you who asks inappropriate questions."

"Have you at least decided on the names yet? Or you want to be surprised too?"

"Yes, I told you: Thorow for a boy and Fina for a girl."

She keeps pimping out the idea to call the baby Thorow Lee or Fina Lee. Lee is her last name, inherited from Josh.

"What are you, twelve? His or her name should be normal if you want me to be an aunt."

"I need a catchy name like Thorow or Fina to sell it on the black market. What the hell am I supposed to do with a Chinese baby?"

I look at her blankly. "What are you on?"

"Lighten up. It was a joke for Christ's sake. You're supposed to laugh. Smile, life is awesome. You quit your sense of humor too?"

I shrug. "Probably."

"Fine. Change of subject then. I can't wait to finally have sex again as soon as the baby gets born. All I think about is sex with a man. I almost jumped on my neighbor the other day and last night I had such a vivid dream about having a sex marathon with Usain Bolt."

"Who's Usain Bolt?"

"The fastest man in the world, hello? Do you ever watch TV? Caly, you're so out of it. You're oblivious about your own culture."

Right, what I need more than anything else at the moment is to know the name of the fastest man in the world. I clear my throat in response. The oven beeps three times, indicating it's preheated to four hundred degrees, ready to turn frozen fries into my comfort food.

Christina purses her lips. "If you're going to sit here all day, you're going to meet dead people looking like Baba Yaga. Go upstairs, get ready, take a shower while I make your favorite holiday drink and finish the emergency fries. Chop-chop. They'll be ready in fifteen, so hurry up."

"Thank you."

"Help me get up."

I help Christina stand up, and she wobbles into the kitchen.

Dutifully, I take my suitcase and Elizabeth up the stairs to the second floor. It's impossible to look *this* bad, especially not like Baba Yaga—an old, crooked-looking, deformed woman who travels on a broom. Christina learned her name from a Slavic folklore book she'd stolen from the library. However, I look in the hallway mirror to prove the exact opposite. Now I can scare people without a costume.

The bedroom is decorated with Halloween stuff: A full-length skeleton is standing in one corner, a cute little Gremlin is sitting on the nightstand, and, of course, a full-blown Baba Yaga is hovering above the bed. There are no murals, just little paper pumpkins taped to the walls.

This is the room Christina plans to devote to the baby, but even though the baby is due soon, the room lacks a crib, baby toys, tiny-knit clothing, and kinky-looking bibs. What an irresponsible thirty-three-year-old.

A candle is flickering on the windowsill, scented with something similar to rosemary. Christina repainted the walls for the first time in ten years, and they look neat. Not even a dust mite in sight. In this house, nothing is out of place because Aunt Sarah loves when things are put away. She dusts too often for my taste.

Elizabeth is doing laps in her pool, swimming in circles rapidly from one side of the container to the other. I place her on a leaning shelf in the bedroom, an eye-leveled shelf next to a small, fat cactus in a metal planter.

I decide to take a quick shower. I unzip the suitcase and pull out a tee, pajama bottoms, and a pair of fresh panties. The bathroom, unlike mine, is roomy with a Halloween-themed shower curtain finished with webs, ghosts, and red spiders. The bathtub is bleached-white since Aunt Sarah is such an OCD. I turn on the water and wait until it warms up, testing the temperature with my thumb. When the water is perfect, I step into the bathtub and flip the switch to start the showerhead. I always thought word "showerhead" had something to do with a word "blowjob."

I wash my hair with Aunt Sarah's $1.99 shampoo to have Christina stop saying it smells like hair. Aunt Sarah never spent more than two bucks on anything. We used to be so poor I learned about how good apple martinis tasted by reading about them in a book. We could never afford alcohol. This was when Christina and I started working as soon as we reached legal age— seven—stealing neighbor's apples from their apple trees and selling them for twenty cents per pound by the Staten Island Ferry.

I massage the conditioner into my hair and leave it on for ten minutes, which makes my hair feel extra silky and smell like coconut. Why do people choose weird produce like coconut for their beauty products? Or why do they wear coconut bras? Why not apple martinis? If my shampoo smelled like apple martini, for instance, why would that be a bad thing?

The "clean smell" bar soap is the only option for body and I lather myself good. They label it "clean smell" as though it was ever possible to have an unclean smell. People would figure out it has a clean smell.

Standing under a hot stream, I can't help but wonder about the séance. Anybody who believes in such stupidity after the age of seven deserves to have a baby with an unknown name and gender. Christina's priorities are messed up. On my other shoulder, an eternal optimist whispers there's a possibility to contact Mom. Even if the séance is bogus, I still have imagination.

But what would I ask her?

Obviously, a question about my future should be the most important, as in: Will I find another job?

Would I rather ask about whether or not I ever get married? None of my family members ever had, despite our ability to procreate without men. Should I ask Mom whether she's in hell or heaven? Can she take a plane from one to the other? And most importantly: Is there any alcohol?

After the shower while toweling myself dry, I call Jessica, but her phone goes straight to voicemail. I put my phone to charge on the nightstand. At 5:00 I head downstairs. Christina's sitting in front of the TV set, knitting her scarf. As promised, she made my favorite holiday drink—eggnog with rum—which she left out on the kitchen table in a glass. Her eggnog is delicious. It reminds me of our holidays with each other when we were kids, minus the alcohol. And why do we never get together like this anymore? Last time I saw Christina and Aunt Sarah was when Christina had no belly. That was four months ago. I was so depressed about something (I forget what it was), and I came over then. I even failed to appear for Christina's birthday as I chose Vegas instead because during happy times family is the last thing on my mind.

But it's a fact: Grief brings families together. We gather during funerals, hospitals, happy hour after work. It's hardly a bad thing, but it's definitely a true thing, since here I am, weeping about my life, disguised as a coconut.

Hocus Pocus is on TV, one of Christina's favorite movies of all time. Mother Goose is knitting her scarf while occasionally watching the screen and laughing. The pink material makes me wonder if she knows something about the baby's sex but pretends she doesn't. What if she's knitting baby clothes after all, acting clueless to piss me off? She loves doing that.

"Did you make my fries?" I ask.

"Listen, we ran into a problem. I realized we're out of emergency fries."

"What!" I run back to the kitchen. The oven has been turned off and there are no fries in the freezer. "Christina, this is why they're called emergency fries—they must be there for an emergency."

"Sorry. I can make you some food."

"I'm not hungry. I needed comfort food."

"There's ice cream in the freezer."

The ice cream she's referring to is butter pecan. The tub is full and I grab a fork, returning to the living room. Christina always makes fun of me for eating ice cream with a fork while I make fun of her for eating fries with ketchup. Gross. I stand in front of the TV and watch the movie, forking the ice cream. I'm still annoyed at Christina, but I decide not to mention it. So séances she sets up, but when it comes to the essentials, she's oblivious. When only half the tub remains, I return it to the freezer and sit on the floor between Christina's legs, using the couch for support.

"Could you braid my hair?" I say. "It now smells like coconut."

"Sure."

Christina places the knitting supplies on the side table while I stretch out my legs, a relaxing pose I was dying for all week. Her hands are soothing, almost magical, comforting me in some way until she actually starts braiding me. She pulls my hair as hard as she can, perhaps trying to lock a look of surprise on my face.

"By the way," she says, "it seemed you needed a catnap. I mixed some good stuff into your drink to calm you down. If you pass out, that's why."

"Thanks." Even though she speaks as though she hates me, the way she acts proves she cares.

I finish the eggnog. I place my hands between my thighs where it's warm and toasty, and soon after I lose control over my body.

WHEN I OPEN MY EYES, I'M ON THE COUCH UNDER A THICK WOOL blanket. The fireplace crinkles with a merry sound of fire, a low-humming conversation heard from the kitchen. The night has consumed the premises; candles lit per Christina and Aunt Sarah's daily custom. They both hate artificial lighting. Candles create an ambivalent atmosphere great for meditation, heart-to-heart discussions, or good ol' drinking. The spooky toys around the house light up once in a while, especially when you least expect them. One toy I hated the most was a dead man with snaggleteeth, who laughed creepily every time something bypassed. He even turned his head around in your direction. Luckily, he's nowhere in sight because last year I "accidentally" spilled an apple martini onto his electrical parts, which did no good. But a pair of scissors fixed him in no time.

The knock on the door comes so unexpectedly I almost jump. I stick my feet under me, ready to cover my head with the blanket in case Freddy Krueger barges in to skin me alive. Christina appears in the living room and walks toward the door, acknowledging the fact I'm awake by waving at me.

"This must be Chucky," she says.

When the front door opens, a rush of chilled night air invites itself in, cross-breezing with an open porch door behind me, which shuts immediately. I never understood the mechanics behind why one door shuts when another one opens, but it must follow the same rule as to why you buy another drink when you finish your first one.

The woman comes in and Christina flips on the hallway light. Her attire is black chador head to toe, wrapped around her like a Christmas present, minus, of course, a bow on top (and minus, unfortunately, the present itself). They embrace each other. The woman looks like a walking skeleton, especially compared to the fat Christina. Maybe she's fasting, or forgot to eat for a few days; maybe she's broke. Whichever came first. I would give her $7 for a burger, but, now that I'm broke too, she can suck it.

"Hey, Calyssa, this is Chucky," Christina says.

I say nothing.

"Hello," Chucky says, businesslike. "Nice to meet you."

Her accent is unmistakable. Black eyes and sunken cheeks give her an appearance—how to say this without being rude?—of a woman who was just hit by a watermelon, after which ants nibbled on her. Chucky proceeds toward the living room while I silently study her. What triggered her parents to call the woman Chucky (the world's most frightening doll) may stay unknown, but what I do know is that with Chucky's influence I may end up with a niece whose name is Fina. I keep an eye on her distrustfully, as though she might ruin the balance of our planet. I never—after the age of seven— trusted anyone who called themselves mind readers, fortune-tellers, or gypsies. Anyone resembling them would only net a laugh from me. How can one take Chucky seriously, especially when she acts all serious? Christina disappears into the kitchen, leaving Chucky and me alone in the living room. Chucky removes the black clogs and claims a spot near me.

"Don't you bask in joy because of the way I rearranged Christina's furniture?" she says. "Now everything is positioned according to Feng Shui. The entire house has such a positive vibe about it. You like?"

To save face I nod, since, in the first place, I was ignorant to even notice the furniture was rearranged. *Bask in joy?* Is she for real? "It's lovely."

"The hex had been placed on this house, and sixteen is an evil number. Hexadecimal is an imbalanced method to count; it disturbs the equilibrium. Now every piece of furniture in the house has a decimal at its base."

Chucky removes clothing from her head and she is, um, bald, and I mean her head looks like that watermelon I thought she was hit with. Not a hair in sight. It was hardly in my plans to stare at her but I do, and she notices it or senses it (whatever), throwing a glimpse at me while removing a deck of cards from a package. Made most likely by a three-year-old girl out of aluminum, Chucky's earrings are palm-sized and triangular, just two antennae catching radio signals.

"Hair disrupts cosmic connection," she says. "It interferes with thoughts. Communicating with the Universe is purely magical. Much better than with humans. The Universe never lies or gossips, and just like with a tree, expect honesty. Her answers are honest. Besides, trees will never get mad at you."

Yeah, right, unless you try to cut them for Christmas or something.

"Ghosts" she adds, "never lie either, despite how tough of a question you ask them. This is why I love séances and love talking to them. This is how I learn the truth. I've been wondering if ghosts are just people who are unwilling to forget their past as humans. And, unfortunately, they may never be ready to give that up."

She produces Whoppers chocolate balls from underneath her chador and crinkles the wrapping until the package is open. When she puts one chocolate ball in her mouth with a delightful crunchy sound, I automatically drool. I guess Chucky notices how hungry I look or senses it (whatever) because she produces several pouches from underneath her chador. After she offers me two pouches (with three balls inside each), I put the first three balls in my mouth at the same time, amazed by how much better chocolate tastes when you're depressed.

"This lady," Chucky says, "Eleanor, we play tennis together, always puts this candy out on her porch in October for Halloween. She's kind, very kind. But she's also very-very bitter. Her husband died three years ago." Chucky takes the cards in her hands and shuffles them. "Eleanor is in denial about his death. She treats him as though he's still alive. She's the black widow, just like the spider. She's crazy."

I look at Chucky unsure whether she's being friendly or just likes to blab about random things. Talk about crazy.

"What happened to you, Calyssa? Your aura is pitch black. Your soul seems to suffer. Share with me, if you wish. If I can't come up with a solution, I'll ask the Universe for you."

"I'm good," I lie. "I was just having a bad day at work."

Chucky fixates her eyes on my forehead with the same squint I reserve for finding Waldo. She shuffles the cards and lays out four on the table, suits up. I wonder if she demands to play poker with her to make extra cash. Broke people tend to do that.

"Interesting. You've got the wind and fire, water and earth. Calyssa, you've been marked by the same hex. It must be bequeathed. You place bets, but you never win." She points at the four of clubs. "You're at a crossroad and you need to make a decision. The two of diamonds represents a money problem. The six of hearts symbolizes jealousy or a feeling of being unloved. The six of spades is your future: but it's unclear. You go through life confused about the next day. You're unsure of yourself."

"Woo-woo," Christina interrupts by entering the room. She's carrying a tray with four tall candles, oatmeal cookies, and her favorite Japanese cast iron teapot set with five cups. Number four is unlucky in Japan, so Christina always adds an extra cup. Aunt Sarah follows her: hair in curlers, face green from a mud mask with only eyes visible. Aunt Sarah places a Ouija board in the middle of the table and instead of saying anything, as though inappropriate during a séance, she kisses me on a cheek, making eye contact. With her eyes, she points toward the cookies she's baked for me, something she does each time I visit. Her cookies are the best, and I promptly shove one in my mouth.

I learned from a credible source—*Rumors Daily*—that so-called future tellers use phycology on us when it comes to their predictions. When Chucky said I had problems with money, I mean who doesn't? Or that I was unsure of myself. Who isn't? Unwilling to be tricked so easily, I straighten my legs and make a mental note not to take whatever Chucky says personally. Will this liar be able to contact Mom? Somehow I doubt it. The cookie, however, tastes delicious, why I take another one and shove it down my windpipe without chewing.

Christina closes the fireplace opening with an iron door. The flames become indiscernible, the crinkling sound muffled. Aunt Sarah pours the tea in each cup, leaving the fifth cup empty. It must be Christina's favorite Japanese green tea she usually serves to her guests. The tea tastes like grass and ass. I always sip on the tea without complaining, because it'd hurt her feelings if I told her the truth. She'd then argue with me and tell me I have no manners and lack a sensible palate. So if I can avoid being humiliated, I will do that. Once Aunt Sarah places a cup before me, I try the tea. It tastes nothing like grass, but fruity. Unstrained, tea leaves are left in the cup for an unidentified reason. Christina only uses loose-leaf tea and claims that teabags are gross.

"Bring a mirror," Chucky tells Christina. "We need a gateway for the spirits."

Within a minute, Christina brings an ancient mirror in a copper frame. Aunt Sarah loves the mirror to death, as it was inherited from her grandmother.

"Let's begin," Chucky says. She slips off the couch, positioning herself in front of the square-shaped coffee table. The three of us follow her example, and each gets her own side. Aunt Sarah sits across from me. I secretly giggle because soon she'll convert into a rock should she fail to wash off the mud mask. She never followed instructions—hated them, in fact—extending mask time from fifteen minutes to an hour and a half. Maybe stewardess Cave got started this way when one day she forgot to wash off hers.

"The moon is about to reach its peak," Chucky says. "Let's lock our hands now." Saying that, Chucky who's sitting on the right side of me and Christina who's on the left, simultaneously, take my hands. "The portal will soon open," Chucky says. "Keep hands locked. Come what may. Come my way. Choose to stay. Don't go away."

Just like in a horror movie, a breeze sweeps through the house. What if spirits are indeed here, floating around and waiting to be contacted? It's hardly a tornado, but moving flames are a good indication (at least for me) something spiritual is happening. Maybe I'll contact Mom after all. Now I need to figure out what question to ask.

"Let go now," say Chucky, releasing my hand. The breeze suddenly stops. The house gets as quiet as my bar on a Thursday night. Only Chucky's voice is heard under a muffled crinkling sound of the fireplace. "The spirits have agreed to talk to us. As per this Ouija board, the spirits have requested to dismiss the alphabet side and have asked us to use the *Yes* or *No* side. We'll honor that. Each will have one person to contact and one question, requiring yes or no, to ask."

I'm first in alphabetical order and I'm first sitting clockwise from Chucky. I'll most likely go first. Chucky looks too serious for my taste and I keep giggling.

"Christina, you start, and we'll go clockwise from you." I squint at Chucky in disbelief. How did she come up with such a weird order, making me go last? "There's enough time before the clouds dissolve, because then, when the first constellation appears in the sky, the spirits will be gone. First, we need to light a candle for each spirit we're inviting."

Too many rules. Even if the séance is legit and Chucky is able to contact the dead, what question should I ask Mom? Chucky lifts up a box with matches, producing a match eleven inches long with a tiny green head at the end. When she strikes the match on the back of the box, she lights up the four tall candles that stood on the tray all along. When she blows out the flame, she places the match on the table next to her.

"Christina," Chucky says, "you may go ahead and name a person you wish to contact."

"I wish to contact Baba Vanga," Christina says without hesitation.

Chucky closes her eyes, connecting her palms in a praying mantis manner. While nobody is paying attention to me, I unwrap the second pouch of Whoppers as quietly as I can. Chucky is prattling something in her native language, whichever language that might be. Her words sound harsh and sassy, not quite believable enough to be a real language. My theory is Chucky just pretends to talk some fancy witchy dialect to show off.

The breeze from earlier begins to wander around, flickering candles in the house. It seems as though the spirits wish to create complete darkness. It makes sense once I think about it: What would I want to do if my descendants tried to contact me? Would I want to appear before humans as a half-skeleton, half-ghost, face half-eaten by worms? Doubtfully so. That is, I presume, the reason behind why the dead wants us to keep it dark and eldritch. The breeze escalates and stops. The four tall candles remain lit while the rest of the candles throughout the house get doused. My heart accelerates, given the séance suddenly took a wrong turn, toward Creepy Street.

I study my fellow séance-attendees. Christina, Aunt Sarah, and Chucky appear younger as though their faces were just lifted by a powerful force of plastic surgeons. Candlelight creates an illusion is what I gather. As soon as I'm forty, dinner under candlelight will be mandatory. Unlike Natalia, I ain't shooting my face with Botox. As long as I can breathe and feel, there's no way I'd voluntarily inject a needle in myself. Nobody, however, seems scared besides me. Christina nonchalantly pours more tea in her cup. Following her example, I rehydrate my throat with one large gulp.

"Baba Vanga has agreed to talk to you," Chucky says without opening her eyes, "and she's on her way. Now, everyone, close your eyes. We must hold hands tight to unlock the gateway in order for the dead to enter our orbit."

When Chucky catches my hand, she fails to notice (due to being in a state of trance) the chocolate balls in my hand. I keep my eyes open as assurance

Baba Vanga doesn't just appear out of nowhere. This way I'm prepared. Veins on Chucky's forehead begin to pump with blood.

"The gateway is now open. Her spirit has arrived. We're now allowed to open our eyes and let go of our hands."

I quickly close my eyes and reopen them again together with the group. Due to our interconnected heat, the chocolate balls melted on my palm, leaving a sticky residue. I quickly lick off the chocolate before it dries.

"Christina," Chucky says, "you may ask Baba Vanga your question."

"Baba Vanga, will Mom and I go on that cruise we wanted?"

"Now all look at the board," Chucky says while she spins the arrow on the Ouija board clockwise. I thought the arrow was supposed to be moved by the dead, but I guess I was mistaken. It's like an advanced version of spin the bottle if only we had men to kiss. With *Yes* printed on the left side of the board and *No* on the opposite side, the arrow spins for about eight seconds, finally stopping at *No*.

Immediately after, one candle near Christina fades out, leaving us with three candles lit. I'm pretty sure just to scare me, Christina extinguished it herself while I was licking off chocolate. Nothing spooky about that. Aunt Sarah rolls her eyes and picks up a cookie from the plate.

"We have to move on," Chucky says. "Sarah, who do you wish to contact?"

"I wish to contact Cleopatra," Aunt Sarah says. Her loud, deep voice—more appropriate for commanding an army—sounds funny in such a ridiculous environment as a séance.

Christina and I turn at the same time. Of all dead people, why Cleopatra? My brain starts a movie, clear images from the hula dance Marcus and I performed at Ke Iki Beach, as a creepy reminder something extraterrestrial is on tonight. Maybe Cleopatra is indeed immortal and will punch me in the face for impersonating her as a trampy little shit. I remember unraveling in Marcus' arms while the band played Hawaiian tunes.

"Why Cleopatra?" Christina whispers.

"I just saw that movie *Cleopatra* with Elizabeth Taylor," Aunt Sarah says loudly. Christina shushes her and politely smiles. Okay, Aunt Sarah's explanation at least makes sense. Christina is still the odd one out with her choice.

"Cleopatra has entered our orbit. Her majesty is awaiting her question. Sarah, please proceed if you may. Choose your question wisely so it could be answered as yes or no."

Someone else's presence can be now felt. Even if I was skeptical before, now it's legit. This is how mind tricks us, making us believe an itchy-bitchy spider is actually a monster.

"Cleopatra," Aunt Sarah says, "say yes if my daughter's baby a boy."

"Mother!" Christina says. "What a sneaky way."

"No worries," Chucky says, "because the baby wants to keep its sex a secret and even Cleopatra is unable to access such knowledge."

"Fine, then," Aunt Sarah says, "I know what sex it will be. Tell me this, Cleopatra: do you believe in love?"

Chucky spins the arrow, this time counterclockwise. I notice her chocolate-stained left hand, which seems to be immaterial to her. Unlike me, though, she's still yet to lick it off. The arrow rotates loop after loop until it slows down and stops at *Yes*. Cleopatra believes in love. Well, weird question, weird answer. The second flame in front of Aunt Sarah goes out within the next three second. This time, I saw nobody blow on it, breathe on it, or even look in its direction.

This is so happening.

I am contacting Mom for real.

Thoughts, my head is full of thoughts.

What question is more important if there's only one chance?

Will I find my true love and get married?

Will I ever find true meaning to life?

Will I ever lose any weight?

"The time has come for me to speak," Chucky says, eyes closed. "Destiny, please step forward." For a second, I wonder whether Chucky means hooker Destiny from Honolulu. Image of Destiny appears in my mind when she was speaking to the bouncer, two sticks in expensive heels. "I wish to contact Jupiter's Amalthea gossamer ring."

She's not at all abnormal, is she? Chucky moves her head in circles and mumbles words. I have to lean in closer to hear her.

"Will the hex be forever cast on this family? Will the hex be cast even after the baby is born? Tell me, Ring, tell me the truth. Will I fail? Will I score a deuce? Tell me even if it blows. Tell me what the Universe knows. Tell me now, tell me here, tell me, Ring, the truth."

She keeps moving her head in circles. Aunt Sarah and I exchange looks. She can't help but silently snicker, luring me to follow. Laughing is not quite contagious as yawning, but in this family, nothing seems normal. Christina gives us both a face, ordering us to stop.

Chucky opens her eyes. Her irises are gone, replaced completely with pupils. Her face radiates heat while the dark sclera reflects the flame from the candle in front of her, making her appear like a complete lunatic. The arrow starts spinning clockwise by itself, which keeps spinning for good ten seconds, during which I'm looking at it with disbelief, mesmerized. The arrow stops at *No* but then it suddenly rotates in an opposite direction for another ten seconds and rapidly, without slowing down first, it stops at *Yes.* The flame before Chucky goes out abruptly. From fear, I even forget what question she asked.

Now with one candle lit, I look at everyone to make sure they're alive after the bloodcurdling moment. I'm the only one who seems to be frightened, though. Chucky swings her eyes at me. They appear cold and lifeless.

"This is the answer I have not anticipated," she says as though nothing magical has just happened.

I'm next.

My turn comes so quickly I still yet to figure out what question to ask. I sit and try to come up with something my head is completely devoid of, which is a brain.

"We need to hurry," Chucky says. "The stars are about to appear in the sky."

Christina hands over her teacup to Chucky. "I finished my tea," she says. "Could you read it?"

Instead of letting me contact my mother, Chucky examines the cup, exploring it like she's some *Dora the Explorer.* Mad, I look at the three of them. What, my turn is over?

"Saptarishi," Chucky says. "A cluster of seven tea leaves at the bottom of your cup is an asterism called the Big Dipper. It symbolizes the seven days of creation. It means in seven days the baby will come to this world—next Friday. So let there be light."

Chucky returns the cup to Christina.

"What about me?" I ask Chucky. "I wish to contact Amelia, my mom."

Chucky's tired, lifeless eyes find mine. "The first constellation has just appeared in the sky, so you need to hurry up. Amelia had been waiting for your question ever since the séance started. Speak now or forever hold your peace."

I feel her presence so strong I want to cry. She's here. My mom is here. Ready to answer my questions. I give the room a quick sweep with my eyes, hoping to see her. The séance may be bogus, but her presence is real. She may be invisible, but she's everywhere. She's everything. She's God, the matter, the air. All these years she's been living only in my imagination and today she's reunited with the humans to make sure I was okay. Suddenly, so many questions I *must* ask her. So many questions I *want* to ask her. Instead, one question I ask her: "Mom, are you proud of me?"

Aunt Sarah, who's sitting right in front of me, gives me a look and drops it just as fast, avoiding further eye contact. Christina averts her eyes as well and makes a closed-mouth smile.

After Chucky swings the arrow counterclockwise, it swirls fast like roulettes do in casinos. My hands start sweating. A tear runs down my face. Just one tear. Without blinking, I watch the board as the arrow goes loop after loop, putting more mileage on its wheels. Christina pats my thigh. I swallow accumulated saliva into the churning stomach. Blood is pulsating in my head as the arrow spins. I hear my heart loud and clear as the arrow spins. Is she proud of me, or is she not proud of me? Yes or No? I will finally learn the answer. In a few seconds, the arrow starts moving slower and slower, until it eventually stops right in between *Yes* and *No*, in a distinct place in the middle called maybe.

The last candle fades out within two seconds, leaving the house pitch-dark and quiet, with a soft crinkling sound of the fireplace on the background.

I stop feeling Mom's presence in the room.

CHAPTER FOURTEEN

Debating

For hours I'm unable to fall asleep, debating my mother's response. That *Maybe* was hostile. That *Maybe* was evil. What does *Maybe* even mean? *Yes* or *No* are two sufficient answers. Hanging from the ceiling above me, Baba Yaga does none in terms of helping me think, but dangles there like a creep, giving me a certain judgmental look while I pray to the Lord she doesn't fall on me in the middle of the night. The wind seems to be picking up outside, whooshing into the window, just a thief trying to break in. The wind is shaking a poor and almost leafless tree back and forth violently. In the blink of an eye, fall will be here.

Who is Chucky, anyway? Knowing Mother Goose Christina, it comes as no surprise she's friends with such weirdos. Did she really contact the other side? As an adult, I try to convince myself it was false, but the desire to believe proves me wrong.

Why would Mom be proud of me in the first place? I hardly achieved anything, didn't set roots anywhere, and made a fool of myself in Honolulu in front of the Tripps sisters. Marcus renamed me Dumb Dumb. Babette won. My bank account is overdrawn and my credit cards are maxed out. Why would I even ask Mom the stupid question I asked, "Are you proud of me?" I should have known the answer from the beginning. I should have played safe and asked her: Is it possible to make apple martinis from scratch?

Unable to quiet my mind, I sit on the side of the bed and look out the window, rubbing my eyes. Clear, cloudless sky, with all its stars spread out like white glitter against black construction paper, hangs heavily and endlessly all the way from top to bottom, Milky Way gazillion miles away crossing the dark ocean of the Universe like a white ship, out of reach and so close at the same time, something so undeniably big and superior, one of those God's inventions to make you think how small, in comparison, your life can really be. What kind of destruction made this happen? Explanation one: the Big Bang theory, even though it's somewhat eerie. Theory of evolution causes air pollution. If you blame God, then I'll argue not.

Fumbling in the Gooseberry, I find the book by Grace Bishop and start reading it. Grace said, "The feeling of unconditional love is the feeling of the new beginning. Family makes you feel important." Maybe this is why as soon as I quit/got fired, I made an unconscious decision to come here for support. I get under the covers and bury my face in the book.

In the morning, Aunt Sarah wakes me up. The wind guides the raindrops in the direction of the window. Quick, loud taps. No good day ahead is guaranteed. After the morning chants, Aunt Sarah gently takes my hands in hers. She's groomed and dressed. Her black hair is shorter than four months ago, just about covering her ears. Her eyeliner, as always, makes her eyes stand out as her most prominent feature. She resembles Mom but looks nothing like Christina, who inherited her dad's Asian looks. She holds my hands tightly.

"How are you feeling?" she asks.

"I'm fine."

"Baby, the question you asked Amelia last night made me worried. You practically galloped upstairs into your room like she pinched you with a needle."

"Her answer scared me."

"You should understand one thing: the whole séance was phony, so you must ignore it. Chucky is a big fat liar."

"A small, skinny liar, that is."

"True. Christina only does it for her because Chucky is a pathetic, miserable creature, who is friendless, lifeless, and without a job. She's vile and worthless. This seems to make Chucky feel important. She makes this stuff up."

"What stuff?"

"About 'talking to the Universe' nonsense. I just hope you understand this without feeling upset about what happened. Christina mentioned you lost your job. Is that what's bugging you? Is that why you freaked out? You know, a job isn't everything."

"I know."

"I know you know, baby. I'm sorry to hear you lost yours. I know how important it was for you to be there for personal and professional reasons. You seemed happy living alone. But maybe you should consider moving back home. With my boss retiring, I'll be working countless hours and Christina needs help. You know how irresponsible she is."

"I can't move back home. I'm thirty."

"Christina is thirty-three. Please, this will save us both time and money."

"Aunt Sarah, we've been over this before. I can't just leave my apartment and come back. Mom is *maybe* proud of me. How am I supposed to make her happy?"

"To make her happy or make yourself happy? It's the same thing."

"Well, if the séance was bogus, how can you explain the moving arrow?"

"I need to check, but I believe the arrow is made out of iron."

"That explains everything," I say. "*Not.*"

"Chucky might have hidden a magnet underneath the table, manipulating the arrow to move."

"Ah."

"Didn't you notice her hands were under the table when it all happened?"

"No, I didn't."

"Baby, I'd like to chat more but I need to leave for work. I just wanted to say hi to make sure you're okay."

"You work on Saturdays?"

"For a while now, baby. Haven't I told you?"

"I don't think so."

How don't I know this? Have I been this long out of touch? "Being an adult" business made me completely oblivious about reality.

"For the next nine months, maybe a year, I'll be working seven days a week. It needs to be done. Money is good and with the baby and Christina not being at the restaurant, extra cash is welcome. Remember, this is your home too. Always remember that, child. I'll see you in the evening. Don't think of the séance any longer. It's unhealthy."

She kisses my forehead. Before I can reply, she leaves the room and heads downstairs, proved by steps creaking slightly under her.

I get up, bed creaking slightly under me, together with my bones. I brush my teeth, wash my face, put on makeup, and feed the fish. Elizabeth, when she notices me, swims to her usual feeding spot right out front. She waits on me impatiently—fins raised, eyes squinted—until I add a few pallets of food in the tank. Then, like an assassin, she jumps on the food with such eagerness, one would assume the food may escape through some invisible channels in her imaginary Chinatown. Emerald green rocks bring out the green color in Elizabeth, flattering her fishy attire.

Downstairs, I find Christina in the kitchen by the stove with a wooden spatula in her hands. She's one of those annoying people who use wooden utensils so as not to scratch the frying pan. She's standing on her left foot, with the right foot on the left knee—a one-legged pelican. She eats nothing but fried chicken, and I'm half-crazed to have some right about now. For breakfast. Her attire is pantyhose and a brown sweater with a big spider as a centerpiece, plus holes here and there, your normal combination if you happen to be a bumlet. First, I notice her fried chicken looks green and has the odor of broccoli. Before I can say anything, I realize she's in fact cooking broccoli. How she could cheat on fried chicken with *that* beats me. I hate broccoli, mainly because it's nutritious and nutritious food tastes like ass. Melodramatically, I clip my nose with one hand, fanning the area around my face with another.

"Since when you eat broccoli?" I say in that annoying voice created by a pinched nose.

"Good morning to you too. It's for the baby, silly. I have to eat healthy, you know."

"Can you make me your famous fried chicken?"

"Sorry, I have nothing except for kale, carrots, and apples. I can make you a smoothie."

"I wanted fried chicken."

"Sorry."

I open the freezer, but there's nothing unhealthy visible in sight. Ditto in the fridge. First, I just want to pour mayo in my mouth, but something stops me. Oh, the common sense. "You don't have to eat healthy all the time. Little drumstick didn't kill the Lees."

"Thorow or Fina must be in good shape when they get here."

"You're joking when you say Thorow or Fina, right? Tell me you're joking."

"Okay, yes. I've decided to call them Sea or Brocco."

"Sea Lee or Brocco Lee? That's even worse. I know you and this is why I'm concerned. You're one of those people who would name her child Dee so that it rhymes with Lee, and I'm worried for my godchild's future. You can't be serious, Christina. Tell me you're not serious."

"Just stop with the naming, I beg of you. Everyone is half-crazed with figuring out baby's sex and what I'm going to name it . . . blah, blah, blah. You guys have to back off." Christina points a spatula in my direction like a sword. "I'll know it when I see it. I'll come up with the name then. Chucky said the baby wants to hide its sex and its name, so let it go."

"Fine. Can we talk about last night? Do you really think Chucky is a vile, worthless creature as Aunt Sarah calls her? Is she indeed a liar?"

"Mom thinks Chucky is a liar because she's heedless of Chucky's power. Watch this—next Friday your Godson or Goddaughter will jump out of me like a toast, as Chucky predicted. Trust me, I've known Chucky for years. Everything she says is true."

"What if she's mistaken?"

"How would I know? Even nature is allowed to make mistakes; here—it allowed me to have this baby grow inside of me, which is clearly a mistake."

"Why is it a mistake?" I say.

"I was joking. Stop taking things so seriously, man. Seriously. Mom's getting on my nerves by pimping out the idea it'll be a boy. What if it's a girl? Will she be unhappy? She keeps insisting I persuade you to live with us, but I know how stubborn you are."

"Maybe it wouldn't be such a surprise if you'd done a sonogram."

"I'm sorry if Mom's getting on your nerves. I'll talk to her."

"Thanks. To be honest, I must confess I felt Mom's presence last night at the séance. She was in the room, sitting with all of us, watching me. She's ashamed of me. Not Chucky, but *I'm* a vile and worthless creature."

The tears I've been holding finally burst out like I'm one defective pipe. Christina pointlessly tries to come up with words of comfort, but I completely shut down, burying myself in her sweater. I return to my bedroom and for the rest of the afternoon, I browse useless sites on the Internet. Later, Christina brings me emergency fries and champagne, and I obediently eat and drink without feeling any better. She became such an adult, I keep thinking. Broccoli, taking care of me and the baby, that healthy glow. And yet at the same time she's worse than a baby: refuses to do a sonogram, jokes about names and gender, and sets up séances like a seven-year-old.

.   .   .

Saturday evening, the three of us watch presidential debates, where two wags answer questions by a smart, intelligent-looking woman with an unfortunate name, Holly Wood. I claim the couch and place myself under the wool blanket while Christina and Aunt Sarah serve themselves a picnic on the floor. Dick Noseknuckle is a Republican, most prominent star while the Democratic Party's fave is Steve Mason. The questions Holly asks are regular and boring, covering the most common topics, including taxes, immigration, Medicare, childcare, and low-income families. Since I hardly fit in any of the categories, I don't care who wins the elections so long as he's a Democrat. The most amusing portion of the debates is to watch Christina and Aunt Sarah discuss each question, talking nonstop like commentators in a football game.

On a question about childcare, Dick, the Republican candidate says, "In my administration, fathers will receive the same rights on a child. Because let me ask you this: is it fair for a baby to be raised by one parent without a father? No. We will ban all sorts of restrictions. A mother will be unable to prevent a father from seeing his child. It takes two people to create a family. Single parents always fail to raise a decent enough person who can accomplish anything in life."

On TV, people who sit in the audience applaud for some reason. I listen to him with disbelief: And if that person is exactly like me—who was raised with neither parent—then who am I, a nickel-and-dime? However, I haven't accomplished much in life so maybe he's got a point, though I won't admit it or give him any credit.

"You, Dick," Christina comments, talking to TV, "are an idiot. Mom, how did this clown ever get on that stage?"

Aunt Sarah shrugs and laughs. "You know this country is messed up, sweetie."

Holly considers the response. "If a father has the same rights on the baby, are you going to ban abortion?"

"Yes," Dick says, "but only until the baby arrives."

Holly looks at him queasily for thirty seconds, eyebrows locked expressing puzzlement. She switches from him to Steve, "What are your thoughts?"

"What have feminists been fighting for all these years?" Steve answers. "Feminists have been fighting for the complete opposite: to be independent from men. By taking these rights away from these autonomous women, we run a risk of pushing the country backward forty to fifty years, something we should avoid at all costs."

"That's telling him, buster," Aunt Sarah says, cracking sunflower seeds in her mouth.

The next question is about whether gay people should be allowed to get married.

"I don't have anything against gay people," the Republican Dick says, "but we must admit we're having problems with reproduction. The only way a gay couple can make a baby is to adopt it from another country. That's the opposite of being patriotic. You know while we're talking about this—what I call a minor issue—we have immigrants trying to crawl from underneath the earth just to live in this country. We need to protect it. In my administration, we will protect the United States."

Holly squints. "To sum this up: no gay marriage?"

"When we resolve immigration we can talk further on the subject."

"What are your thoughts?" Holly asks the Democratic candidate.

"If we don't support minorities," Steve says, "who are we as a nation? The Democratic society becomes a repressive society. We need to learn to love one another regardless of sex, skin color, or sexuality. Why do I fully support gay marriage? Because it's the right thing to do."

The last sentence nets the candidate applause, both from the audience and from the living room.

On a question about raising the minimum wage, the Republican candidate makes an annoyed face. "The only way to earn more money is to attend college. How can all these losers without education imagine they deserve as much money as would a lawyer? This is why our economy is unstable, because of dumb protests from minimum wage workers who are too lazy to commit to finishing school. I'm talking high school dropouts specifically: nobody twisted their arms. You want to earn a decent wage? Stay longer with your company and prove your loyalty. This is why I think there are so many obese people in this country."

Holly crosses her eyes. "Because of minimum wage?"

"Of course, because they work in fast food industry. Give them more money and they'll eat double."

"I disagree," says Steve Mason. "Increasing minimum wage has been proven to skyrocket the economy. Why does increasing minimum wage improve lives? Because even though for 1 percent of the population thirty cents may mean nothing, for 99 percent of us it's the matter of life and death."

On and on the debates continue, along with babble and comments from

Christina and Aunt Sarah while I consider both sides of each story. For Marcus, the Republican approach is best, because in that case Cynthia will be unable to forbid him from seeing Lydia; for Christina, the opposite. Over three hundred million people live in this country, so how can one president make everyone happy? I can't even make *myself* happy at this point. Politics is the precise reason *why* I stay away politics: too many unanswered questions.

At night, Baba Yaga looks fierce: She just uselessly remains on the ceiling, attracting dust and germs. I lie in bed, wondering whether I quit my job at Shred Unread too soon. Could I withstand humiliation of sleeping with my boss for more money, or would people treat me as a cheap hooklet? Knowing men when it comes to gossip, it would surprise me not if Mr. Grunt just *told* people he sleeps with me to degrade me in the eyes of the others. I'd have to either "know my place" or beat it. There are always ways to come back. All I have to do is show up on Monday and act as though nothing happened. Until I submit my resignation letter I still technically work for Shred Unread. What do they really shred? Humans.

Sunday afternoon, Christina throws me out of the house to go for a walk with her in the neighborhood. She reasons with me that lying in bed burns no calories unless my goal is to fatten up; that makes me get up. We walk up a steep street at an incline my calves were unprepared for, but a spry Christina claims she needs the exercise. The rain finished its work, but apparently so did the sun. Clouds covered most of the sky, and crows, like little witches, fly above us in circles, chanting. The air smells fresh, however. Pine needles and wet cement. A squirrel jumps in front of us with a nut in her mouth and climbs a tree, carefully watching us from a height where she's out of reach. Puddles accumulated in road intersections and in crevices between sidewalk squares, grass a vivid dark green. At the crest, we turn right to another quiet street. In this neighborhood, each intersection ends with a STOP sign, and on weekends traffic is sparse, allowing kids and parents to play freely. Christina rummages through some junk at a garage sale down the street while I patiently wait. After, we pass Willowbrook Hospital, the place where she plans to give birth. She makes me promise to be there with her. She then leads us toward a newly opened café where unlimited mimosa and Bellini brunch is served until two o'clock on weekends. Christina insists on eating. The only reason she can talk me into it is because I can drink all I want for $14 and she picks up the tab, which is why I order an extra order of fries together with an extra Panini for dinner.

Drunkenly, I verbally vomit to Christina about the Hawaiian shenanigans. Christina listens without commenting, but she continues eating a salad, occasionally nodding. I find the picture of Marcus and me on my phone. Marcus is even cuter than I remembered, but that's what alcohol does—it makes people twice as attractive. "Ugly people need to get laid too," alcohol said.

After brunch, plastered, I return to the house, just as unhappy as I was before. In the evening, home alone and restless while Christina and Aunt Sarah go out to play canasta with the neighbors, I flip through channels on TV, dwelling on some unknown feeling of boredom. This is the only weekend in a year when I'm out of place and miserable, let alone jobless. I drunkenly call Chloe without any luck getting her on the line. Natalia doesn't pick up, but I leave her voicemail. And Lindsay, who isn't even a friend, fails to pick up her phone as well. Just to speak to someone, I call one of those numbers on TV doing infomercials and order a set of knives for cooking for $12.99, with two more blades for chopping and dicing for $10.99 extra. As a bonus, they throw in a lunch bag and an amazing cast iron frying pan for only $9.99. The shipping is free, which is good. On the couch, with hair still braided and smelling like hair, I pass out, thinking it's impossible to feel more friendless, watching reruns of *Friends* alone.

MONDAY MORNING, MY PHONE WAKES ME UP BY VIBRATING ON the nightstand. Sunshine peeks through the curtains, making me squint. From the caller ID I learn Natalia is calling and I pick up the phone, unrecognizing my hoarse voice. We hadn't talked since last week when she told me she was on her way to LEGS, the Ladies' Elite Gambling Society, for a scrutiny. After the preliminary, introductory greetings, I realize she's sobbing.

"What's the matter?" I say.

"I feel so stupid. I thought I could fit into that society, you know? I thought I could be one of the ladies."

"What happened?"

"The interview went well. They told me I was in."

"Congratulations!"

"They seemed full of themselves, which I assumed they would be. We were served tea and sandwiches, followed by cocktails and the portion where they asked lots of questions. Another woman was interviewed together with me, Sandra. She's thin, so she got drunk fast and made no sense when she talked."

"It sounds so formal," I say.

"It was. After the tea, the ladies decided to go gambling, this way they could see us in action. Thirty minutes later, Sandra became even drunker and got embarrassingly too loud, to the point when the ladies decided to leave the casino. They immediately considered her a write-off. They stood up to leave Sandra behind and asked me to follow. I told the society's president, Miriam, that we should look after Sandra or she might hurt herself, to which Miriam replied, 'If you want to stay with her, you can. You should forget, of course, about being a part of our society. Remember, I created this for ladies only, not for sloppy drunkards or ladies with penises.' After I made a face, she continued, 'Have you not noticed Sandra has a penis? She's just a chick with a dick, and we don't need those here. Your decision, Natalia.'"

"What a bitch."

"Obviously, they knew nothing about me being transgender, and I didn't know about Sandra either. If I became a member, it would be such a validation for me as a woman. So I debated."

"What were you debating?"

"Next time one of us gets drunk, then what? We leave her alone to possibly die and be robbed? What kind of society is it? It's almost like being racist or almost like allowing women earn less money and pretend it's okay. What kind of friendship could I have with those sons-a-bitches? So I thought better of it and showed Miriam my middle finger and my crotch. She rolled her eyes and left. Earlier, Sandra had mentioned she stayed one floor below me, so I took her to her room and put her to sleep. How could Miriam and the others be so ignorant? How? How could I ever become a woman in a world where women try to act like men while men who try to become women are transgender freaks?"

"I'm sorry," I say. "They are stupid. They don't deserve you."

"Yeah, right," she says sarcastically. "The only way to be accepted as a woman is to cut the pistol."

"What pistol?"

"You know, the tool."

"What tool?"

"My member."

"I don't understand, Natalia. What member?"

"Cock, goddammit. I need to cut my cock."

"Sorry, I'm slow today. Anything I can do to help?"

"Have a drink with me."

"*That* I can do."

We make plans to play by ear and meet at our bar sometime this week, possibly closer to the weekend. I tell Natalia about what happened on Friday to which she snorted something in Russian and thought Mr. Grunt reminded her of Miriam. Afterward, I trudge downstairs. Monday is a groundhog day, some sort of a Saturday/Sunday reprise: broccoli, pelican-pose Christina, her bulging belly. She prepared breakfast some time ago and arranged it on the kitchen table on a tray. She's blabbing on the phone, so I take the tray and give her a buss on a cheek, mouthing "thank you."

With a tray full of breakfast items—a whole wheat toast, a cup of green tea, and a gross egg whites/kale omelet—I jump back in bed. While eating, I replay my conversation with Natalia, wondering whether Christina ran out of salt. Aunt Sarah started a low-sodium diet six months ago, but I don't understand why I have to suffer through that as well. Chewing the buttered toast, I can't help seeing the obvious parallel between Natalia and me. She decided to quit rather than being humiliated and faking to act like someone she's not, even though her decision made her unhappy. What is it about the human mind and letting us choose one option versus another? Are self-respect and dignity more important than praise and stability?

Once again I dial Jessica, and her phone rings continuously until voicemail kicks in. I'm glad to hear her prerecorded voice. "Hi, you've reached Jessica Hirezy. Sorry, I can't pick up. Call me later or briefly describe the nature of your call, and I'll get back to you as soon as I can." An automated voice follows, asking me to leave a message after the tone. Jessica is in a pickle because of me, and I blame her none for refusing to speak. If she hasn't lost her position at Shred Unread, she's then at work and unavailable. Time is 10:15. She'll come around at some point in future, so I decide against leaving her a message and hang up.

Elizabeth demands food. She swims from one side of the tank to the other. Under the bright sun, the fish appears extra beautiful as though dressed for prom. I grab my camera in haste and start shooting. After taking a bunch of photos, I drop several pallets in water, which she skillfully catches and hides in the bush.

I remove the flash card and plug it into my laptop. When I open the folder, I enlarge each photo, picking the best seven. Afterward, I brainstorm ideas how to edit them to post on social networks. I hate those bitches who post pictures of their dogs and children twice a day, so I'll do the same with the same gusto to show them how annoying it is. Hopefully, they'll get the message. On the flash card, there are also blurry photos of Adam, which Chloe took at Ke Iki Beach. None of these were acceptable enough as blackmail, but, on some, his plastered face is clearly visible, with some drool around his mouth. Would serve him right if I cropped his face and pasted it on a chimpanzee like I did with Babette.

It strikes me so suddenly I want to punch myself in the face for not doing it sooner. Being a whiz when it comes to editing photos, I don't understand what stopped me before. I'll photoshop him. I'll place his face on provocative photos, and nobody will be able to tell the photos are fake. I'm *that* good. Mom's hostile *Maybe* will turn to a definite *Yes.* I'll have Adam solicit my job for me. It's called blackmail, and the fat ass deserves it.

I download a picture of a donkey, Godzilla, and most importantly one of a naked woman. From a porn site, I also download a photo of a guy with a similar look and skin tone, who's having sex with a hairy man. Let's spread a rumor he's gay. Why not? If Adam refuses to help me, all four photos will make him the laughing stock of the office, after I send the photos to the right people.

I start editing, but another great idea comes to me. (I must be on a roll; if I were in Vegas I'd win big bucks.) Marcus could blackmail Cynthia the same way she's blackmailing him. So simple! He'll get Lydia back in no time, and before I know it, I'm dialing his cell phone number printed on the back of his business card.

"Hello?" he says.

"Hey, it's me. Calyssa Pantaleo. Do you have a minute?"

A breath of hesitation. "What is it?"

"First of all, I'm quite well, thanks for asking. How are you? Second, I have an idea how to get Lydia back."

Silence. He snorts something in response. "Sorry, I'm busy."

"It'll only take a second. I don't like what happened between the two of us, so I want to make amends."

"Seriously? Why do you care? We met once. Okay, twice. Okay, three times."

"I had no chance to explain what happened with Adam. Let's call it a big misunderstanding. You'll laugh your ass off."

"I'm sure I will."

"Do you want to hear what happened?"

"Why not?"

"I was on a verge of getting fired so I flew to Honolulu to find Adam, get him drunk, and take pictures of him naked. I was going to use it as blackmail to get my job back. Really, I was desperate and my plan failed. I got fired—quit myself, actually—on Friday." I pause.

"And?"

"You should blackmail Cynthia. Hire a private detective or dig your inbox for some provocative emails, or, even better, send me her photo and I'll photoshop it for you."

"Cynthia already filed a restraining order as she'd promised, and blackmail will only make it worse."

"She did? Then that's it. This will help her withdraw."

"Blackmail is the lowest thing a person can do."

"Isn't it what she's doing to you?"

"She's hurt because I cheated on her. I deserve this. Not only is blackmail against my nature, but it's also against the law. Do you want to go to prison? Be my guest. Can't believe you suggested a stupid idea like that. Please, never call me again."

Marcus hangs up. Oh, so blackmail is the lowest thing? The poor thing's unhinged. I hold the phone in my hands, getting angry—so angry—with Adam. I don't need my job back, I need revenge. Devil inside of me uses my body like I'm a string-puppet, my hands carefully adding Adam's face to the four pictures I've downloaded. The whole process takes me an hour and a half. Right after, I sign into my email account and compose an email. I type two hundred angry words and attach the four pictures, admiring my editing skills. One question remains: should I send the pictures to Adam first, to test his reaction, or should I also send carbon copies to Jessica, Mr. Grunt, and even Babette to show Adam I ain't playing games here. While I'm thinking of the consequences, I notice Adam shows up online on instant messaging.

"Calyssa!" he messages me.

"I hope you're happy," I type. "Thanks for such great reviews in Mr. Grunt's office last week."

"Thank God, you're online. I've been trying to reach you since Friday, but you were offline. You said your phone was stolen, so I didn't bother calling. I apologize for what happened."

"Really."

"If I lose my job I'm fucked."

"Why's that?"

"Last week, Eve told me she's knocked up. She wants to keep the baby because it's a boy. You know, Jewish people always want a boy; it means a blessing."

"Congratulations."

"Thank you. We're both thrilled, but we need to purchase a buttload of stuff for the baby: crib, clothes, toys. With the recent pay cut, we can't afford losing our jobs. I told Mr. Grunt what he wanted to hear. I was protecting my family."

"I understand."

"You can always use me as a reference for another job, just make sure your résumé is edited. By the way, I heard what happened in Mr. Grunt's office. You gave him such a wallop."

"He told me you had told him I sleep around."

"Are you kidding? What a moron. He misunderstood. He's an old asshole and can't hear a thing. I'm glad someone had the nerve to punch the punk. Your impudence is what everyone loves about you, Calyssa. You either have it your way or no way."

I suddenly realize if I want a real blackmail, I should take a screenshot of our chat and send it to Mr. Grunt. But I'm not done yet; evidence is already being collected regardless. "So you say you didn't spread the rumor?"

"Of course not. The whole team loves you, Calyssa. You're the funniest person."

When people start praising you like that—they're lying. When they say you're the funniest person—you're screwed. There's something else I need to know. "Is Jessica okay? She never answered her phone."

"She's fine. She's worked for Shred Unread for years. She received a promotion if you want to know the truth. She had nothing to do with you being hired. Apparently, Mr. Grunt wanted to hear your reaction. He was the one who hired you because he liked your 'aura,' how he put it."

Jessica's fine! I breathe in deeply with revelation, and type, "Is Babette happy? She seemed pretty happy last I saw her."

"You won't believe what happened. After you left the office on Friday, so did Babette. Today she called out sick while I got my hands on a confidential email from Babette to HR, in which she states she's leaving the company! Ding-dong, the witch is dead. You won!"

"No way. What happened?"

"Her mom was diagnosed with stage IV lung cancer, which is fatal. Babette will be taking care of her in Arizona, of all shitty places to live. The email said Babette was going to come back on Thursday to pick up her personal things and sign a resignation letter, but that's all I know. I'm glad the bitch is gone. She was such a nag."

I can't believe what I'm seeing in front of me. Babette's mom is dying, and all Adam's gabbing about is what a nag Babette was. I feel so disgusted by him, vomit piles up in my esophagus. How can he be saying that? Clenching my teeth, I shut my laptop, unwilling to type another word.

Unsettled, I sit on the side of the bed and look at Elizabeth, who slowly glides around her tank. I can't help but feel bad for Babette. Stage IV cancer is a terminal illness, kind of like walking on a ledge of a tall building, ready to be swept into the abyss any minute. Knowing your parent has one foot in the grave must be the worst thing happen to you. My mom died suddenly in a car crash and was announced dead on arrival, and I hope she felt no pain. Why did I pick a fight with Babette and photoshop her face on a monkey?

This will haunt me forever.

Adam is a liar and a sissy who cheats, drinks, and gambles. Nothing will change his attitude on life, not the raise, not the blackmail. Plus, what the hell was I thinking when I decided to send these photoshopped images out into the universe along with bad karma?

I'm better than that.

To prove I'm better than that, I nosedive downstairs and pour myself a strong apple martini, leftover from last night. It's only one o'clock, but it's five o'clock somewhere. Besides, discriminating against the time when to drink—same as what Natalia said about LEGS—is like being racist. I realize that after chatting with Adam, I was sitting on my bed for hours, absolutely transfixed, brooding about life. I felt translucent. A puppet in a show. Guilt is a hard emotion to shake, especially when you're guilty to the core and half covered in shit.

Christina's not home. She's probably walking around, 'exercising' as she put it, perhaps fingering through another garage sale. The martini instantly clears my head from all the negativity I've just experienced. The martini, also, decides to mind someone else's business, and it wants me to find Cynthia Truman to beat some sense into that bitch.

Then, Common Sense stops me halfway through the thinking process, saying, "You're acting like a stalker. What are you doing, and why do you care?"

Apple Martini answers, "Because she's a good person and she doesn't like loose ends."

Common Sense argues, "What if she makes things worse?"

Apple Martini says, "Apple martini wasn't shaken in a day."

I like the way Apple Martini thinks. Besides, what if Marcus gets diagnosed with a terminal disease, then what? Cynthia will never forgive herself. To release Cynthia from committing suicide, I must intervene. Also, my selfish side is desperate to change *Maybe* to *Yes* and make Mom proud. Plus, Apple Martini was right: I hate loose ends. Even if I never see Marcus again, I want him to think of me as a normal woman being, not a lunatic from Honolulu.

The New York City telephone directory, a gigantic yellow book sitting near the home phone, is covered in dust. I wet my finger, going page after page, making fun of weird last names in the process. Last name Ball always got me. "Look who's here, the Balls are here."

Just for fun, I look up Pantaleo, but only two other families with such a name exist. There are three pages of Lees. Bacon, Hanus, and Trickle are funkiest three I come across while leafing through the book. When on T, last name Truman takes half a page. I groan with displeasure, but swiftly find one with a name Marcus attached to it.

After a sip of my drink, I dial the number.

"Hello," a woman says. Her voice is cheerleader-like, for I instantly cheer up.

"Hi, I'm trying to reach Cynthia."

"This is she."

I replace the receiver into the cradle. Our conversation must be face-to-face. In person, she won't be able to hang up on me. I note the address, scribble it down on a sticky note, and picture the fancy apartment. People who live in Gramercy are usually extremely smart, or stupid but married to the rich. No wonder Cynthia settled for Marcus' apartment right away.

THE FIVE-STORY TOWNHOUSE IS RIGHT OFF IRVING AND 16TH Street, a mere ten-minute subway ride on the express train. Attached to the door, a picture of a ghost greets me. A pumpkin by the steps is carved into a cheesy face with a lit candle inside. Two pots with evergreen shrubs are decorated with webs, spiders, and orange-colored balls. I buzz in, realizing I forgot to create a plan. After taking a bus, a ferry, and a train, there was plenty of time to figure something out, yet instead, I occupied my time being paranoid someone would catch on I have a water bottle filled with an apple martini. Christina had nothing else in the house I could take as a roadie.

"Who is this?"

"Cynthia Truman?"

"Yes."

"My name is Laura . . . Gitis? I'm conducting a survey about the elections. It'll only take a few minutes. Mind if I come in?"

The pause takes longer than expected, as though she's looking up an answer online. Never in the world would I resemble a surveyor even if I wore a *Vote Now* button, had a legit-looking clipboard, and was dressed in business attire.

"I've already sent my ballot," she finally says. A cheesy answer from an unreliable website.

I buzz once again.

"Yes?"

"Ms. Truman, it was a school joke. I'm a teacher from Lydia's school and we must discuss in private her . . . grades."

After preliminary hesitation, Cynthia buzzes me in fourteen seconds later. Fourteen seconds? She's clearly irritated, and I write a mental sticky note to avoid annoying her any further.

In the foyer, a bulletin board takes up part of the wall to the left. The board is divided into two parts. The right side is marked as *Complaints*, with some notes clipped to it with pins. The left side is dedicated to family-friendly activities, with Halloween being the most current. The old-looking wallpaper —together with ugly carpeting—should be stripped off. Being absolutely clueless when it comes to real estate, price $9,000 a month to rent in the building sounds legit to me. People who rent here must be Harvard graduates and really good tippers in strip clubs. Come to think of it, money Lindsay makes may partially come from men who live in this neighborhood.

The apartment in question is located on the fourth floor, which I have to learn the hard way. I climb up, completely out of breath, wishing for an elevator and some food. Cynthia waits by the door, scrutinizing me. Even from halfway through I notice her perfect makeup, perfect hair, and perfect body. The entire ride to Manhattan I imaged her having saggy breasts, crooked teeth, and a mole. Cynthia is leotarded as though ready to hit the gym. Although the fact I just almost suffocated from walking mere sixteen steps should put me to shame, it doesn't.

She has a bitch face. Her pursed lips express hostility. With her arms crossed, she looks as friendly as a monkey with a gun.

"Take off your shoes," she demands.

Following her, I enter the apartment and compliantly place my sneakers in the corner. Now an inch shorter, I step on a cold tile floor. Her eclectic taste brings a wide variety of mismatched colors to the room: a red couch, an orange chair, and a cherry table with mahogany stools.

Cynthia leads toward the kitchen without saying a word, her demeanor cold and uninviting. I follow her through an extremely narrow hallway, imagining how Adam with his belly would get stuck in the middle. The hallway is floor-to-ceiling mirrors, as though all she does all day is looks at herself. In the kitchen, she claims the top of the dining room table, inviting me to take a chair. When I notice cookies on a plate neatly arranged in a circle, my saliva starts flowing.

"What is it about again?" she says.

"As I understand," I say, sitting, "Lydia lives without her father?"

"So what?"

"She told me you and Marcus had divorced in May. Do you want to talk about this?"

"Not in particular."

"Well, I do." I take a cookie from the plate to replenish my strength after the walking-up-the-steps workout. "Without a dad, Lydia is pretty much doomed. You might want to reconsider withdrawing the restraining order you filed."

"I see. What's your name again?" she says, blinking rapidly. Her generous eyelashes remind me of butterfly wings. I'm afraid she may just fly away.

"Lauren Gitis."

I bite into the stale, two-day-old cookie—no match to Aunt Sarah's. Cynthia grins and makes her way toward the fridge where she finds a bottle of milk. On the fridge door, there is a picture of a little girl's face and shoulders, and I catch myself on wishing to ask whether she's Lydia, but I stop myself right on time. I'm her teacher, so how can I be clueless what Lydia looks like? Lydia's wearing purple and has a thatch of blond hair. She inherited Cynthia's pedigree beauty, but Marcus' handsome smile.

Cynthia pours half a glass of milk. "And you are Lydia's teacher?"

"Yes, a new teacher. Today was my fifth day at work, actually."

"And what is it that bothers you? I filed a restraining order because Marcus is an alcoholic. I'm afraid he might hurt us."

"I've met with Marcus and I don't think he's an alcoholic. Also, imagine if he gets diagnosed with stage IV lung cancer. You'll blame yourself for the rest of your life."

"Was he diagnosed?"

"As far as I know Marcus is as healthy as a horse." As soon as I say it I bite my tongue. "Actually, last time I saw him he coughed a lot. He's really taking it hard."

"Interesting, Laura. Was it Laura or Lauren?"

"Oh, call me Laura or Lauren. Kids call me Pinocchio, even though my nose ain't big." I force a laugh, which comes out creepy.

"Pinocchio is right. You should look in the mirror because your nose is twenty feet long."

"Pardon?" I say.

"I'm Lydia's mother. You think I wouldn't be personally introduced to all the teachers, even new ones? You must be stupid. I don't know who you are, and this is precisely why I let you in. Before I call the cops, you better tell me what you want from me and my daughter." She picks up a cell phone from the windowsill, keying in 9-1-1.

I choke on the cookie and gag. I clear my throat with milk and fan my face to reduce the heat that has just rushed in. I decide to tell her my real name, which I disguise as Shakira Melano.

"I'm sorry I lied about being Lydia's teacher. I met Marcus in Hawaii last week. Actually, we met on the plane; I was drinking, he wasn't. He was talking about Lydia nonstop when we met at the beach the next day. Again, I brought margaritas, but he refused to have any. We quickly became friends— no sex or anything; I have a boyfriend, Adam—and Marcus shared with me he'd cheated on you. He admits it was the biggest mistake of his life. He loved you, but your love life was lost. Happens to 90 percent of all married couples."

"Says who?"

"*Staten Island Tribune*. Even if he drinks a little, so what? Who doesn't indulge in such deliciousness?"

"I don't."

No wonder she's so pissed with life! "Not the point I tried to make. So what if he cheated on you? He slipped. Big deal. Again, he wasn't the first and he won't be the last."

"I'm sorry, but how is it your business? He entered a monogamous relationship, in which I was a virgin."

"You have to forgive him. If you take his daughter away from him, not him but Lydia will hate you in the future. One day you'll realize what a dope you've been. Oh well, too late now. Trust me, as a child without a father, I know how she feels: miserable and incomplete. Marcus loves her. What, you're just going to call the cops when Lydia wants to see her dad? You're just a lazy, stubborn, soulless woman who refuses to forgive once." More or less I resemble a politician trying to win a vote. Now *that* was a failure for sure.

She grins. "You're falling for him, aren't you? You think by making me change my mind, you win Marcus. The moon has two sides, so let me tell you something about him. His penis is too small. His mother is all *nice to see you*, but she's as stupid as he is. Every weekend he would come home drunk. I had to call the cops on several occasions because he couldn't control himself. I don't need this."

"That's what drunk people do."

"I need a respectable husband who doesn't drink." Her smile makes me want to smack her in the face.

I get up. "You're such an idiot. It's not Marcus I came to discuss, but Lydia. His penis isn't relevant to me because I'm not sleeping with him. We live in a Democratic society—let Lydia choose her own life, and make her own decisions."

"She's incapable of making her own decisions."

"She's smarter than you that's for sure."

"Get the hell out of my house, you bitch!"

I back out, grabbing my shoes. She cusses behind my back with a rolling pin in hands like she'd have the nerve to use it. I unlatch the door and scoot. Stepping into my sneakers, I jump down three steps at a time. They should vacuum the carpet. I exit, taking the bulletin board off its hooks. It flies down with glass scattering all over the marble floor. Loudly. I can't control my body. Rage took over. It's clear to me Cynthia married Marcus to be a housewife and do nothing. She stopped sleeping with him, sabotaging him to cheat. Manipulative bitch made him ask alcohol for answers as soon as he slept with the twins. Now he's an alcoholic after she called the cops on him. A report is proof he drinks heavily. As soon as an excuse presented itself, she took the apartment and now lives off his money.

I feel ridiculously sorry for Marcus, but more so for Lydia, who has to live with that hooker.

Outside, I kick the cheesy-smiling pumpkin so hard, it flies through the fence and smashes on the sidewalk. I rip the ghost off the entrance door and step on its face. I push one pot down the steps. Soil, worms, and the plant get scattered all over. A window on the side of the building opens and a man sticks out his head. "What the hell are you doing?"

Before he locks my face features in his mind, I sprint down the steps and rush past the gate as though stung by a bee. I round the corner of the building like a sports car in three seconds. I park my rear end on the sidewalk, trying to catch up on my breathing. That's some dangerous living, I tell myself, a fast ride to a heart attack.

Two minutes later, somewhat calmer, I decide to reward myself with chocolate. I did the best I could is what matters. A grocery store is located on a nearby street with the temperature inside dropped severely. Bread and water are gone from the shelves. What in the world is going on?

I find my treat in aisle five and proceed toward the checkout. A gentleman ahead of me in line carries a basket full of bread. When my turn comes, I hand the chocolate bar to the cashier. "Your bread is completely gone. What's up with that?"

"People are stocking up for the hurricane," she says, scanning my indulgence. "The power may be off for days. We're closed on Friday and probably the weekend."

"I heard of a possible hurricane earlier this morning, but I thought it was a joke. Hurricane in New York? I thought it would never make it here."

"You wish. It's so happening. It was just officially announced. Thursday night."

I TAKE THE 6 TRAIN TO ITS LAST STOP, CITY HALL. WALKING down Broadway, I note how all the business people being very businessy. Some talk on their cell phones; some eat a sandwich on the go.

According to the business card Marcus provided, his building is located near Fulton Street, where tourists, in packs of two or three, linger around. Times Square is insufficient for them anymore. Now everyone needs to walk the Brooklyn Bridge.

The sugar from the chocolate gave me such a blast of courage and confidence that I decided to tie loose ends with Marcus and kiss him goodbye. I plan to share the highlights from my visit to his ex-wife. As Cynthia inclined, the moon has two sides, which makes me want to hear Marcus' before I make any decisions. How can the moon have two sides, if it's round like a basketball? She'd make more sense making an analogy between two butt cheeks or two brands of vodka.

The façade of Marcus' building is unimpressive: just a standard thirty-something story building, shabby-looking, old. I enter the lobby and get less impressed by the interior. A gigantic chandelier located right above the receptionist is too ugly. Red walls, metal tables, tall straws sticking out from vases are nuances that make this place hard to compliment. Marcus failed to put out candy in the lobby, ignoring the fact Halloween is nearing. There's a scaffolding to the right, as though the building is undergoing construction.

The receptionist is an Eskimo lady or maybe a gentleman, nevertheless a human (an *it*). Its garments are better described as though it killed a bear and was now sitting in the bear's fur. Since I'm clueless when it comes to style, I'm debating whether the bear outfit is fashion or trashion. I know for a fact I'd never wear that animal, though. They build a bear in stores for kids, they *skin* a bear in stores for adults. Now, imagine trying to explain this to a kid while reading a fairytale about the Three Bears? The notion behind overdressing in fur must be because of the freezing lobby. Cheap shams, I think, saving up on heat.

"May I help you?" the receptionist says. Still sexless. So far the receptionist lacks a traceable Adam's apple or Eve's feminism. Its accent is Chinese, teeth perfectly intact.

"I'm here to see Marcus Truman, the architect. Tell him it's Calyssa Pantaleo, the shredder." I laugh, but net a blank stare from the Eskimo.

"One second," it says.

While the epicene receptionist dials Marcus' office, I find on its badge an ambiguous, sexless name: Laruza Somo. I guess the only way to find out its sex is to follow Laruza to the restrooms to see which door it chooses, Men's or Women's. Unless, of course, Laruza goes to the family unisex one and then I'm screwed.

Maybe Laruza's parents, like Christina, went too far with keeping the sex a secret that now everyone else is confused with its gender, including Laruza. Satisfied with my theory, I unwrap the remnants of the chocolate and shove the rest in my mouth.

"Mr. Truman is in a meeting right now," Laruza says.

"I'll wait."

"It will take a long time."

"Fine. I'm jobless, so one thing I have plenty of is time. Anyone hiring in this building by any chance?"

"He's very busy," Laruza says angrily. "He asked me to tell you to never come back."

"Are you serious?"

"Leave."

"Why did you say he was at a meeting when there's no meeting?"

"I said so to be nice."

"What's so nice about lying?"

Laruza gives me a death stare, ready to skin me alive. The bear stood no chance against that beast. With its index claw, Laruza points toward the exit. "Get out."

Before Laruza pulls out a tranquilizer gun I leave.

"But I'll return" is what I tell her implicitly.

CHAPTER FIFTEEN

A Catch

Tuesday night I return home to Queens. Like vectors, pedestrians aim to get from point A to point B, without interacting with one another. I love that New Yorkers are focused. I quickly ease out of the station, bypassing my fellow subway riders, and round the corner. Familiarity feels great. The new twenty-four-hour Laundromat is open, which put the old nine-to-five Laundromat out of business. I know this because of the sign on the window that says: "Out of Business." The old Laundromat is incapable to catch up with its old washers and dryers, machines so ancient Einstein washed his pants there. I've lived in this neighborhood long enough to deserve a Laundromat that works late at night, so I could wash my clothes whenever. Other than the Laundromat, in Astoria we have bodegas that are open around the clock, along with subway stations and one pizza joint (even as an embarrassment for Italians everywhere). Once a Chinese takeout is available 24/7, my life will be complete.

Last night, I made up my mind and decided to talk to Babette. Two days from now, on Thursday. Adam mentioned she'd be coming into the office to sign some papers. This is where I come in. The catch is we aren't friends, and her reaction will be hostile. Even so, I need to apologize, not to get it off my chest, but to take full responsibility. I have tomorrow to actually figure out what to say. It won't make it any better for her, but it can't make it any worse either. When my mom passed away, each word, each reassurance that everything will be okay, each sentiment counted, even from people who I hadn't met. I counted on it.

My apartment, I learn as I walk in, is devoid of clothes pyramids and pets, dishes all but washed and put away. Bathtub is clear of fish and the toilet smells of bleach. Chloe is stretched out on the couch in her pajamas, catching a snooze with Anubis on her stomach.

The TV set is tuned to a news channel. "Hurricane Amelia is at her peak, swooshing a hundred and twenty-five miles per hour up the East coast, projected to affect at least eighteen states. Florida and North Carolina have already suffered thirty-seven fatalities due to the storm. The high wind speeds put the storm into category two, a scary destructive cyclone with incredible strength. Many flights across the region are being cancelled. Please, check with your airline to see if your flight is affected."

Damn, I think, dragging myself to the bedroom without making any noise. The hurricane is getting more serious than I thought. I've never heard of such a thing as hurricane in New York, but there's always the first time. I leave the fish on the dresser and shrug into my sleeping attire. After I close the bedroom door, I lie down, and fall asleep immediately.

I see such a vivid dream about my mom that when I open my eyes, the images stay strong in my head. We're shopping at the mall. I tell her about my trip to Hawaii, the missing wallet, the strip club while remembering to include Marcus, Lydia, Cynthia, and Grace Bishop. At the food court she orders herself a salad. For me she asks for fried chicken and the biggest soda, which will make me pee every five minutes irritating her no end. The strangest thing is the fact she and I are peers and we look exactly alike. She was thirty years old when she died, forever locking her age in a prison of moment. If she suddenly woke up alive she'd be my contemporary. Actually, as bizarre as it sounds, I'm actually older than her by maybe a week. Mom's name was Amelia, and I can't help seeing a correlation between that and the fact the hurricane was named after her. I don't believe in coincidences, so this thought woke me up. Even to the most atheistic, theoretical, deny-existence-of-after-life human, this should be a sign. But for what? I just tried to contact her and now a hurricane named after her will be sweeping New York. What is she trying to tell me, if anything?

I sit up and turn on the lamp on the nightstand. I must see her. The photo album is located inside of the nightstand next to my bed. The year her last photo was taken is when I'm ten. She's thirty, an absolute reflection of me in the mirror (minus the belly and the triple chin). Her hair is cut short, however, and her figure is perfect, placed into an actual dress. Not to bitch, but I'm sure I'd be slim in those days, because the food wouldn't be filled with growth hormones. Plus, Mom scarcely ate meat. After I clip the photo to my bulletin board, I imagine her alive today, turning fifty in two weeks, on a day coincided with the Election Day. She would still look slender and beautiful, with Aunt Sarah's short hair and my big, black eyes.

She died in a car crash, when an eighteen-wheeler dragged the cab forty meters along the interstate. It was January, just three months after she'd turned thirty. At the time, the two of us lived with Aunt Sarah, Christina, and Cheng, who was Aunt Sarah's boyfriend/Christina's dad. The two never married, even though they had a child by that union—Christina. Cheng left Aunt Sarah for another woman and I was glad he was gone because they argued a lot and his armpits smelled. Also, when he spoke he'd spit in your face—how I learned patience when it came to spitting camels and anything with teeth larger than a poker chip.

Mom felt like a burden in their Staten Island home while I couldn't get enough of making fun of acne-faced Christina who was going through puberty. Her bust was growing and I hated that mine was out drinking. It came at twelve, mostly sober. When I heard about the road accident, I was at school, drawing a caricature of my math teacher who I couldn't stand. The rest of the day went as a blur. Twenty years later, the funeral remains as a painting in my mind, not at all as a dragged-out movie with numerous details. Just one painting with an open casket. People gathered around her. Crying. Orange hues, burning incense, and a distant organ.

Sleep decides to leave me alone. I had troubles last night too, turning and grunting, but unable to clear my mind. It was filled with voices. I thought about life on different planets after watching a Discovery Channel documentary with Christina. Aunt Sarah made us the broccoli and carrot soup we both love so much. Why I never learned to cook such a simple recipe beats me. I glue a mental sticky note to ask Aunt Sarah for it.

I light an apple-and-cinnamon scented candle bought several weeks back. As I blow out the match, Elizabeth appears near the front of her tank, demanding food. She comes to her feeding spot every time she sees me. Fish, I learned from observation, lack a sense of time. She thinks she's hungry when I stand in front of her. She became codependent, just like a child. Elizabeth swims before me in circles, then toward her bushy plant where she likes to hide, and then back to the front. I drop five pallets above her but she fails to notice. As with her sense of time, she lacks a sense of smell. Elizabeth continues swimming in circles until the first pallet starts to free-fall. She catches it in the middle of the tank. When the second pallet falls down slowly, she snatches it as swiftly. She loves action. She loves when her food moves. When she hides in her bushy plant, the rest of the pallets descend to the very bottom and get lost in the emerald pebbles. She returns to the top, demanding more food, but I jump in bed, covering myself with a blanket. With the candle flickering on the shelf, I close my eyes.

I WAKE UP AT 7:00 AND BRING A BUNCH OF LAUNDRY TO THE Laundromat. There are more than thirty machines in total and the premises are almost empty, with just two washers and dryers operating. Today is Wednesday. Tomorrow, Babette will stop by the office and I'll finally talk to her. Earlier this morning while the laundry was being tumbled dried, I finally sent a resignation letter. Jessica replied back and we chatted for a while. It was awesome to know she's not mad at me. We made plans to meet up for lunch next week to catch up. Jessica promised to text me as soon as Babette comes to the office tomorrow so I'll know when to leave my house and catch her on time.

Chloe departs in the morning, taking the black Anubis with her. She permanently deleted her profile from the online dating website so I follow suit. Bars are the best way to meet men. The few men I've met at Mario's were no Channing Tatums, but at least they were real. A drink in a hand is worth two in the bush. Chloe seems better, different, defeated but happier. She finally confessed she'd used someone else's picture in her dating profile, some girl in a bikini: small, slender, and skinny. When the guy saw real Chloe—not because she's unattractive but because she's not the same person as on the photo—he freaked out, blocked her, and wrote her off as a psycho. After the high school reunion fiasco, she hasn't lied once. She learned her lesson: lies are good only when the truth hurts no one. Chloe returned all the pets back to the shelter, admitting she had no home for them.

Later in the afternoon, I edit my résumé, a piece of paper so tragic to look at I wonder whether that was how Shakespeare started, writing his tragic drama playwrights. He was applying for a job, see, but instead he wrote *Romeo and Juliet* by mistake. I eradicate Mr. Periwinkle from the résumé, because if I'm serious about finding a job, I need a serious approach. I add Adam Klutz as a reference since he volunteered for the job, even if I can't bear the thought of speaking to him at the moment. As soon as I submit my résumé to several places online, I make myself a congratulatory drink—an apple martini in a genuine martini glass stolen from Waikiki Beach Palace.

My cell phone rings as I was just getting comfortable on the couch. I stand up and walk to the bedroom where the beast is plugged in to charge. The caller ID comes blocked. I love and hate when people block their numbers for at least two good reasons (not necessarily good reasons though): (1) if I know who's calling, I'd most likely ignore, and (2) because the number is blocked I must pick up to see who it is. What a sneaky way to get my attention by bringing some catch-22 to the table.

"Hello?"

"Good afternoon, I'm trying to reach Calyssa Pantaleo." Her voice comes distorted as though she's calling from the Lincoln Tunnel.

"Speaking."

"Sorry, you're breaking up."

"Calyssa here, speaking."

"Oh, hi. This is Lucky Knotts. I'm calling about Lindsay Goldplenty. She left me your number as a reference. She said she worked for you and was in charge of the girls. Are you the house mom?"

I roll my eyes with disbelief. "Yes, I'm the house mom."

"Good, me too. Did Lindsay do a good job?" Lucky says. She sounds like Destiny, the pencil-legged hooker. I stuff my other ear with a finger to eliminate the background noise.

"Yes, love," I say, lowering my voice to resemble Cassidy, gaining an English accent in the process. "Lindsay was in charge of the girls because they didn't listen to me. I needed a replacement, someone with confidence. Lindsay dances like a bird of paradise before the prenuptial agreement."

"Fabulous. Maybe Lindsay can teach my girls how to dance."

"Oh, yes, love, she can. I saw it myself how flawlessly she worked that pole like a lollipop."

Lucky sniffs something indecipherable. "Can she call shots? I need someone with strong discipline."

"She's good at making shots, yes, and telling people they resemble clowns."

"She sounds lovely. I like when people can call shots. How old were your girls?"

"Depends. Twenty-one, twenty-five. One girl was seventeen, but she liked to strip too much so I had to fire her."

"And you would highly recommend Lindsay?"

"Yes, of course. She'll bring quite a clientele to your club. Just look at her body. She likes to cook in glory, that ham."

"We are Jewish. We don't eat ham."

"Oh."

"Lindsay is a fantastic candidate. I hope you won't miss her too much, but since you're a house mom you can take care of the girls yourself."

"Yes, they never complained about how I run business in this house. But get Lindsay before I change my mind."

"You got it, because Lindsay sounds like a catch. Anything else you could add?"

Add? How many more girls does this needy woman need? "I can throw in my DJ but I'd have to speak to him first."

She laughs. "That's okay, sweetheart. You've been tremendous help. Goodbye," she sings.

"Goodbye," I sing back.

When I hang up, infuriated, I dial Lindsay but the hooklet ignores my call. The bitch is now a liar, using my hairstyle and my name, and now I'm her reference. She's pimping me out as a house mom. She's lying exactly how I taught her. Now other house mamas are calling me asking how well she danced. This is no good. I wanted Lindsay to lie a little bit, not through her teeth.

I finish laundry, fold clothes, and buy a pumpkin to carve. I carve a pyramid, which ends up looking like a triangle, but pyramid is triangular so I believe I did a bang-up job.

I dilly-dally for the rest of the day doing nothing in particular. I watch some TV, make frozen pizza, and talk on the phone with Christina.

THURSDAY MORNING DURING BREAKFAST, I TUNE INTO THE NEWS channel. Apparently, the hurricane started moving faster than expected and by 8:00 P.M. Amelia's heavy winds will destroy everything they touch. "We're waiting with anticipation, hoping the hurricane changes its course. Amelia is the first hurricane in a century to bring such mass destruction to the land, leaving nothing but ruin, fatalities, and uncertainty."

The mayor recommends having five gallons of water per person per day as a guideline, plus a bunch of nonperishable edibles in case a power outage occurs. I fill up cooking pots, empty bottles, carafes, jars, and vases with water. After a quick shower, I fill up the bathtub as well, just in case. I'd rather drink water than stay clean. I write a list of products to purchase, following the mayor's guidelines that fit my budget, since economizing is the key when you lose your job. My last paycheck will be mailed soon and it'll pay for rent and a few (but not all) bills. When the grocery list is written, I walk the short six blocks to the grocery store. Sign "WE HAVE WATER" welcomes me by the entrance.

Circling the store, I follow the shopping list I've created, just occasionally, on impulse, picking items I wasn't planning on buying. The store is out of bread, among other foodstuffs (including, but not limited to): milk, ice cream, and water, despite what the outside sign states. Like we're shopping after an apocalypse. The real downturn to my neighborhood is that all the big grocery stores are too far of a walk and all the small ones, especially bodegas, always run out of the essentials. Perhaps bathtub full of water was a great idea after all. Into the basket I put cans of fruit, beans, cooked rice, ramen noodles, cheese, dried Turkish apricots, crackers, cereal, chocolate, protein bars, and apples. After I check out, just to madden Mother Nature even more, I stop at a liquor store and get a premixed cocktail called Hurricane, which is some sort of a kinkier version of Long Island Iced Tea. At home, after all the groceries have been put away, I receive a text message from Lindsay.

"How's it shaking, sister?"

Sister, my ass. In response, I send her a smiley face, still mad at her for giving my number to Lucky Knotts without asking for my written permission.

"Caly," she writes, "I'm back in New York. Surprise, surprise! Come out for a drink with me."

I type: "Gee, I wish I could."

"I'm going to that bar in Spanish Harlem. Please, come."

"Gee, I wish I could," repeating myself, I type, but I don't wish I could.

"In case you change your mind I'll be there anyway. It's happy hour."

In that dive bar, happy hour is every hour. I ignore.

"Drinks on me," she writes thirty seconds later.

"I'll think about it."

No replies follow.

I wonder what Lindsay is up to. Yes, she's not a thief (after all, Natalia's wallet wasn't stolen), but we aren't such close friends to hang out and have drinks. Perhaps if we met at Mario's on several other occasions, then maybe I'd consider it. That's how both Chloe and Natalia became my friends. We kept bumping into one another and became close. Natalia bought us tickets to Vegas, and with her I visited Atlantic City for the first time. In bars, after two drinks, even enemies call for a ceasefire. The more drinks, the tighter the bond.

Would it be terrible if I come out for just one cocktail with her? Besides, she said she'd pay for my drinks and, being broke, I can't at least deny it's a tempting offer.

Another message pops on my phone from Jessica. Babette has just walked into the HR office. In haste, I put on my favorite green hoody, jeans that look good on my booty, and a pair of UGGs that don't rhyme with "booty." I grab my bag and my phone and flee the premises. Wind outside is quite unusual, singing a fifteen-mile-per-hour tune. Pieces of paper and dust fly in my face and I have to maneuver around them on the way to the subway, feeling frisky. Going down the steps, I hear an approaching train and I run, trying to catch it. No such luck. The turnstile fails to accept my MetroCard, stating I'm out of funds. That's how I miss my train. Another train will arrive in five minutes and I load my MetroCard with $10.

I get off the subway and hurry the few blocks to my old building, realizing the wind is nothing when compared to this frost biting my skin. I shiver involuntarily. As I enter, I spot a security guard by the elevator, the one I used to make fun of, by placing whoopee cushions on his chair. The lobby is fully decorated with Halloween junk.

"May I help you?" he says.

"Do you remember me?"

"I'll never forget you."

"Perfect. I need to get upstairs to talk to Babette."

"Do you have your badge?"

I shake my head. "I forgot it at home."

"Only coworkers are allowed upstairs. When you forget your badge you need to call your employer to make sure they let us know. Which company do you work for?"

"Shred Unread."

"Give me a minute and I'll call them."

"To be honest, I quit last week. But I really need to talk to Babette Hook."

"I'm sorry, but I cannot let you in."

"Please, pretty please, with sugar on top?"

"Ma'am, even if you put organic sugar on top, visitors are verboten to go upstairs unless you're employed."

I make a face by squinting and pursing my lips. I notice a journal entry that Babette Hook has entered the building less than an hour ago without leaving. I decide to wait.

"Thanks for being so helpful," I tell him nastily. "I'll call tomorrow to complain. Good luck getting fired." I don't know where the anger comes from, but I don't see why he makes such a big deal out of it.

Due to the upcoming Halloween, an orange cover's been placed on the couch by the entrance. Next to it stands a side table full of candy. Might as well get myself useful while here, and dutifully walk in that direction. I sit down, happy I'm waiting in warmth after watching shivering people passing by outside. I grab a handful of candy, putting most of it in my hoody pocket. Before I can unwrap my first treat, someone taps my shoulder. I turn around to find the security guy.

"Ma'am," he says, "you need to vacate your seat. No employment? The couch is not for your enjoyment. If you need to wait, I'll agree for a small rate."

"How much?" I say.

"One thousand dollars."

"You want me to bribe you? Sorry but I'm out of funds."

"Then, please leave the lobby and wait outside. Return when you attain a different disposition."

"But it's cold cat and fish out there."

"Make sure you wear a coat next time you're being rude to people."

"When was I being rude?"

"Just two minutes ago, on Fridays, and every day I saw you."

Before I could answer, he shoves me through the revolving door. Once outside, I peg the temperature to be negative. The darkness has eaten through the sunlight, leaving murky patches in its wake. The clouds move fast and cover the entire perimeter of the sky, just like a thick massive duvet. The security guy stands by the door, watching me with expression of pity. Indeed, I'm the pity one—an icicle in the middle of winter, teeth clamping in a merry chorus. I try to sneak back in, but he locks the door.

I realize he was right about me being rude, but there's nothing I can do to offset this. I did nothing but make fun of him in the past, like a little girl. Maybe this *could* teach me a lesson. Maybe this *would* teach me a lesson. Maybe this *should* teach me a lesson. *Maybe.*

The wind blows in my ear, suggesting to leave and go home. But I need to talk to Babette. I need to apologize for photoshopping her face to a monkey and for the fight we had and for being mean to her.

Was I mean to everyone in that building or what? I just thought I was making jokes and making people happy, but I possibly went overboard. The first time Lindsay and I met, she told me I was brainwashed by the media. I was definitely someone else, a career-obsessed, manipulative, careless nine-to-fiver. While I was on the thirteenth floor "working," my manners stayed downstairs. Power changes people and maybe I wasn't ready for a real job at a real office. Christina said I was unappreciated, but truthfully I didn't even try. I was always late, I always ate, and while at work, I kept chatting online in order to snatch a date. I read in a magazine the main reason why a worker slacks off is because they are bored, disinterested, or not challenged enough. I loved the pay but hated the atmosphere. Maybe the time has come to find a job where I can have fun, something social rather than sitting in a boring office all day.

Time is dragging slower than Caisha's hag. At least inside of a car I could have turned on the heater, played some music, or even made out with a man. To comfort myself, I eat another candy, unwrapping it first with my blue hands. If I had balls, I wonder if they would also be blue.

I notice my nails should be done.

A café across the street appears closed, so is the restaurant adjacent to it. Other businesses have shut down early too, due to the hurricane. A cab charges fifty cents per thirty seconds or something similar, the amount of money too precious to spend until there's steady income in my bank.

Come on, Babette, come out already.

The security guy returns to his desk. I make my way to the door but I forgot the sucker locked it. I look through the glass to find him laughing at me as though I were some sort of a joke.

I *am* a joke, ain't I?

My feet get pierced with cold. Moving them will help me warm up. My limbs are heavy as a reminder I may turn to stone by the end of the night. Cold slows my heart rate, and I'm running a risk of getting hypothermia. In the meantime, I blow on my hands only to realize my breath makes them thaw for exactly two seconds before they turn back to icicles. The subway is too far. If I go there to wait, I'll miss Babette. Where else can I wait in warmth? Bars in my vicinity have signs "CLOSED" on their doors. A liquor store has its lights off. A grocery store has closed early. One would assume (driving by) people in New York City are dead.

To preserve heat, I cross my arms in front of my chest, with my feet doing a fusty polka dance, which must look as though I'm auditioning for a Broadway show. I'm sure many an actress was discovered in such an adventurous way, if only I were talented enough to be an actress. Several crooked people bypass without paying any attention, but they seem in a hurry to reach home.

I must get going, but I need to speak with Babette. I touch my nose but no longer can feel it. Lord, I've suffered enough cold for one day. The wind blows harder, whistling a cold, naughty tune to humiliate me even further: "Here comes the sun, little darling." And like in good ol' days, the record gets stuck repeating: "Here comes the sun, here comes the sun, here comes the sun . . ."

By the time the sun actually comes, falls the nighttime. Heavy clouds have covered the sky without letting a single sun ray to break through. The area that surrounds me is desolated, as though a battleground at the end of a war: a sad, cold, and empty place. Even crooked people stopped walking by and I'm standing all by myself, sadder than wind, colder than air, and emptier than shelves with bread (should such a thing exist).

A bus full of people halts at a stop. Nobody enters, nobody leaves. Street lamps come off, illuminating the perimeter somewhat. Litter is being thrown by the wind: paper, cigarette butts, plastic bottles. People are nasty, man. Why do we litter? Especially in a city the size of New York. If each person throws one cigarette butt, there will be thirty million of them at the end of the day.

The wind is so strong it pushes me forward and backward.

I decide to dance another Broadway performance to warm up. Two more minutes of this nonsense and I'm going home. I'm craving hot ramen noodle soup and a cup of herb tea.

Babette appears in the lobby. She exchanges words with the security guy and proceeds toward the exit. Relief washes over me. There's the same sensation in my body when my TV cable was installed and I groaned with pleasure: Finally, we have Internet! Babette scans the image in front of her —me on the other side of the glass doors—her mouth open. I want to wave but my hands are frozen. She lifts up her chin and gains a look of indifference. As soon as Babette exits, she sharply turns, avoiding eye contact.

"Babette, wait," I say, my voice raspy from the cold. Without responding, she keeps walking. I catch up. "I need to talk to you," I say, grabbing her coat. The wind muffles my words.

She breaks free from my grip. "Stay away from me."

"I know about your mom and I'm sorry."

She stops. "What?"

"I know about your mom's lung cancer. Adam said it was fatal. If I knew any of this, I would never pick a fight with you. I'm here to apologize for photoshopping your face on a monkey. You deserve better. A lion, at least."

"You're such a dummy, Calyssa, just like the rest of them."

"What do you mean?"

"My mother's not sick at all."

"She's not?"

"No, she's been dead for twenty years."

"I don't understand," I say.

"I was raised by my father."

"Then why did you say she was sick?"

"So nobody could suspect me in quitting."

"You lost me," I say, squinting.

"To save face I made up this whole ordeal."

I stare at her blankly, partially relieved, partially angry. "Why did you decide to quit?"

"Look, why do I have to explain anything to you? You and I were never friends. Why do you care? I accept your apology but it's too late. We'll never see each other again."

"I know," I say. "Whatever happened between the two of us is over. I left, you left. Come on, tell me what happened. Why did you quit?"

Shivering, Babette shilly-shallies with a look of distrust on her face. She places her hands in her coat pockets. "What Mr. Petticoat said about me was enough to realize I was unwanted there. He offered you my place and said I was ugly. I heard the entire conversation because I was listening by the door. Am I *that* ugly?"

Babette starts crying, her one eyebrow scrunched in the middle. I always thought she was incapable of emotions. It was easy to forget Babette was human when we were rivals. Now that we're equals I realize she doesn't deserve to work for that company. Mr. Grunt is just one nasty man who needs to be castrated and hung upside down like a piñata.

Lindsay mentioned she'd be at Mario's. With her makeup abilities she can fix Babette in no time, and perhaps fix me too. The best way to feel better about yourself is to have a few drinks and speak up what's on your mind. Especially now, more than ever, Babette needs girls on her side.

"I have a friend in town who will help you," I say.

"Help with what?"

"Beauty tips. For both of us, I mean. Let's go."

"Now?"

"Yes."

She's uncertain how to react to such a proposition but she argues not. I grab her hand, dragging her to the subway.

Spanish Harlem is located three stops away on the express train, and twelve mere minutes later we enter my favorite establishment. The warmth welcomes us, as though Fibonacci and Afrodite have practiced their occult little tricks here.

Two patrons are chatting idly by the beer pumps in the middle of the bar, another one's standing by the jukebox, perhaps picking a song. Chloe's chatting with a guy without noticing me. In her orange sweater and bleached blond platinum hair, she resembles a grandma. Far back, Natalia is on the phone at the table we usually claim as ours. She's wearing workout clothes: a bright pink top and bright green tights. I've never seen Natalia wearing anything but designer clothes. She waves, lifting her index finger to indicate she'll soon be finished.

Lindsay is sitting by herself at the very corner of the bar, watching TV. She's wrapped in a white furry shawl underneath which peeks a burgundy dress. Her hair is an unmistakable wig: long, black, cheap-looking. Her bubble braid style imitates Princess Jasmine (aka me). She must be trick-or-treating, and I'd give her some candy I stole from the wooden bowl earlier, but I only have enough for myself.

"I need to use the ladies' room," Babette says without making eye contact. She probably wants to blast a dookie but afraid to admit it. "I'll be right back."

I approach the bar. Upon seeing me, Lindsay stretches a smile, jumps off the stool, and gives me a hug. She acts like a Chihuahua who's been reunited with her owner.

"Look at me," she says, twirling twice. I do as I'm told: Her lips are burgundy red to match the dress, with a beauty spot on her cheek imitating Marilyn Monroe.

"Who are you supposed to be?"

"Fifties glamor: Marilyn, Audrey, maybe even Elizabeth Taylor. I'm all three. Can you imagine this whole outfit only cost $700?"

"Fifties glamour is not an outfit. Kids won't know who you are."

"I'm not dressing up for the kids. For myself. You like my pearl necklace?"

"No. Too early for Halloween."

"Early? Stop being silly. You're allowed to dress up for the entire month of October." She makes eye contact with Mario, who's cutting limes.

"Apple martini, please." After Mario and I wave at each other, he starts juggling bottles in the air. I missed his strong drinks is what precisely I wish to tell him, hug him, lift up his little butt, and kiss him, but decide better of it.

I didn't mean to come off hostile, but my anger at Lindsay has been building up ever since Lucky Knotts called me. The hooklet's disposition seems different, on the cheerful side, her voice easier to digest on an empty stomach. Before, she spoke as though she was afraid of her own voice. Today Mario has no problems understanding her.

I finally start thawing as I arrange myself on a stool next to her. I wish Lindsay told me she was wearing a dress so I could match. Now I just resemble her pimp, in this hoody, in these jeans that look good on my booty, and the UGGs that don't rhyme with "booty." Lindsay's skinny pink suitcase is parked next to her, which means she might be looking for a place to stay. She ordered a drink for me as means of bribery, the way Chloe had when she brought Elizabeth in a condom. My apple martini magically appears before me and I take a sip.

"Cheers," Lindsay says happily, lifting her glass, also an apple martini. A pouch of dried Turkish apricots rests next to her. Not only the bitchlet stole my name, my haircut, and calls me a house mama, but she stole my drink and my food. Anger overwhelms me to the point where I have cartoon steam puffing off my nose.

"Let's cut to the chase, bitch: What's this all about?" I say, squinting.

"I don't know what you mean."

"This," I say, circling my finger in her face. "You, inviting me for a drink."

"I got the job! Thanks to you, that is."

"So now you utilize my name as a reference? Now I'm your house mama? I'm waiting for an apology."

Her smile changes to frown. "House mama? What do you mean by that? I'm sorry I used your name without asking. I thought you wouldn't mind."

"Apologies accepted. Under normal circumstances I wouldn't mind. But now you might as well be me." I point at the apricots and her drink.

"I thought you'd be flattered I want to act like you. I love your audacity."

"Oh, I'm flattered all right." I purse my lips to indicate the opposite.

"Are you okay? I'm sorry if I made you mad. I didn't mean to."

"I'm mad because I know nothing about stripping. If she asked me a strip club jargon term you'd be kissing that pole goodbye." I take three apricots and shove them in my mouth.

"What's stripping got to do with anything?"

"Well, the lady who called me said she was a house mama from another strip club. She's the one who hired you, I presume."

"Lucky Knotts?"

I nod, chewing. Lindsay starts suffocating from a laugh. "You misunderstood. She's a housewife. Lucky doesn't like term 'housewife,' so she calls herself a house mom. Now she wants to go to school full-time, why she needs a live-in babysitter for Dana and Charlotte."

In my head I replay my conversation with Lucky, wondering how that scored in Lindsay's favor and landed her a job. I'm pretty sure I was sober then. "To be clear: Lucky Knotts is not a house mama from a strip club?"

"Correct," Lindsay says.

"And you will be a babysitter?"

"Yes, this job is a perfect set up for me. I'll be a live-in nanny for an older kid and Charlotte, who is four. Remember when I told you I wished I had a home? Well, now I finally have it. I will no longer need to search for a couch at the end of the day. The money's good. Really, just watching two tots is a stable job, and it will teach me responsibility, until I decide what I should proceed doing next."

"Congratulations."

"Thank you. I have a hotel for the weekend in midtown, and I start working Monday."

"So no more stripping?"

She shakes her head. "After what Wolfgang told me, I knew I needed to respect myself more. Stripping is a great way to make money, but I had low self-esteem, and therefore nobody respected me in return. Once I realized that, with respect came confidence, and there I was, confident enough to apply for a real job. I hate that I had to lie to Lucky but you were right: lying didn't kill the cat, the lack of confidence did."

While she looked for ways to kill cats, I take a sip of my drink. Gone is the feeling of anger. Lindsay received what she wanted—a home—right after Wolfgang humiliated her, calling her crooked legs. All Lindsay needed was to realize she deserved to be treated as a human, not a secondhand employee whose proprietor is allowed to say anything he wishes, just because he conjectures if he owns the job then he owns you with it. After a short silence, I briefly tell Lindsay about my job, the séance, and other shenanigans, bringing her up to speed. She reapplies lipstick and looks at me with a smile.

"Caly, I remember when we first met, you said you always wondered what your mom thought of you. Did the séance answer your question?"

"The séance was bogus."

"But it bugs you."

"It bugs me because I thought Mom would be happy for me. I finally made it on my own, had my own apartment, had no accidental pregnancies. Why did she still say *Maybe*?"

"Maybe she wants you to be happy with yourself as you are."

"Right. *Maybe*."

Mario turns up the volume on the TV, interrupting our conversation: "Because of Amelia, the Staten Island Ferry was shut down at five o'clock until further notice. The waves make the harbor unsafe. Ferries to the Liberty and Ellis Islands were cancelled as well. If you need to travel to Staten Island, take the Verrazano Bridge."

Time is 5:25. I hope Christina and Aunt Sarah are safe in their Staten Island home. Chucky predicted tomorrow the baby will be born, but just like the séance, her predictions were untrue.

Babette returns from the bathroom. She definitely must have been laying brown dumplings, why she took so long. Her hands smell like bananas. Realizing the Cute Mango dispenser was gone, Mario must have purchased a pack with variety of different flavors, and I can't wait to try them all. The current one is perhaps called Atlanta's Bananas or something along the lines. After I introduce the two, Lindsay studies Babette with caution.

"Is she the same Babette who got you fired?"

"Yes," I say, "the same Babette. She's not involved because I quit."

"Actually," Babette says, "I'm kind of involved. When I found your résumé, I was the one who brought it to Mr. Petticoat's attention."

"But I was the one who photoshopped your face on a monkey first."

"But I was the one who started a fight with you in the bathroom."

Lindsay stretches out her hands like a referee at a boxing tournament. "Hold up. Nothing personal, sister," she tells Babette, "but you got to take that breath under control."

I'm glad she doesn't get personal. Babette turns red, covering her mouth with a hand. Her breath doesn't smell *that* bad, but Lindsay fans the area near her face melodramatically, as though Babette's erupted an anal volcano.

"Here's an easy fix," Lindsay continues. "Order a mojito and chew on the mint. The drink will freshen up your breath in seconds. I always make guys do that before I kiss them. Next, I'll teach you how to floss." She orders a mojito for Babette, asking for twice the mint. "You're paying for your own drinks," Lindsay clarifies to Babette.

When a mojito arrives, Babette instantly digs in for some fresh mint leaves with a thick straw that came with it. As Lindsay predicted, her fowl breath instantly disappears. With the mojito in hands, she sits on a stool next to me, making bubbles through the straw.

"Lindsay," I say, "could you do Babette a favor? She needs recommendations how to look more attractive." Babette turns away as though she's not involved in the conversation.

Lindsay's forehead muscles twitch. "Nothing too much. I strive for a natural look on a woman. Maybe if you tweeze your eyebrows, because you resemble a Cyclops. Also, smoky eyes do the trick. What are you wearing? Your outfit is masculine enough for you to have balls. You must pay attention to details and accessories, sister. Guys are careless when it comes to clothes you wear, but more interested in your sleekness."

"What do you mean?" Babette says. "I don't understand any of it."

"It's common sense, all in the brain," Lindsay says and taps the side of her head. "Have you ever looked in the mirror and thought how unnatural you looked? To look natural for a woman is to look as fake as possible."

"Could you be more specific?" says clueless Babette.

"Come with me, kid," Lindsay says and sighs. She stands up, drink in hand. "Let's go to the bathroom—where there's better lighting—and I'll show you a few tricks how to apply makeup and stuff. Just be thankful I brought my makeup kit with me or you'd be screwed. Just bring that mojito with you, and keep eating that mint."

Before the two of them saunter toward the ladies' room, Lindsay pulls out a makeup bag from her skinny pink suitcase. I like how Lindsay's advice —a girl who *never lies*—involves faking.

Bored, I study the guy Chloe's with. The last couple of month she was afraid going on dates, hiding behind a keyboard, so I'm glad she's back on the horse. I can't see Chloe's visage because her rear faces me, but he's sitting clearly in my line of sight. His skin color of café au lait. He's thirty-four, if a day. He's no model but cute in a way. He's wearing a plain gray tee and jeans, a sturdy jacket on an empty table next to him. His hair is combed back and he's wearing glasses. They have just finished their beer, and Pedro Grande picks up the empty pitcher. I can't eavesdrop on their conversation, but the guy uses his fingers to imitate a pen in what could only be his request for a check. Chloe throws a peanut in the air and it lands in the guy's mouth. They both laugh. The guy puts on his jacket and zigzags in the direction of the baños.

Using the free moment, taking my drink along, I position myself on the guy's chair in front of Chloe. She smirks in a silly way, surprised, and reaches for a hug during which we bounce around a ball of hellos.

"Who's the guy?" I say when we sit back.

"His name is Eddy. He came here by himself and we started chatting because nobody else was here. He's super sweet and smart. He works for an IT company, some computer stuff I know nothing about. He said we should go back to his place to play doctor."

While she takes a sip of her beer, finishing the glass, I take a note of the natural state of her skin. Her fake tan is washed off, no makeup, gone are the gigantic lashes. Still, there's the orange sweater. Even though there isn't an uglier sweater being sold, it compliments her skin tone. Her confidence in herself, especially by wearing something quite disturbing, can be almost touched.

"I'm happy for you. He looks almost as cute as Moshe. I'm sure his penis doesn't curve in any direction."

"I hope it does. I need some extra pleasure today."

"How's your mom? You guys made up?"

"Yup. She agreed on keeping Anubis. To be honest, it was extremely hard on me taking care of those pets, so I quit volunteering. I thought I was doing good for the pets while in reality I was trying to feel good about myself. Selfishness; what can we do? I was doing the right thing, but for the wrong reason."

"I wish you didn't go to that reunion."

"I'm glad I did," she says.

"You are? Amanda Gellar made you feel awful about yourself."

"Amanda Gellar can penetrate herself with a cactus. She made me feel horrible the day we met, true. But you know what I realized? She's got this fake confidence because she's got money, but when she invited people back to her hotel—the expensive Plaza—for an after-party, no one went. She was acting like the Queen of England. You know the kind? *I'm better than you, I'm richer than you, I'm prettier than you.* Her attitude pissed people off. I don't want that. I don't need fake confidence. She's lying to herself about being fabulous while in reality she's got no friends. Nobody, except for her sorry-ass-self, will ever love her for *her*. I'm happy to have real friends."

"Me too," I say.

"And I know if I had an after-party you'd be the first one to bring us drinks."

"You couldn't be further from the truth."

"I realized I was good enough as is, the entire package, and it made me more appealing and attractive. And hey, I snatched a date without having to pretend anything. With Eddy I'm planning to play doctor until he needs an actual doctor. It's been a while for me, if you know what I mean." She winks.

"Chloe, you were right about me blaming others for my own mistakes. So I apologized to Babette for photoshopping her head onto a chimpanzee."

"What did she say?"

"We haven't discussed it at length, but maybe we can become friends."

"Maybe."

In the meantime, Eddy returns from the bathroom. Chloe introduces us, after which Eddy pays his tab and the two of them leave for the "hospital."

The next five minutes I enjoy my drink and check the news on my phone, occasionally giving Natalia a look indicating she needs to hang up. There's an interactive way to track Amelia's epicenter, as a dot moving slowly up the East Coast. Luckily, the epicenter is miles away, terrorizing nothing but the cold waters of the Atlantic Ocean. Pedro Grande stops by my table.

"Order, ma'am?" he says.

"Let's see. Has the flyer been fixed?"

"Yes, ma'am."

"Has the potato man come?"

"Yes, ma'am."

"Will you please stop calling me ma'am?"

"Si."

"Nothing for me, thanks."

Pedro Grande seems insulted and unsure how to react. "No fries?" he says in a way as though I just denied an invitation to the White House by the President himself.

"Not unless they will chisel away my three chins."

Dumbstruck, he keeps staring at me. I should know better than using real words in this bar aside from yes, no, and maybe. "No fries?" he repeats and I shake my head. Pedro Grande dismisses himself at the same as when Natalia hangs up her phone. I join her at our table, with half a martini still left in my glass.

"Who was that on the phone?" I ask.

"Remember Sandra?" I nod but I don't remember. "She was another transgender lady in Vegas. We stayed in touch. She lives in Trinidad."

"Trinidad and Tobago?"

"No, Trinidad, Colorado, a transgender capital of the States. Might as well be called *Trannydad*. Anyway, she invited me to visit sometime next month. She says I'll love Trinidad and should move."

"That's great."

"No, it's not."

"Why not?"

"Just because I'm transgender doesn't mean I should live in a community with only transgender people. Why does it matter if I'm a man or a woman? I'm a person."

"I'll drink to that," I say, and to prove I mean it, I actually drink to that. Maybe gender is no longer real. Elizabeth is confused about her gender, being a male with a female name. Laruza Somo's gender is impossible to trace. Finally, even Christina's baby is gynandromorph until proved otherwise. "So you declined Sandra's invitation?"

"I may consider a visit but I'll never move. I love my life in New York. I love how my friends treat me as a woman. I value our friendship more than belonging to a fake society or living in a city full of transgender women."

"Good point."

"And more importantly, guess what I've got."

"A new housekeep?" I say, thinking whether Natalia found Lupita and shaved her pussel.

"No, think harder. Lucille Roberts."

"A white housekeep?"

"Don't be silly. Use your brain."

"Natalia, I don't have one. Obviously."

"I signed up for a gym called Lucille Roberts."

"Is there anything special about the gym, or why are you so happy?"

"The gym is for chicks only. Men are prohibited inside."

Her wide smile might as well be an accordion. I haven't seen her happier. After the mishap in Vegas, where she had a choice to remain herself or to lie, she chose correctly and was awarded with validation of her female gender.

I finish my apple martini. "I've never heard of such a gym."

"Because you don't exercise. There are several locations in Manhattan. I just finished my first training session with the fittest chick I know. She tested my strength first, then placed me on a treadmill, and at the end we came up with a plan. Girl, I am exhausted. My next session is next week."

Suddenly I get jealous, for soon Natalia will be the fittest chick I know, making my triple chin double in her presence. Maybe I should start dieting. If only I had Christina nagging me with her newly found fetish for healthy foods for the "baby." Mario appears with an apple martini and what looks like a Sex on the Beach. Finally, a girly drink for Natalia. He sets down our respective glasses by a bowl of peanuts while I wonder whether I got so drunk already and forgot I'd requested two drinks.

"We didn't order these," I say.

"On the house," he says. "Friday night special for ladies."

"But today is Thursday," I say, wishing for once I kept my big mouth shut.

"We're closed tomorrow because of the hurricane. So they're on the house today. For you, ladies."

When he hides behind the bar, Natalia lifts up her drink. "See? For the ladies."

With a smile on her face Natalia enjoys a sip of her Sex on the Beach while I understand why I love my ugly baby—the bar—because sometimes they treat us like royalty. Free drinks here and there, cozy atmosphere, and good food.

"Calyssa, have you found a job yet?"

"Nope."

"I need a housekeeper. The job is yours."

"I ain't cleaning no houses."

"Speak like a normal person. I'll pay $20 an hour if you're willing to learn how to make empanadas."

"Natalia, your proposition is out of the question."

"Call me later if you change your mind." Her phone rings and vibrates, its buzz of a bee against the window trapped inside. "Sandra's calling again. Ah, women are so needy. Nothing personal. I'll take this and scoot. Bye."

Natalia finishes her drink and leaves after kissing me on a cheek. Her ass looks great in the bright green tights, and as she walks toward the door, the few present patrons follow her with their eyes.

Mario switches the news channel to a cooking show. A lady chef prepares a catfish for an appetizer. Catfish sounds like a monstrosity. It's not a cat, not yet a fish, like a gross combination of Anubis and Elizabeth in one package. The chef dips the catfish into cornmeal batter and places it in a deep fryer. I swear on my apple martini I'd never eat something like this in reverence to both Anubis and Elizabeth.

Lindsay and Babette exit the bathroom. They find me in the process of cropping Marcus out of the picture we took in the VIP lounge. I'm ready to part with him, but I'll finish him off later. I say it like a real criminal. Tweezing gave Babette's forehead a red halo, with two distinct eyebrows instead of one. She's got the double deuce, I say and laugh to myself. With makeup she looks prettier. Lindsay cut her hair short and styled it messy. Her eyes are outlined with thick eyeliner, the way Cassidy's were.

"Look at the razor cut," Lindsay says proudly. "I learned it from my friend Delight. You like? And what about the smoky eyes? Aren't they a piece of art? She has three different tints, a trick I learned from Cassidy."

"I can't recognize her," I say. "Babette, what do you think?"

"I can't recognize myself either," she says. "I was raised by a man, my father, and he never helped me with any makeup tricks. I grew up as a tomboy, but I love the way makeup looks on me."

Lindsay messes Babette's mop a bit more. "Remember the tricks I taught you. I'll text you tomorrow. Calyssa," she says, turning to me, "I have to leave. The hurricane will hit us soon and I want to check into my hotel prior to that."

"Thanks for helping her," I say.

"You're welcome. You're next."

She embraces me and presses her lips against my ear. "Babette is such a great gal," she whispers. "But you're still my favorite."

Lindsay picks up her skinny pink suitcase, pays her tab, and out the door she goes. When the door opens, in comes the cold air. After finishing my drink, I'll get going as well. Babette and I are sitting in silence. We've never hung out together and I don't know how to start a conversation. She eats the remaining mint while I give her a closed-mouth smile.

"Babette—" I say.

"Calyssa, don't. I know what you want to say and it's unnecessary."

I'm glad she knows what I was going to say because I don't. I just started, hoping Blabber would pick up from there.

"We were never friends," she continues, "but we're girls and we must stick together. You came all the way back to apologize. You're brave."

"To be honest, I don't know what it was. When Adam told me about your imaginary mom, it made my anus cringe at a thought I'll never see *my* mom, and the fact you're losing *yours*. That feeling alone was strong enough to forget that I wanted to kill you by feeding you to my fish."

"Good thing you didn't go through with your plan."

"Oh, please," I say, "if that failed, I was planning to feed you falafel until you choked to death."

She bursts out laughing and covers her mouth, not realizing I was serious. "I'm sorry I lied about having a mom."

"That's what we have in common, I guess. Both moms are dead. How old were you? What happened, if you don't mind me asking?"

"I don't mind. I was fifteen. She worked in sales and was scarcely home, driving from one state to the next. Dad is an accountant. He could stay at home whenever, so he was raising me. Mom was at a big sale in Minnesota, stuff she planned to resell at a retail price later on, and as soon as the store opened, hundreds of women barged in. She was killed in a stampede."

"Holy crap."

"This is why I stay away from clothes and stores. How about you?"

"I was ten and she was my age, thirty. She died in a cab en route to the airport, and I wonder whether it has anything to do with me being afraid of flying. But at this point in life Mom and I are the same age. I may die tomorrow and what kind of memory will I leave behind? The reverend will say, 'Calyssa was great at photoshopping people's faces on monkeys. We won't miss her, but a martini glass will.'"

"You sound as though you're looking for forgiveness. I forgive you, if it makes you feel any better."

"I promise it does," I say. "What is your plan now, in terms of work?"

"No idea. Working for Shred Unread taught me a few things, mainly that if you feel unappreciated at your job you should quit. Even if the money is good, emotionally it isn't worth it. Over the course of three years, I was promoted twice but was never chosen as coworker of the month. Money is money but praise and recognition are more important for an employee. We want to feel wanted and loved at our job."

"You're right, but let me add something. My friends were looking for recognition, and they found it within themselves."

"How?"

"The same way you found yours. Through humiliation."

"Interesting," she says. "Can you elaborate?"

"After humiliation came revelation. They were destroyed emotionally. They felt like failures. Not literal destruction, of course, but in their mind. When you know you can't go on feeling like this. When what you really needed was in front of you, but you couldn't understand it at the time. As soon as they failed, there was no way to move but up. They seem happier knowing that after destruction comes creation. A friend of mine said catastrophes cause evolution. Now I understand what she meant."

"What about you?"

"What about me?"

"Lindsay told me you'd traveled all the way to Hawaii to attain blackmail material on Adam. You obviously haven't found your revelation. What holds you back?"

"I'm afraid of failure."

"Maybe that's exactly what you need to move on."

"Maybe."

Babette slurps up the rest of the mojito. "Well, Lindsay was right. We need to leave before the hurricane gets out of control. Let's stay in touch and have a drink sometime. I'd like to hear the entire Hawaiian story."

I nod and we quickly exchange phone numbers. What a difference it makes when you stop hating a person. I never noticed what a nice smile she had. Babette leaves while I lick the last bits of my drink, hoping the subway is still running. My phone rings when I get up.

"Hey, it's me," Christina says. "I'm in labor. I'm in the cab to the Willowbrook."

"Where's Aunt Sarah?"

"She's on her way from work. She said she'd be coming straight to the hospital."

"Are you okay?"

"Yes, but I hope the baby won't crawl out of me in the car. I'll see you there."

"I can't—the Ferry was shut down at five."

"Calyssa, you promised."

"I'm telling you the truth, though."

"Sorry I didn't hear what you said. See you soon. Thanks!" She hangs up.

The Verrazano-Narrows Bridge will be closed in twenty-five minutes. There are no other ways to reach Staten Island, unless I swim by hand. One thing Christina expects from me is to join her in the delivery room. I might have missed her birthday or forgot to return her calls, but babies don't happen every year. I'll assume responsibility without making any more excuses. Because I need not pay for my drinks—first paid by Lindsay, second by Mario—I leave, saying goodbye to my two men, kissing the air in their general direction. I place $5 on the bar for good measure.

For the next five minutes, I unsuccessfully try to catch a cab. Instead, I take the express 4 train to Bowling Green Station, located near the Brooklyn-Battery Tunnel. The train arrives a minute before eight o'clock. Even if I were Wonder Woman, there's no way I'll reach the Verrazano Bridge on time before they shut it down. However, I decide to take a leap of faith. Hailing a cab nets me one. The driver rolls down his window. His face is covered in beard with only eyes visible.

"Where are you headed?" he asks. His mouth is invisible under all the hair as though he's using his mind to communicate with me. Although I try to open the door without saying my destination, I realize the door is locked.

"Staten Island," I say.

He rolls back his window and off he drives. The wind intensifies, growling like a hungry animal. The darkness turned Manhattan into a black hole. Just like we learned in school about the general theory of relativity, Manhattan (a black hole) is a region from which gravity prevents anything to escape (me). The surface called "an event horizon"—the point of no return—surrounds Staten Island. Another cab stops, its door locked, a terrorist-looking hag sitting behind the wheel.

"Where are you going?" he says after he rolls down his window.

"Brooklyn," I say, hoping Brooklyn sounds less crude than Staten Island.

He gives me the finger and pulls left toward the road. It dazes me how sneaky the cab drivers are, locking you out when it suits them. If I felt warmer, I'd write down the number of his license's plate and report him to the New York City Department of Transportation. If cab is palace and Caesar is driver, Cleopatra needs to roll herself into the carpet to sneak in. The more I think of a warm carpet though, the colder I feel. Lying will be the only option to sneak inside.

I decide to walk because standing is certainly unhelpful. If I try to walk all the way to Staten Island, I'll be DOA. With my arm extended, I'm hoping to catch a fish. A cab pulls in next to me. The driver unravels the window just a tiny bit. A woman sits behind the wheel. Her nationality is to be determined later but she's certainly of Persian origin.

"Where are you going?" she says with a strong accent. I rarely catch females driving cabs, and that's encouraging. Her voice is soothing. I can't lie to her even in my condition.

"My cousin is giving birth, but it's all the way on Staten Island. You might as well drive off."

"Get in."

She unlocks the door. My brain blows a fuse, but I argue not and claim a seat as soon as I step in. Through the opening in the Plexiglas partition, I throw in two Jackson to show her I'm willing to pay double. On her license tag, her name appears as Scheherazade. "Thank you so much. Nobody else would take me."

"You're welcome."

"You heard it right, right? Staten Island."

"I know. I was born there." She revs up the engine and we're on the way to Brooklyn. Not to be rude, but forget about being born here, she sounds like she *just* stepped off the ship. I wonder what prompted her to help, when others were so reluctant. But no more questioning.

In Brooklyn, when we merge to the Brooklyn-Queens Expressway, traffic gets heavy. In ten minutes, we only cover seven blocks, from 85th Street to

92th Street. Slowly we merge, and Scheherazade takes the higher level of the bridge. From here, blurry Manhattan lights are visible through the darkness, just like stars on a cloudy night. Almost in the middle of the bridge, our speed descends and we stop completely. The cab meter keeps running while I note the amount owed: $31.90. Honks are heard. Voices. An ambulance. The wind whistles from the cab crevices. I keep my palms warm between my thighs, watching the darkness as though I might somehow X-ray through the cars ahead. We haven't moved in five minutes. Suddenly, cars start moving backward. 9:00. They've just shut down the bridge and they want everyone off it.

CHAPTER SIXTEEN

Boy or Girl

THE WIND IN THE MIDDLE OF THE BRIDGE IS WHISTLING fiercely, beating against the window as though trying to break in. Scheherazade is blabbing on the phone, unconcerned with the hurricane or the fact that the left lane is moving backward like a conveyor belt. I'd put three cents to the table that, even if we started falling down, she'd remember to call all of her relatives to say goodbye. At least I've warmed up. Even after I bang on the glass to get Scheherazade's attention, she keeps blabbing to her husbands like I'm invisible. I pull out another two $20 bills and shove the money through the Plexiglas, exiting the cab right away. That's $80 of cab fare I'd have to somehow deduct the following tax season.

The chill instantly bites into my skin and the gust of wind pushes me from behind toward Staten Island. I hover along the road and cars honk at me as a reminder of my stupidity, but it's beyond me—my mind is too frozen at this point. I'm unaware I break into a trot until I start sweating when the cold air frosts my damp clothes as I run. I vaguely notice the reason for the created conveyor belt—two cars are smooching each other in the middle of the road. Past them, the bridge is otherwise empty. Staten Island is perhaps three hundred feet away, and I keep running, unable to feel my legs or arms, head tucked in the hood. If I were Mae Mobley from *The Help*, (a movie the three of us watched over the weekend), I just imagine Aibileen telling me, "You is kind. You is important. You ain't smart though. You is stupid. Very, very stupid."

A towing truck along with an ambulance and two police cars drive by, and if any of them notice me, they fail to indicate. Is it legal to attempt crossing a bridge that's been shut down? Behind me, I sense an approaching vehicle, headlights more and more visible on the pavement ahead of me. They honk. I take it as a clue to stop. I turn around and get blinded by the bright light. I cover my eyes with a sleeve, shivering. The cops bypass without stopping. Jumping to get their attention, I realize I better get arrested than freeze to death. The cops, it seems, have more important things to do like shooting black folks or men in wheelchairs.

The cold nibbles on my skin. One bite after another. I pause, unable to walk. The hurricane has numbed my limbs to the point where I imagine being glued together from six different pieces like a papier-mâché. My otherwise finesse hoody has become inept against the wind. There's ringing in my ears. Even though I try answering the phone, nobody picks up. Someone is shooting cannonballs out of me. Fireworks. I must return to the cab and have Scheherazade drive me to Queens.

The sound of an ambulance seems close, but when I turn my head, its remote colorful lights are far in the distance. Apparently, somehow half-asleep, I've reached the end of the Verrazano Bridge. Lights are approaching. Sauntering to the middle of the road, I pause motionlessly, incapable to locomote. Should've ordered the fries for extra energy. There's candy in my pocket, but it hurts to even wiggle my fingers. I close my eyes, fully aware I'm passing out. Screeching of wheels.

"Lady, what are you doing?" a man yells through the wind. I open my eyes. Ahead, there's a van with a logo in extra-large lettering: "BABY DON'T QUIVER, FOOD WE'LL DELIVER." A Staten Island grocery store chain —Larry's—offers free delivery on orders $50 or more. He must be finishing his shift or something.

"I need to get to Staten Island."

"Obviously."

"Give me a ride?"

"It depends on where you're going."

"Willowbrook Hospital."

"Get in." Word *stupid* at the end was nonexistent, but I heard it nevertheless. He opens the door and I get inside. My teeth are jiggling like two maracas, my throat raw. He keeps talking to me, even though my brain registers none of it. I close my eyes. The man revs up the engine and we suddenly stop, about ten seconds later.

"Lady, we've arrived," he says and nudges me with a knuckle.

I open my eyes. The Willowbrook Hospital building greets me to my right. I obviously snoozed, because it's about seven miles between the two places—ten, maybe fifteen minutes away.

"I don't know what's the matter with you," he says. "Maybe you're suffering a stroke, plain stupid and/or Republican, but please stay inside until the hurricane is over, okay?"

I nod and exit the car, saying, "Hello," copying Grace Bishop. Like a marionette, I'm directed toward the hospital by some invisible force. The wind whistles, but the surrounding complex acts as a windshield. The trees are being punished with one tree lying flat on the ground in front of the entrance while other trees are being violently choked. Leaves are flying around like confetti. We're celebrating the end of fall.

Inside, shaking, I crawl toward the receptionist, who happens to be a pirate in a nurse's costume. The eye patch makes her appear scary, together with an oversized safety pin for an earring. I know it's almost Halloween, but come on, girl. If a baby sees this creature, she'll be scarred for life or pee her pants. The badge introduces her as Marina Bobrova. She smiles, revealing a gap between her teeth. The rest of her teeth resemble the Manhattan's skyline: crooked and uneven. She blows a bubble that could only happen after chewing a whole pack of gum, spearminty from the smell of it.

"Hello," she says with a thick accent. "You're looking for something?" She asks it in the same manner a visitor is asked, "Are you here on business or pleasure?"

"Business."

"Excuse me?"

"My cousin's giving birth. Christina Lee. How can I find her?"

"Oh, the Chinese girl who wants to be surprised. Are you her partner?"

"Gross. She's my cousin."

"You don't say. You don't look alike whatsoever."

"She just really got undeveloped. How can I find her?"

"Did you have different fathers?"

"That's what cousins usually have, yes."

Marina blows another bubble. It burst on half of her face and she shoves it back into her mouth with her fingers. "Did you know when a baby gets born during a hurricane it means good luck? Especially if they're twins."

"According to who, Tila Tequila?"

"I read that in *The Staten Islander* this week."

"Well, that's a legit source."

"No kidding. The baby's a Libra, just two days before becoming a Scorpio. You'll easily get along with Libras. They're friendly, social, clever, self-motivated, optimistic. But they can be really unreliable. The baby won't show up until it wants to. I read one time a Libra made a mother wait for a whole week, and when it came out it was an octopus. I saw this once on Discovery Channel: this Libra woman committed suicide because her husband fed her with pickles. She couldn't take any more of his pickles."

"Marina, could you please let me know how to find Christina? I'm not in the mood for chitchat."

"Go to the waiting room," she says and averts her eyes. "Thought I was giving helpful information." Without moving from her chair, Marina points to the right with her finger. A gem the size of the Cullinan diamond sits on her pinkie.

"I swear you were. I'm sorry. I just want to see Christina."

"That's okay. I just have nobody to talk to and you look like an easy-going person. I'm sure you're a Sagittarius."

"I'm a Leo, actually."

"My ex-boyfriend was a Leo. What a whacko. He was good in bed though, but stupid. One time we were on vacation in Michigan, and he," she looks around and moves closer to me, whispering, "decided it was finally time for anal."

"Marina, are you still *with* me?"

"What? A little contraception story for the road: no condoms needed."

"Marina, Christina? Let's talk anal some other time."

"Sorry, got carried away. I love astrology."

"And drinking, I presume?"

"Go this way and you'll find the waiting room at the end of the hallway to the right. Follow signs for maternity. Let's hope they're twins."

"Thank you," I say, wondering whether Christina can have twins. I just imagine the surprise on Christina's face while I chime in, "Told ya so. Should have done the sonogram." I always want to use the phrase "Told ya so" on Christina, but so far she is the only person who's used that in our relationship.

The hospital corridors are eerily too empty. Just occasionally I'd pass somebody with a broken leg, or an older person with an I.V. stand next to them. I'm not a frequent hospital visitor, mostly because I like to self-administer the pills I personally prescribe myself *by myself*, and I always feel uneasy in such facilities. I pass a row of empty gurneys parked by the wall, and find maternity. Hospital: a place where we come to life and say goodbye to life.

The waiting room is at the end of the corridor, and I push the door to open. Aunt Sarah, spread out on a chair, is molesting a daisy. There's nobody else beside her. She pulls one daisy leaf at a time, mouthing, "Boy, girl, boy, girl, boy, girl . . ."

"Hi, Aunt Sarah."

She follows me with her gaze, and after pulling the last leaf, she tosses the stem into a nearby trash can. "It'll be a girl," she says. That's coming from somebody who just made fun of the séance. Aunt Sarah says she isn't superstitious, but then would toss the salt behind her shoulder after spilling it. She stands up to embrace me, her hands as hot as lava, compared to my frozen skin. She takes my face into her boiling hands, awaking me in a second. Her lips sting as she gives me a kiss. She sits back in her chair. "Thanks for coming, Calyssa. It's taking longer than expected, and I'm about to climb this wall. Guess *what* your cousin did?"

"She pooped herself."

"No."

"Well, nothing else would be funny."

"She made sure nobody enters the delivery room but her and the nurse."

"Why?"

"Exactly. Like I never gave birth myself."

Aunt Sarah was dying to be with Christina in the delivery room while I dreaded it. At least for once, she listened to my pleas. Without makeup, Aunt Sarah is a copy of my mother. Her coal-black hair is collected on top of her head in a bun with a large golden clip. Several pink barrettes hold her long bangs on either side of the face. I can't help thinking this is how Amelia would look like if she were alive.

I claim a chair next to hers, promptly removing a book of baby names from under me. A plump toddler on the cover is playing with blocks, building a structure reminding of a house. A future Marcus Truman.

"Whose book is this?" I say.

"Mine. I was reading name meanings, trying to figure out whether or not I like James or Walter. Any thoughts?"

"What if she's girl?"

She makes a face. The eyeliner makes her coal-black eyes pop out. "If it's a girl, I was thinking Amelia . . . after your mother. The receptionist said the hurricane means luck and prosperity. What do you think?"

"I think the bitch is drunk. Was my mom born during a hurricane?"

"Child, your mother was born when they elected a Republican. *That* I'll never forget. I was three at the time, and a big democratic supporter. That's why our country was so messed up back then. You were unable to perform an abortion, let alone be a single mother like Christina. You know, before Christina, I had two abortions, a doctor friend of mine helped me perform illegally. But your mom would never even . . . do one." Aunt Sarah takes the book away from my hands and covers her face.

"My mom would never even do what?"

Aunt Sarah wets her finger and flips pages while whistling a tune. "What?"

"You said my mom would never consider an abortion?"

"Silly Calyssa. I was reciting poetry."

"Please, tell me," I say.

"'My desolation does begin to make a better life. 'Tis paltry to be Caesar—'"

"Not that. About my mom."

She sighs deeply, and peeks from behind the book. "Why taunting the past, Calyssa?"

"Because it'll help me understand."

"There's nothing to understand. Stop disturbing the dead."

"Please, tell me what happened. I feel entrapped. In just the past two weeks I lost my job, embarrassed myself in Honolulu, and got a message from my mom she's *possibly* proud of me. I'm at a crossroad, and it's also the dead end."

"Baby, I wish you told me you were feeling this way. Ever since you moved, you're drifting farther and farther away. No *wonder* you're lost."

"My hooker friend told me I'm brainwashed by the media."

"You have a hooker friend?"

I laugh, wondering whether it's worth an explanation. "Can't discriminate based on gender, sexual orientation, skin color, or occupation. Money don't smell. But she told me I have a fear of rejection. That I'm trying to be like everybody else by blending into the working world."

"Smart hooker. And you're right: Can't discriminate. You know, the reason I went out with Cheng and got knocked up with Christina was because of Amelia. She was courted by your father, the Middle Eastern hottie from Turkey or whatever. She kept saying white guys are bad in bed. You know, Cheng's penis was a real schlung."

"Aunt Sarah, can we please have the penis conversations at a cocktail hour?"

"Glad you asked, love." She browses around the room in a sketchy manner. She then leans into her purse and gets a flask. "I brought my own whiskey, figured they don't serve this brand at the hospital." She unscrews the top and takes a sip, offering the flask to me. I promptly take it, memories of the last time I had whiskey surfacing: I ended up as a carcass under Marcus. "Now that it's cocktail hour, where was I?"

"Can you tell me more about the guy from Turkey or whatever?"

"I don't know the size of his penis, dear."

"I mean random information. We never talked about it, but it doesn't mean I wasn't interested."

She pauses to consider. "It *just* hit me: you're an adult now. Wow. You're old enough not to judge her, I guess."

"Why would I judge her?"

Aunt Sarah takes a deep breath. "She's a liar, for one. She said the Turkey-or-whatever left her, when in fact it was the opposite. When she introduced him to me, he looked like an extravagant kiwi in a bag of yellow onions. They just pretty much graduated high school: he was around twenty and she was nineteen. This was when she got pregnant. As much as I tried to talk her out of having the baby—you—Amelia protested. She was a rebel, for sure. Girls in our family always do the opposite of what's told. All of a sudden, she moves to the East Coast without telling anyone. She stopped talking to me *and* your grandmother."

"What was she after?"

"The same thing you're after: She thought she wasn't good enough. She finally came back a month before giving birth and stayed put. Turkey-or-whatever never knew about you."

"She said he left us," I say.

"She said a lot of things. She didn't want to appear trampy and so she did this by making *him* sound bad. She wanted to make you proud. And now it's the opposite. She was afraid you would blame her for being a lousy parent, but truth be told, she was not the one to grow up, that's for sure." Aunt Sarah takes the flask, chugs some whiskey, and passes it back.

"We don't sound dissimilar."

"Exactly," she says and releases a breath of liberation. "Are you judging her?"

I shake my head. "Why would I?"

"Because she never achieved what she wanted. She was a dreamer more than a doer, unlike you. She was raised without a father, and her entire life she was judging your grandmother for the life she had as an abandoned child;

Amelia liked to play the victim. I was afraid you'd act like her. Affection is an irrational thing, a foolish combination of love at first sight and the smell of sex. Your grandmother, Amelia, me, *and* Christina are the victims of that. The *baby* is the victim of that. Even Chucky said we'd had a hex put on our family, and for sixteen generations we will suffer. Single women with children. I'm glad you didn't get pregnant to get even with Amelia just to blame everyone else for your own pratfalls."

"That's why you got pregnant with Christina?"

"Of course. If my mom did so, I had to do so too. Our entire clan acts out the same pattern over and over again. I mistakenly thought you'd do something unwise, like stop talking to us, stop drinking, or do drugs. Never do drugs, child, you know how I feel about Cheng's addiction. Unlike all of us, though, you've managed to keep it together, and I'm very proud of you. We're the only coterie in our history that remains intact. Let's keep it that way."

Processing the information, I look up. The TV set mounted to the wall is tuned to the news channel, where a story is being covered about how the hurricane affected Atlantic City. One after another, footages of flooded sidewalks and broken houses are followed by empty streets of New York City. A ghost town. Subtitles mention power outages have begun occurring, and that several subway stations have already been shut down due to being full of water. Unfortunate choice of advertising follows the news, selling home insurance, cheap tickets to Hawaii with its beaches and sun, and an upcoming event at Macy's, which I must attend because of a great sale. Aunt Sarah takes a Styrofoam cup off the nearby table, a cup that unmistakably smells of coffee. She drinks the remnants and takes off the lid.

"It's a boy. Look." She shows me the inside of the cup, where coffee stains on the bottom created something reminding of a boy's reproductive organ. "You see it? Little James or Walter."

Agreeing, I nod. Yes, and they'll grow up to be *big* James or Walter. What the world needs, another man. Her eagerness to learn the sex before the baby gets here is amusing, but I decide to switch gears. "Tell me, Aunt Sarah, are you proud of Christina?"

Playing basketball, she throws the cup into the trash can without standing up. She takes my hands into hers, gently. Her patchy nails beg for a manicure. "Baby, we love our children unconditionally. You work or choose to be a housewife. You can be a mother of six or be a spinster forever. Nobody can tell you who you should become, and I wouldn't dare tell Christina how to live her life."

"What if some people suggest how to live our lives?"

"If somebody tells you *what* you must be, they're jealous. Jealous people plug every hole in every conversation because they feel left out. Life must be about choices and freedom. Just think about nature, how animals do whatever they wish. All animals. But I'm not speaking dolphins here; I hate those people-humping, always smiling assholes. Life is what you make of it, Calyssa. You want to be a hooker, then be a hooker. Who cares? Life is who you are. With her looks, if Christina ended up in Chinatown giving massages, I'd love her anyway. I'm joking. Not really." She pauses and makes a confused face as though she lost her train of thought. "Of course I'm proud of her, silly. She's my daughter. You're my daughter too and I'm proud of you just as much. I can't and wouldn't want to change a single bolt within you. You are who you are."

"People keep saying that, but what does it mean? Who *am* I?"

"You is smart, you is funny, and you loves people. You've grown so much; just look at yourself. You stopped crying about boys, you work, you make money, you're young and beautiful. You're my partner when we try kicking Christina's ass at board games."

"She really needs to learn how to lose."

"Competing in sports is one thing, but competing with your friends or family is another. You don't have to be superhuman to be loved. That's who you are, baby. You're a strong, opinionated woman who will make some men very happy, hopefully not all at the same time. I can't imagine you in a gang bang. And not with your ex-boyfriend, who was a loser."

"He was so hot though."

"I thought he looked like a wazoo."

"But this is my exact point, Aunt Sarah: I'm thirty years old, and I haven't accomplished anything. Thirty is one of those numbers you start thinking seriously about. Will life be getting in the right direction, or will I keep being lost? How do I know my life's on the right path?"

"Only you can answer that question, baby."

The door to the waiting room opens with a squeak. A nurse in a nurse's costume enters, and if I must say something nice about her, I like the healthy glow on her fatty cheeks. "Guess who's here? The baby's here," she says quietly. "Follow me, Christina wants to see you immediately." A smear of lipstick on her chin is like an indication she blew a janitor in a broom closet.

"Who is it?" Aunt Sarah says, flying up. "Boy or girl?"

"You'll see," the nurse says and leaves. Her hips are extraordinary too wide, which makes me wonder: If she ran at full speed, would she be able to make a turn, or would she hit the wall? You know, like, at full speed big objects have trouble navigating. Never mind. I also wonder if she ate the janitor.

Aunt Sarah runs after the nurse while I get up from my seat slowly, my heartbeat accelerated for some reason. Before I exit, I glance at the digital clock above the door: 12:43 A.M.

Friday.

Exactly seven days after Chucky's prediction.

The delivery room smells like ass. The nurse withdraws, leaving the four of us alone. Christina is lying in bed with the baby, a doll wrapped into a blanket. We approach the bed (me tiptoeing for some reason). Christina's doomed without makeup. Her hair smells like hair and the outfit she's wearing is *so* last season. She hardly has cucumber eyes, but I can paint a pretty picture of what I looked like a week ago (and it's not a pretty picture, by the way). Nobody says a word. Christina guards the doll without letting anyone touch it, with a smile on her face two feet long. The baby's itsy-bitsy. I was skeptical before, but now I'm convinced I'm an aunt.

"She's a baby girl," Christina says, whispering, as though the baby isn't supposed to know.

"A girl," Aunt Sarah repeats.

I watch the baby's face, wondering the following question: How does Christina know it's a baby girl? How much different a baby boy looks like? Would he have an elephant trunk out front? Fina Lee. No, not Christina, the *baby* is doomed.

"Look at how gorgeous she is," Christina says.

"I knew the baby was going to be a she," Aunt Sarah finally says. "It's in our DNA. All women in our family gave birth to girls. Christina, I asked you for a boy; now look what you've done." Aunt Sarah mocks Christina and kisses her forehead.

"Mom," Christina says, "you smell like coffee. Get away from me."

"Whatever. I'm a freaking grandmother."

"Not with that breath, you're not. I told you: stop talking or I'll throw up. My stomach is super sensitive."

"I can smell like whatever I want to—I'm a grandmother for fuck's sake."

"Mother, language!"

"Mother? I told you, don't call me mother. Mother is the most impersonal word on this planet."

"Okay, father."

"Don't be a smart aleck now. Back to business. Is her name Fina?"

"She's too beautiful for Fina," Christina says. "China maybe . . . But I think I know what to call her. Are you ready?" We both nod. "Grace."

"Grace," Aunt Sarah repeats.

"Grace Lee," I mouth.

Christina purses her lips. "I can't believe neither of you remembered."

"Remembered what?" Aunt Sarah and I say in unison.

"That I loved Grace Kelly so much and made a promise to name my daughter Grace."

"You never told me," Aunt Sarah says.

But I so clearly see Christina and myself sitting on the floor in our living room. We're five and eight and we're playing dolls. This is the story Mom would tell everybody who ever ended up staying at our house. I clearly have no recollection of anything, except for her green high heels that I loved so much.

"I'll call my daughter Grace."

"Mine will be Elizabeth."

"Why?"

"Elizabeth Taylor!"

Mom walked in then. She looked tender and beautiful. She was wearing the shoes, four and a half inch heels, which I put on privately numerous times.

"Aunt Amelia, which name do you like better?" Christina said. "Grace or Elizabeth."

"Hm, let me think about that. I like them both."

The memories come so vivid, tears swell up in my eyes and I look at Christina. "Do you remember what I wanted to name my daughter?"

"Elizabeth. Like your fish."

"What was my favorite color?"

"Green. You were after Aunt Amelia's shoes like a crazy person. And your hoody; there's always something green on you."

"What was my favorite Disney character?"

"Princess Jasmine. You always imitated her hair. Case in point." She indicates my hair. "What are you driving at?"

Everything I do in my adulthood is the exact mirror reflection of my youth. When adults did shots, I did shots of juice in secrecy under the table—a place where I'd sleep a lot as an adult. Maybe I'll never grow up. I watch how Christina holds Grace with such love that of course Mom would be proud of me. How could I be so crazy to think otherwise? Even if I looked like a zombie, smelled like Cute Mango, or drank like a fish. (Well, we can debate about the last one later. Besides, I doubt the idiom is any longer true, for Elizabeth never officially complained about being hungover or asked for any painkillers.)

"Are you okay?" Aunt Sarah asks and hugs me.

"Calyssa, what's the matter?" Christina asks me, patting my arm.

But I can't help it. My defective pipes pour down tears. I may never grow up, but just being with the three of them makes me feel wanted and loved. This is what an emotional bottom must have felt like for the girls: unfair, taunting, exhausting. Emotions overwhelm me. Living by myself seems right but for all the wrong reasons, just like Chloe and the pets she watched. Having a good job may seem respectful, but unless I'm happy there, just like Lindsay is happy now, I won't have respect for myself or for others. Natalia felt accepted as long as she accepted herself.

I feel tired and defeated. I wish to crawl under blankets and stay there for a week. However, despite everything I did, despite all the lies and judgmental comments I made, despite the dumbass decisions, Mom would always love me. It's easy to lose yourself, and I think living alone taught me that. I'm lost, and there's only one way to get myself back.

Chucky enters the room, a bouquet of flowers in hands. She's wrapped into the same black chador she was wearing last Friday.

"Hi, Chucky," Christina says.

Chucky shoves the bouquet in my hands and examines Grace. "She's gorgeous. Grace has arrived into this family. I *knew* it. I kept it a secret at the séance, but Grace appeared before me and told me she'd be here Friday. The hex is now gone. The aura is white. You're all free. Seventeenth generation starts with Grace." Chucky starts sniffing the air in the room, moving hands up and down, then side to side. "And foremost, the hurricane is a positive sign. When a baby gets born during a hurricane, expect a miracle to happen. And it happened."

"By the way, Chucky," I say, "how did you make it through the hurricane?"

"Hurricane?" Chucky meets my eyes. "Hurricane ended hours ago."

I reach the only window ahead of me. As I roll the sheers, the sun rays instantly brighten up the room. 6:57 A.M. I'm impressed by how we've spent six hours blabbing with each other without even noticing how the night passed us by. I literally feel like I just walked in. The only tree growing in the yard with its bare, leafless branches—is standing still—a sign that hurricane Amelia left New York to rest in peace. Tree leaves cover the pavement of an empty parking lot, a red-and-yellow carpet as an indication for the end of fall.

Aunt Sarah joins me by the window and hooks her arm into mine, tears of joy in her eyes. We're both sobbing quietly, both for different reasons. Christina hates when the two of us go into our sobbing fits, so most of the time we do this without indicating anything, in complete quietness.

"I want to move back home," I say, sniffling between each word. This is not what Mom or Aunt Sarah wants. This is what I want.

And it is real.

Aunt Sarah just nods, and the two of us start hiccupping. Fries would be nice right about now.

IN JUST OVER A WEEK, ON TUESDAY, OCTOBER 31, THE AIR IS finally crisp and fresh, a perfect weather for my favorite holiday: Halloween. After hurricane Amelia pacified her needs, the weather in New York warmed up, right before the cold weather, which is predicted to overwhelm the city, is about to strike again. Today the sun shines brightly, the temperature a record seventy-three degrees. Without a single cloud in the sky together with low humidity, today is paradise for the beginning of winter. Enjoying while it lasts, I even decide to wear a skirt for the first time in ages, borrowed from Christina.

An army of trick-or-treating kids, dressed in costumes, walks up and down the streets in Astoria with their parents. Unlike other states in the country where people actually own homes, Astoria is a neighborhood lacking such privileges due to (but not limited to) compact living, expensive apartments, and because people who reside here want Astoria to look like a city, as opposed to the rural-village look the rest of the country seems to be sticking with. Therefore, kids use 30th Avenue, Astoria Boulevard, and Steinway Street, terrorizing local businesses as the only available option to get candy.

I guess apartment buildings are a tough bet because most people are (1) at work and (2) too lazy to go down four to six flights of stairs every time a little child, dressed as a superman, wants sweets. I mean, I'd never go down four to six flights of stairs every time a little child, dressed as a superman, wanted sweets. I'm on my way to Manhattan. I'm drinking champagne that's camouflaged as lemonade in a lemonade bottle (courtesy of Lindsay with her idea of camouflaging wine in a cranberry juice bottle).

Ever since Grace was born, I've devoted my time helping Mama Goose with the baby since Aunt Sarah is mostly at work.

I no longer live by myself.

I dropped off my keys at the landlord's apartment downstairs. I was able to break the lease. My landlord wanted to renovate for a long time, because my apartment needed a facial badly, but he was unable to do so with me living there. He says once he's finished, he'll rent it for an extra $700. So I doubt he'll miss me.

I sent back the couch a few days ago, loaded up a U-Haul, and had Christina drive me home. She's the only person in our family with a driver's license. It was wise to move back in with Christina and Aunt Sarah. It's a full house, but it's a fun house. At first, it seemed impossible, I felt like a failure, but I knew Mom would want it that way. No. I want it that way. Plus, I won't slack off because I was hired to work as a sales associate at a jewelry store in Manhattan. They said I had this "customer service" face, which I believe is a flowery way to say I don't look like a complete bitch. I start next week.

I came back to Astoria to drop off the keys and to give my old neighborhood one last walkthrough. In my old apartment, I touched its empty walls and eyed its beautiful wood floors. I was never sentimental, reason why I did this in ten minutes flat. Kind of reminded me of the last time I had sex: got in, got out, bye.

Drinking the champagne, I wonder why I felt like I wasn't good enough. New Yorkers are ambitious; if you don't make the money you won't fit in. But fit into what? The modern world is cruel, making you believe you're only half-good or half-bad. And today everything became so complicated in my mind I wanted to erase and start over. I will stop listening to what is told and open my own horizons. If they—whoever I meet—dislike me for who I am, I will need to tell them to suck it.

The emotional bottom: not the end but a place to start over.

I realized this, so let's hope Marcus Truman realized it as well. I'm on my way to see him.

I return to the subway stop and take the N train to Lexington Avenue, where I transfer to the downtown 5 train. I exit on Fulton Street, hoping Laruza Somo took a day off.

Marcus' building is half covered in scaffolding. The interior walls have been painted in warm pastels. Paintings of sakura blossoms make the lobby nice and cozy. The weird chandelier above the receptionist has been removed.

On my way to the elevators, I hide my face away from the receptionist, but Laruza's voice stops me cold. "Where are you going? I told you before, you're not allowed in the building." Laruza gives me a nasty look and stands up. "And if you're not out the door in exactly four seconds, I'll call the police."

In exactly four seconds, I'm out the door.

Dammit!

With my heart racing as though I just swam across the Atlantic Ocean by hand (I say it like I know how that feels), I gasp for air, almost choking in the process. Laruza is an equivalent of an electrified fence for dogs. I expected such a turnaround, but the eternal optimist kept whispering in my ear: drink, drink, fries. Wait, I'm confusing two thoughts. Must be the champagne. The workers bring in materials, along with brushes, cans of paint, and carpeting. I hate construction, so once outside I'm relieved, I survived the chemical fumes.

I guess I'll never see Marcus again.

In all honesty, it beats me why I decided to bother him. Unfinished business is unfinished business, however, and I wondered if he felt the same way. At least now I know my answer. I advise myself to finish the champagne, and I do as advised.

While catching up on my breathing, I try to guesstimate a proper term for Laruza's sex: a girl and a boy together—a goy. Or, possibly, a boy and a girl together—a birl. A goy and a birl together must be something from science fiction.

Kids, in costumes, walk in and out of adjacent buildings, bags of candy in their tiny rascal hands. A costume store, in fact, is located across the street with "50 PERCENT OFF" sign placed neatly on the window. If I ever want to buy a Halloween costume, I should purchase it tomorrow when the junk goes on 90-percent sale. But what idiot shops a year in advance for something so trivial? I've done that in the past, so I guess I am that idiot. I haven't acquired a costume yet, but tonight the girls and I are going on the town. I wanted to borrow Christina's Japanese kimono for a geisha girl outfit, but Christina distrusts me with keeping it safe. I know this because she said she "can't find it anywhere," which means she hid it, and tomorrow it will magically reappear. Maybe I should rummage through the store and see what they've got.

Inside the Halloween store, the shelves appear empty, granted the merchandise is almost sold in its entirety while only a few unwanted pieces remain. A painter's costume is only ten bucks. Would teach Laruza a lesson if I bought this costume and some sort of a wig, and pretended to be one of the construction boys, an idea empowered by the champagne, I must admit. Cleopatra's costume costs $25.99, as though telling me I should go out as Queen of the Nile tonight. Inside the package, I find a black wig with bangs, an asp, a tiara, and a necklace. Why not? After all, I've already been Cleopatra, so I might as well play her again.

A vampire dressed as a cashieress scans the package. "This is the ugliest Cleopatra costume I've ever seen. You'll just look like a tacky old thing. Get the nurse. She's much more popular."

"And twenty dollars extra. Just this."

"At least buy the toga too. It's just $15."

"A toga? I have a white sheet at home for free."

"How about—"

"How about just this?" I say. Working in retail in the past, I know what she's doing: she's upselling. People aren't stupid, and they'd clue in she's trying to make an extra sale.

"Someone cranky today, huh? Your total is $25.99. Would you like to donate a dollar for the Children International? It's an organization that helps children, internationally."

I shake my head in the negative, thinking of the nonexistent Children International. I bet an organization called Cashiers Local does exist, where she'd really donate the money to: into her own pocket. After I fumble in the Gooseberry, searching for my wallet, I realize the bag is one disorganized mess as always. Plus, the consumed champagne helps none in terms of helping with concentration. The wallet is hidden at the very bottom, and once I pull out my debit card, I hand it to the cashieress. She swipes it, eyes devoted to the window behind me.

"Those sexy Latino guys who are bringing in the carpet look oh-so-yummy," she says and drools. "I'd eat them alive."

I turn around to see what she's gabbing about, and I notice the sexy Latino guys who look oh-so-yummy, and who are bringing in the carpet into Marcus' building. It strikes me so suddenly I jump and high-five myself.

"Carpet!" I exclaim.

"Ex-squeeze-me?"

"Carpet. We have Cleopatra *and* we have carpet! It's your lucky day: I'm buying the toga as well."

Without taking my receipt—after all, all sales are final as indicated by the door sign—I flee the store in five seconds flat.

For fifteen extra dollars, I make a deal with the driver of the carpet truck to have the workers roll me into one of their carpets. I lie to them, of course, saying I need to surprise my boyfriend. I change into Cleopatra's costume at the back of the truck. This is *my* version of the Trojan horse. To come up with something of this magnitude, Achilles must've been drunk with champagne too, the way I am.

Cleopatra was a trooper, I think while being carried into the building. We finally pass Laruza's desk and get into the elevator. Without knocking on the door, the men who are carrying me enter (what I presume) Marcus' office, and carelessly drop me on the floor. One of them kicks me and the carpet starts unrolling. When I'm totally unfolded, I stand up. Marcus is sitting at a desk ahead, a perplexed look on his face. Nay-nay, I want to mock him to tell him his dog down in the lobby is poor protection. If she were a condom, someone just got knocked up.

"Calyssa?" he says and stands up. "What are you doing?"

"Kill me now, Caesar, or listen to what I have to say."

He can't help but smile. "Okay."

"To be honest, I don't know what I'm doing. First, I wanted to apologize for going to Cynthia's apartment. I had no business going there. But she pissed me off. Oh, by the way, do you have a minute to talk?"

"Actually, Cleopatra," he says and interlocks his arms in front of his chest, "I'm busy at the moment."

"Well, I'm busy too so we're doing this. Maybe it's the dance we performed on that stage or the kiss in the lounge. We liked each other. I'm not saying sexually, though I can't deny I have thought of you that way. I even have a picture of you and me on my phone, which somehow, magically, survived. Plus, I thought we had great chemistry together."

"So did I, but so what?"

"So that maybe we could at least become friends. You think low of yourself for cheating on Cynthia, but I'd also cheat on that bitch. She thinks the moon has two sides. Who is she, anyway? I know nothing of you, true, but I believe you're handsome, a great kisser, and you should respect yourself more. Everybody makes mistakes. What counts is what you learn from them. You're not as bad as you think you are." *And not as muscular as I wish you were*, I want to add, but decide to hold my horses.

Marcus smiles, puzzlement on his face replaced by amusement. "It certainly takes guts, Queen of the Nile, to barge in here, despite the fact I told Laruza to keep you out."

"By the way, is Laruza a man or a woman?"

"You're seriously asking me this? You're nuts."

"I *am*," I say and make two steps forward. "But so what? You're the one who imbibes at nine in the morning, by the way. I went to Hawaii for a wrong reason, but like Grace Bishop said, 'Nothing happens for no reason at all.'"

"I did like you and I thought of you last week."

"You did?"

"Yes. I appreciate you talking to Cynthia. Aside from the blackmail plan, I think what you did was courageous."

"Then, you want to remain friends?"

"Can we finish this some other time? I appreciate you coming and I promise I'll call you. I'm in the middle of something here."

I've been in his office for less than two minutes, and only now I hear a royal flush of the toilet in his private bathroom. What a hag I am. He's with someone, reason why he's *in the middle of something*. Quickly, I glance around the room for an opened condom but find none, which means they haven't started having sex yet. And what a stupid idea. Why would the condom be open if she's in the bathroom cleaning her cooch?

"I'm sorry," I say, backing out. "It's okay. Let's halt our friendship right here. Bye, Marcus."

"Calyssa, wait."

As I grab the handle, the bathroom door opens with a squeak. I give a dirty look to that woman. But it's not a woman. I squint. It's a little girl. She's around five, and I realize she must be Lydia. I stop by the door, mesmerized by her pretty face and gorgeous blonde hair, wondering whether she could have just jumped into our reality from a Disney book in that purple dress. I watch the two them as though stoned, unable to move, my feet shackled by the ball and chain. The girl watches me in the exact same way.

"Hi," I carefully say, as though to a stray cat who might run away.

Lydia comes closer. "What's *your* costume?" she exclaims. Her directness shocks me because I thought kids were supposed to be shy.

"I'm Cleopatra. What's yours?"

"I'm Rapunzel. She's my favorite princess. Do you like my dress?" She twirls.

"Yes, I do. Very much so."

"Is Cleopatra a princess or a queen?"

"She used to be at some point, something for sure . . . I think?" I say, trailing off, unsure of the answer. I eye Marcus for help, as by now he should know how to answer those tricky kid questions, but he just shrugs in response. Other than being used for sex, sometimes men just prove how useless they can be.

Lydia examines my costume. She touches my bracelet and the toga while I examine her: her eyes are the lightest shade of blue. She's almost like the exact copy of Marcus, but much, much prettier.

"You're beautiful," she finally says. "You look like a queen."

I can't believe a five-year-old child is telling me I'm beautiful. Where are *your* manners, Marcus? I blush (underneath, of course, three layers of makeup).

"Thanks, Rapunzel. You're beautiful, too. What's the difference, princess or queen?"

"Only adults can be queens." She states it so clearly, my eyes pop open in surprise. There was no trace of doubt. Absolutely a firm statement.

And here it is: my revelation. I don't know why I needed this little girl to remind me what I already knew, that I am *indeed* Queen of the Nile, that I'm *indeed* an adult. I smile from one ear to the other, thinking that so long as there are kids, there are adults.

After the emotional bottom comes the time of revelation. Everything I knew appears at a different angle, in a different light.

I believe I'm actually going into the right direction in life. To remain myself would be the hardest thing to do, but I'll keep trying. I may never be an "adult" by someone else's standards, but I am an adult by my own standards. I might as well be five years old, be called names, and live in a bowl of water, but I'll always do my best. I'll try not to do what "I'm supposed to" just because someone told me so.

I is human. I is adult. I is Queen of the Nile.

Damn, that was a lot of champagne, man.

"I'm five," Lydia adds out of the blue while I kept staring at her with my jaw half open. "Do you want to color princesses with me?"

There's only one answer to a question like that and it's never a lie. "I'd love to."

Lydia takes my hand and pulls me toward Marcus' desk, which is full of crayons and paper. Life may be a gamble, but life is also a choice. I choose to do this because we girls must stick together. I give Marcus a superior look, like, *Now try to kick me out, bitch.*

EPILOGUE

After the elections, which brought us a Democrat (at last!) for the next four years, Chloe mentioned she's confident enough to attend her high school reunion next year. It didn't go far with the guy from the bar, but at least she had wild sex. Her imaginary friend Matilda hasn't shown up yet. She also introduced me to her mom, a lovely woman who made us dinner and took us for a drink in their neighborhood bar in Murray Hill.

By Thanksgiving, Lindsay was still working as a live-in nanny. Lindsay is teaching the little girl, Charlotte, how to dance for the beauty pageant. The other girl is too old for a babysitter, and she's such a brat. Lucky Knotts is pleased with Lindsay, but because of our shenanigans a couple of weeks prior, Lindsay now has a curfew during the week. Lindsay said she had never learned discipline, and that she not only doesn't mind the curfew, she actually likes it. The curfew lets her know that someone is looking after her.

Natalia hired a new housekeeper, Conchita. I was suspicious of the name at first, but Natalia explained she had made her up. Whenever she needs her apartment cleaned, she puts on an apron and scrubs the apartment herself. Natalia imagines she's the housekeeper because she must learn ladies' duties and to understand how hard Lupita worked. Indeed, it appeared hard, why Natalia quit and hired a professional service, the one that offers a twenty-minute massage. Somehow, I must have misread the ad or mixed it up with another ad, because in the maid package there wasn't a massage offered at all. Natalia had to learn this the hard way when she had oiled herself all up before the maid showed up with a vacuum cleaner in hands.

We went to Vegas one more time, but what happened in Vegas stayed in Vegas, so I ain't telling you nothing.

Babette and I remained in touch. We had coffee the other day. What I like about her is that she loves kids and she's helped me babysit Grace on numerous occasions when I needed a drink. Speaking of Grace, I hate to admit this, but she isn't as needy as I thought she'd be. She stays in Christina's room into which we placed a crib. Now that I work at the jewelry store, I can afford stuff, and I've even bought baby toys, having discovered Toys "R" Us. I love working with gems at the jewelry store. And most importantly, I get commission. Though because I never sold more than $10,000 in one consecutive month, I haven't yet gotten any. Elizabeth is still alive, though I wonder whether or not she'll keep. We all placed bets, and mine was she'd commit suicide by March.

By December, Marcus and I officially started dating, and I finally got penetrated. Yes, the beast wouldn't sleep with me until then, a gentleman he is. On December 10, however, everything changed. I never knew men pretended to "wait." For revenge, I plan to give him blue balls, but a chance hasn't come up yet.

The morning after New Year's Eve, I wake up constipated from all the food and so hungover I promise myself never to drink again, knowing perfectly well the promise would last no longer than a week. Jim Morrison was right when he said drinking is like gambling, that "you don't know where you're going to end up the next day." I can't give up the opportunity of being thrilled with the unknown, but I took an oath to quit drinking as soon as I birth an apple, and so far nothing.

I finish a whole bottle of coconut water, a drink Marcus bought for me last night. (Something about hydration, potassium, and blah blah blah.) I return to bed and position myself next to him, wondering why I just consumed all these calories for no effect. I spent the night at his place in Brooklyn where Marcus rents a spare room from his friend until further notice.

Fully awake, I'm thinking should we ever get married—hypothetically, mind you—how ironic I would sound with a name like Calyssa Truman. But I believe irony is good because irony was in part involved in making my friendship with the fish a legit union. I don't know if my relationship with Marcus will last, but these days I'm living one day at a time. There's no need to live in the past, there's no need to live in the future, but living in the present is what I'm precisely learning to do. The future and the past hold us back.

As a Christmas present for myself I bought a membership to Natalia's gym because I need to chisel away my triple chin, but every time I'm pumped to work out is during the time the gym is closed, which is between 12:00 A.M. and 6:00 A.M. So it's not really my fault they can't tailor their hours to my needs.

On a thought of how funny it would be if our wedding cake was shaped like a martini glass with a giant edible fish on top resembling Elizabeth, I close my eyes, and drift back into sleep, knowing perfectly well I would never "seriously" grow up with my imagination suitable only for children.

I see a quick dream about hanging out with my mother: me as her parent, her as my child. Well, that's not creepy at all. From this point on, however, I'll always be older than Mom while she'll remain imprisoned in my mind as my child. When I'm sixty she'll be thirty, but even then I'll still be her little Calyssa. In the dream, she first diminishes in size, turns green, and becomes a betta fish. Suspicious, I pick her up as she swims around the martini glass. In the dream she talks, though I'm very concerned about my mom being a fish. I handle her carefully without dropping—which is an accomplishment on its own.

Eye level with her, I watch her swim in circles and I slur, "There's nothing like a strong drink after a day of hard work, Amelia," and proceed to drink her together with the martini.

"Calyssa," she screams fishingly (it makes sense in a dream) and backs out farther and farther. "What is wrong with you, mama?"

I spit her out into a condom filled with water and tie it up.

I fly up awake, thinking, *I drank too much coconut water.*

The rest is a blur.

THE END

ACKNOWLEDGMENTS

Spasibo (Russian for "thank you") to everyone who believed in me: Andean Publishing, Andrés, Gian, Claire, Rhonda, and Amber. Over the years, while this book was in production, your insights were invaluable and really appreciated. A special *spasibo* to Chrissy, my book editor, and Vicky, the interior designer.

ABOUT THE AUTHOR

Jeremy Taylor was raised in Siberia and Kazakhstan and moved to the United States in 2007 at the age of nineteen. He received political asylum on the basis of being gay and now lives and writes in West New York, NJ.

The Girl and Apple Martinis is a debut novel.

Find out more on his website:
WWW.JEREMYTAYLOR.ONLINE

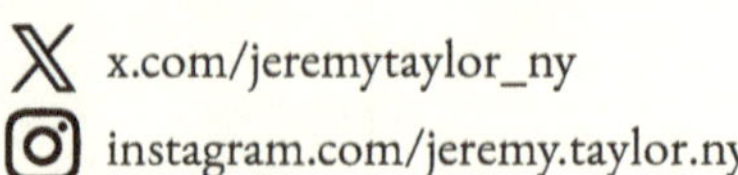

x.com/jeremytaylor_ny

instagram.com/jeremy.taylor.ny

BOOKS BY JEREMY TAYLOR

Puss on the Loose

Diary of a Mad Gay Man

The Cornerstones of Happiness

One Hundred and Eleven People I Can't Stand

Smart Casual and Other Expressions I Hate

*Noodles with Grandma and Other Stories from
Our Homestead in Kazakhstan*